The Paralegal's Guide to the Microsoft® Office System

PUBLISHED BY

Agility Press - An imprint of the Mann Publishing Group
208 Post Road, Suite 102
Greenland, NH 03840, USA
www.agilitypress.com
www.mannpublishing.com
+1 (603) 601-0325

ISBN: 1-932577-10-6
Library of Congress Control Number (LCCN): 2004115497
Printed and bound in the United States of America.
10 9 8 7 6 5 4 3 2 1

Credits

Authors:	Dorian S. Berger, Anthony T. Mann
Copy Editor:	Jeff Edman
Book Layout:	Molly Barnaby
Cover Design:	Marcelo Paiva
Indexer:	Buz Riley
Legal IT Advisors:	Jean Champagney, Lori Ann Page

All Mann Publishing Group books may be purchased at bulk discounts.

The Paralegal's Guide to the Microsoft® Office System

agility PRESS

Dorian S. Berger
Anthony T. Mann

About the Authors

Dorian S. Berger

Dorian Berger is a Product Manager at Microsoft Corporation. He specializes in the legal profession's use of technology. He teachers a number of Continuing Legal Education Courses (CLE) through the Washington State Bar Association and other groups. Prior to coming to work at Microsoft, he worked at Realnetworks, Sun Technology Ventures, and for brief time at the NBC Television Soap Opera *Passions*. He has done extensive training on Microsoft Office for a range of audiences. When he is not avoiding helping people with their computer problems, he lives in Seattle's Belltown Neighborhood. He is a graduate of Harvard College. He can be reached for comment or feedback about this book at `dorianberger@gmail.com`.

Anthony T. Mann

Anthony T. Mann is the President/CEO of the Mann Publishing Group, which specializes in publishing business and technology titles, including this book (under the Agility Press imprint). He typically focuses on writing and teaching Microsoft-based technologies, including Microsoft Office and many software development technologies. His 11 prior books include *The Rational Guide To: Microsoft® Virtual PC 2004* (Rational Press), *The Rational Guide To: SQL Server Reporting Services* (Rational Press), *.NET Web Services for Dummies* (John Wiley & Sons), *Microsoft SQL Server 2000 for Dummies* (John Wiley & Sons), *SharePoint Portal Server: A Beginner's Guide* (Osborne/McGraw-Hill), and *Microsoft SQL Server 7 for Dummies* (John Wiley & Sons). He can be reached for comment or feedback about this book at `tmann@mannpublishing.com`.

Acknowledgements

Dorian S. Berger

I always thought I would be thanking people in the Kodak Theater during the Academy Awards. But this will do. I would like to thank my coauthor Anthony T. Mann who has been incredible to work with and forced me to turn around drafts with the speed of a fairly old 486 computer. At Microsoft I would like to thank my managers Melanie Cosklo, John Smithwick, and Robert Crissman for the tremendous support they have given me. This book is not the first book I have written and a number of other manuscripts lie behind my laundry basket. I would like to thank the editors of those manuscripts: Anne Enquist and Judy Wacht. My parents Marilyn and Albert Berger, who have been incredibly supportive during my time at Microsoft and give me wonderful advice and wisdom—which I usually argue with and fail to follow.

Anthony T. Mann

I would like to express my sincere appreciation to everyone who has painstakingly produced this book. There are many people behind the scenes that work on a complex book like this one. I'd like to specifically thank Jeff Edman, who has done his usual outstanding job of copy editing, as well as conducting much research for the book. A very special thank you goes out to Jean Champagney and Lori Ann Page from SoftWise. They have provided outstanding expertise and advice on the content in this book. I also want to thank my coauthor, Dorian Berger, who conceived this series of books. Without his vision, you'd be reading something else right now. Last, but certainly not least, I would like to thank my wife, Alison. Once again, her unwavering support meant my countless late nights yielded a book of the highest quality.

Conventions Used In This Book

The following conventions are used throughout this book:

- *Italics* — First introduction of a term.
- **Bold** — Exact name of an item or object that appears on the computer screen, such as menus, buttons, dropdown lists, or links.
- `Mono-spaced text` — Used to show a Web URL address, computer language code, or expressions as you must exactly type them.
- **Menu1⇨Menu2** — Hierarchical Windows menus in the order you must select them.

NOTE

This box gives you additional information to keep in mind as you read.

TIP

This box gives you additional technical advice about the option, procedure, or step being explained in the chapter.

CAUTION

This box alerts you to special considerations or additional advice.

In Practice

This box contains statements from legal professionals about how they take advantage of Microsoft Office to perform Paralegal tasks.

Preface

Something bad was awaiting me in the conference room. I had received an e-mail that morning from the lawyer who supported our group. It was the kind of short e-mail that you fear—without a greeting, but including a time and a place. And I especially feared it since I had only been working at my company for one month.

I tried to think about what I could have done. Perhaps I was parking in somebody else's space. I always parked by the loading dock in a space that *could* be legal if viewed from an angle. Or maybe I was being called in to the lawyer's office for egregious use of the printer. I print almost everything I receive, and my weakness is for printing it all in color. At our company, everybody seemed to be moving toward a paperless office, so the printers were always festooned with messages about recycling and stopping waste. The printed PowerPoint decks and Word documents piled up on my floor were my Great Wall against the invasion of the paperless office.

I had spent all morning coming up with ever more horrific explanations for the purpose of the meeting, and the half moons of sweat under my arms were converging on the front of my shirt like a logo gone horribly wrong. I dragged my feet to the conference room.

Joan—the Paralegal who supported our group—was sitting at one end of the table and the attorney for our group at the other. I took a seat between them.

"Your mother wouldn't be very happy with you," Joan the Paralegal said. Joan took to giving motherly and stern advice to people in our group. Since I was in charge of negotiations surrounding the acquisition of content for an obscure part of our company's product, Joan had given me tips on negotiating, and told me how I should talk on the phone. "Stop using the word 'like'—you're not in college anymore," she'd say. She had also taught me how to track changes, format documents to meet her needs, and schedule appointments in her Outlook calendar.

Joan had been at the company for so long that her stock awards had vested and she could be seen speeding around the campus in a green Porsche 911. (It was a hideous color, but Joan had said it reminded her of a swaying tree.)

The lawyer at the end of the table was silent as Joan continued to eye me. "Very, very bad," she continued. "Do you at least know what you did?"

I stumbled for an answer.

"You don't know?" She rapped her pad against the table. "If I wasn't such a forgiving person, if I hadn't been here for thirteen years—and let me tell you I've seen it all—then it would be worse."

The lawyer for the group was silent. He was somewhat hunched over in his chair. With his thinning hair, he seemed like a shrunken presence sitting next to Joan, like a tree which had lost most of its leaves. It certainly wasn't the kind of tree that Joan thought her car resembled.

"Joan, I'm really sorry," I said, although I wasn't sure what for. But when you get your first job out of college you learn to apologize for most things that you do.

Joan drew herself back, and nodded. "So I sent you the contract as a Word document. And what exactly did you do with it?"

Now I knew what we were here for. Earlier in the week Joan had sent me a contract we were negotiating with a client. I was really very proud of my work on the contract and had gone in and made a series of changes which seemed appropriate before sending it along to the client to sign and return. I had turned the entire contract around and got it signed in less than a week. My co-workers said these contracts would take a month of going back and forth. Somehow I had figured out a shortcut.

Joan cocked her head, "And what did you do with the contract?"

"I made some changes in it," I responded.

"Are you a Paralegal or a lawyer?"

I wasn't a lawyer. I spent a good deal of time watching *Law and Order*, but as Joan and the other lawyers in our group had told me, this did not make me a lawyer or a Paralegal. It merely made me someone acquainted with the law. But as Joan pointed out, felons were also acquainted with the law.

I was silent as Joan continued, "Did you get permission to change the contract?"

I had not, but it seemed like a good idea. Sometimes I'm like that. I come up with ideas which come back later to haunt me. The changes I had made to the contract were extensive.

Joan opened her laptop to reveal my edited contract on the screen. Joan believed in the paperless office.

"This here," she pointed at the screen, "this isn't even English."

"But it is legal language," I replied. Sometimes when I am in a meeting, a funny comment comes to me and I can't help myself from saying it. I had told myself that in my new job I must stop doing that.

"Very funny." Joan did not look very amused. "And no, it is not even legal language. Here you seem to have added whole sections surrounding the delivery of materials. I compared this in Microsoft Word with the original contract I sent you and they don't even look like the same document. Do you see all the black lines on the side? These show me the differences between the two versions."

"I thought it would save you time," I answered. I really had thought this. Joan was very busy and I didn't want to bother her.

"Well, with your newly edited contract, you help no one. I want you to repeat after me… I will not edit my own contracts. I will not expose us to legal risks. I will not do things without my Paralegal's approval."

I repeated what she said. And Joan for the first time started to smile—out of the side of her mouth.

"And one last thing, Dorian. If you ever do this again—if you start home-brewing legal agreements—then you won't be talking with just me. Got it?"

"Got it."

It has been a number of years now since my 'homemade contract.' Since then, I have been careful to get approval from Joan or from the subsequent Paralegals I have worked with. But Joan also ensured that in the future I didn't make too many mistakes. She would put a lock on documents so I couldn't go in and change them. Joan was a master of Microsoft Office and knew how to use it. She used Word and Outlook not just to help her be more efficient but also to make sure that folks like me didn't create problems for her.

This book distills the key things that Paralegals need to know about Microsoft Office. In writing this book, we interviewed Paralegals from across the nation, from big firms and small, to make sure we are providing you with the key things you need to learn to use Microsoft Office like Joan does. This book provides you with the same kind of knowledge that Joan has, so that when you come across a fresh employee or a difficult task, you can use Microsoft Office to your benefit.

- Dorian S. Berger

Contents

Part I

My Office

Chapter 1

Introduction

The purpose of this book is to demystify the complex and seemingly confusing world of Microsoft Office. The idea behind this book is to focus on your job—the tasks you perform every day as a Paralegal—rather than the all too common software-centric approach that many other technology books habitually adopt. It is written using a friendly and sometimes humorous style, so you will not be intimidated by learning such a complex topic. You'll be able to learn and laugh at the same time (or at least smile).

Other Microsoft Office books on the market for the legal profession are often difficult to understand because they largely address an Information Technology (IT) audience, cover too many professions in a single book, or are so large (more than 800 pages) as to be overwhelming. This book was written from scratch with a Paralegal in mind. No ifs, ands, or buts. In fact, this book was developed by consulting and interviewing industry experts, legal trainers, technology experts, attorneys, and of course, Paralegals. We learned exactly which topics were most troublesome for Paralegals, and made sure to explain them thoroughly.

While the tasks discussed in this book may not exactly apply to your specific practice area, these tasks were determined to be appropriate for this book because they satisfied the "80/20 rule," where at least 80% of the time, Paralegals said they perform the tasks outlined in this book. If a particular task is not part of your job at present, it is worthwhile to learn the concepts, since you may find that your job will expand to encompass these tasks. And of course, it's likely that by the time you finish this book, you will learn new uses for Microsoft Office that may have been unknown to you or seemed too daunting to tackle. All the Paralegals interviewed for this book used Word, Excel, and to a slightly lesser extent, PowerPoint. However, many admitted that they knew they were not using these applications to their full potential because the learning curve was too steep. Certainly, Outlook was the prevailing e-mail application, but some Paralegals were either unaware of all the features that Outlook offers, or were unsure where to begin the process of finding out. OneNote is not yet part of every Paralegal's experience, mainly because it is a relatively new product, but it offers great potential in the hands of anyone in the legal profession. Given the many ways these Office applications can be used to increase the productivity and efficiency of Paralegals, this book is an easy way to dive into them.

The goal of productivity software is to make you more productive—not to weigh you down with complexities and steep learning curves. This book will help you cut through the hard stuff, and make Microsoft Office work for *you*.

How This Book is Organized

This book is organized into these parts:

- **Part I: My Office** — Discusses Microsoft Office 2003 as a whole, including Word 2003, Excel 2003, PowerPoint 2003, Outlook 2003, and OneNote 2003. This part shows you product-specific features that you will care about as a Paralegal, but is not focused on specific daily tasks.
- **Part II: My Tasks** — Discusses specific tasks that you do as a Paralegal and shows step-by-step instructions on how to perform those tasks using Microsoft Office. While most legal tasks are done in Microsoft Word, this part of the book shows how to perform the task regardless of the Office product needed to perform it.
- **Part III: Extras** — Contains additional information, such as the glossary, index, and more.

How to Read this Book

This book was written as a reference for you, knowing that not every possible task covered will apply to you. As such, it is not necessary to read this book cover-to-cover. However, because Part I of this book covers basics that apply to specific Microsoft Office 2003 products, it is recommended that you first read Part I in its entirety. Then, you can discover the tasks in Part II of this book that apply to whatever tasks you need to perform on any given day. It is recommended that you keep this book by your computer at work as a handy reference.

What's With All Those Version Numbers?

While the book is specifically written for Microsoft Office 2003, most of the topics covered also apply to prior versions of Office. The two immediately prior versions of Office were as follows:

- Office XP (includes the "2002" versions of Word, Excel, PowerPoint, and Outlook)
- Office 2000 (includes the "2000" versions of Word, Excel, PowerPoint, and Outlook)

To determine which version you are using, simply click the **Help⇨About** menu item in any Office product.

Bonus Materials

This book comes with valuable bonus materials. To receive these materials, you must register you book on the Web, but that's only a two-minute process. To see how to register, refer to the last page of this book.

There's More Coming...

As you already know, this book was written specifically for Paralegals. Agility Press realizes that there are more people in your firm in different roles who could benefit from a book that is geared specifically to them. Look for these upcoming legal books in the VertiGuide series from Agility Press:

- *The Attorney's Guide to the Microsoft Office System*, ISBN 1-932577-11-4
- *The Sole Practitioner's Guide to the Microsoft Office System*, ISBN 1-932577-12-2

We Welcome Feedback

The publisher and authors wish to thank you for reading this book. Your feedback, both positive and negative, is greatly appreciated. Suggestions are also welcomed. Please send any feedback at all to `legalbooks@agilitypress.com`.

Chapter 2

Paralegal Challenges

In the last two decades, technology has transformed the legal profession. Twenty years ago, few people in the legal profession were preparing electronic briefs, editing documents on computers, using e-mail, or preparing case preparations with computer graphics. There are still folks out there in the legal profession who have refused to move to computers, but they are becoming fewer and fewer—the last of the mastodons. In the course of writing this book, we have come across many approaches to technology in law offices. At one firm, every aspect of the work had been digitized. In client meetings, the lawyers would take notes on Tablet PCs that allowed them to write directly on their screens with a stylus. On the other end of the spectrum, there are some law firms where senior partners have refused to learn how to use e-mail and have requested that their secretaries print out their e-mail so they can reply to it in long hand.

Even as computers are touching more and more aspects of the legal profession, most people don't know how to harness the power of these applications. A recent study of the ways in which people use Microsoft Office showed that most users employ only around 10-20% of the features that apply to them. This is like using only one or two fingers on your hand to type (although there are some folks who attempt this and can even get proficient at it). By the end of this book, you'll feel that you are using more than two fingers—or at least that your fingers have not been chopped off. This book is targeted specifically at Paralegals and looks at key technologies that legal professionals can use to become more efficient in their jobs. It serves as a guide to help you learn how to accomplish specific tasks associated with the Paralegal profession.

Before jumping into the specific programs and tasks that can help you, let's take a broad look at some of the major technology issues that face the legal profession.

Document Preparation

Twenty years ago, most law office documents were painstakingly typed—using carbon paper, typewriters, and sweat. The advent of word processing programs during the 1980s has transformed how legal documents are prepared. Now you can track the changes in a document, compare different versions, and submit them to courts and clients in a variety of formats. In addition, more and more courts are moving toward all-digital document delivery. This means that a growing number of courts will only accept documents in digital format. The day when you run to the clerk's office to submit a stack of paper is quickly becoming a thing of the past. Understanding how to prepare electronic documents in the most efficient manner is becoming much more important. This book shows you the tricks of efficiently preparing a document.

Document Management and Security

Legal offices used to (and in many cases still do) store documents in immense warehouses, but now they are increasingly stored on disks and hard drives. The digitization of documents has created a wealth of opportunities and a good number of risks. This book covers two of the major advantages of electronic documents. First, electronic documents can be stored and sent efficiently and quickly. Second, you can quickly compare different versions of electronic documents and edit them.

Electronic documents have also created risks. The sheer volume of electronic documents means that it is important to come up with an efficient way of organizing documents for yourself or for your firm. Many large legal firms use outside companies to manage and store their documents. If you are part of a smaller firm it is important to figure out your own classification system. Also, digital documents can be altered and moved around the globe, so it is important that sensitive documents be protected. This book discusses features in Microsoft Office that deal with securing your documents so that they cannot be altered or e-mailed.

Presentations

Graphics have always played an important part in the presenting of arguments to the court or to a client. Twenty years ago, few lawyers used computer programs to illustrate key parts in a case. At that time, the law profession used either poster-sized illustrations on paper or an ELMO Projector. But digital illustrations can be incredibly powerful tools to present either to the other party or to a court. In the O.J. Simpson trial, PowerPoint was used to illustrate key exhibits. There are two primary ways that products such as PowerPoint are changing the way legal cases are presented. First, because of the low cost and simplicity of creating PowerPoint slides, the use of graphics and illustrations is expanding. For example, in a recent settlement conference for a personal injury case involving a snowplow which had run over and killed a woman, the plaintiff's lawyer prepared a 10-minute video embedded in a PowerPoint slide deck to show the arc of the victim's life. The second way in which the expanding use of presentations is influencing the legal profession is in the creation of presentations for internal use. Increasingly, lawyers are using programs such as PowerPoint to create presentations for marketing their firm's services, to show changes in the firm, or even to illustrate the steps in preparing a case. The simplicity of PowerPoint allows legal professionals to use graphics as an internal and external communications tool.

E-mail and Time Management

For many people, remembering a time without e-mail is like peering into the distant past. E-mail is playing an increasingly central role in the legal professional's life. Not only is it a way of communicating efficiently with clients and co-workers, but more importantly, e-mail is quickly becoming the tool in which we are doing most of our writing. This book focuses on some key ways in which e-mail is changing jobs in the legal profession. First, understanding how to efficiently manage e-mail is becoming more and more important. Organization of folders and messages can play an important role in ensuring that you respond to your clients. Second, e-mail is becoming increasingly tied to setting up appointments in a calendar. Understanding how to efficiently set up and manage your time using a computer can provide you with an edge.

Law Office Management

Technology has made the management of a legal office more simple, but at the same time more complex. With tools such as Excel, it is easier to measure the efficiency of lawyers or clients and to keep track of costs. A variety of billing programs can be tied to Excel, allowing you to carefully analyze a firm's billings. Also, the advent of word processing and scheduling products means that individuals in a law firm are increasingly playing a more active role in a wider variety of activities. More and more legal professionals are becoming responsible for a wider variety of tasks, such as editing documents, drafting contracts, or managing schedules.

This book provides you with information on the Microsoft Office System as it pertains to Paralegals, which will help you address the major technology issues that are affecting the legal profession.

Chapter 3

Microsoft Office 2003 Overview

Chapter At A Glance

WHY YOU SHOULD READ THIS CHAPTER:

The Microsoft Office System is comprised of many different products, such as Word 2003, Excel 2003, PowerPoint 2003, Outlook 2003, and OneNote 2003. Each product has specific benefits and features that are outlined in other Part I chapters of this book. However, there are many things that these products have in common. This chapter is a good primer on the common features found in all Microsoft Office System products. This chapter can help Paralegals perform daily tasks.

PRODUCT OUTLINED IN THIS CHAPTER:

- Microsoft Office 2003

PRODUCT FEATURES AND TECHNOLOGIES COVERED IN THIS CHAPTER:

- Collaboration
- Spelling and Grammar
- Research
- Templates
- Metadata

Microsoft Office is a comprehensive suite of applications, tools, and technologies that assist you in your daily tasks. All of these applications packaged together are known as the *Microsoft Office System*. This book does not cover every application that makes up the Microsoft Office System, but concentrates on the ones that you are likely to encounter as a Paralegal:

- **Word 2003** — Feature-rich word processing program that allows multiple users to work on documents, such as legal pleadings, legal briefs, leases, agreements, wills, memos, and more.
- **Excel 2003** — Powerful spreadsheet program to perform extensive calculations for applications such as fee billing, expense calculation, time tracking, and more.
- **PowerPoint 2003** — Graphical presentation program that is very useful for presenting to clients, courts, and within your firm.
- **OneNote 2003** — Program for taking notes with your computer and allowing you to electronically classify and categorize those notes. You can use OneNote 2003 on your desktop PC, a laptop, or a Tablet PC. If you use a Tablet PC, OneNote 2003 will use its built-in handwriting recognition, which saves you lots of time over needing to transcribe notes. It even has speech recognition to allow you to talk to your computer.
- **Outlook 2003** — Program that lets you manage all forms of electronic communication, including schedules, contacts, and e-mail. It is also used during the process of mail merging, as contact information for the merge comes from Outlook 2003.

NOTE

The Microsoft Office System actually includes a whole slew of additional products to help you be more productive, such as Access, FrontPage, InfoPath, LiveMeeting, Project, Publisher, and Visio. However, it is not possible to cover these products in one book, so we chose the ones that are most likely to be used in law firms. If you want additional information on these other products, visit the Microsoft Office Web site at `http://office.microsoft.com`.

As you read through the rest of this book, you'll discover how to use each of these Microsoft Office programs to perform the tasks you are most likely to face as a Paralegal.

Microsoft Office 2003—for Paralegals?

While some law firms use WordPerfect as a word processing program and GroupWise for e-mail, the majority of firms use Microsoft Office, including Word and Outlook. Still, some programs that are part of the Microsoft Office System, such as OneNote, are less known by Paralegals. The point of this book is to illustrate how these programs work together to give you a consistent and productive user experience that lets technology work for you, not the other way around. It will also introduce you to some Office System programs that you may not be familiar with.

Based on research conducted for this book, as a Paralegal you will likely perform the tasks outlined in Part II, "My Tasks." You should find that those tasks map closely to the tasks you perform in your daily job. However, to understand more about the individual products that make up the Microsoft Office System, see the chapters in Part I, "Overview." This will give you a good overview of the products that are outlined throughout the book.

This chapter covers a few things that you must know first about Microsoft Office in general before you dive head-first into the rest of this book:

- Collaboration
- Spelling and Grammar Checking
- Research Task Pane
- Templates (a must!)
- Metadata
- Office Viewers

These features are common to all the Office applications, and you are likely to take advantage of them in every application you use. Let's look at each.

Collaboration

Microsoft Office and all of its applications allow you to work on documents and share them with other people. This is known as *collaboration*. Collaborating on documents allows for tight teamwork and more efficient document creation. The term "documents," in this context, does not only mean Word documents. It also means Excel spreadsheets, PowerPoint presentations, and OneNote notes. These programs all output documents that can be worked on by multiple people.

As a Paralegal, you need to understand the concept of collaboration because it enables you and your firm to save time and money, and to be more productive. Imagine a scenario where you draft a legal pleading on behalf of two attorneys at your firm that are working on a case. Without collaboration, you would have to work on the document first, send it to attorney #1, wait for comments, send the document to attorney #2, and wait for those comments as well before you can do anything with the document. The document flows from one person to another and stops the workflow process until each person comments and releases the document. This is known as a *serial* process. The serial workflow process is depicted in Figure 3.1.

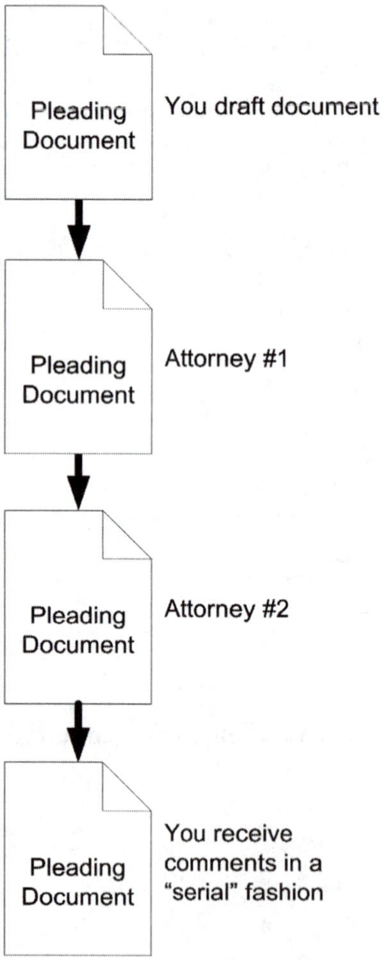

Figure 3.1: Document Workflow without Collaboration.

However, if you use the collaboration features built into Microsoft Office, multiple people can work on the document at the same time. Each attorney can send you the document when it is finished and not have to wait for each other to work on the document. Working on the document at the same time is known as a *parallel* process and is depicted in Figure 3.2.

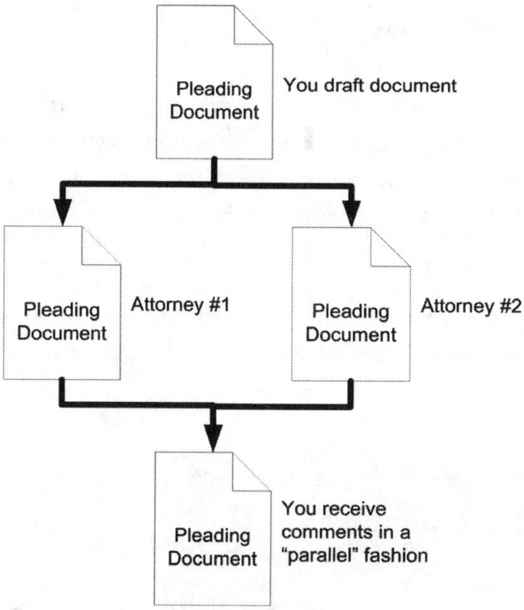

Figure 3.2: Document Workflow with Collaboration.

NOTE

There are many ways to collaborate on documents, but they are not all covered in this book because there are just too many products in the Microsoft Office System that enable collaboration. However, you should be aware that Microsoft has very effective technology that will allow users to store documents in a central repository. This technology is called SharePoint.

SharePoint has two "flavors:" one that provides basic collaboration services (Windows SharePoint Services) and another that adds additional "portal" functionality (SharePoint Portal Server). If your firm uses Windows Server 2003, Windows SharePoint Services is built-in, so you may want to ask your IT department about looking into this functionality.

In a nutshell, SharePoint technologies will allow any user with appropriate security permissions to work on a document. The advantage of using SharePoint technologies is it allows any user to "check out" a document from the library, which prevents other users from making changes. When it is checked in, it will be available for other users. If the document is stored on a file server without SharePoint, you cannot prevent multiple people from changing the file inadvertently. SharePoint also enables users to comment on documents in real-time without having to check the document out.

How's Your Spelling and Grammar?

Too often, people send out documents without checking them for spelling or grammar. It's exceptionally easy to do, so why not do it? Spell checking and grammar checking together are referred to as *proofing tools*. The proofing tools work in all Microsoft Office programs. In fact, the dictionary that contains the list of words for use with the spell checker is the very same dictionary in all Microsoft Office programs.

In any Microsoft Office program, to begin spell checking and grammar checking, simply press the **F7** key, or the **Tools⇨ Spelling and Grammar** menu item. Either way, when an error is found, you'll see the screen shown in Figure 3.3.

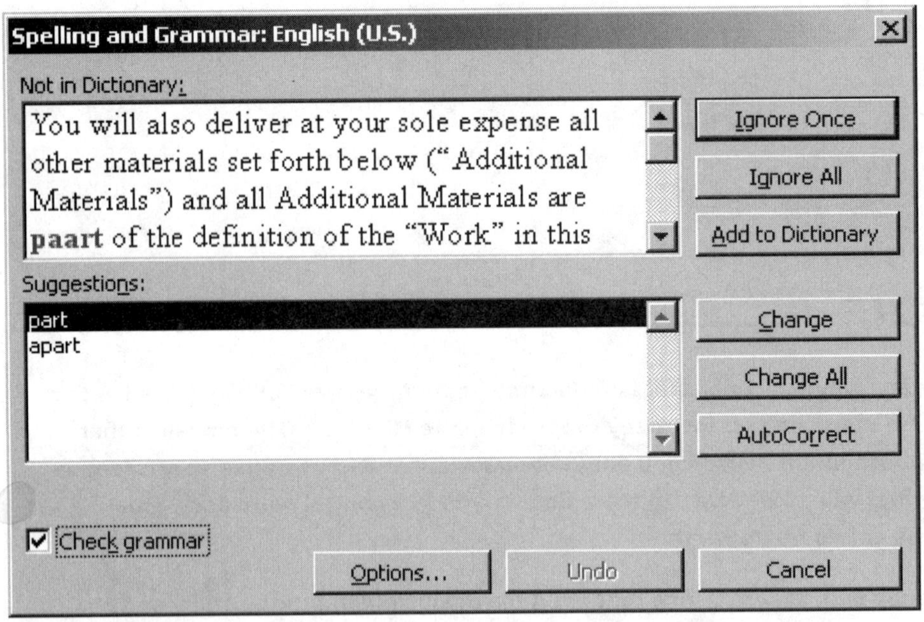

Figure 3.3: Spelling Error Found in Microsoft Word.

Notice in Figure 3.3 that the word or phrase in question is highlighted (shown in red), with suggested words in the **Suggestions** box below. The words in the **Suggestions** box are presented in the order that the Office proofing tools thinks are most likely the correct choice. In the case of Figure 3.3, it is absolutely correct. The incorrect word "paart" has an extra "a" in it. The correct word is "part." To use the corrected word from the **Suggestions** box, simply ensure it is selected and click the **Change** button. In fact, here is a summary of what the buttons on the screen do:

- **Ignore Once** — Disregards the current incorrect word, but if it is encountered again, the proofing tools will prompt you again.

- **Ignore All** — Disregards all occurrences of the incorrect word throughout the entire document.
- **Add to Dictionary** — Adds the current incorrect word to the dictionary so that it will not be incorrect again in this or any document.
- **Change** — Changes only one occurrence of the current incorrect word to the word selected in the **Suggestions** box.
- **Change All** — Changes all occurrences of the current incorrect word to the word selected in the **Suggestions** box.
- **AutoCorrect** — Enters the current incorrect word into the AutoCorrect database so that next time you type it incorrectly, it will automatically be fixed for you. Voila!
- **Options** — Brings up the screen to allow you to specify proofing tools options. This book does not go into these additional options, but you can feel comfortable that the default operation of the proofing tools is suitable for most law firms. The only thing that you'll want to do is add words to the dictionary.
- **Undo** — If you accepted any changes using the proofing tools, you can immediately undo those changes by clicking this button.
- **Cancel** — Closes this screen and returns to your document.

There is one further option that you should know about on the **Spelling and Grammar** screen shown in Figure 3.3. There is a **Check Grammar** option at the bottom of the screen. By default, it is checked, but if you uncheck this option, grammar will be ignored. Grammar is a little difficult in legal documents, which don't necessarily follow Standard English grammar. You may want to turn this option off.

Research is the Key to Success

As a Paralegal, you most likely do research every day. You probably spend half your day on the Internet. However, did you know that there is much you can do from within Microsoft Office to conduct research? This is done through the **Research** task pane.

NOTE

The Research task pane is only available in Office 2003, not any of the prior versions.

Here's how you do research using the Microsoft Office Research task pane:

1. Click the **View⇨ Task Pane** menu item, or press the **CTRL+F1** keys. Doing so brings up a window on the right-hand part of the screen, called the *task pane* . There are many types of tasks that can be shown in the pane — one of which is **Research.**

2. Using the dropdown arrow at the top of the pane (next to the "x"), click the **Research** menu item. This shows the pane in Figure 3.4.

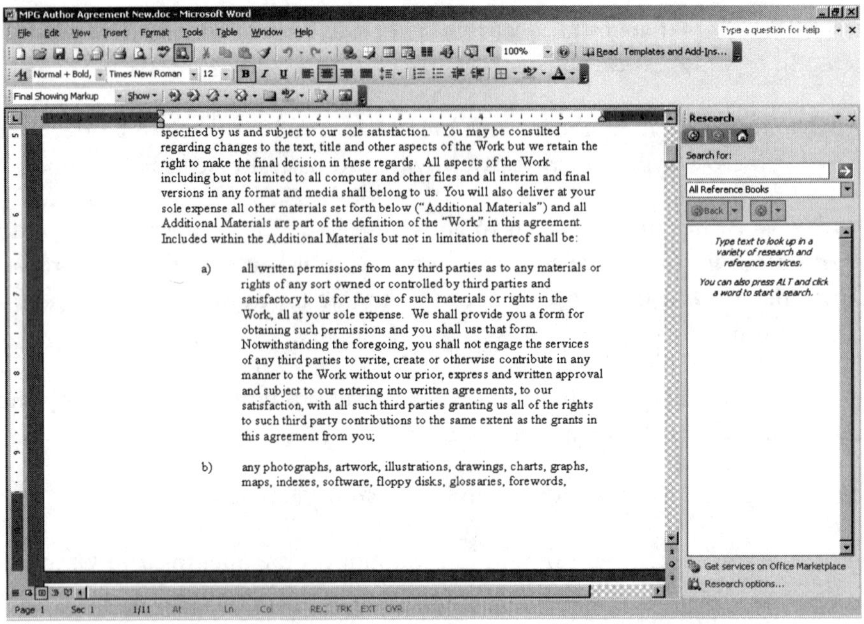

Figure 3.4: Research Task Pane.

Using the **Research** task pane is as simple as typing in a word and clicking the green button to start a search. However, the research that you can do depends on the services that you have installed. This is not unlike any service that you subscribe to for your job, such as LexisNexis. However, some services are free and some are available for an additional fee. The following services are installed and configured when you installed Microsoft Office:

- Encarta Dictionary — Free dictionary service
- Thesaurus — Free thesaurus service
- Translation — Free word and phrase translation service
- eLibrary
- Encarta Encyclopedia

- Factiva iWorks
- MSN Search
- MSN Money Stock Quotes
- Thompson Gale Company Profiles

Templates: Models for Success

One of the greatest things about Microsoft Office is its ability to use templates. *Templates* are a way to create new documents based on another that is already formatted with spacing, fonts, images, margins, form fields, and more. You can create your own templates, or get them from Microsoft—for free!

Templates are available for all Office applications that are covered in this book. Some of them are specific to the legal industry, while others are not. There are hundreds of templates available for you to download and use. To find them, point your browser to `http://office.microsoft.com/templates`, which can be seen in Figure 3.5.

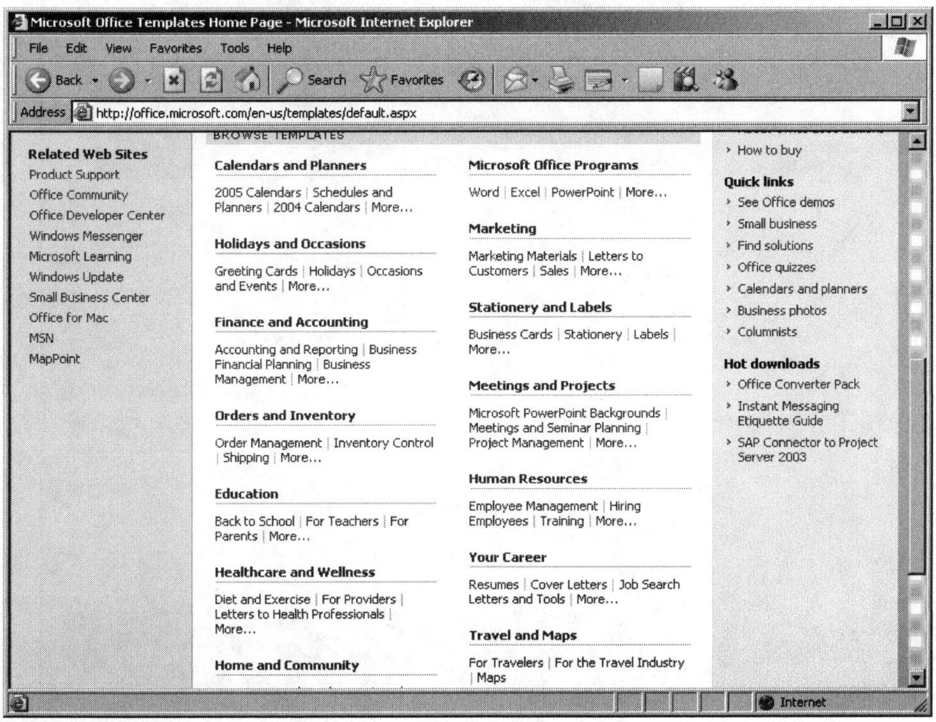

Figure 3.5: Templates Available on the Microsoft Office Web Site.

Templates are available by category (such as **Legal**) or by product. For example, if you wanted to see templates that are available for Microsoft Excel, simply click the **Excel** link under the **Microsoft Office Programs** heading. On the other hand, if you wanted to see what templates are available for family law, you would click the **Family Law** link under the **Legal** heading. The latter would show you the templates available in that category for all Microsoft Office System products. Likewise, you can click the heading itself to show all available templates for the heading in a new Web page. This is sometimes easier to navigate.

To know what product a template is available for, you would simply look at the icon next to the listing. For example, if you click the **Legal** heading in Figure 3.5, you'll be presented with the categories of legal templates available, such as those shown in Figure 3.6.

NOTE

Microsoft develops new templates all the time, so the ones you see in Figure 3.6 might be different than the ones you see online.

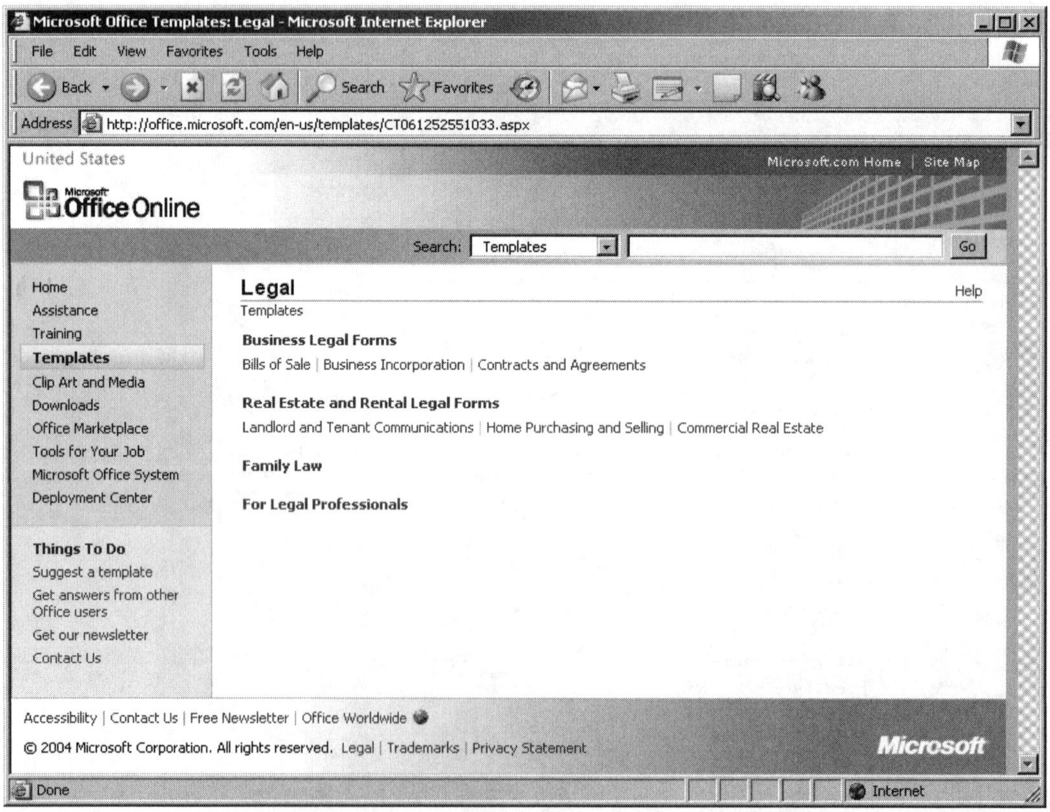

Figure 3.6: Legal Templates Available on the Microsoft Office Web Site.

If you click the **For Legal Professionals** link, you'll see a lot of templates available to you as a legal professional. Each of these shows the icon of the Microsoft Office program that it is assigned to. Figure 3.7 shows the templates available when you click this link.

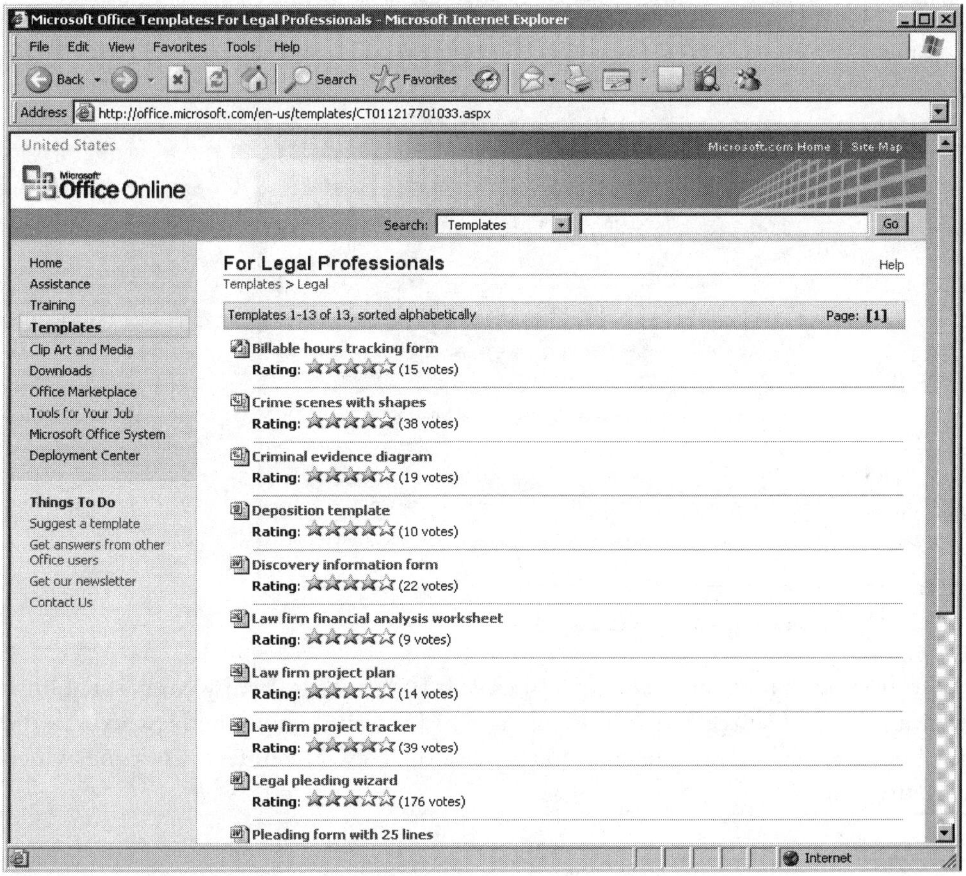

Figure 3.7: Legal Professional Templates Available on the Microsoft Office Web Site.

To understand which icons are represented in Figure 3.7, refer to Table 3.1 for a brief explanation.

Icon	Microsoft Office Program	Description
	Word	Word processing program that is covered in Chapter 4
	Excel	Spreadsheet program that is covered in Chapter 5.
	PowerPoint	Presentation program that is covered in Chapter 6
	OneNote	Note-taking program that is covered in Chapter 7
None	Outlook	Email and contact program that is covered in Chapter 8
	Access	User database that is not covered in this book
	InfoPath	Information gathering program for filling-in forms; not covered in this book
	Project	Program for tracking projects and their tasks; not covered in this book
	Publisher	Desktop publishing program that is not covered in this book
	Visio	Diagramming tool that is not covered in this book
	FrontPage	Web page creation program that is not covered in this book

Table 3.1: Template Icons Used on the Microsoft Office Web Site.

Another way to search for templates is within Microsoft Office itself. In any Microsoft Office 2003 application, if you click the **File⇨ New** menu item (not by clicking the **New** icon in the toolbar), you'll be given a choice of file types to create in the **New Document** task pane, which is shown in Figure 3.8.

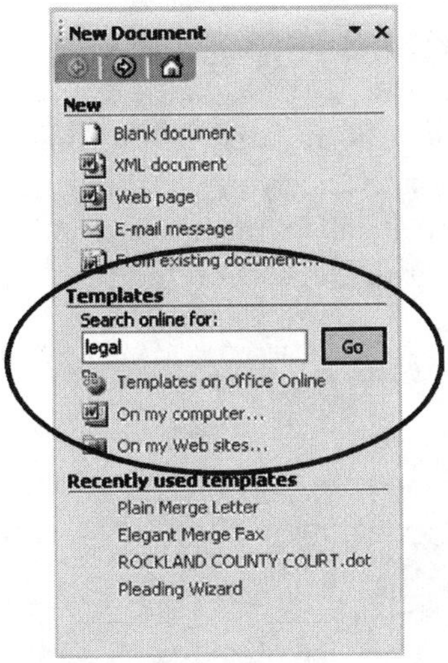

Figure 3.8: New Document Task Pane.

In Figure 3.8, the circled area shows where you search online for a template. One option is to search for templates online. If you type a search value in the box provided, such as **legal**, and you click the **Go** button, you'll see all available legal templates. You can also be more specific about your search, such as looking for **Real Estate**. Figure 3.9 shows the results of searching for **Real Estate** in the online templates.

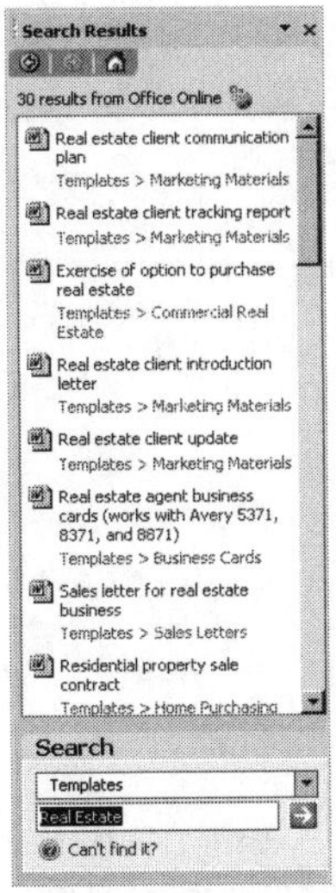

Figure 3.9: Searching for Real Estate Templates.

To use one of the templates, simply click the desired template name and you are prompted to download and install automatically.

Downloading and Installing Templates

Downloading templates from the Microsoft Office Web site couldn't be any easier. You simply navigate to the desired template by choosing a product or category. Once you see the list of templates, click the name of the template, which will show you more detailed information about the specific template, as shown in Figure 3.10. This example is for the **Deposition template** in the **Legal Professionals** category.

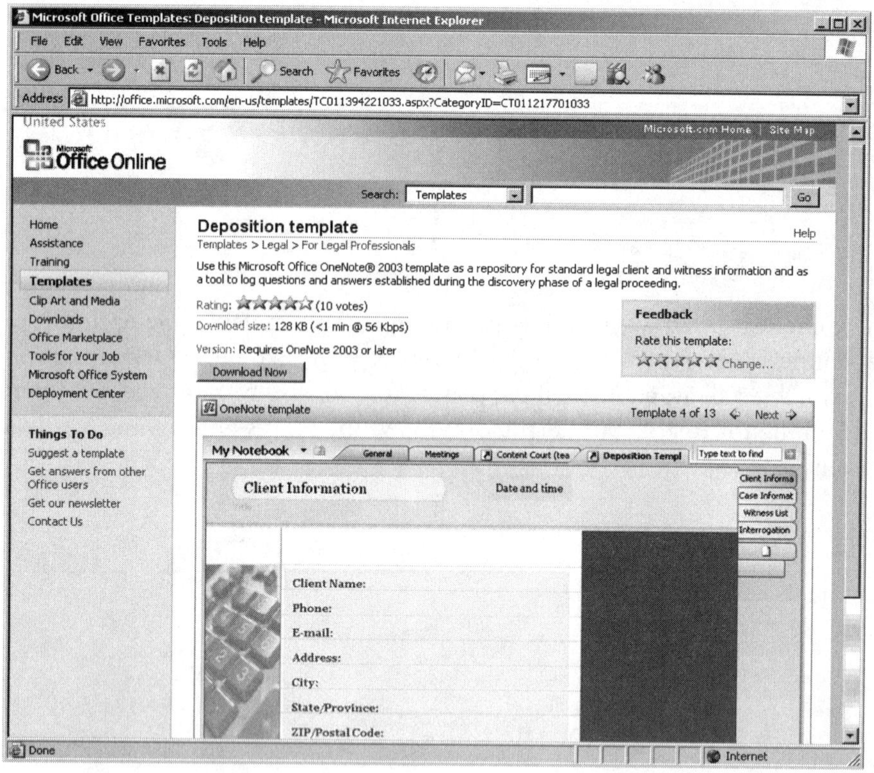

Figure 3.10: Viewing Detailed Information about a Template.

You'll see the following information available for a template:

- **DESCRIPTION** — Shows a more detailed description of the selected template.
- **RATING** — Shows ratings of the template, as rated by general users to the site, from one to five stars. Any user can rate a template. You also see the number of people who voted to arrive at the overall (averaged) rating.
- **DOWNLOAD NOW BUTTON** — Clicking this button begins the download process.
- **PREVIEW** — A preview of what the template looks like.

After you click the **Download Now** button, the template will be downloaded and automatically installed. To see how to use the templates for a specific program, refer to that program's chapter in Part I of this book. After a template is installed, you use it by opening the Office application that knows about the template, such as Microsoft Word. Then, you open the template by creating a new document based on that template. More information about how to do this for each of the Microsoft Office applications covered in this book is shown in the respective chapters of Part I of this book.

What in the World is Metadata?

The technical definition of *metadata* is data that describes data. Isn't that clear? Well, in case it isn't, did you know that your name, your firm's name, and some of your computer information is automatically stored in your documents? Well, it is! Because all of these bits are data that describes data, it is referred to as metadata! Metadata affects only Microsoft Word, Excel, and PowerPoint documents.

Metadata sounds like a good thing, right? It can be, but it can also cause privacy issues. Metadata can even be used against you in the discovery process, as unwanted data can be stored in your document. For example, Office documents can contain metadata such as this:

- Your name
- Your initials
- Change tracking information
- Company or firm name
- Computer name
- Network server and file names and locations
- Template used to create the document
- Comments
- Miscellaneous information about embedded objects

If you are concerned about circulating your documents with this information stored as metadata inside the document, you should know that there are steps you can take to remove it. The next two sections describe two ways to remove this metadata, should you wish to do so:

- Access the "Save As" feature of each of the Microsoft Office applications.
- Use the Remove Hidden Data Tool, which is a Microsoft Office Add-In.

Save As

All Microsoft Office programs except for OneNote have "Save As" functionality, which allows you to save a file as a different name. While you probably don't care about saving a file with a different name, the "Save As" feature allows you to specify additional options during the saving process. Therefore, you can access the special features that allow you to remove personal information. Because the way you access each of these options is specific to the Microsoft Office application that you are using, each is covered in its respective chapter in Part I of this book.

Remove Hidden Data Tool

The Remove Hidden Data (RHD) Tool is a special program that works with Microsoft Office. This program is called an Add-In because it extends the functionality of Microsoft Office. The RHD tool is available on the Microsoft Office Web site. To find it, simply point your browser to `www.microsoft.com`. In the search box at the top of the screen, type `rhdtool`. You'll see a list of RHD tools for the version of Office that you are running. Choose the appropriate one and download it by following the instructions on the screen.

To install the RHD tool, simply run the installation program after you download it and follow the simple directions. After you install the tool, make sure that you quit all Microsoft Office applications. When you reopen then, you'll see a new menu item under the **File** menu, called **Remove Hidden Data.** If you click this menu item, the currently open file will be saved as a new file name that you are prompted for. During the process of creating the new file, all personal information will be removed.

NOTE

There are other non-Microsoft tools available for removing Metadata, such as Out-of-Sight, from SoftWise. For more information, visit their Web site at `www.softwise.net`.

It's No Mattel View-Master, but...

Suppose you don't have Microsoft Office and someone sends you a document. What are you to do? Rush right out and buy Office? Well, you could! On the other hand, you can open most Office documents with a free viewer from Microsoft.

An Office *viewer* is a program that you install on your computer that allows you to open Microsoft Office documents in read-only mode. In other words, you cannot save any changes or create new documents with the viewer, but at least you can open them. If you are reading this book, you likely already have Microsoft Office 2003 installed, so you won't need a viewer. However, if you send a document to one of your clients and they don't have Office installed, they *will* need a viewer to open the document that you send.

These Office viewers are available from Microsoft for no charge:

- Access 2003 Snapshot Viewer
- Excel 2003
- PowerPoint 2003
- Project 2003
- Visio 2003
- Word 2003
- Word 2003 XML Viewer

This is the easiest way to find the viewers:

1. Open a Web browser.
2. Enter the Web address, `http://office.microsoft.com`.
3. In the search box, type `viewer`.
4. Click the **Go** button.
5. You'll see the results of all available viewers. There may be some available that were not at the time of this writing, so following the above procedure will give you the latest results.

Once you have installed a viewer, you can open the document type appropriate for the viewer. Pretty great, huh? If you already have the Office application, there's no point in installing the same viewer for that application.

Conclusion

The Microsoft Office System and all of its associated applications provide a very robust collaborative framework for you to perform all of your Paralegal tasks. While this book cannot cover each of the applications that make up the entire Office System, it does cover the most commonly used ones for a Paralegal, such as Word, Excel, PowerPoint, OneNote, and Outlook. If you don't have the full or updated application for a file that someone sends to you, you can either purchase and install the required Microsoft Office program or download the free viewer that Microsoft provides on the Office Web site. This chapter showed you how to use the research pane to conduct research without leaving Microsoft Office. It also discussed what metadata is and how you can remove it from your documents. You also learned about collaboration and the reason why collaboration can aid in productivity.

To enhance your experience with Office, Microsoft makes countless templates available for all Office System applications. These templates automatically provide formatting, sizing, and layout of common documents. There are many legal-specific templates available to you as well. Along with templates, all Microsoft Office applications come with spelling and grammar checking, also known as proofing tools. While this seems like an easy enough to use feature, this chapter gives some pointers to be more effective with your proofing.

Chapter 4

Microsoft Word 2003

Chapter At A Glance

WHY YOU SHOULD READ THIS CHAPTER:

Being in the legal profession, you create lots of documents. Some documents can get quite complex, but Word can handle even the most complex legal documents. This chapter focuses on general issues surrounding Microsoft Word 2003, while most of the chapters in the rest of this book show how to perform specific tasks.

PRODUCT OUTLINED IN THIS CHAPTER:

- Word 2003

PRODUCT FEATURES COVERED IN THIS CHAPTER:

- Toolbars
- Templates
- Removing Metadata
- Word Counts
- Revealing Formatting

Virtually nobody in the free world is unfamiliar with Microsoft Word. However, even with this vast penetration in the market, it sometimes takes a back seat to WordPerfect in the legal industry. WordPerfect has a legacy in the legal industry, but more firms actually use Word as their word processing program. Microsoft Word 2003 enables you to do such things as:

- Create legal documents, forms, and labels
- Format documents according to court specifications
- Reuse styles to provide a consistent look and feel in your documents
- Conduct research
- Compare and merge documents
- Track changes for multiple-user collaboration
- Secure your documents
- Include Headers and Footers
- Cross-reference other areas of the document, such as a Table of Authorities and a Table of Contents
- Send bulk e-mails and letters

In an effort to keep this chapter as brief as possible, you'll learn an overview of what Word can do for you, but most tasks that a Paralegal uses a word processor for are covered in Part II of this book.

Microsoft Word 2003—for Paralegals?

Microsoft Word is a word processing program that helps you construct documents of all types. You can construct legal documents, agreements, pleadings, forms, labels, and more. Microsoft even makes the process of creating legal documents easy by providing lots of templates that guide you through the process of creating documents. This chapter is geared towards you getting your feet wet with using Microsoft Word.

As a Paralegal, you perform many tasks that are centered on creating documents. You draft agreements, pleadings, wills, and contracts. You also create labels, letters, and memos. These things are by no means a comprehensive list, but the bottom line is that you generate lots of documents. Therefore, you use a word processor every day. There are two basic choices for a word processing program: WordPerfect and Word. Word has emerged as the leader in no small part because of the rest of the Microsoft Office programs that easily integrate with it, such as Excel, PowerPoint, Outlook, and OneNote.

Toolbars

Microsoft Word has many toolbars that help you to perform quick actions. The most common of these toolbars are the **Standard** toolbar, as shown in Figure 4.1, and the **Formatting** toolbar, which is shown in Figure 4.2.

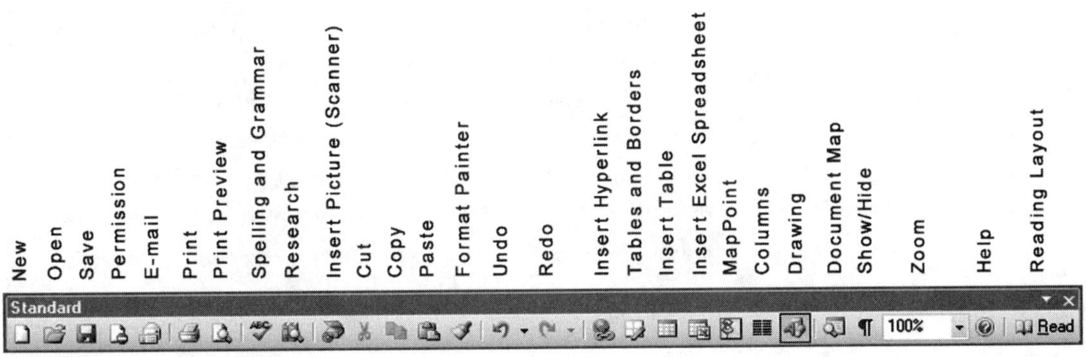

Figure 4.1: Word 2003 Standard Toolbar.

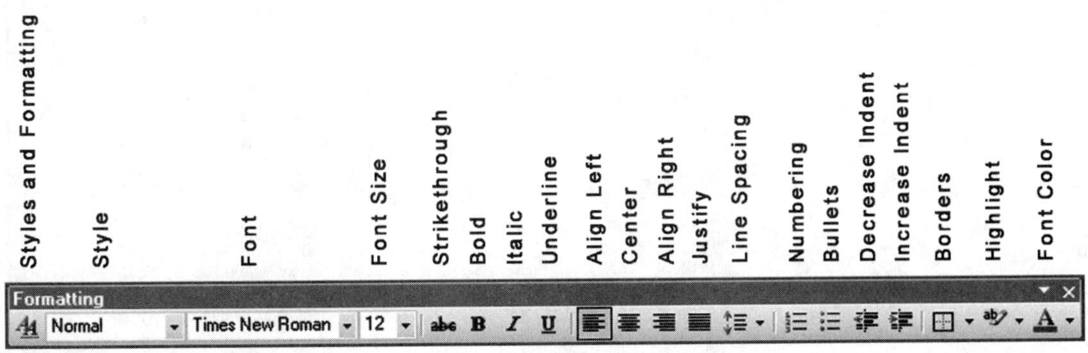

Figure 4.2: Word 2003 Formatting Toolbar.

To show any toolbar, click the **View⇨ Toolbars** menu item and you'll see a list of possible toolbars to display. Simply select the desired menu for the toolbar that you want to display. Depending on any special software that you have installed, you may see more than the out-of-the box Word toolbars.

Legal Templates

There are lots of legal templates on the Microsoft Office Web site that you can download and install for free. You can search for these templates at `http://office.microsoft.com/templates`. The downloading and installation of templates is covered in Chapter 3. Templates are also available by using the *task pane*, which is also discussed in Chapter 3. Table 4.1 lists some of the legal templates that are available for Microsoft Word at the time of this writing.

Agreement between carrier and shipper	Deed granting easement	Patent license agreement
Agreement to assign	Demand for payment: In default of agreement	Petition for simplified divorce
Agreement to rescind contract of sale	Demand for rent	Pleading form with 25 lines
Annual Shareholders' Meeting Minutes	Exercise of option to purchase land	Pleading form with 26 lines
Apartment lease	Exercise of option to purchase leased premises	Pleading form with 28 lines
Application for variance	Exercise of option to purchase real estate	Pleading form with 32 lines
Arbitration agreement	General release	Power of attorney
Authorization for sale of assets	Indemnity agreement	Pre-incorporation agreement for existing business
Authorization to release healthcare information	Installment payment clause for sales contract	Pre-incorporation agreement for new business
Authorization to release healthcare information (online)	Joint venture agreement	Pre-incorporation designation of directors
Automobile bill of sale	Lease option clause	Promise to buy and sell corporation
Basic deed	Legal firm accountant resume	Property management agreement
Basic stock agreement	Legal Pleading Wizard	Rental application
Business corporation bylaws	Letter from attorney about debt	Request for medical records
Checklist for sale of business	Letter of credit	Residential lease
Commercial partnership agreement	Mediation agreement	Residential property sale contract
Confirmation of agreement	Modification of lease	Response to proposal with modifications
Confirmation of contract details	Net lease of business premises	Revocation of "S" Corporation election
Consignment agreement	Notice of annual meeting of shareholders	Sales agency agreement
Contract for manufacture and sale of goods	Notice of legal action after repossession attempt	Shareholders' proxy
Contract for sale of commercial property	Notice of regular directors' meeting	Standard "Work for Hire" contract
Contract for sale of goods	Notice of special directors' meeting	Stock agreement between corporations
Contract for storage of goods	Notice of special meeting of shareholders	Sublease of office space
Corporate bill of sale	Option to purchase	Terms and conditions of contract
Corporate promissory note	Partnership dissolution agreement	Terms and conditions of informal agreement

Table 4.1: Free Legal Templates Available for Microsoft Word.

Creating Custom Templates

In Chapter 3, you learned all about how to download and install templates. However, did you know you can create your own? Well you can, and it's quite easy. Before you create any templates, you should format your document according to the formatting techniques found in this chapter and throughout the rest of this book. Then, when the document looks exactly as you want it, save it as a template.

Let's look at why you would want to create your own templates. A *template* is just a format from which a document is based when it is created. Think of a template in this way. If you were making a batch of cookies shaped in a star, would you cut out the star for each cookie? No! It would be must easier to use a cookie cutter that is already in the shape of the star on which you will base each cookie. Well, Word documents (and all other Microsoft Office templates as well) can benefit from such an approach. Therefore, if you create your own templates you can gain the advantage of creating documents based on that template.

Creating a custom template is very easy. To create a custom template, just follow these simple steps:

1. Create a document that will be used as a template.
2. Click the **File⇨ Save As** menu item.
3. Select **Document Template (*.dot)** in the **Save as type** dropdown list.
4. Give the template a name in the **File name** field. This name is what you'll see every time you want to create a document based on the new template, so make sure you use an obvious name.
5. Click the **Save** button to create your new template.

Removing Metadata

As you learned in Chapter 3, you can use the Remove Hidden Data tool to remove metadata from your Word documents, but that requires an extra installation of a program. Microsoft Word has a built-in feature to remove metadata as well, so you should know how to use it. There are some security implications for not removing metadata from your Word documents, so be sure to check out Chapter 3 for an explanation of metadata.

Metadata can be removed by doing this:

1. Click the **File⇨ Save As** menu item.
2. In the top-right part of the screen, you'll see the **Tools** button, which shows a popup menu.
3. Choose **Security Options** from the popup menu. This brings up the screen shown in Figure 4.3.

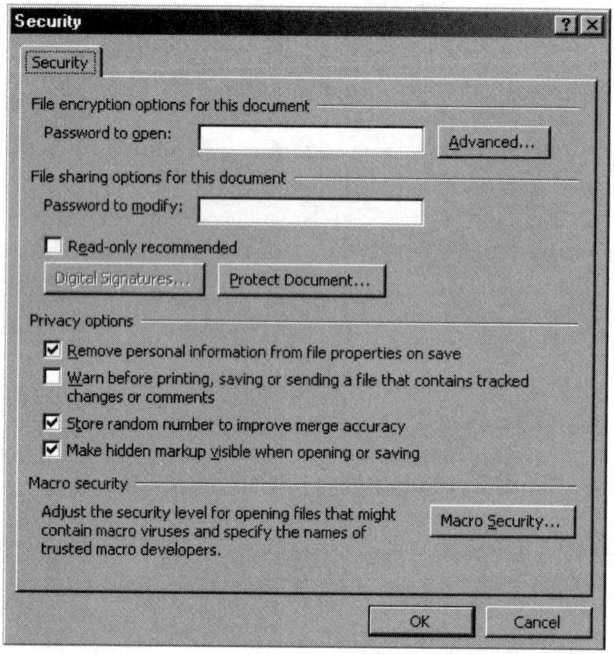

Figure 4.3: Security Options for a Word 2003 Document.

4. Click the **Remove personal information from file properties on save** option.
5. Click the **OK** button. Note that this is only to set the security options, not to actually save the document. After you click the **OK** button, the screen is closed, but you are returned to the **Save As** screen.
6. Click the **Save** button to save your file with the metadata removed.

Wordy Word Words

Many types of documents must be a certain size, or certain clauses in documents can only be so long. For example, you might have a court that requires a legal brief to be a specific number of words, paragraphs, or pages. Instead of taking off your gloves and shoes to prepare for counting the words manually, you can have Microsoft Word count those words for you with a couple of mouse clicks. Here's how:

1. Open your document.
2. If you wish to count all words in the document, ensure that no text is selected. If you want to count only the words in a particular section of the document, such as a sentence or a paragraph, select (or highlight) that text in the document.
3. Click the **Tools⇨ Word Count** menu item. This brings up the screen shown in Figure 4.4.

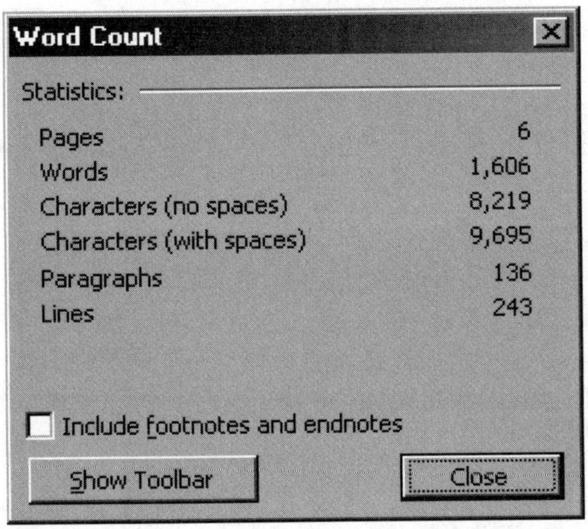

Figure 4.4: Word Count in Microsoft Word 2003.

4. If you wish to include footnotes and endnotes in the count, click the **Include footnotes and endnotes** option, but it is not selected by default.
5. If you plan to use the Word Count feature often, you can show the **Word Count** Toolbar by clicking the **Show Toolbar** button. This shows a toolbar that is displayed all the time that continually counts words, based on text that you have selected in the document.
6. Click the **Close** button when you are finished counting words.

How Many Carats Does Word Have?

Believe it or not, Microsoft Word has one carat. It's the name given to the "I" cursor in your documents. Technically, it's not a pointer, as that refers to the mouse pointer. Figure 4.5 shows a magnified document to illustrate where the carat is located, just to make sure you are clear on this because many chapters in Part II of this book refer to the carat.

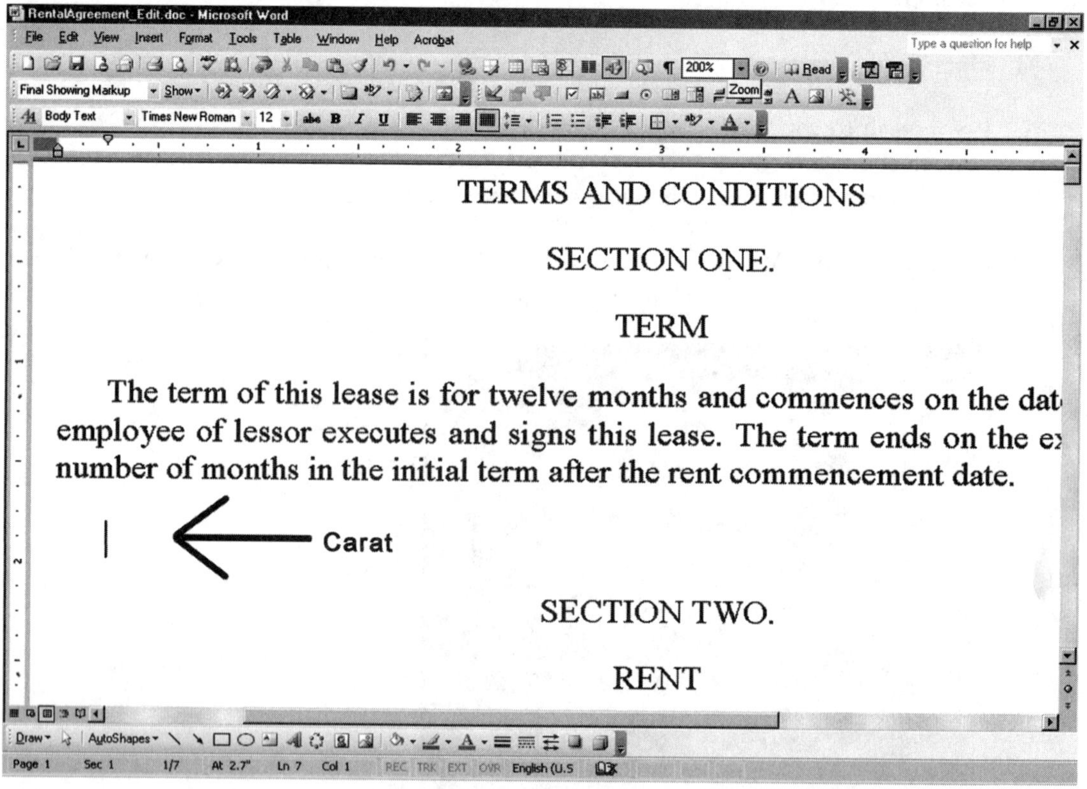

Figure 4.5: Locating Word's Carat.

Revealing Formatting

Formatting your legal documents is very important. A properly formatted document can dictate whether a court will accept or reject your document. While this book can't help you to understand the formatting requirements of courts, it can help you to understand how to format documents for any given situation. Specific formatting techniques for your documents are covered in Chapters 17 and 18. However, you should know how to quickly reveal the formatting of the text where the carat is currently located.

Revealing Formatting is a term used to describe the **Reveal Formatting** pane where the attributes of the selected text are displayed in a hierarchical fashion. Take a look at Figure 4.6, which shows the **Reveal Formatting** Pane.

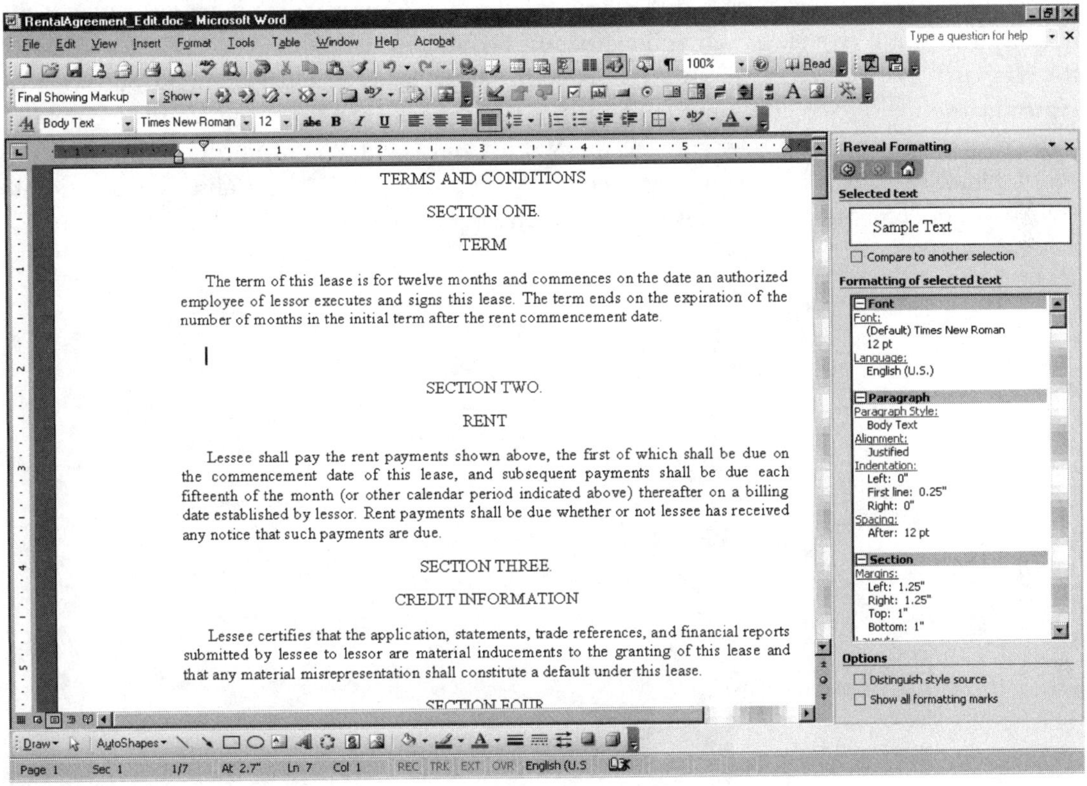

Figure 4.6: Reveal Formatting Pane.

Notice the **Reveal Formatting** pane on the right-hand part of the screen. All the attributes of the text where the carat is located are displayed. For example, you can see in a very quick glance that the left and right margins are set at 1.25" and the top and bottom margins are set at 1". One very convenient feature of the **Reveal Formatting** pane is that if you wish to change any of the formatting, simply click on the provided link (such as **Font, Language, Paragraph Style**, etc.). You'll immediately see a screen pop up that lets you change the selected value. This makes it very quick to review and change your formatting.

Conclusion

Microsoft Word 2003 has some great features to let you construct your legal documents. This chapter introduced you to some basic concepts that are needed before you dive into the rest of the book. This chapter discussed the legal-specific Word templates that are available on the Microsoft Office Web site, as well as how to create your own templates. You also learned about the standard and formatting toolbars available in Word. These toolbars contain buttons that represent the majority of the functionality that you'll need while creating Word documents. This chapter also outlined how you use the **Word Count** and **Reveal Formatting** features of Word. Finally, you even learned what a carat is. While security is an important consideration in your Word documents, it wasn't covered in this chapter because it is covered in Chapter 16.

Chapter 5

Microsoft Excel 2003

Chapter At A Glance

WHY YOU SHOULD READ THIS CHAPTER:

Microsoft Excel 2003 is a spreadsheet program that law firms use to track all sorts of information, including timesheets, billable hours, project planning, contact lists, and more. If you want to learn about the main features of Microsoft Excel 2003 and how it can help you in your firm's activities, you should read this chapter.

PRODUCT OUTLINED IN THIS CHAPTER:

- Excel 2003

PRODUCT FEATURES COVERED IN THIS CHAPTER:

- Toolbars
- Templates
- Formulas
- Quick Summaries
- Formatting
- Pivot Tables
- Security

Microsoft Excel 2003 is one of the applications built into the Microsoft Office System. Microsoft Excel is not used as much in the legal industry as Microsoft Word is, simply because the legal industry is centered on creating legal documents with a word processor. However, spreadsheet programs like Microsoft Excel have their rightful place in the legal world. They can be used to track and calculate all types of financially-related information, such as timesheets, client billing, profit and loss statements, and more. This chapter gives you an overview of using Microsoft Excel 2003 to help with your Paralegal tasks.

In Practice

"I use Excel to create detailed document lists where information can be easily edited, sorted, linked to document databases, and then sent to third parties to comply with production requests."

— Mark Callahan, Paralegal
Nutter, McClennan & Fish, LLP

Microsoft Excel 2003—for Paralegals?

Excel can help you with all sorts of Paralegal tasks. How involved you get into your firm's financial activities will dictate how often you use Microsoft Excel and in what capacity. Many firms use Excel for their own finances, as well as for client and project tracking. Excel can be as complex as you let it be, or you can use its basic calculation functionality. It is completely up to you and your firm's business needs. While this chapter gives you an overview of some of the things you can do with Excel 2003, it only scratches the surface of its capabilities. However, it is enough to get you started in your Paralegal tasks.

Toolbars

Microsoft Excel has a few toolbars that help you to perform quick actions. The most common of these toolbars are the **Standard** toolbar, as shown in Figure 5.1 and the **Formatting** toolbar, which is shown in Figure 5.2.

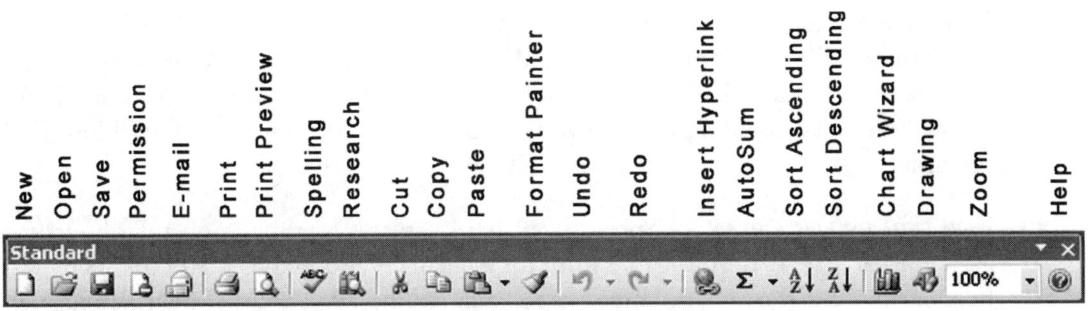

Figure 5.1: Excel 2003 Standard Toolbar.

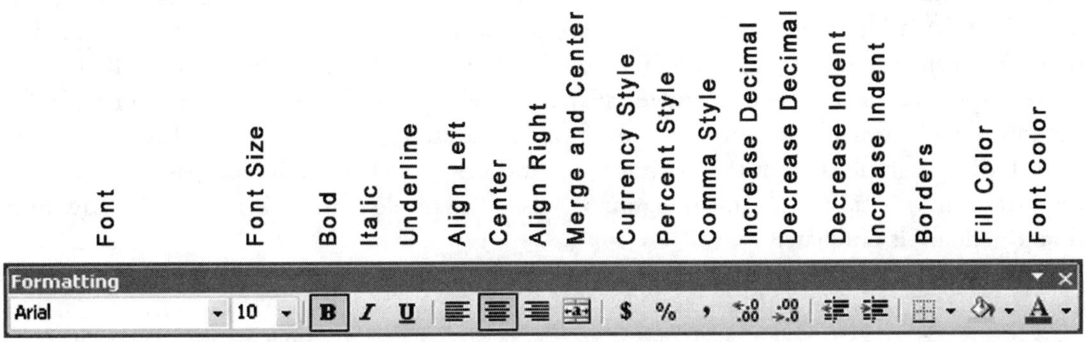

Figure 5.2: Excel 2003 Formatting Toolbar.

To show any toolbar, click the **View⇨ Toolbars** menu item and you'll see a list of possible toolbars to display. Simply select the desired menu that you want to display. Depending on any special software that you have installed, you may see more than the standard Excel toolbars.

Legal Templates

Legal templates on the Microsoft Office Web site can provide good examples of what Excel can be used for. There are a few legal templates available on the Microsoft Office Web site for use with Microsoft Excel. You can search for these templates at `http://office.microsoft.com/templates`. The downloading and installation of templates is covered in Chapter 3. Templates are also available by using the task pane, which is also discussed in Chapter 3. These templates are available for Microsoft Excel at the time of this writing:

- **LAW FIRM PROJECT TRACKER** — Spreadsheet that calculates planned and actual totals for hours and billings for each resource that works on a project. It also graphs the planned vs. actual hours and billings so you can compare how accurate your estimates are.

- **Law firm financial analysis worksheet** — Spreadsheet that calculates and tracks actual time and billings for all clients and provides totals and graphs for every month. The graphs provide calculations for not only monthly billings, but also cumulative billings. Cumulative billings enable you to easily view trends in the financial health of the firm.

- **Law firm project plan** — Spreadsheet that calculates total cost and total hours for all resources that perform billable work for a client. It also graphs the hours spent and billable amounts for each resource, so you can see the relative time spent amongst all resources in a graphical format.

The legal Excel templates give you a great starting point for any of your project tracking and financial calculation needs. Even if these templates don't exactly suit you, you can modify them. You can even take them one step further and see how they are doing the calculations by viewing the example formulas in the template. This will enhance your knowledge of Excel for use in your job. You'll be surprised at how easily some things are accomplished in Excel, such as including a graph. Graphics also impress attorneys and clients alike because they convey important information at a glance. Figure 5.3 shows a sample graph taken from the **Law firm financial analysis** template.

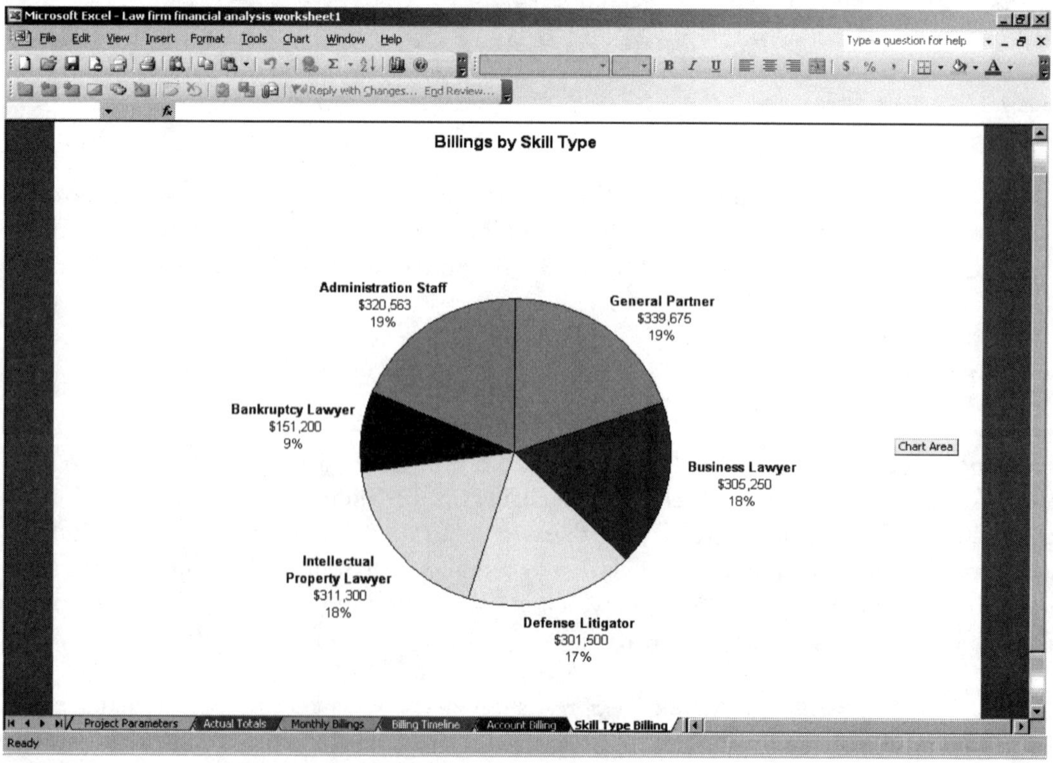

Figure 5.3: Billings by Skill Type Example from the Law Firm Financial Analysis Worksheet Template.

Anatomy of an Excel Workbook

When you open Excel 2003 (and prior versions too), a workbook is created with three worksheets. A *workbook* is a container of related spreadsheets. A workbook is saved on your hard drive or a network drive with an .xls file extension. A *worksheet* is the same as a single spreadsheet. Worksheets are displayed as a series of tabs at the bottom of the screen. Notice in Figure 5.3 the tabs (worksheets) are labeled **Project Parameters, Actual Totals, Monthly Billings, Billing Timeline, Account Billing**, and **Skill Type Billing**. The **Skill Type Billing** tab is currently selected in Figure 5.3, as it is shown in front of the other tabs.

When a blank workbook is created, as shown in Figure 5.4, it has three tabs labeled **Sheet1, Sheet2**, and **Sheet3**.

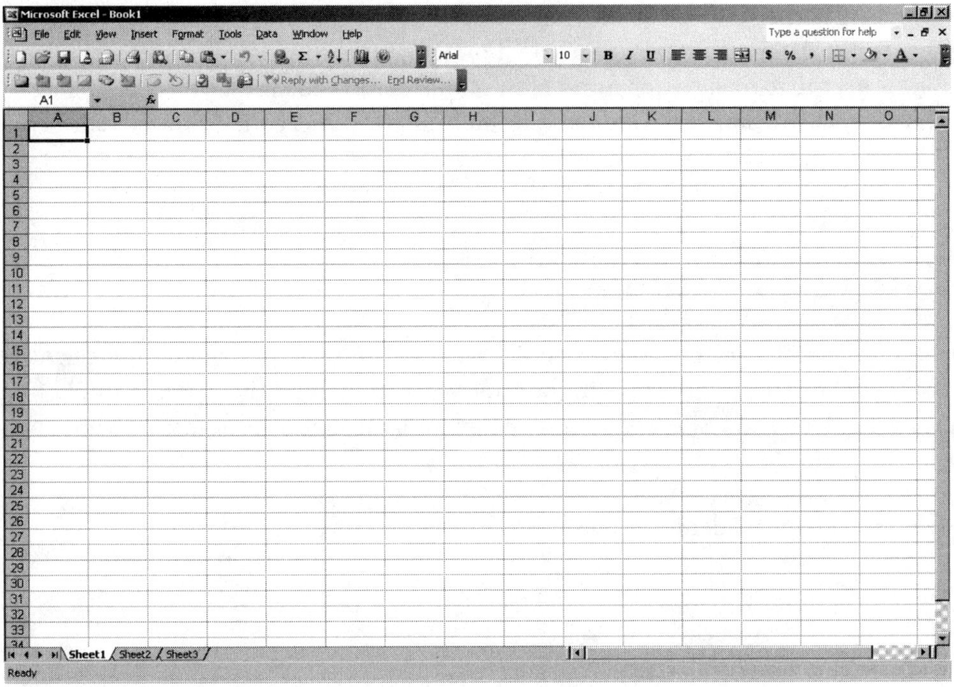

Figure 5.4: New Blank Workbook with Three Worksheets.

If you need more or less tabs (worksheets), you can add or remove them by right-clicking the desired tab and choosing the **Insert** or **Delete** option from the popup menu. You can also rename the tabs, again by right-clicking on the tab, and choosing the **Rename** option from the popup menu.

So, when do you create multiple worksheets vs. using multiple workbooks? As usual, the answer varies. Table 5.1 illustrates some examples of when you would use either scenario.

Scenario	Single Workbook with Multiple Worksheets	Multiple Workbooks with a Single Worksheet
Single physical file on the hard drive	X	
Related sets of self-contained calculations	X	X
Worksheets refer to each other in formulas	X	
Security Protection	X	X

Table 5.1: Multiple Worksheets vs. Workbooks Scenarios.

To see an example of how Table 5.1 works, suppose that you have a spreadsheet of clients and the number of billed hours to those clients for the current month. You want to have another spreadsheet that tracks the same information for all prior months in the current year. You want yet a third spreadsheet that tracks your firm's billing information for prior years. Therefore, it would make sense to have a single workbook with multiple worksheets that can reference each other.

Formulating a Formula

The main feature of Excel is to create formulas. Formulas are used to dynamically calculate values based on values in one or more cells in the same or different worksheet. For example, you can sum a list of hours in a timesheet to see how many billable hours are worked by members of your firm.

Each cell is referenced in a standard way, with the following syntax:

```
[Sheet!]ColumnRow
```

The above syntax uses three variables, which are:

- **Sheet** — The name of the spreadsheet (tab) in a workbook. This is optional (as noted by the "[]" brackets) if the referenced cell is on the same sheet.
- **Row** — The row to be referenced in the formula. Rows begin with the number **1** and can go all the way up to **65536**. Rows are situated horizontally in the spreadsheet.

- **Column** — The letter corresponding to the column to be referenced in the formula. Columns begin with the letter **A** and go all the way up to column **IV**. This may look strange, but after the twenty-sixth column (column **Z**), columns are labeled with double letters, such as **AA**, **AB**, **AC**, etc. Columns are situated vertically in the spreadsheet.

According to the syntax above, the top left cell is referred to as **A1**. Similarly, the top left cell on a worksheet called **Client** would be referenced as **Client!A1**. Formulas are always prefaced by the equals (=) sign. Therefore, to create a formula in a cell that adds cell **A1** and **A2** and **A3** and place the result into cell **A4**, you would simple enter this into cell **A4**:

```
=A1+A2+A3
```

However, it is not practical to enter a formula like this:

```
=A1+A2+A3+A4+A5+A6+A7+A8+A9+A10
```

Instead, you would enter the formula using the **SUM** function in this way:

```
=SUM(A1:A10)
```

Notice that the **SUM** function forces you to place the cell range that you wish to add inside parentheses and separated by a colon, so this type of function is sometimes referred to as a *range function*. This colon is used to specify a range of cells. In other words, you can think of a range as being from cell **A1** to **A10**. Using a range function is very helpful if you are summing many cells at once.

To help make summing a little easier, there is actually an **AutoSum** button on the **Standard** toolbar. To use it, follow these simple directions:

1. Select the cell where you want the formula to be entered.

2. Click the **AutoSum** button on the **Standard** toolbar. You'll see a bounding box (which looks like a rubber band around cells) that automatically selects the most likely candidate for the cells that will be summed. The **AutoSum** button is shown in Figure 5.1.

3. Change the selected cells with the keyboard or mouse, if desired.

4. Press the **Enter** key. You'll see the new formula in the cell that you selected in Step 1. The formula will use the **SUM** function.

Following the same concept for entering formulas into a cell for addition, you can use the information shown in Table 5.2 to perform additional calculations.

Operations	Symbol	Range Function
Addition	+	SUM
Subtraction	-	None
Multiplication	*	PRODUCT
Division	/	None

Table 5.2: Common Operations for Excel Formulas.

In Table 5.2, notice that there is no range function for either subtraction or division. This is because, if you remember back to your arithmetic days, it makes no sense to perform subtraction and division on a bunch of values at once because you can't specify the order of operations. However, you can use the symbols shown in Table 5.2 in your formulas to do subtraction and multiplication. For example, here's how you subtract cell **B2** from **A1**:

```
=A1-B2
```

Use these concepts of formulas to make your spreadsheets very functional. You should also peruse the online help to understand the hundreds of functions available for your spreadsheet formulas.

Quick Summaries

It is a little known fact that Excel lets you do a quick summary of items in your spreadsheet without needing to enter a formula. These quick summaries are useful for temporary calculations inside your spreadsheets. The funny thing about these calculations is that you don't have to do anything special to get this to work. Suppose you are using the **Law firm project tracker** template. It provides example columns that might not necessarily be used in your firm, but they are used for illustration purposes only.

On the **Planned Totals** tab, there are a bunch of billable hours values in the spreadsheet as samples. Suppose you wanted to do a quick summary of all billable hours for cells in the **General Partner** column, but only for the rows labeled **Coho Vineyard**, **Coho Winery**, and **Coho Vineyard and Winery**. All you have to do is select all cells in the spreadsheet that comprise these values. In the bottom right-hand part of the screen, you'll see a summary of the selected cells. This is shown in Figure 5.5.

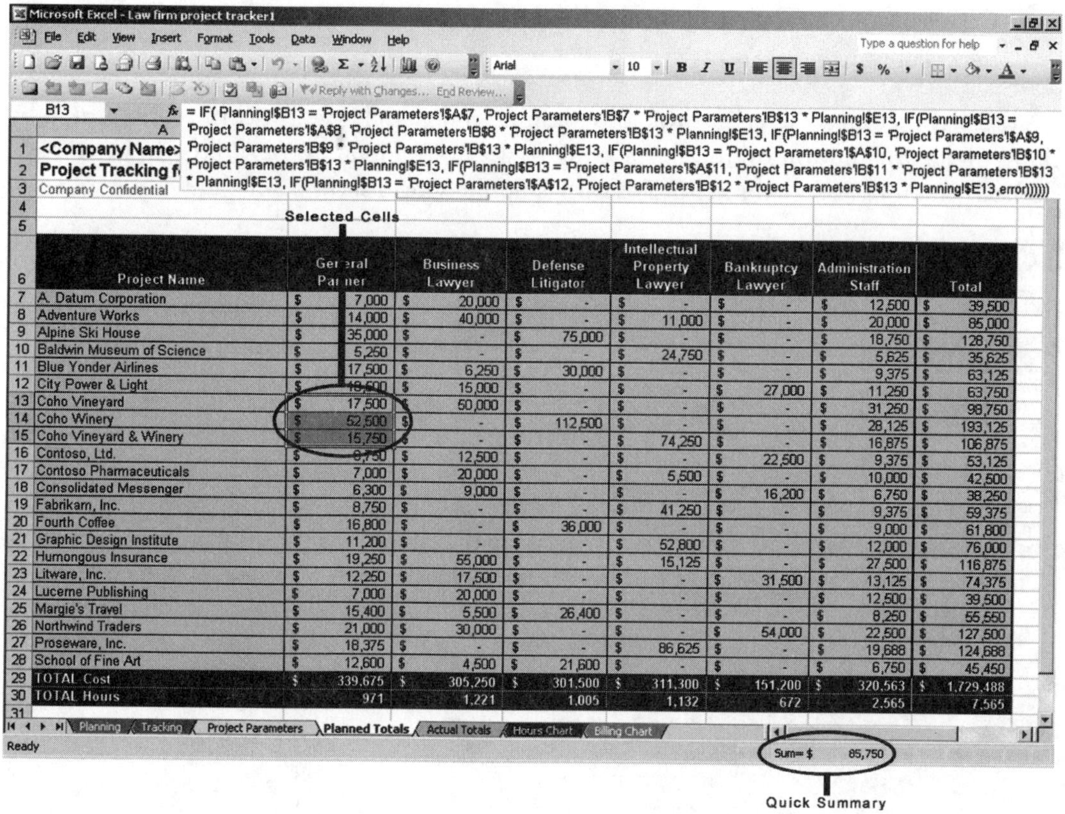

Figure 5.5: Performing a Quick Summary.

Formatting a Spreadsheet

You have just about as many formatting options for Excel spreadsheets as you do for Word documents. You can change font styles, colors, cell background colors, borders, alignments, and more. Just as with your Word documents, you highlight the desired text before you change the format of it. In the case of Microsoft Excel, you select one or more cells before selecting the desired formatting option.

Excel allows you to select these things in your spreadsheets:

- **SINGLE CELL** — Simply click the desired cell.
- **MULTIPLE CELLS** — With the **Shift** key, you can select multiple sequential cells with the mouse. Using the **Ctrl** key, you can select multiple miscellaneous cells with the mouse.
- **ROWS** — Click the row numbers (using the **Shift** and **Ctrl** keys if desired) to select rows in a spreadsheet.

- **Columns** — Click the row header letters (using the **Shift** and **Ctrl** keys if desired) to select columns in a spreadsheet.

Once you have selected the cells, rows, or columns, you can choose the formatting option by clicking the desired button on the **Formatting** toolbar (see Figure 5.2). Alternatively, you can click the **Format⇨ Cells** menu item. This brings up the screen shown in Figure 5.6.

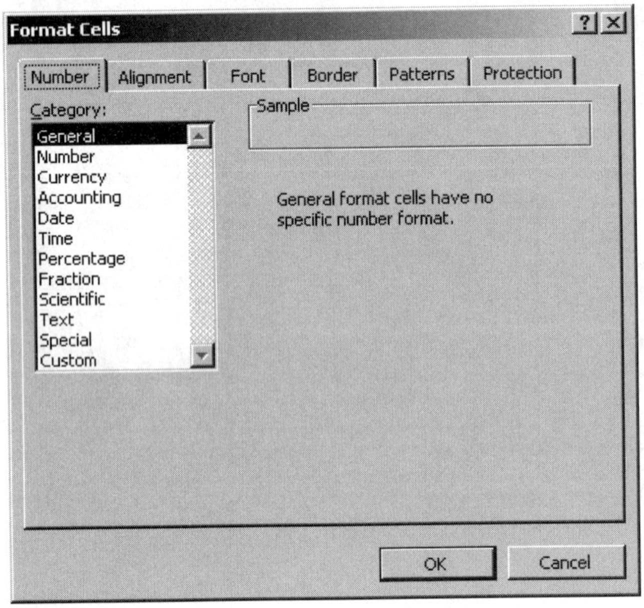

Figure 5.6: Formatting Cells in Excel 2003.

Your formatting options using the screen shown in Figure 5.6 are more advanced and are more flexible than those available in the **Formatting** toolbar. You can specify formatting in these tabs:

- **Number** — Allows you to specify the formatting of values displayed in a cell.
- **Alignment** — Used to align text (including indenting) and text direction and rotation.
- **Font** — Used to specify not only the font name and size, but also whether the font should be strikethrough, superscript, or subscript.
- **Border** — Used to specify the border style, line weight, and color for the selected cells.
- **Patterns** — Allows you to indicate the shading and pattern to use for the background of the selected cells.

- **Protection** — Used to indicate the protection of selected cells. This is covered in the "Excel-erating Security" section later in this chapter.

Pivoting Your Tables

If you have never worked with pivot tables before, they can be a little scary to deal with because Excel gives you so many options for viewing your data. However, you're going to learn how to deal with them the easy way and how they can help you to analyze valuable data in no time.

A pivot table, strangely enough, is just like it sounds. It lets you pivot data. Consider a situation where you have rows and columns of data in a spreadsheet. Rows and columns collectively are known as a table. Unless you perform major surgery on your spreadsheet, the columns that you set up will always be presented as columns, and the rows are always presented as rows. However, you can switch them to get a different view of the data. In other words, you can pivot the rows and columns; hence the term, pivot tables. Pivot tables provide more functionality than just swapping rows for columns and vice versa. Pivot tables allow you to analyze data in a spreadsheet by enabling you to filter the columns and rows that you are viewing to just a subset of your spreadsheet. You can also place columns or rows side-by-side to let you see trends in data that you didn't even know existed.

For law firms, pivot tables are not used every day, but they are included in this chapter to illustrate the power of Excel and to get you thinking about ways to be innovative in using your data. A law firm might use a pivot table to determine which clients are the most profitable. Alternatively, suppose you had a spreadsheet where you tracked billable hours for individuals working on a project; you could use a pivot table to display the results of billable hours by legal department instead of by individual. A pivot table could interpolate this information if you had a listing of which individuals belonged to each department that was included in your spreadsheet.

Excel 2003 provides a wizard to help you manage your pivot tables. Here's how to use it:

1. Open the desired spreadsheet that contains the data you wish to pivot.
2. Highlight all cells in the spreadsheet that will be contained in the pivot table. Make sure that you do not include any cells or columns that are not to be included. As an example, open a new spreadsheet based on the **Law firm project tracker** template. Select the data in the **Actual Totals** worksheet by starting with the column names and selecting all cells up to the total line.
3. Click the **Data⇨ PivotTable and PivotChart** menu item. A wizard is shown with three steps.

4. In Step 1 of the wizard, make sure you select the **Microsoft Office Excel list or database** option.

5. Click the **Next** button. Step 2 of the wizard appears.

6. Step 2 of the wizard is used to select the range of cells that you will use in the pivot table, but that was already done, so just click the **Next** button again. Step 3 of the wizard appears.

7. Select the **New** worksheet option to create a new worksheet in the current workbook.

8. Click the **Finish** button to create the new worksheet and pivot table. This new worksheet contains a list of all data items from your original spreadsheet and a special control surface where you drag and drop data items. This new worksheet shown in Figure 5.7.

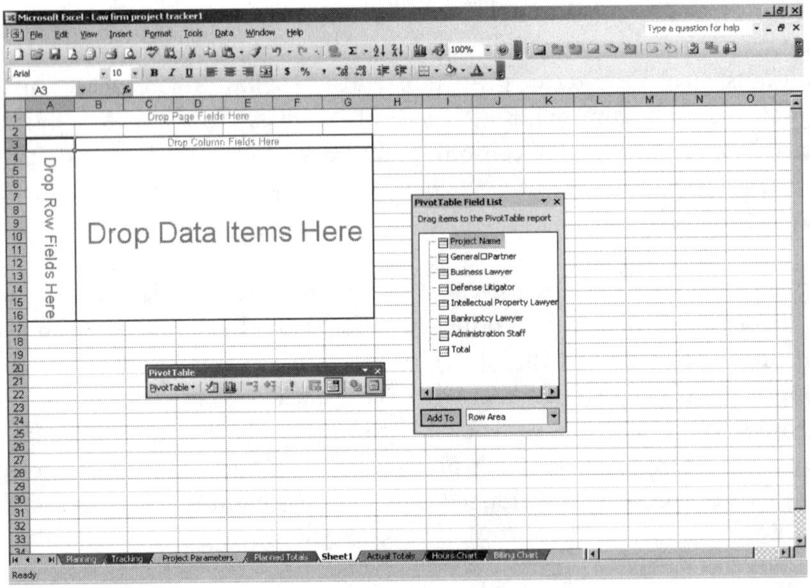

Figure 5.7: New Worksheet Containing Pivot Table.

Notice in Figure 5.7 that the field list has the names of the columns that were selected in Step 2. These field names will be dragged and dropped onto the control surface that is labeled **Drop Column Fields Here**, **Drop Row Fields Here**, and **Drop Data Items Here.**

9. Drag the desired fields from the **PivotTable Field List** box onto the area that is listed as **Drop Column Fields Here.** These fields will have their headings and data values presented as columns. For example, if you wanted to see the project names in each column (where they were in each row in the original spreadsheet), simply drag the **Project Name** field onto the **Drop Column Fields Here** area.

10. Drag the desired fields from the **PivotTable Field List** box onto the area that is listed as **Drop Row Fields Here.** These fields will have their headings and data values presented as rows. Depending on what you are trying to do in your pivot table, this step may not be necessary. For example, if you only want to see the items in the **PivotTable Field List** box on each row, you can skip this step.

11. Drag the desired fields from the **PivotTable Field List** box onto the area that is listed as **Drop Data Items Here.** The fields you choose here are the data items that you wish to view for each row and column. For example, drag **General Partner, Business Lawyer,** and the other fields into the **Drop Data Items Here** area. Drag them in the order which you would like to see them. Because the values stored with these fields will be in the center area, a summary heading for each field will automatically be displayed in the **Drop Row Fields Here** area. (That's why Step 10 was optional).

NOTE

Remember, these fields came from the sample spreadsheet in the template and might not be applicable to your firm.

Figure 5.8 shows the spreadsheet after you drag the fields onto the control surface to swap columns and rows from the original spreadsheet.

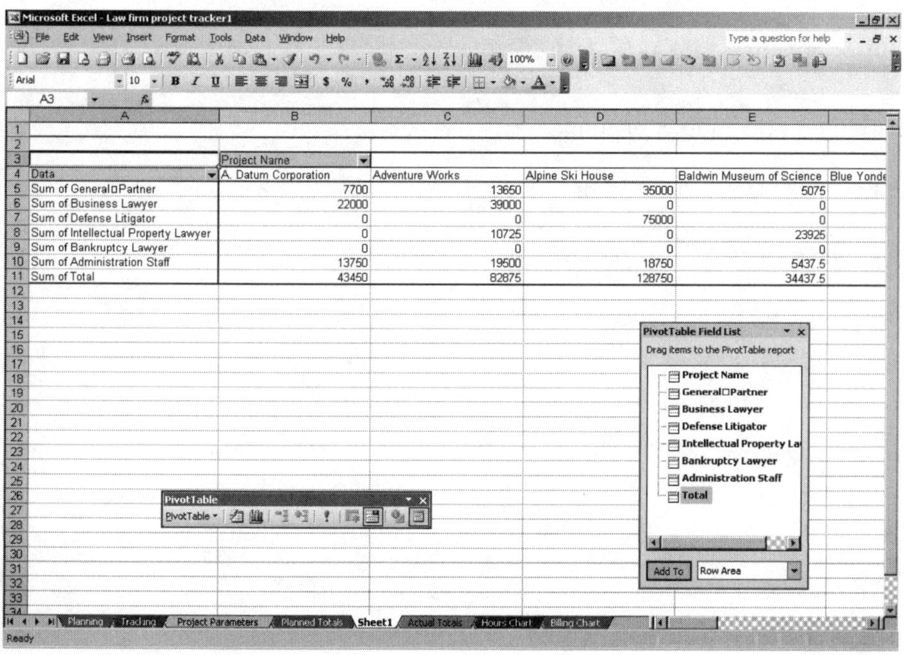

Figure 5.8: Pivot Table After Dragging Fields onto Control Surface.

It's hard to really illustrate the power of pivot tables in a small section of a chapter, but it is a great idea for you to further explore how you can utilize pivot tables to analyze your data.

Excel-erating Security

Security is at the forefront of everyone's thoughts. This is especially true in law firms where data needs to be protected from unauthorized access, as well as unauthorized changing of data in an Excel spreadsheet. Excel allows you to protect both workbooks and individual worksheets within those workbooks; it's your choice.

Protecting Worksheets

Before you protect a worksheet (spreadsheet), you can decide if you want any cells in the worksheet to be locked or hidden. A locked cell will prevent a user from editing the contents of the cell unless the correct password is entered. A hidden cell is not what it sounds like. It does not actually hide the cell itself, but instead, it hides the formula inside the cell. This can be advantageous in situations where you want to send the spreadsheet to someone, but you don't want them to see how you calculated the values. For example, if you have a special way of calculating billing for a client, but don't want them to know all the details, you can hide those cells.

To lock or hide cells, follow this procedure:

1. Select the desired cells to lock or hide.
2. Click the **Format⇨ Cells** menu item.
3. Click the **Protection** tab. You'll see the screen shown in Figure 5.9.

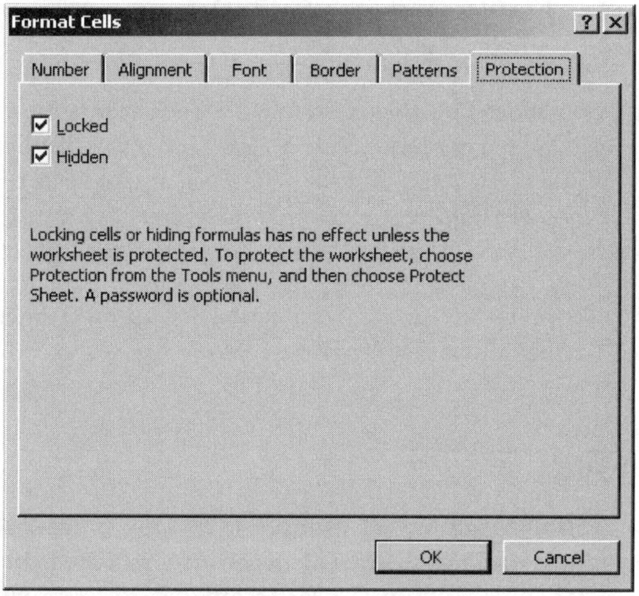

Figure 5.9: Protection Options for Selected Cells in Excel 2003.

4. Select either the **Locked** and/or **Hidden** options.

5. Click the **OK** button to apply the indicated options to the selected cells.

6. Click the **Tools⇨ Protection⇨ Protect Sheet** menu item. This applies the protection to the cells that you specified in Steps 1–5. You'll see the screen shown in Figure 5.10.

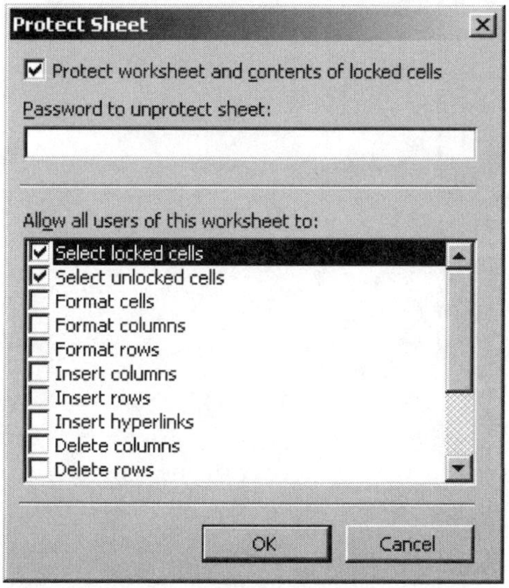

Figure 5.10: Protecting an Excel Worksheet.

7. Enter a password in the **Password to unprotect sheet** field. You must remember this password, as there's no way to recover it if you lose it.

8. Select the options that a user should be able to have while the sheet is protected. By default, all users can select cells that are locked (see Step 4) and also cells that are not locked. In other words, all users can select all cells. However, if you want to prevent someone from being able to select and copy cells that you have locked (unless they know the password), you might want to uncheck the **Select locked cells** option.

9. To unprotect the worksheet, click the **Tools⇨Protection⇨Unprotect Sheet** menu item. You'll be prompted for the password to unprotect the worksheet.

Protecting Workbooks

When you protect a workbook, you don't protect all worksheets in the workbook, but you do protect the workbook from having worksheets inserted, renamed, or deleted. In the case of a workbook such as the templates available from the Microsoft Web site, you have many worksheets that contain complex formulas that reference values in other worksheets within the same workbook. Therefore, you probably want to protect the entire workbook to avoid problems with worksheets that reference each other. Here's how you protect a workbook:

1. Click the **Tools⇨Protection⇨Protect Workbook** menu item. You'll see the screen shown in Figure 5.11.

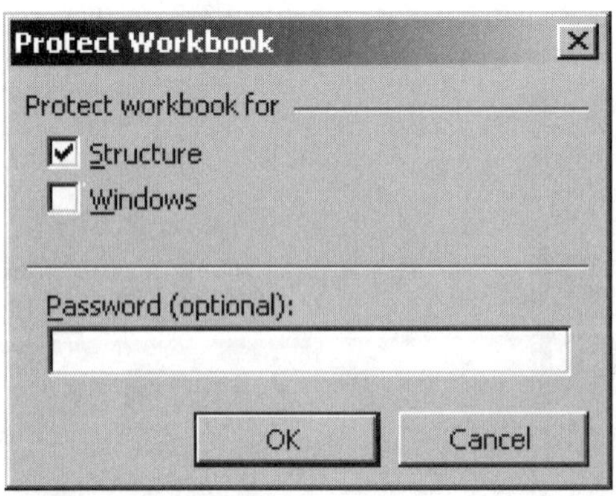

Figure 5.11: Protecting an Excel Workbook.

2. Ensure the **Structure** option is checked, so that nobody can insert, update, or delete worksheets in the workbook.

3. Click the **OK** button to protect your workbook structure.

That's all there is to it!

Conclusion

Microsoft Excel 2003 has some great features that you can use in your law firm. Since Paralegal tasks sometimes include time and billing activities for clients, it is very likely that you and Excel will cross paths. This chapter showed you the Excel templates that are available on the Microsoft Office Web site. It also showed you how to enter formulas into your spreadsheet, formatting, and quick summaries. You learned how powerful (and sometimes confusing) pivot tables can be, but saw how they enable very quick analysis of data in a spreadsheet. Finally, this chapter showed you how to protect your worksheets and workbooks with the security options built into Excel 2003.

Did you know?

An Excel 2003 Workbook can contain up to 256 worksheets. It would be very difficult to manage that number of worksheets, but if you were to use Excel for very sophisticated and complex financial models, you might approach this limit. It is likely not to happen in the legal industry.

Chapter 6

Microsoft PowerPoint 2003

Chapter At A Glance

WHY YOU SHOULD READ THIS CHAPTER:

Microsoft PowerPoint is increasingly used in the legal industry. Graphical presentations can be made using a projector, computer monitor, or laptop for clients and even in some courts. If you are interested in becoming proficient at creating PowerPoint presentations, you should read this chapter.

PRODUCT OUTLINED IN THIS CHAPTER:

- PowerPoint 2003

PRODUCT FEATURES COVERED IN THIS CHAPTER:

- Toolbars
- Templates
- Presentations
- Charts and Graphs
- Hyperlinks
- Handouts and Notes

Law firms sometimes use PowerPoint to deliver presentations to jurors, judges, clients, conference audiences, and members of their own firms. The availability of audio/video equipment in conference rooms and in courts is becoming more commonplace. If you don't currently use PowerPoint, you'll get a lot out of this chapter to understand how it can help you to prepare visual presentations. Of course, this single chapter cannot cover everything you need to know about Microsoft PowerPoint, but it does cover the basics and point out some useful tips for Paralegals. This chapter does not go into enhancing your presentations with transition effects, animations, and sounds. While these things can be really cool, they don't have much place in a legal presentation, so they are not covered. For these features, you might want to consult the online help.

In Practice

"PowerPoint lets me create impressive-looking trial exhibits that can easily be edited at the last moment—something every Paralegal knows to expect!"

— Jennifer Colman, Litigation Paralegal
Nutter, McClennan & Fish, LLP

Microsoft PowerPoint 2003—for Paralegals?

Paralegals are often tasked with helping to prepare or update PowerPoint presentations. Gone are the days of whiteboards, slide projectors, and plastic strips on overhead projectors. Today's presentations may instantly and seamlessly move from bulleted lists to enhanced photographs to detailed charts, and even animations and sound recordings. PowerPoint presentations can even show key points of evidence, such as a list of phone calls, dated letters, or forensic evidence. You can also show a summary of arguments, a list of legal cases you are citing, or even a sequence of events that are crucial to a case. Whether presenting evidence to a jury in a compelling way or detailing a strategy for a client, Paralegals can use PowerPoint to help the attorney deliver the facts and the message in a strong visual manner that audiences will understand and retain.

Microsoft PowerPoint 2003 has many features that will help your law firm make effective presentations:

- Offers a presenter maximum control over all the elements of a presentation
- Allows you to print handouts and notes
- Allows collaboration between experts

- Brings together photographs, drawings, graphs, flowcharts
- Offers the use of Animation and Sound
- Supports live links to external information sources
- Provides security for sensitive content
- Free viewer application so that PowerPoint documents are readable by users who do not own Microsoft Office

As much an organizational tool as a graphics presentation application, PowerPoint can marshal all the facts in an easily navigable series of notes that replaces the old legal notepad. This chapter will show you how to quickly create notes and handouts.

Anatomy of a PowerPoint Presentation

A PowerPoint presentation is comprised of a series of individual screens, known as *slides*. The presentation is given to your client or a court, much like an old-time slide show with one slide presented after another. Your slides can include links that jump to specific parts of the presentation if desired. Every slide in the presentation does not have to be displayed exactly one after another. A PowerPoint presentation is also known as a *slide deck* because it contains lots of individual slide screens.

PowerPoint is also useful as a teaching aid for clients or other attorneys on a point of law or point of order. For example, Figure 6.1 below shows a slide from a PowerPoint presentation intended to instruct a client (in this case, a homeowners association) in the rules and regulations relating to rules violations. This chapter will show you how to work with text and lists in your slides.

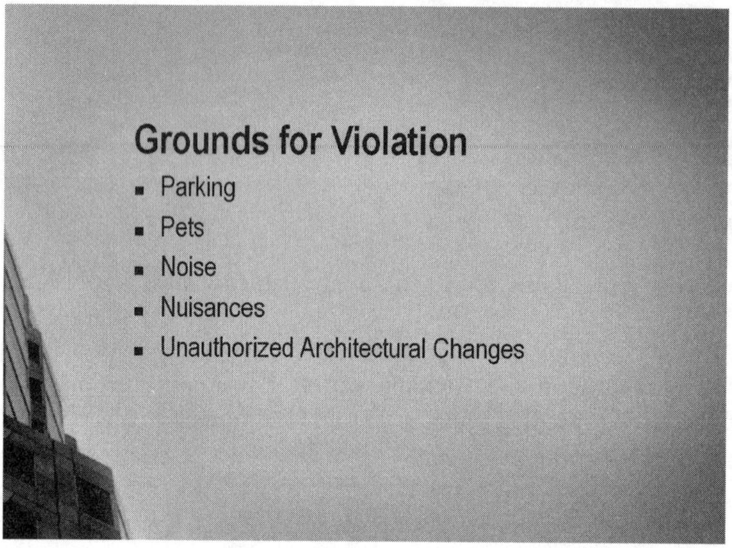

Figure 6.1: Sample PowerPoint Slide as Teaching Tool for a Client.

Toolbars

Microsoft PowerPoint has a few toolbars that help you to perform quick actions. The most common of these toolbars are the **Standard** toolbar, as shown in Figure 6.2, and the **Formatting** toolbar, which is shown in Figure 6.3.

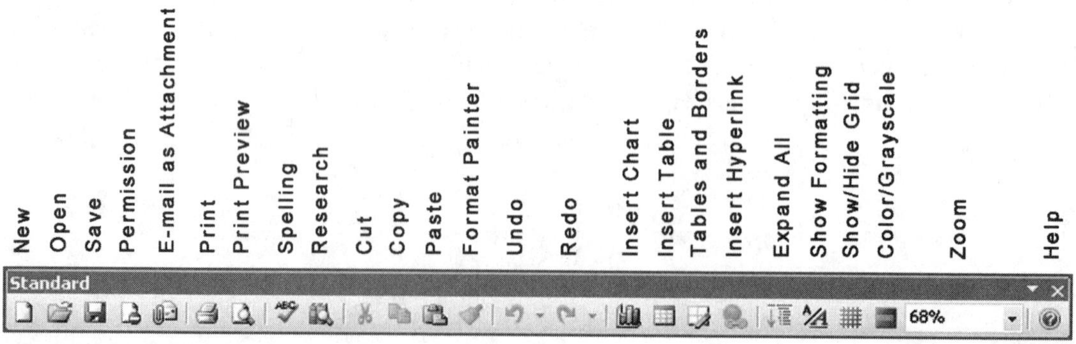

Figure 6.2: PowerPoint 2003 Standard Toolbar.

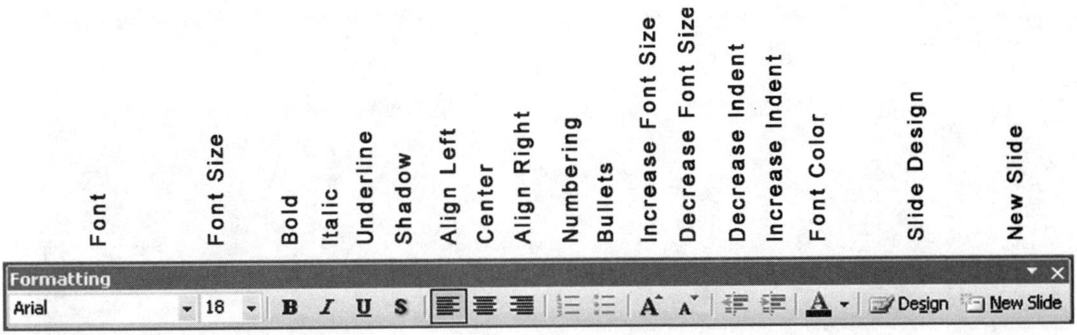

Figure 6.3: PowerPoint 2003 Formatting Toolbar.

To show any toolbar, click the **View⇨ Toolbars** menu item and you'll see a list of possible toolbars to display. Simply select the desired menu that you want to display. Depending on any special software that you have installed, you may see more than the standard PowerPoint toolbars.

Legal Templates

At the time of this writing, there were no PowerPoint templates specifically designed for legal usage on the Microsoft Office Web site. However, there are lots of other templates that can be used as backgrounds for your legal presentations. To find these templates, simply search for PowerPoint templates at `http://office.microsoft.com/templates`. The downloading and installation of templates is covered in Chapter 3. Templates are also available by using the task pane, which is also discussed in Chapter 3.

PowerPoint templates give you a great starting point for your presentations. Not only do these templates place background images into your presentations, they also set up a theme for all slides in your presentation that includes fonts, text placement, and more. Figure 6.4 shows the **Presentation for strategy recommendation** PowerPoint template. While this template is not a specific legal template, it could be used in certain types of presentations.

Figure 6.4: Sample PowerPoint Template.

Creating a New PowerPoint Presentation

A PowerPoint *presentation* consists of one or more *slides*, each of which can contain text, effects, images, sounds, and links. To create a new presentation, do the following:

1. Click the **File⇨ New** menu item.
2. In the **New Presentation** pane, you can choose from several default presentation options, as shown in Figure 6.5.

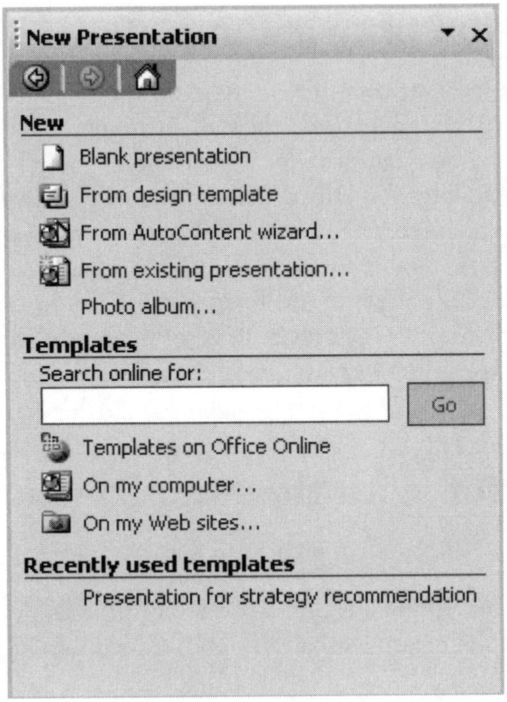

Figure 6.5: Choices Available for Creating a New PowerPoint Presentation.

You can create a new presentation from these options:

- **Blank presentation** — Creates a blank presentation and allows you to choose from a variety of default text and content layouts.
- **From design template** — Allows you to choose from a variety of Design Templates, Color Schemes, and Animation Schemes.
- **From AutoContent wizard** — Runs a wizard to assist you in defining the appearance and content of your presentation. For more information, see the section "Creating a New Presentation with the AutoContent Wizard" below.
- **From existing presentation** — Opens an existing presentation to use as a starting point for a new presentation.
- **Photo album** — Allows you to easily create a presentation of pictures as a photo album.

Creating a New Presentation from a Template

You can also choose a template as the basis for your new presentation. As shown in Figure 6.5, clicking the **File⇨ New** menu item brings up the task pane on the right-hand part of the screen, which enables you create a presentation based on a template located online, on your computer, or on a personal Web site. Clicking the **Templates for Office Online** link will take you to the Microsoft Office Templates Homepage (`http://office.microsoft.com/en-us/templates`), where you can search or browse for a template suitable for your needs. The advantage of using templates is that they contain slides with default content and formatting that you can use or modify to suit your needs. It can also be beneficial to investigate some of the products available from the National Institute for Trial Advocacy, at `http://www.nita.org`.

Creating a New Presentation with the AutoContent Wizard

The AutoContent wizard makes creating new presentations a breeze by prompting you for options and guiding you through the process of creating a PowerPoint presentation. Here's how to do it:

1. Click the **File⇨ New** menu item.
2. Click the **From AutoContent wizard** link in the task pane on the right-hand side of the screen. The wizard will take you through a series of screens where you will choose a type of presentation, the ways in which your presentation will be used, output options, and summary profile information.
3. When you have completed all the screens in the wizard, click the **Finish** button to see the new presentation. You will, of course, have to modify the new presentation to suit your needs and your specific content.

Sliding into PowerPoint

Once you have created a new presentation, you're free to start adding slides and content to your slide deck. The next few sections show you how to do that.

What a View!

Views are simply ways of looking at your presentation when you are creating and editing it. Once you have created a new presentation, you can work on your slides in any of the following views. (To switch between views, use the **View** menu or the view buttons at the bottom of the left-hand pane).

- **NORMAL VIEW** — This is the most commonly used view for creating and editing presentations. It contains four working areas:
    - The **Slides** tab shows thumbnail images of your slides.
    - The **Outline** tab displays an outline of your slide text and gives you an overall view of your presentation's content.
    - The **Notes** pane allows you to enter, edit, and view notes that accompany a slide. You can choose whether to display or hide these notes during your presentation.
    - The **Slides** pane shows a larger view of the current slide.
- **SLIDE SORTER VIEW** — Shows thumbnail images of your slides, giving you a quick overview of their layout and sequence.
- **SLIDE SHOW VIEW** — Runs a full-screen slide show of your presentation, showing all images, effects, and multimedia elements exactly how your audience will see them.
- **NOTES PAGE** — Allows you to enter, edit, and view notes that accompany a slide.
- **MASTER** — Three master views (**Slide Master**, **Handout Master**, and **Notes Master**) allow you to make global changes (such as adding your firm's name or logo) to all the slides, handouts, or notes in your presentation.

Adding New Slides

Since the fundamental mechanism of your PowerPoint presentation is a slide show, you will use slides as the basic container components of your information, whether it be text, graphics, charts, animation, or sound. Think of blank slides as a painter's canvas, where you place the content anywhere within that canvas. You add slides wherever you need them in your presentation. Here's how you do it:

1. Click the **New Slide** button on the **Formatting** toolbar (or simply press the **Ctrl** and **M** keys). The **Slide Layout** pane comes up, as shown in Figure 6.6.

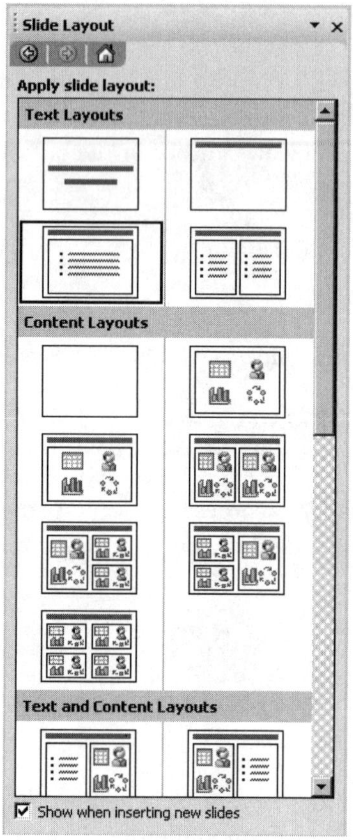

Figure 6.6: Choosing a Layout for a New Slide.

2. Choose your desired layout by simply clicking on the picture that is most like the layout you are interested in.

The Object of Your Desire

Now that you know how to create presentations and insert slides, it's time to explore PowerPoint objects — the sorts of things you can actually put in your slides. These are the most commonly used PowerPoint objects:

- **Text boxes** — These are boxes containing text or images. They can be resized and placed anywhere on a slide.

- **SHAPES** — These consist of circles, rectangles, lines, connectors, arrows, flowchart symbols, and more. Shapes can be rotated, flipped, resized, colored, or have text added to them.

- **PICTURES** — These are graphics files that you can add to a slide.

Working with Text

You can add and edit text for your slides by typing in the **Outline** tab (available in the **Normal** view), or add and edit text directly in a slide in the following locations:

- **PLACEHOLDERS** — Boxes containing body and title text for images, charts, or tables. Placeholders are usually part of the default layout of a slide and have dotted or cross-hatched borders. Changing the placeholder in the **Slide Master** view will effect a global change to all slides.

- **TEXT BOXES** — Boxes containing text or images that can be resized and placed anywhere on a slide. You can add a text box to a slide by clicking the **Text Box** button in the **Drawing** toolbar.

- **AUTOSHAPES** — Stock images for geometric shapes, flowcharts, symbols, banners, callouts, or arrows. Text that is attached to an AutoShape will conform to the shape and formatting of the AutoShape. You can add an AutoShape to a slide by clicking the **AutoShape** button in the **Drawing** toolbar, and choosing a shape from the **AutoShape** menu.

- **WORDART** — Text objects with special formatting and effects, such as stretching, rotation, colors, or a 3-D appearance. You can add WordArt to a slide by clicking the **Insert WordArt** button in the **Drawing** toolbar and choosing an effect from the gallery.

You can create numbered and bulleted lists by selecting the desired text and clicking either the **Bullets** button or **Numbering** button on the **Formatting** toolbar. To create subordinate lists within the main list, select the desired text and click the **Increase Indent** button on the **Formatting** toolbar. An example of using text in your presentations is to show an evidence timeline, which is shown in Figure 6.7. This is a powerful way to convey a lot of information at a single glance.

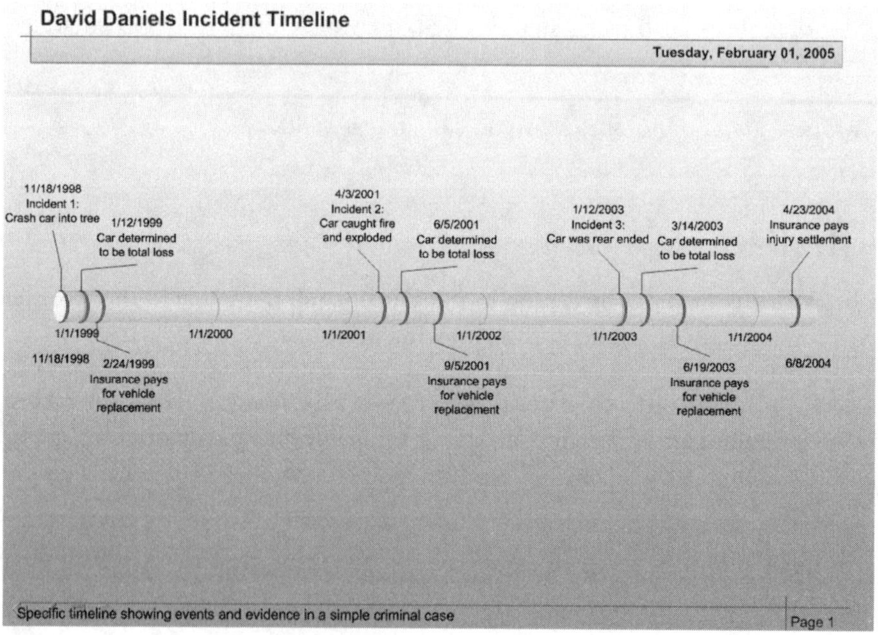

Figure 6.7: Sample Slide Showing Evidence Timeline.

To add a text box to a slide, click the **Text Box** button in the **Drawing** toolbar and click the place on the slide where you want the new text box to go. You can place multiple text boxes on a single slide.

TIP

Don't try to put too much text on a single slide. Too much information will be hard for the audience to focus on, and harder still for them to remember. The same advice applies no matter who your audience is—even if the slides are only intended for an attorney to use as notes in court. For example, it is a best practice is to use bullets to stress or summarize the key points of a speech. Use your slides as a guide to organizing, summarizing, and delivering your speech. Don't try to put the whole speech on a single slide! It *has* been tried, and seldom works out well.

Adding Shapes and Pictures

Shapes (such as lines and other geometric shapes) and pictures can really spruce up your presentations. They add visually appealing elements without being too flashy. In fact, shapes and pictures can tell the entire story, such as the picture displayed in Figure 6.8.

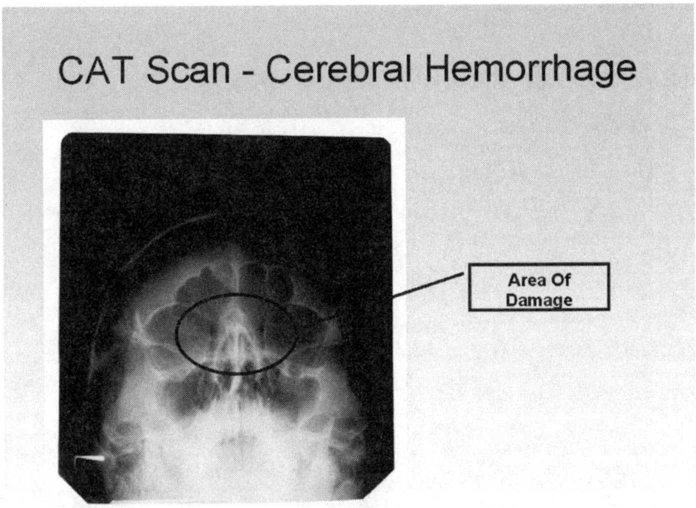

Figure 6.8: Sample Slide Showing the Impact of Pictures.

It is very easy to add shapes and pictures. To add a shape to a slide, do the following:

1. On the **Drawing** toolbar, click the **AutoShapes** button and choose a shape from the available categories. You can choose from several ready-made, basic shapes, such as circles, rectangles, lines, connectors, arrows, flowchart symbols, and more.

2. Click the place in the slide where you want to add the AutoShape.

To add a picture to a slide, do the following:

1. On the **Drawing** toolbar, click the **Insert Picture** button.

2. Navigate to the graphic file you want to add and select it.

3. To embed the picture into your PowerPoint document, click the **Insert** button. To merely link to the picture (on your hard drive or at an external location), click the down arrow on the **Insert** button and choose **Link to File**.

In Practice

"We use PowerPoint for delivering presentations in the courtroom, and also internally for things like year-end presentations. We like the fact that PowerPoint uses a lot of the same features that we're already familiar with from other applications like Word. I make use of imported charts, tables, timelines and graphs from Excel. An audience will respond to strong visual information, as long as the presentation is not too cluttered or overloaded with information. Simple and streamlined is best. Less is more."

**— Suzanne Scanlon, Litigation Technology Specialist
Goodwin Procter, LLP**

Incorporating Charts and Graphs

You can create charts and graphs in PowerPoint using its bundled default application, Microsoft Graph. Creating a chart this way is as easy as clicking the **Insert⇨ Chart** menu item. You can also import charts and graphs from other programs such as Microsoft Excel or Lotus 1-2-3, and this is most likely the way you will add such items to your presentations. Figure 6.9 shows how powerful it is to use a graph in a presentation. In Figure 6.9, it is obvious at a glance which practice area is generating the most revenue.

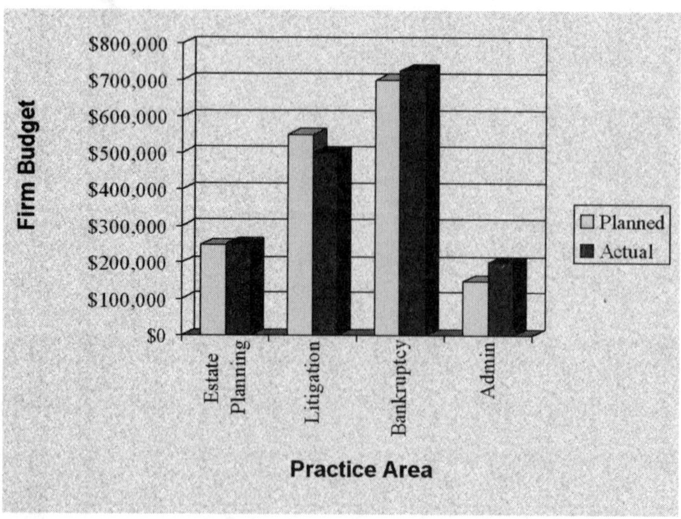

Figure 6.9: Sample Slide Showing a Graph of Billing Information.

Here's how to add a chart from Microsoft Excel:

1. Click the **Insert⇨ Chart** menu item.
2. When the datasheet appears, be sure it is selected (click the **View⇨ Datasheet** menu item if necessary).
3. Select the cell where the imported data should begin.
4. Click the **Edit⇨ Import File** menu item.
5. Navigate to the desired Excel file and click the **Open** button.
6. In the **Import Data Options** screen, select the appropriate sheet to import.
7. To import all the data, click the **Entire sheet** button. To import only part of the data, enter the cell range in the **Range** box.

Flowcharts allow you to show a sequence of events or the logical flow of a procedure. To create a flowchart, do the following:

1. Click the **AutoShapes⇨ Flowchart** menu item in the **Drawing** toolbar.
2. Click the area on the slide where you want to place the flowchart, and add shapes, connectors, and text.

Becoming Hyper About Hyperlinks

When delivering a presentation, it may be useful to be able to navigate quickly from one slide to a non-adjacent slide elsewhere in the presentation, or to instantly access an external Web page or file that contains supplementary information. For example, if you are in a client meeting and you need to skip ahead to certain slides due to time constraints, you want to have hyperlinks in your presentation to enable on-the-fly tailoring of your presentations. A *hyperlink* is simply an object that, when clicked, takes you directly to a specified slide, URL, or file path. You can attach hyperlinks to text, pictures, shapes, graphs, WordArt, or customized buttons.

NOTE

Hyperlinks only work when you are running your presentation—not when you are creating or editing your slides.

Creating Hyperlinks to Slides

To create a hyperlink to another slide in the presentation, follow these steps:

1. Select the text or object that will activate the hyperlink when clicked.
2. Click the **Insert⇨ Hyperlink** menu item (or simply press the **Ctrl** and **K** keys).
3. Under **Link to**, click **Place in This Document.**
4. Select the destination slide for the hyperlink, as shown in Figure 6.10.

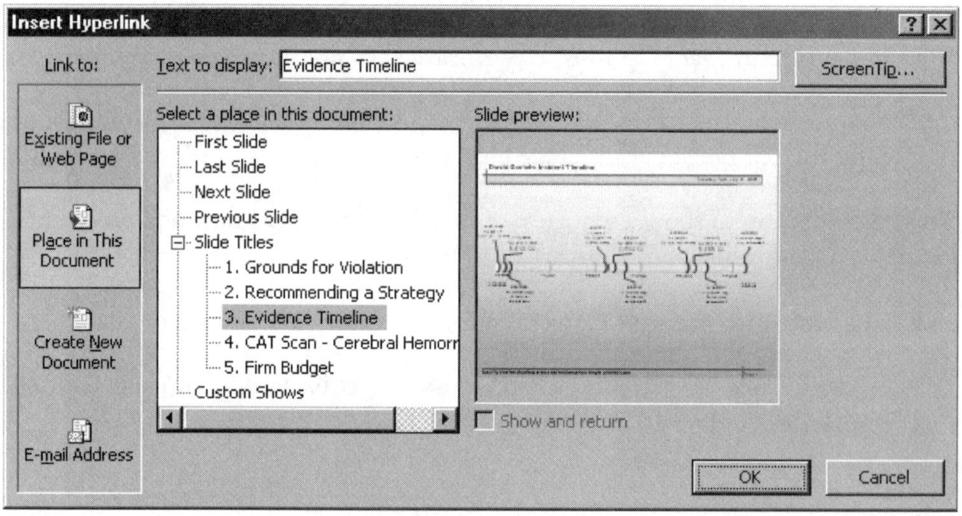

Figure 6.10: Setting a PowerPoint Hyperlink between Slides.

NOTE

If you need to change the hyperlink later, right-click the text or object to which the hyperlink is attached and choose the Hyperlink menu item. A screen similar to that in Figure 6.10 will appear, allowing you to reset or alter the hyperlink.

Creating Hyperlinks to a File or Web Page

Much like creating hyperlinks to slides in a presentation, you can also create a hyperlink to a Web page or file. Here how you do it:

1. Select the text or object that will activate the hyperlink when clicked.

2. Click the **Insert⇨ Hyperlink** menu item (or simply press the **Ctrl** and **K** keys).

3. Under **Link to**, click **Existing File or Web Page**.

4. Under **Look in**, select **Current Folder**, **Browsed Pages** (for URLs), or **Recent Files**, and navigate to the file or URL that will be the destination for the hyperlink, as shown in Figure 6.11. (You can also type in the file path or URL in the **Address** box).

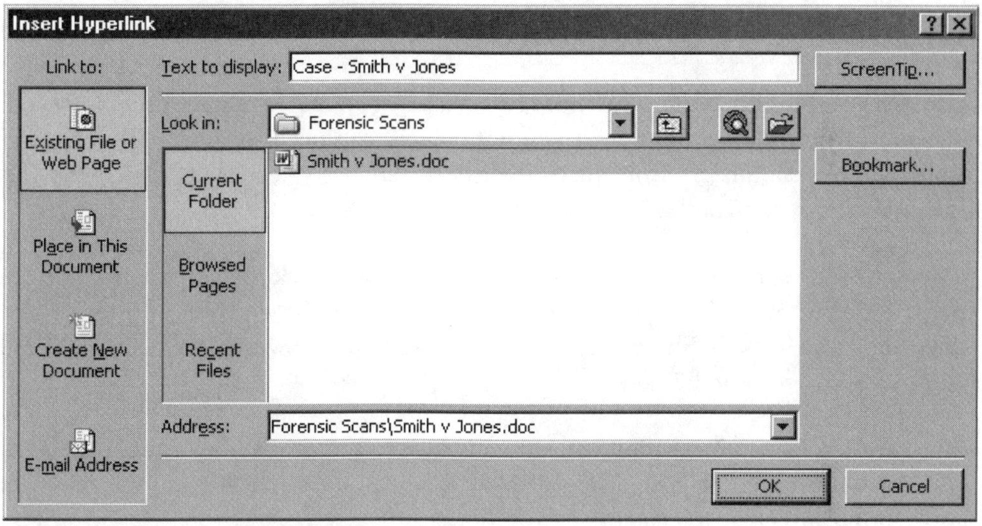

Figure 6.11: Setting a PowerPoint Hyperlink to a File.

⚠ CAUTION

If you define a hyperlink to an external URL, always be sure to test the link before you give your presentation in court or to a client! Web sites can move, alter, or go down.

Creating Handouts and Notes

Handouts are printed versions of your presentation that you can pass out to your audience. Often, the handouts are the real end product of a Paralegal's use of PowerPoint. You may find that the handouts are more valuable than the actual slide show, since they can provide the attorney with a well-organized way of delivering a summary of key points to an audience. You can choose how many slides to include on each page of your printed handouts and whether to include lined space for the audience to take notes.

Notes are typed comments that you may choose to include with each slide. Using notes allows you to make the most of PowerPoint as an organizational tool, as well as a presentation application. When creating your presentation, simply type your notes in the **Notes** pane of the **Normal** view, or in the **Notes Page** view, where you can add pictures, charts, or tables. You can print your notes as an aid for delivering your presentation, or for distribution to your audience.

To print handouts and notes, simply click the **File⇨ Print** menu item. Then, select either **Handouts** or **Notes Pages** from the **Print What** dropdown list.

Running the Slide Show

Up to this point in the chapter, you have been creating your PowerPoint presentation. However, when you present your slide show to your audience, you need to run the slide show. This will enable the presentation to display with the full screen, activate all hyperlinks, and include any additional effects that you have added to your presentation.

To view the slide show, simply open the presentation and click the very small **Slide Show from current slide** button at the lower left corner of the window (in a cluster of three small buttons), or you can click the **Slide Show⇨ View Show** menu item. However, the easiest way to run your slide show is to press the **F5** key.

While running your presentation, you can advance to the next slide by clicking the left mouse button or by pressing the space bar or **ENTER** key. You can back up to the previous slide by right-clicking and choosing the **Previous** menu item.

Conclusion

Whether you are preparing a case, delivering an educational presentation to a client, or conducting internal training for your firm's staff, PowerPoint slides can show key points of your argument or speech (such as a list of evidence, legal cases, events, or anything you choose). It can also deliver a concise and visually compelling summary of arguments. PowerPoint can serve as an organizational tool, allowing you and your attorneys to come prepared with all the facts in an easily accessible series of hyperlinked slides. Notes and handouts are easily generated from these slides. This chapter showed you the basic PowerPoint activities of working with slides, adding charts and graphs, using hyperlinks, and creating notes and handouts.

There are additional features of PowerPoint that are not explicitly covered in this chapter, such as automating PowerPoint with macros, adding full-motion movies to your presentation, and other enhancements. For additional information, visit the PowerPoint Web site at `www.microsoft.com/powerpoint`. For information on document security in PowerPoint, see Chapter 16.

Chapter 7

Microsoft OneNote 2003

Chapter At A Glance

WHY YOU SHOULD READ THIS CHAPTER:

During the course of performing your Paralegal duties, you no doubt take lots of handwritten notes on legal pads. You might give these notes to a Legal Secretary to transcribe into an electronic format, such as a Microsoft Word document, or you might do it yourself. All these paper notes means that you have lots of paper lying around in files, even after your cases are closed. They are sometimes hard to locate and very difficult to search. A great alternative is to use Microsoft OneNote 2003 to take electronic notes in court, meetings, depositions, and more. This chapter explores the use of OneNote 2003, which allows you to electronically take notes, categorize them, and share those notes with others.

PRODUCT OUTLINED IN THIS CHAPTER:

- OneNote 2003

PRODUCT FEATURE COVERED IN THIS CHAPTER:

- Taking Notes

When you are in client meetings or in court you no doubt take lots of notes. You have to document absolutely everything! There are many challenges surrounding the copious handwritten notes that you take as a Paralegal. Here are some of those challenges:

- You don't have the time to transcribe those notes into a computer format.
- It is difficult to share your notes with others.
- You must physically store those notes in enormous files and cabinets.
- It is time consuming to search handwritten documents.
- It is difficult or impossible to protect handwritten notes from fire or theft.

There must be a better way. There is, but many in a legal profession don't know about it!

Microsoft OneNote 2003 — for Paralegals?

Microsoft OneNote is just that…One product for taking, filing, and storing notes. Not only does it allow you to enter, categorize and file your notes electronically, but depending on the type of computer you have, you can even write your notes on the screen and have OneNote automatically recognize your handwriting.

Microsoft OneNote 2003 is the latest (and first) version of the product and is part of the Microsoft Office System. It does not come with Office 2003 (either standard or professional editions), but it is a separately licensed product. However, if you purchase a Tablet PC (one that allows you to write on the screen like a pad of paper), OneNote will likely be preinstalled already. Figure 7.1 shows what a Tablet PC looks like.

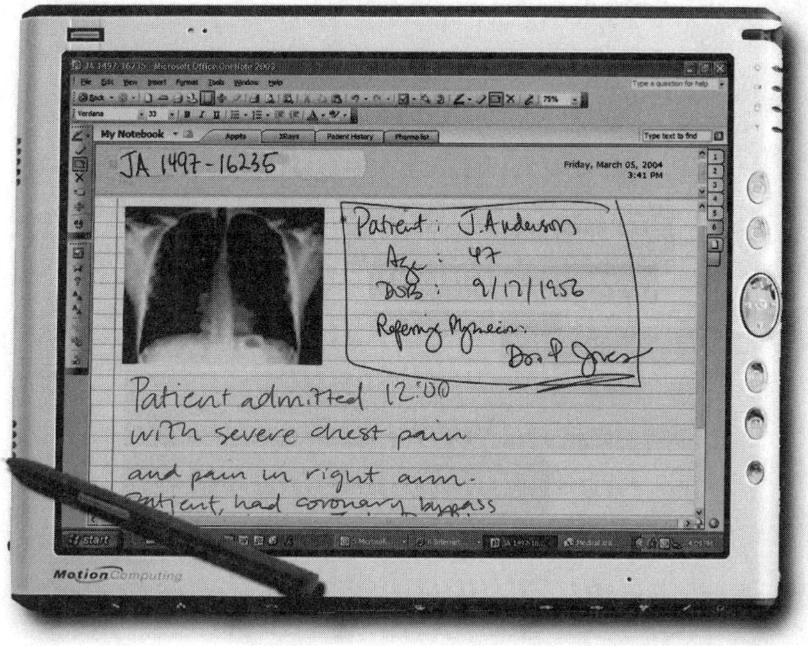

Figure 7.1: Motion Computing M1400 Tablet PC.

A Tablet PC can greatly enhance your effectiveness in taking notes because it comes with a special pen called a *stylus* (which is shown lying on the screen in Figure 7.1). This stylus can be used to write directly on the actual screen of the tablet PC in your own handwriting. Storing notes in this fashion allows you to already have an electronic copy of your notes without needing reams of paper.

While OneNote is a really cool product and will enhance your note taking abilities, this one chapter cannot cover everything you need to know about OneNote, but it does touch on the highlights of what OneNote can do for you. However, if you are interested in finding out more about how to perform Paralegal tasks with OneNote, flip to Chapter 10, which shows you how to take notes with OneNote 2003. If you've never seen OneNote before, take a look at Figure 7.2, which shows a OneNote document as it looks after you've typed some notes into it using a keyboard.

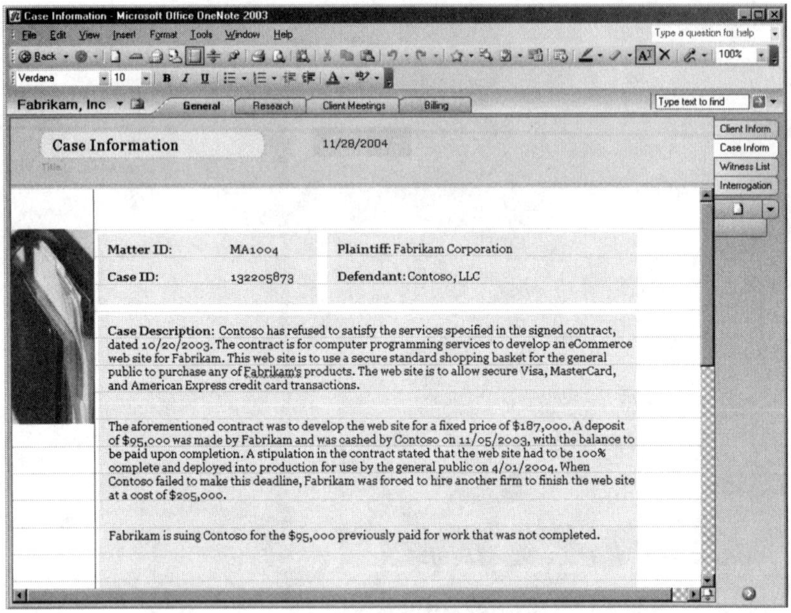

Figure 7.2: Microsoft OneNote 2003, Showing Typed Document.

The screen shown in Figure 7.2 was generated using a Deposition Template that was downloaded from the Microsoft Office Web site. To show the very powerful features of using OneNote 2003 on a Tablet PC, Figure 7.3 shows the same screen shown in Figure 7.2, but with handwritten notes instead of notes entered with a keyboard.

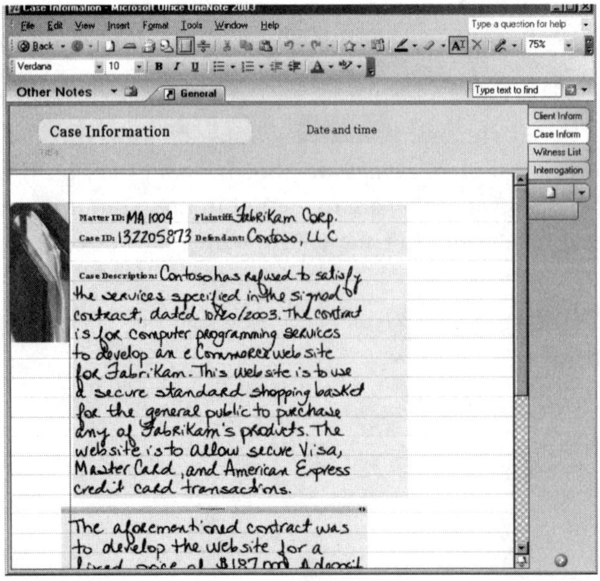

Figure 7.3: Microsoft OneNote 2003, Showing Handwritten Document.

If you have a Tablet PC, handwriting recognition is built-in, so all you have to do to produce the screen shown in Figure 7.3 is to simply write on the screen using a special pen called a stylus. What's more, you can convert your handwritten words into text with the click of a single button. You don't even need any additional software to do it. For more information about handwriting notes and converting handwriting to text, see Chapter 10.

Features of OneNote

Microsoft OneNote 2003 has a whole slew of very cool features that you can take advantage of, but some that will particularly suit you in your law office are:

- Easily take notes by typing or writing on the screen (assuming you are using a Tablet PC, as shown in Figure 7.1).
- Categorize your notes in any way you see fit—into folders, sections, and pages.
- Share your documents or collaborate with other users in your office.
- Import/Export documents into other Microsoft Office System products, such as Word, Excel, PowerPoint, or Outlook.
- Create and store audio or video clips with your notes, using a computer's built-in microphone or camera.

Anatomy of OneNote 2003

OneNote 2003 organizes your notes into a hierarchy of OneNote objects, as shown in Figure 7.4.

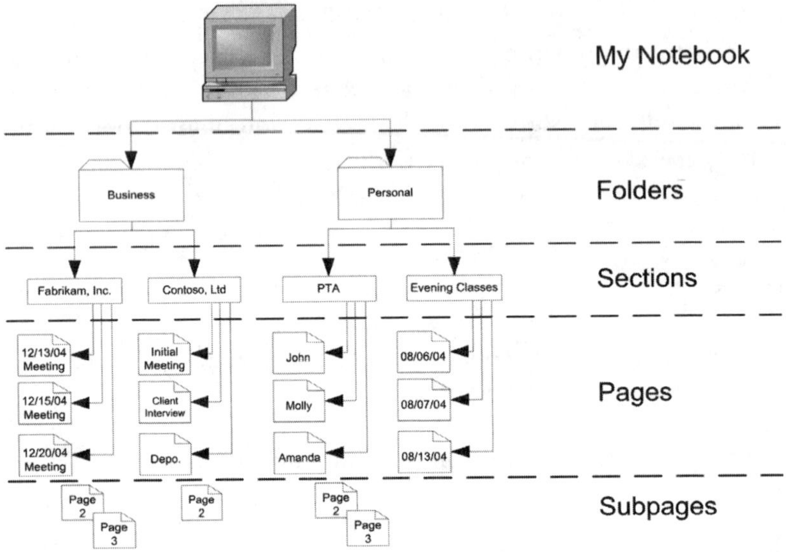

Figure 7.4: Hierarchy of OneNote Objects.

You will likely be familiar with these objects, as they follow the paradigm of a logical categorization of notes, as follows:

- **FOLDERS** — Physical and logical storage unit under which you will place your notes. An unlimited number of folders or subfolders can be created in order to logically categorize your notes. A folder might be named **Business**, **Personal**, or any other grouping for files.

- **SECTIONS** — Logical grouping within a folder. A single folder can contain any number of sections. Sections are created within OneNote and appear as tabs at the top of the screen. A section is stored as a separate physical file in a folder with the `.one` file extension. For example, if you have a section named **Research**, OneNote will automatically create a file named `Research.one` in the appropriate folder, and all objects under the section are stored within that one file. Other examples of sections are shown in Figure 7.4, such as **Fabrikam** and **Contoso** under the **Business** folder and **PTA** and **Evening Classes** under the **Personal** folder.

- **PAGES** — A page of notes that appears within a section. You can have an unlimited number of pages within a section. Each of the pages in a section is stored within the file that is associated with a section. Pages within a section have a title, such as **Meeting Minutes 10/22/2004**.

- **SUBPAGES** — Additional pages that appear after a page. Subpages do not have their own title. A subpage is really just a continuation of notes on the same topic that simply doesn't fit on one page, such as page **1 of 4**, **2 of 4**, and so on.

You can specify any number of these items and organize them in any way you see fit. The **My Notebook** folder is at the top of the hierarchy of folders and files. The rest of this chapter will refer to this folder as the *root* folder because it is at the top of the hierarchy. By default, this folder is actually named **My Notebook** and is located just under the **My Documents** folder, which is available in Windows XP anytime you are presented with a list of folders to search. A sample **My Documents** folder (which will look slightly different than on your own computer) is shown in Figure 7.5. Notice the selected (highlighted) folder, named **My Notebook**.

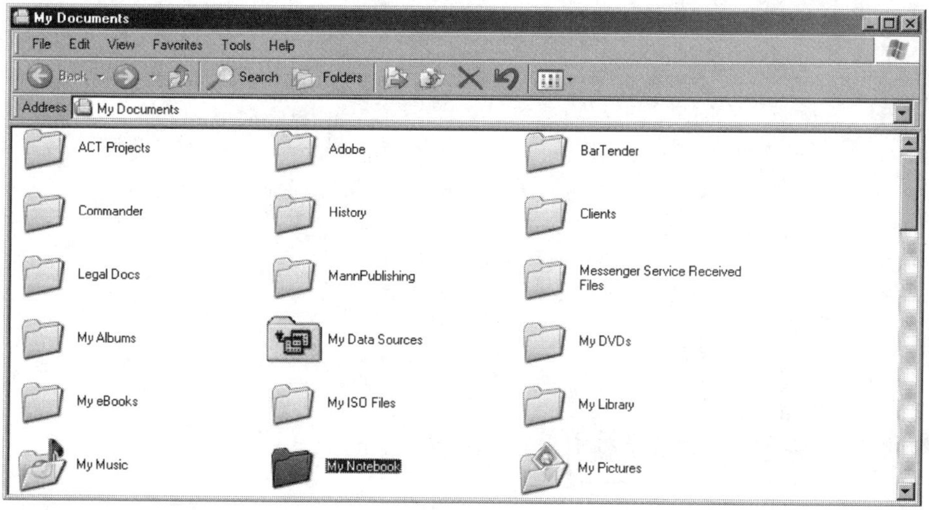

Figure 7.5: My Documents Folder Showing the My Notebook Folder Selected.

The **My Notebook** folder is the beginning point of the hierarchy. Under this folder, you will create additional folders that make sense for you and your firm. For example, under the **My Notebook** folder, you may want a folder for each client. However, it might make sense to create a **Clients** folder within the **My Notebook** folder, which could distinguish client-related items from personal items. Your personal items could be placed in a **Personal** folder within the **My Notebook** folder.

Toolbars

Microsoft OneNote has a few toolbars that help you to perform quick actions. The most common of these toolbars are the **Standard** toolbar, as shown in Figure 7.6, and the **Formatting** toolbar, which is shown in Figure 7.7.

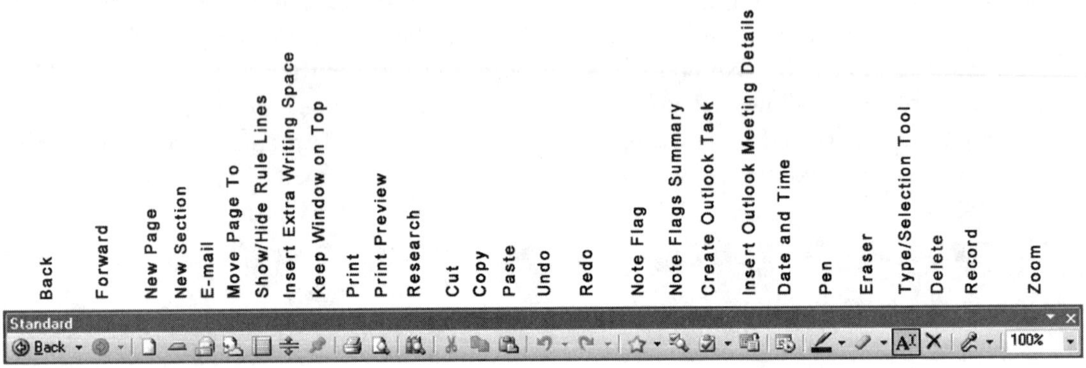

Figure 7.6: OneNote 2003 Standard Toolbar.

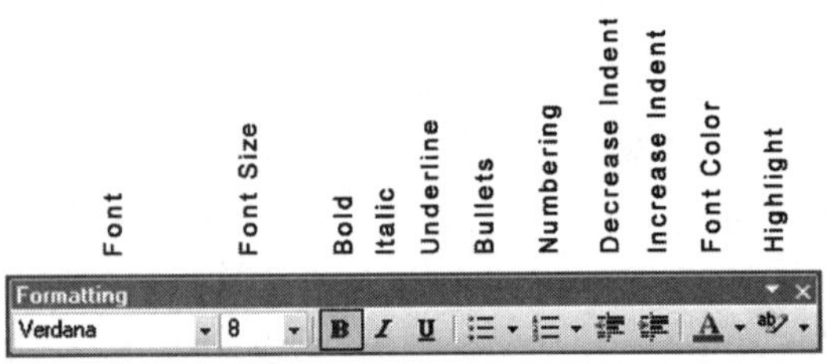

Figure 7.7: OneNote 2003 Formatting Toolbar.

To show any toolbar, click the **View⇨ Toolbars** menu item and you'll see a list of possible toolbars to display. Simply select the desired menu that you want to display.

Legal Templates

There are two legal templates available on the Microsoft Office Web site for use with Microsoft OneNote 2003. You can search for these templates at `http://office.microsoft.com/templates`. While the downloading and installation of templates is covered in Chapter 3, you should know that these templates are available for Microsoft OneNote 2003 at the time of this writing:

- **Deposition template** — OneNote template that includes places to take notes for client information, case information, witness list, and interrogation.
- **Case brief** — OneNote template that includes places to take notes relating to a brief, such as the parties, heading, procedural history, the facts of the case, the issues in the case, the holding, the court's reasoning, and other important items.

The template shown in Figures 7.2 and 7.3 is the Deposition Template. These templates are very effective in providing fields to use in your legal and personal endeavors instead of having to face a blank screen every time you want to take notes.

Setting Up Your Notebook

The first thing you'll want to do is decide how you will organize your notes. Believe it or not, this is not a simple task. You need to think long and hard about this organization. Organize your folders in any way that makes sense to you and your firm, but read the rest of this chapter first to understand the hierarchy of how OneNote stores notes.

Creating a New Folder

To create a new folder, you must understand where you are currently positioned in the hierarchy. It is a good idea to navigate to the top of the hierarchy (in the **My Notebook** folder) before you create a folder. This will ensure that you know where you are in the hierarchy and will eliminate the possibility of creating a folder in the wrong place. An example of a folder is in Figure 7.2, where the folder is called **Fabrikam**, which is located under the **Clients** folder, even though you do not see the entire hierarchy.

Here are the steps to create a new folder.

1. Open OneNote 2003 by clicking the **Start**⇨ **Programs**⇨ **Microsoft Office**⇨ **Microsoft Office OneNote 2003** menu item.
2. Navigate to the top of the hierarchy by clicking the dropdown button on the toolbar. Doing so brings up a list of folders, which you can see in Figure 7.8.

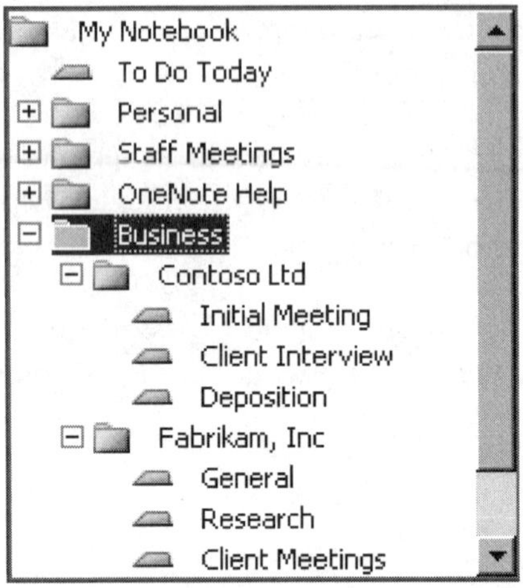

Figure 7.8: Sample Folder Hierarchy.

3. Continue to navigate to the folder under which you will create a new folder. For example, if you want to create a new folder directly under the root folder, click the **My Notebook** folder.

4. Click the **Insert⇨ New Folder** menu item. A new folder is created.

> **NOTE**
>
> **If you browse for the new folder using Windows Explorer, you'll see a physical folder with the same name as the one you just created.**

5. Continue navigating and creating folders until you have the structure that you wish to use to store your notes.

Creating a New Section

Again, a section can be equated to a tab in a notebook. You may opt to have each client be a section within a folder, but it will be more likely that you will have each client assigned to their own folder and sections (tabs) across the top for storing individual notes, such as **Research**, **Contacts**, **Matters**, **Meetings**, **Tasks**, etc. You may or may not duplicate these sections for each client, depending on what makes sense for your firm. For example, see the sections in Figure 7.2, which are named **General**, **Research**, and **Billing**.

Creating a new section involves these simple steps.

1. Navigate to the folder in the hierarchy that will contain the new section. If you have not created any sections in a folder, you'll receive the informational message shown in Figure 7.9.

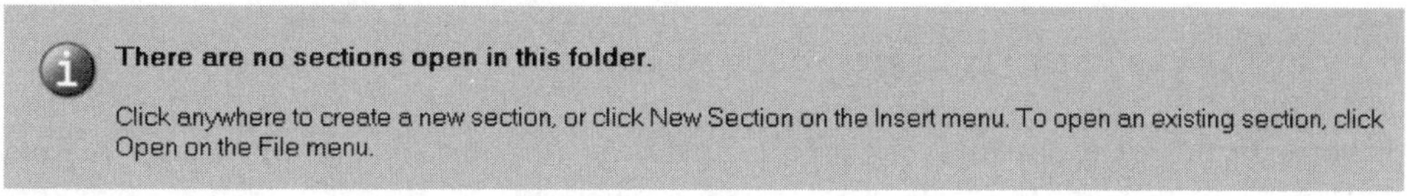

Figure 7.9: Informational Message for New Folder.

If you see the message shown in Figure 7.9, simply click anywhere in the screen to create a new section. If you don't see this message, click the **Insert⇨ New Section** menu item. You'll see a new tab at the top of the screen.

2. Change the name of the section. After you create a new section, the system will be in edit mode, allowing you to rename the section. If not, simply right-click the tab representing the new section and click the **Rename** menu item.

3. Press the **Enter** key to save your changes.

> NOTE
>
> **If you browse to the folder containing the new section, you'll see a file with the name of the section, followed by** `.one`**.**

Creating a Page

To create a new page (which is where you'll actually take your notes), navigate to the desired folder and section within the folder. When you create a new section, a new page is automatically created and named **Untitled page**. Otherwise, if you want to create an additional page, simply click the **Insert⇨ New Page** menu item. Each subsequent new page will also be named **Untitled page**.

To see an example of OneNote pages, see Figure 7.2, where there are four pages within the **Fabrikam** section (shown on the right-hand part of the screen) labeled **Client Information**, **Case Information**, **Witness List**, and **Interrogation Questions**. These pages were created using the Deposition Template described earlier in this chapter.

Pages are renamed by giving them a title. To give a page a title, simply do this:

1. Place the cursor in the area of the screen marked **Title**.
2. Type or write (if you are using a Tablet PC) the desired title for the page, such as **Meeting Minutes 10/22/2004**.
3. Press the **Enter** key to save your changes.

If you run out of room in a single page and need to continue, simply click the **Insert⇨ New Subpage** menu item. This will create a new page, but logically link it to the preceding page, so it won't have its own title.

Taking Notes

Once you have created a new page (or subpage), you are ready to start taking notes. To take notes, either position the cursor in the desired location on the screen and start typing, or if using a Tablet PC, simply start writing on the screen of the Tablet PC by using the stylus.

⚠ CAUTION

If you use any other pointing device besides the supplied stylus on the screen of a Tablet PC, you will damage the screen. You must use the stylus supplied with your Tablet PC when you write on the screen.

Again, it is not possible to cover all the features of OneNote 2003 in a single chapter, but this is a high-level list of the things that you can adjust in your notes:

- Font
- Font Size
- Section Color
- Line spacing
- Showing ruled lines

- Stationary
- Pen color (for Tablet PCs only)
- Pen width (for Tablet PCs only)

What's the Big Deal About a Tablet PC?

A picture of a Tablet PC is shown in Figure 7.1. A Tablet PC allows you to use a stylus to write your notes on the screen instead of typing them with a keyboard. This makes for more of a natural experience, not to mention a quiet one. Imagine typing with a noisy keyboard in court or in front of a client at a meeting? In fact, this is why a court stenographer's machine is designed to be so quiet. It is incredibly important not to distract anyone in court or in a meeting. As an example, Figure 7.10 shows a drawing made on a Tablet PC to sketch the layout of the room in a deposition.

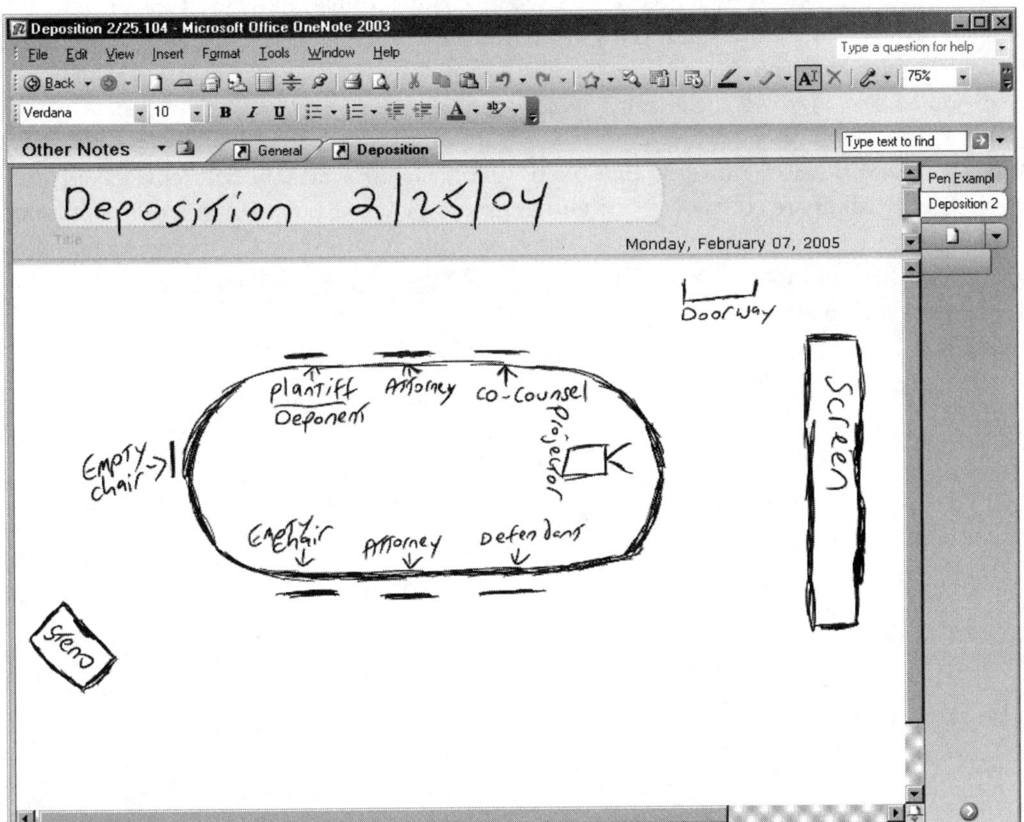

Figure 7.10: Sketch of Room Layout in a Deposition.

The Tablet PC runs a special edition of Windows XP, known as Windows XP Tablet PC Edition. It operates just like Windows XP, but has special goodies built right in, like handwriting recognition, speech recognition, and more. For more information about this edition of Windows, simply point your browser to `www.microsoft.com/tabletpc`.

With a Tablet PC, you write your notes on the screen just like it was a piece of paper. However, because you are taking notes with OneNote 2003, these notes are already in an electronic format. There's no need to have a Legal Secretary transcribe those notes into an electronic format so that you can archive them or share them with others. This time-saving measure will pay for the cost of a Tablet PC in no time.

Conclusion

Microsoft OneNote 2003 is a very powerful program that allows you to take and categorize notes in a series of folders and sections. If you make the investment in a Tablet PC, you can even use a stylus to actually write notes on the screen in your own handwriting. You can actually convert your handwritten notes to text by using automatic handwriting recognition already built into the Tablet PC. This is made possible by Windows XP Tablet PC Edition, which is a special edition of Windows XP specifically for Tablet PCs.

There are some additional features of OneNote 2003 that are not explicitly covered in this chapter, such as the ability to collaborate with other users on your notes or send them to someone in an e-mail. You can even include audio or video recordings into your OneNote documents. This can be very helpful in situations such as legal meetings, where you record depositions. Be sure to visit the OneNote Web site at `www.microsoft.com/onenote`.

Chapter 8

Microsoft Outlook 2003

Chapter At A Glance

WHY YOU SHOULD READ THIS CHAPTER:

Outlook 2003 is part of the Microsoft Office System and is a centralized way to manage everything related to communication, such as e-mail, contacts, and appointments. Outlook even lets you schedule appointments on someone else's behalf, so you can schedule an appointment for an attorney and have it placed in his or her calendar automatically. This chapter shows the basic features of Outlook 2003, while the specific tasks you might do in Outlook are covered in Part II of this book.

PRODUCT OUTLINED IN THIS CHAPTER:

- Outlook 2003
- Outlook Express 2003

PRODUCT FEATURES COVERED IN THIS CHAPTER:

- Mail
- Calendar
- Contacts
- Tasks
- Notes
- Views

Microsoft Outlook 2003 is a communications program that is part of the Microsoft Office System. It handles e-mail, appointments, contacts, and tasks—all in one package. Most law firms use either Microsoft Outlook or GroupWise, with Outlook being the prevailing program. With Outlook, you can not only manage your own information, but also that of someone else who has given you permission to do so. For example, you can use Outlook to manage an attorney's calendar and appointments. This chapter covers the basic features of Microsoft Outlook 2003. Much like the way a pocket knife has multiple tools, Microsoft Outlook is actually comprised of these five individual programs:

- **Mail** — Used for sending e-mail.
- **Calendar** — Used for creating appointments. Appointments are covered in detail in Chapter 15.
- **Contacts** — Used for managing contact information, such as addresses and phone numbers. Managing contacts is covered in detail in Chapter 13.
- **Tasks** — Used for managing one-time or recurring tasks.
- **Notes** — Used for jotting down notes, much like an electronic sticky note.

In an effort to keep this chapter as brief as possible, you'll learn an overview of all five individual programs in Microsoft Outlook 2003, but the main emphasis is on the Mail program. Outlook has many more advanced features that are beyond the scope of this book, but you should realize there's more under the hood. Check out the Microsoft Office Web site to learn how to expand your use of Outlook. Some features (such as Public Folders) require your IT department to configure.

In Practice

"Our Paralegals use Microsoft Outlook very heavily. Not only is it relied upon it for the majority of our internal and external communication, but we use the Public Folder structure of Outlook to organize contacts specific to certain practices. For example, our Intellectual Property practice maintains their shared international contacts, while the Litigation group maintains vendor contacts for the entire department. It's quick and easy to access vendor contact information, from scanning and coding vendors to forensic e-discovery and trial presentation vendors. In addition, some practice groups use the Public Folder Calendars—sorted by practice—to track vacations so that they have access to lawyer and staff time availability. Because of the shared nature of the Public Folders, they are maintained as a group and don't require a full-time person to keep them up-to-date."

— Julia C. Forbes, Paralegal and IS Special Projects
Mintz Levin Cohn Ferris Glovsky and Popeo PC

Microsoft Outlook 2003—for Paralegals?

Outlook 2003 is a very useful program for a Paralegal, as well as everyone else in your law firm. Not only does it enable you to send and receive e-mail, but it also lets you store your contact information and schedule time in the calendar on behalf of someone else, such as an attorney. This can be a very important feature so that you can support the attorneys in your firm by using the technology that is likely already on your desktop. Outlook can even let you schedule tasks, such as "To Do" lists. The bottom line is that Outlook has lots of applications to make a Paralegal's life easier, but you have to know about the features to use them. To learn how to manage client contacts, see Chapter 13. The scheduling features of Outlook 2003 are covered in Chapter 15. Make sure to check out these chapters to gain the most insight into how to become more efficient with Outlook 2003.

Outlook vs. Outlook Express

Outlook Express is an e-mail program that is completely free of charge from Microsoft. It provides basic e-mail capabilities for sending and receiving messages. However, Outlook provides many additional features for a fully-integrated system for managing messages, contacts, and tasks. Your firm will likely want to use Outlook because it is feature-rich. However, if you don't have Microsoft Office and your firm has no intention of buying it (although we know that would never happen), you probably want to stick with Outlook Express.

NOTE

You should know that no specific features of Outlook Express are covered in this book because it is not technically part of the Microsoft Office System. It is part of Windows and Internet Explorer.

To understand the feature differences between Outlook and Outlook Express, see Table 8.1, which lists the features for each product.

Features	Outlook	Outlook Express
Send and receive e-mail messages	Yes	Yes
Connect to Microsoft Exchange Server for enhanced collaboration, scheduling with free/busy information, and online forms	Yes	No
Connect to POP3 Internet e-mail servers	Yes	Yes
Address Book and Contacts folder to store and retrieve e-mail addresses	Yes	Yes
Out of Office Assistant that automatically sends a reply to incoming messages while you are out of the office	Yes	No
Multiple address books	Yes	No
Fully integrated Calendar, including meeting and event scheduling, appointments, and group calendars	Yes	No
Reminders for e-mail messages, calendar events, tasks, and notes	Yes	No
Information Rights Management (IRM) functionality that allows you to control whether recipients can print, copy, or forward your e-mail messages	Yes	No
Integration with Windows SharePoint sites	Yes	No
Auto backup (archive) functionality to keep your mailbox manageable. Store old items that you want to keep but don't need immediate access to, and move those old items to the archive location automatically	Yes	No
Microsoft Office Word as your e-mail editor to provide access to additional formatting and style options	Yes	No

Table 8.1: Outlook and Outlook Express Features.

Features	Outlook	Outlook Express
Categories for organizing your items	Yes	No
Side-by-side calendars where you can view multiple calendars and drag items between them	Yes	No
Tasks folder to keep lists of personal or work-related errands that you want to track from start to finish	Yes	No
Junk e-mail message filter	Yes	No
Notes folder—the electronic equivalent of paper sticky notes	Yes	No
Access to NNTP newsgroups	No	Yes
Signatures and stationery	Yes	Yes
Secure e-mail messaging	Yes	Yes

Table 8.1 (continued): Outlook and Outlook Express Features.

There is only one feature that Outlook Express does that's better than Outlook. This is in the area of connecting to newsgroups. If you have any legal newsgroups that you regularly participate in, Outlook won't do it for you. You'll need to install another newsgroup reader to read or respond to these newsgroups.

Outlook Web Access

In addition to accessing your data by using Outlook, you can also use a program from Microsoft called Outlook Web Access, or OWA. OWA is a program that enables you to access your e-mail, contacts, and appointments by using a Web browser, such as Microsoft Internet Explorer. To use OWA, you must be using Microsoft Exchange Server as a mail server. When Exchange Server is managing your e-mail, data such as messages, contacts, and appointments are all stored on the server itself—not your workstation. Therefore, you can access the same data by either Outlook or OWA. Want to see proof of this? Just take a look at Figure 8.1. When you compare it to Figure 8.2 in the next section, they are virtually identical.

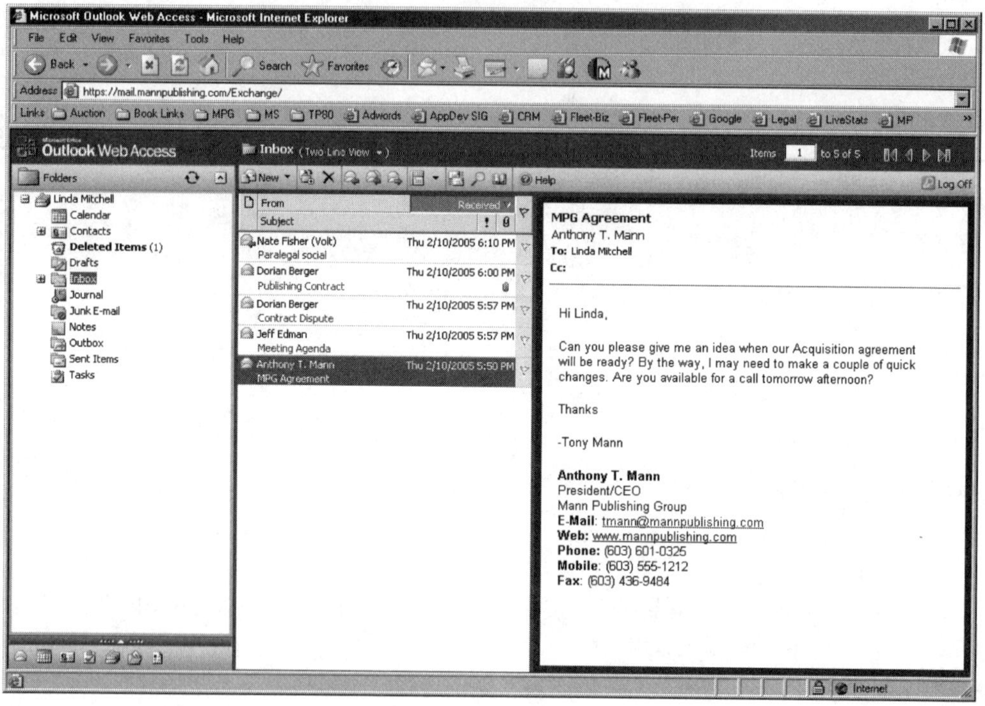

Figure 8.1: Outlook Web Access (OWA) Shown in Internet Explorer.

OWA can be a very convenient and efficient way to access your e-mail when you are not in the office. You can access OWA by using any computer that has a browser with access to the Internet. Therefore, you can retrieve your e-mail, look up calendar appointments, or retrieve contact information at a client site, while on vacation, or even with mobile devices when you are commuting.

> **NOTE**
>
> **If you are not sure if you use Microsoft Exchange Server as a mail server or if OWA has been configured, check with your IT department.**

Mail Program

The Mail program in Outlook 2003 is probably the most often used functionality in Microsoft Outlook. It handles the sending and receiving of e-mail. When you receive a message, it is placed into a special folder called your **Inbox**. However, after that point, you can place it into any custom hierarchy that you wish for easy reference. To enter the Calendar program, from within Outlook, simply click the **Mail** folder, or click the **Go⇨ Mail** menu item. When you do, you'll see a screen like the one shown in Figure 8.2, which shows a sample hierarchy of folders.

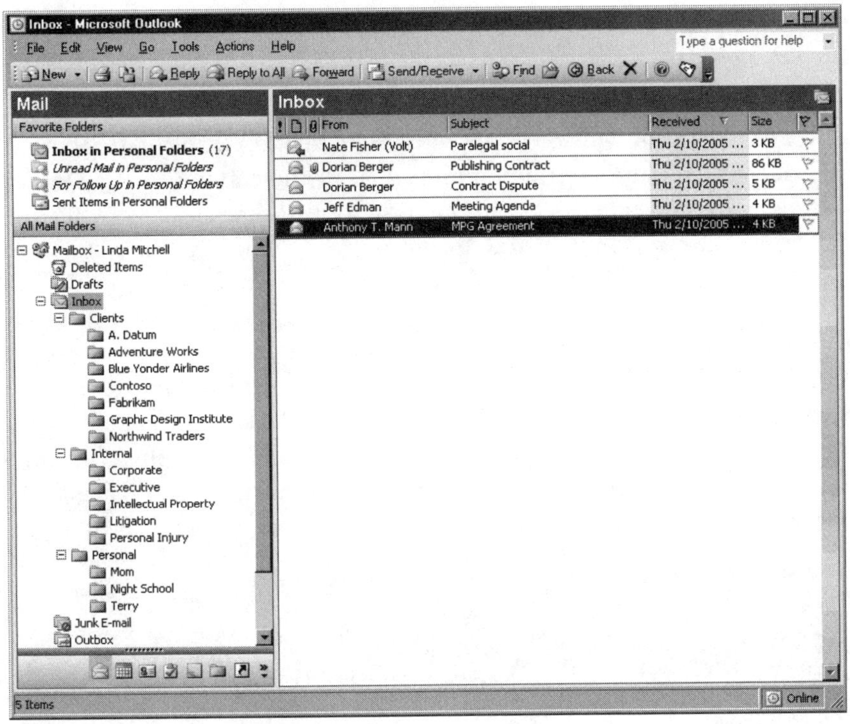

Figure 8.2: Outlook 2003 Mail Program.

In the example shown in Figure 8.2, you'll see a series of folders that were created specifically to illustrate how a Paralegal might want to store e-mail. In the pane that reads **All Mail Folders**, you'll notice a hierarchy of folders under the **Inbox** folder. Under **Inbox** are folders named **Clients**, **Internal**, and **Personal**. Under the **Clients** folder is a folder listing of clients, such as **A. Datum**, **Adventure Works**, **Blue Yonder Airlines**, and so on. When an e-mail arrives in your **Inbox**, you can simply move it to the desired folder by dragging it from the **Inbox** and dropping it into the desired folder. In Figure 8.2, the **Inbox** folder is selected, so the right-hand pane, labeled **Inbox**, displays the mail that has been received and not yet moved into your hierarchy of folders.

NOTE

Notice the folder structure in Figure 8.2 is the same as what's shown in Figure 8.1. This is because both OWA and Outlook read data from the same Exchange mail server.

To create a new e-mail, click the **New** button in the toolbar and construct your e-mail. In the **To**, **Cc**, or **Bcc** lines, you can select any contact from your electronic address book. For more information about this, see "Contacts Program" later in this chapter and also Chapter 13.

Calendar Program

The Calendar program is a feature of Microsoft Outlook lets you schedule appointments for yourself or someone else. Not only will these appointments be placed into an electronic calendar, but you can have Outlook automatically remind you of these appointments with a popup notice. For example, you can create an appointment for a court date and have it remind you two hours in advance so you have enough time to run out the door, beat the traffic, and arrive on time.

The Calendar feature also lets you schedule an appointment as a recurring task. For example, if you have a regular staff meeting every week on the same day and time, you'll want to enter this appointment only once, not for every week of the year. You can even take your appointments one step further and invite attendees to the appointment to schedule a meeting. To enter the Calendar program, from within Outlook, simply click the **Calendar** folder, or click the **Go⇨ Calendar** menu item. When you do, you'll see a screen like the one in Figure 8.3.

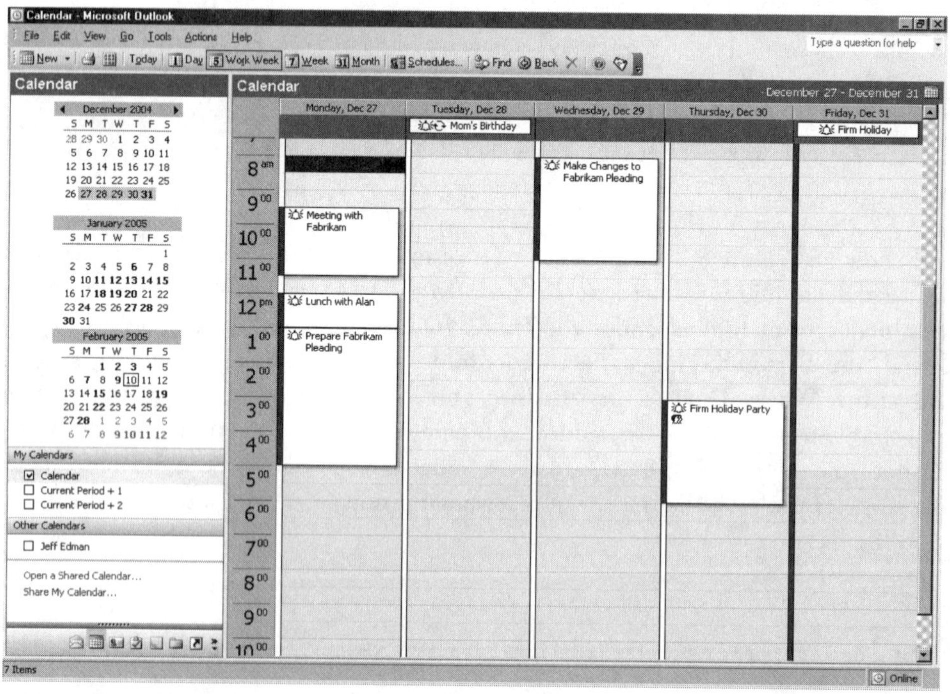

Figure 8.3: Outlook 2003 Calendar Program.

Notice the first day displayed is **Monday, Dec 27**. There are three appointments scheduled. These appointments have definite start and stop times. The first appointment, which is a meeting with Fabrikam, begins at 9:30am and ends at 11:30am. That gives you just enough time to run over to have lunch with Alan from 12:00pm to 1:00pm. Fortunately, the café at which you will be having lunch is next door to your office so you can begin to prepare the Fabrikam pleading in your office for the rest of the day.

On **Tuesday, Dec 28**, you don't have any scheduled meetings or appointments, but there is a recurring event labeled **Mom's Birthday**. It does not have a definitive start and stop time, only a specific date. This is referred to as an *All-Day Event*.

On **Wednesday, Dec 29**, you have a single appointment scheduled from 8:00am to 11:00am to make changes to the Fabrikam pleading. You don't expect this to take more than three hours because you will have read Chapter 23, "Drafting Legal Pleadings."

On **Thursday, Dec 30**, you also have a single appointment, which is the firm's holiday party in the office. It is scheduled from 3:00pm to 6:00pm.

On **Friday, Dec 31**, you have an All-Day appointment, just as you did for **Tuesday, Dec 28**. However, you'll notice a thick dark line (blue on a color screen) to the left of the time slots in the day. This is a visual clue that the blocked-out time is flagged as being "busy." Busy time means that you are doing other tasks and nobody can schedule additional time with you. After all, you can only be in one place at one time (unlike Dolly the sheep). By contrast, the appointment on **Tuesday, Dec 28** does not have this same line, but it is an All-Day appointment. The difference is that someone else can schedule time with you on that day. After all, you can't call your mother's birthday "busy time." You'll also notice that the other appointments in the calendar also have this thick line to the left. It doesn't run for the entire day because those aren't All-Day appointments, but they do flag that you are busy for certain periods of time.

The seven appointments shown in Figure 8.3 highlight the main types of appointments that you can schedule using the Calendar feature of Outlook 2003. You can learn more details about these features by checking out Chapter 15.

Contacts Program

The Contacts program is a feature of Microsoft Outlook that lets you manage contact information for all of your clients, vendors, friends, relatives, co-workers, and more. Contact information includes things like e-mail addresses, mailing addresses, phone numbers (home, work, and mobile), company names, Web page addresses, notes about a contact, and lots of other details. Once you enter your contact information, you can actually share it with others. Having your contact information in one place ensures that everyone in your office is using the same information. It also helps to ensure that you don't make any typographical errors when you type someone's e-mail address into Outlook's Mail program. This program can simply look up your contacts. To enter the Contacts program, from within Outlook, simply click the **Contacts** folder, or click the **Go⇨ Contacts** menu item. When you do, you'll see a screen like the one in Figure 8.4.

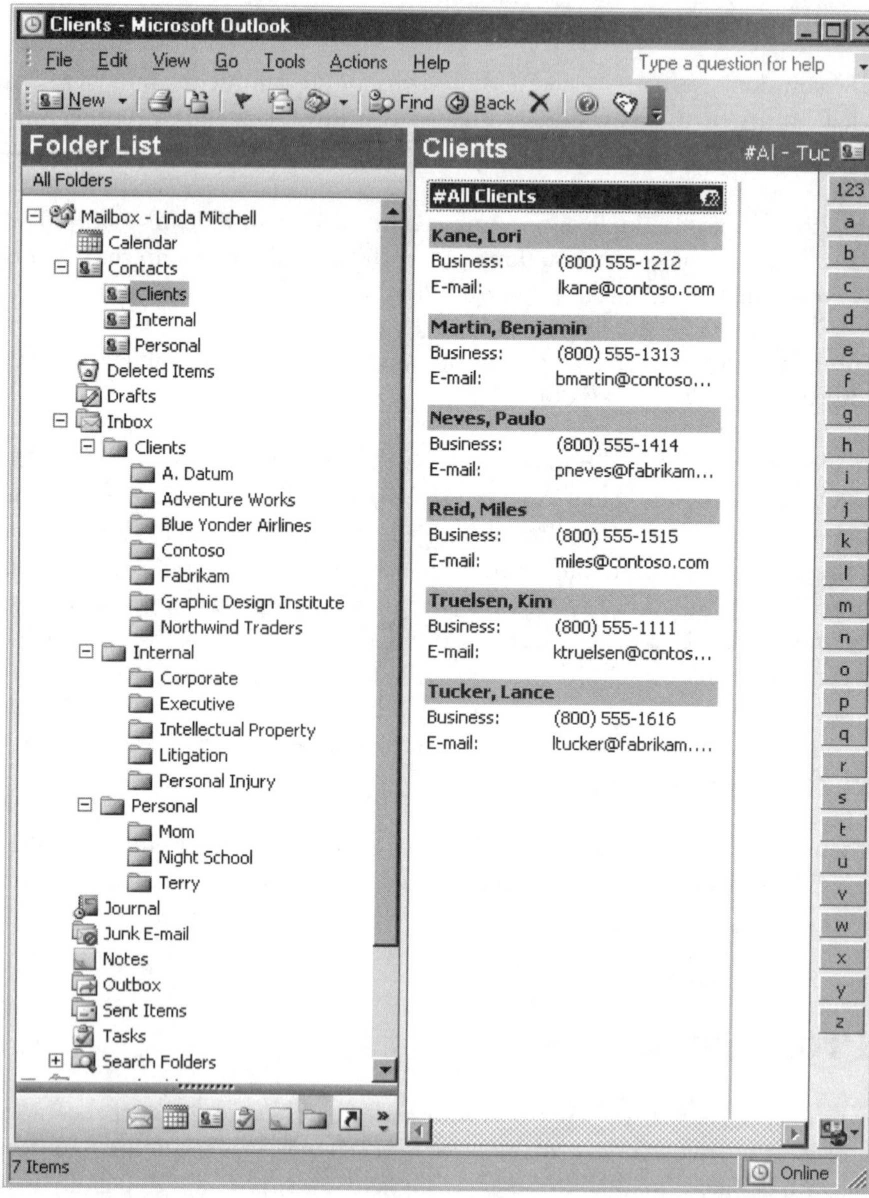

Figure 8.4: Outlook 2003 Contacts Program.

Notice in Figure 8.4 under the **Contacts** folder, there are three other folders that were created for this example: **Clients**, **Internal**, and **Personal**. Creating folders in this way enables you to store your contact in a hierarchical format so that they are classified in a way that makes sense to you. The sample contacts that you see in Figure 8.4 are all in the **Clients** folder. See Chapter 13 for more information about managing contacts.

Tasks Program

The Tasks program is a feature of Microsoft Outlook that lets you create lists of task-related items. Some people refer to tasks as "To Do" lists. Tasks can be useful in situations where you cannot schedule a specific amount of time to complete an activity. For example, you can have a task named **Grocery Shopping**. It does not matter if you shop today or tomorrow, so it wouldn't make sense to schedule the time in your calendar. It's just a pending or open task. Other possibilities for tasks include one named **Fabrikam Pleading**, where the individual items in the task might be bullet points of items that need to be included. You can even assign start and end dates to your tasks so that you can track if you are behind or ahead of schedule.

To enter the Tasks program, from within Outlook, simply click the **Tasks** folder, or click the **Go⇨ Tasks** menu item. Doing so brings up tasks similar to those shown in Figure 8.5.

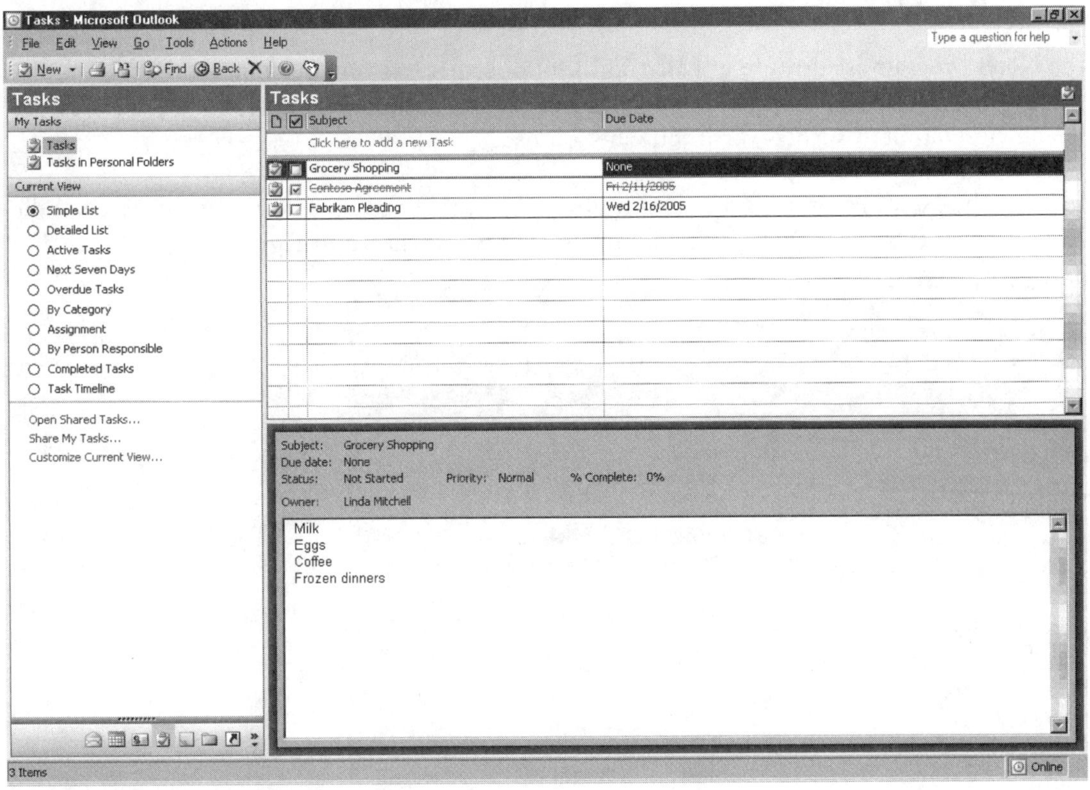

Figure 8.5: Outlook 2003 Tasks Program.

In Figure 8.5, there are a couple of things to notice. The very first task is named **Grocery Shopping.** It contains task items which are the items you wish to purchase at the store. It can be very convenient to have Outlook 2003 handle personal tasks as well as firm tasks. The second task, **Contoso Agreement**, has a line through it. That's because it is a completed task. The last task, **Fabrikam Pleading,** is still open, so there is no line through it. The bottom of the screen shows a preview window that contains a quick view of the items in the selected task. More information about views is available in the section "Views" later in this chapter.

To create a new task, right-click in the right-hand pane labeled **Tasks**. From the popup menu, click **New Task** to open a new task. You simply type the items that are related to your task. Every time you create a new task, you'll see it listed in the window behind.

Notes Program

The Notes program is a feature of Microsoft Outlook that lets you create notes that are similar to sticky notes that you might place on your monitor or desk. Sticky notes are good for things like quick reminders, such as "Call John at Contoso."

To enter the Notes program, from within Outlook, simply click the **Notes** folder, or click the **Go⇨ Notes** menu item. Doing so brings up your notes, as shown in Figure 8.6.

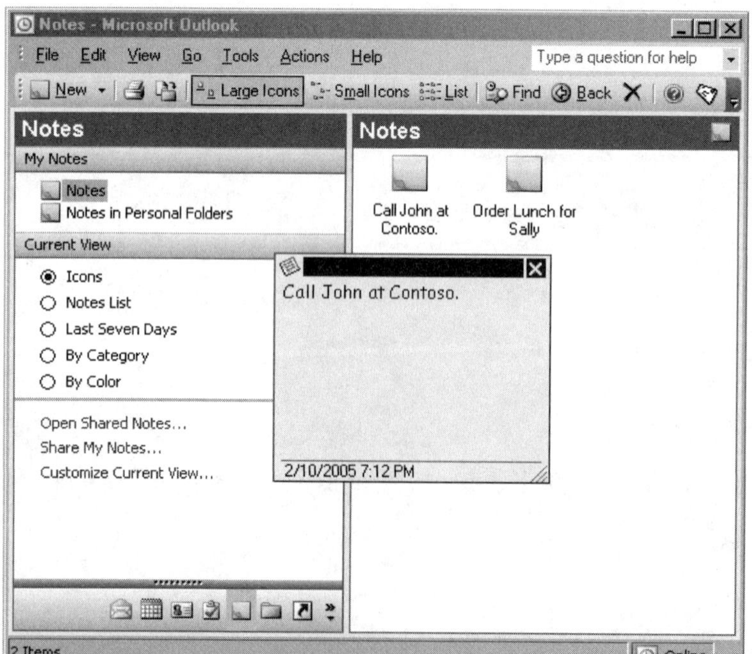

Figure 8.6: Outlook 2003 Notes Program.

To create a new note, right-click in the right-hand pane called **Notes**. Click the **New Note** menu item from the displayed popup menu. A new sticky note window appears where you simply type your text that makes up the note. Every time you create a new note, you'll see it listed in the window behind.

Views

As with almost everything Microsoft produces, Outlook is customizable so that your user experience can be tailored to suit you. You can customize the way your Outlook programs (Mail, Calendar, Contacts, Tasks, and Notes) appear, the level of detail that you see on your screens, and even which panes appear in the Outlook window. Many users of Outlook customize the way their e-mail is displayed so they can quickly preview and prioritize messages that require prompt responses.

> **NOTE**
>
> **To not overload you with information about views, this chapter focuses on the views in the Mail program, but the same concept applies to the other programs as well.**

A *view* defines what you see in Outlook—how data such as e-mails is sorted and displayed. Outlook includes some predefined views that are suitable for most users. In the event that these built-in views do not suit your needs, you should know that you can build your own views. However, building custom views is beyond the scope of this book.

Before diving into views, it's important to describe a couple of terms that are used to define views. First, refer back to Figure 8.2, which shows a basic listing of messages.

Now, take a look at Figure 8.7, which shows AutoPreview. *AutoPreview* is an expanded listing of data that gives you more detail, but also takes more space on the screen. AutoPreview is a good option when you need to know more than just the sender or subject of an e-mail. For example, suppose you receive an e-mail from a client whose subject is **Legal Info**. This subject line is so vague that you need to open it right away to see if it contains important information that needs immediate attention. Instead of opening the message, you could use AutoPreview to see the first few lines of the body of the e-mail. This will likely give you a feel for the message contained in the e-mail.

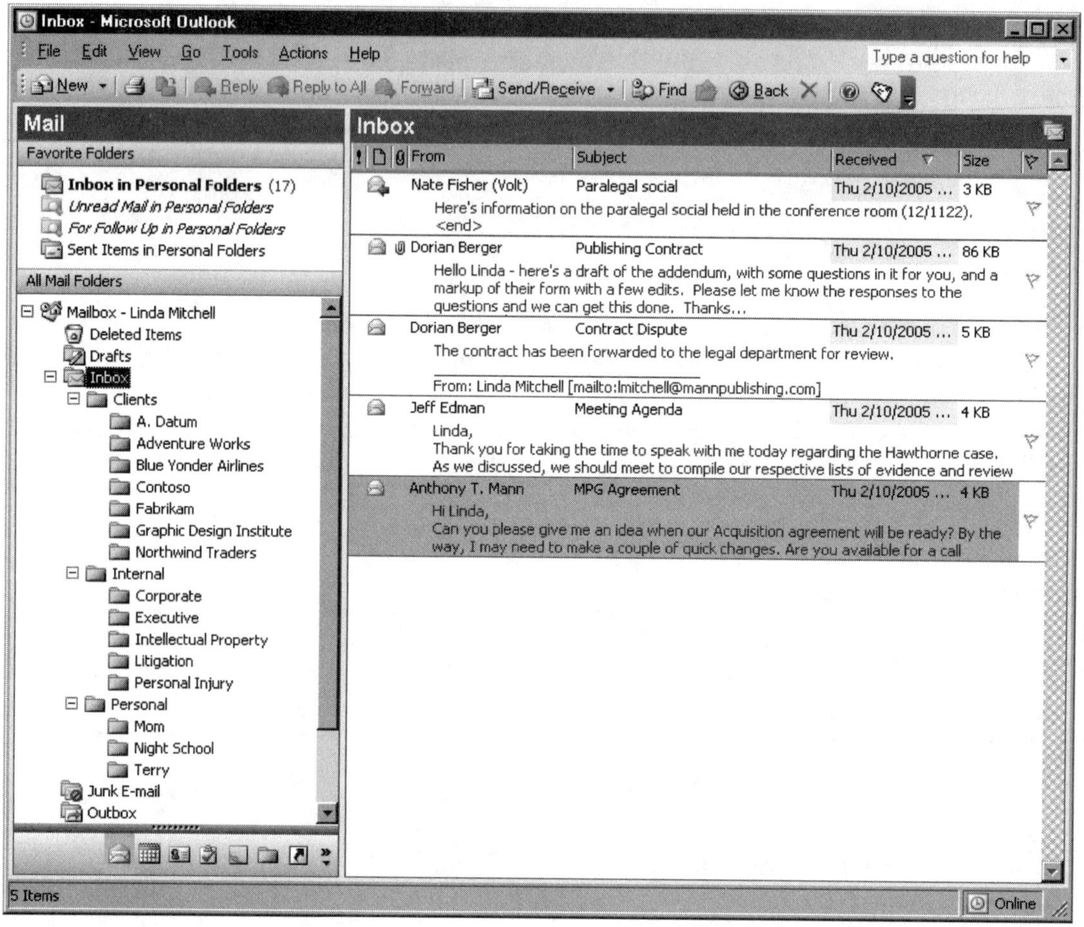

Figure 8.7: Outlook 2003 Message with AutoPreview.

In contrast to AutoPreview, the Reading Pane gives you a window that shows the entire content of a message without needing to open the message. The Reading Pane can be very useful, but takes up lots of screen real estate. The Reading Pane is shown in Figure 8.8.

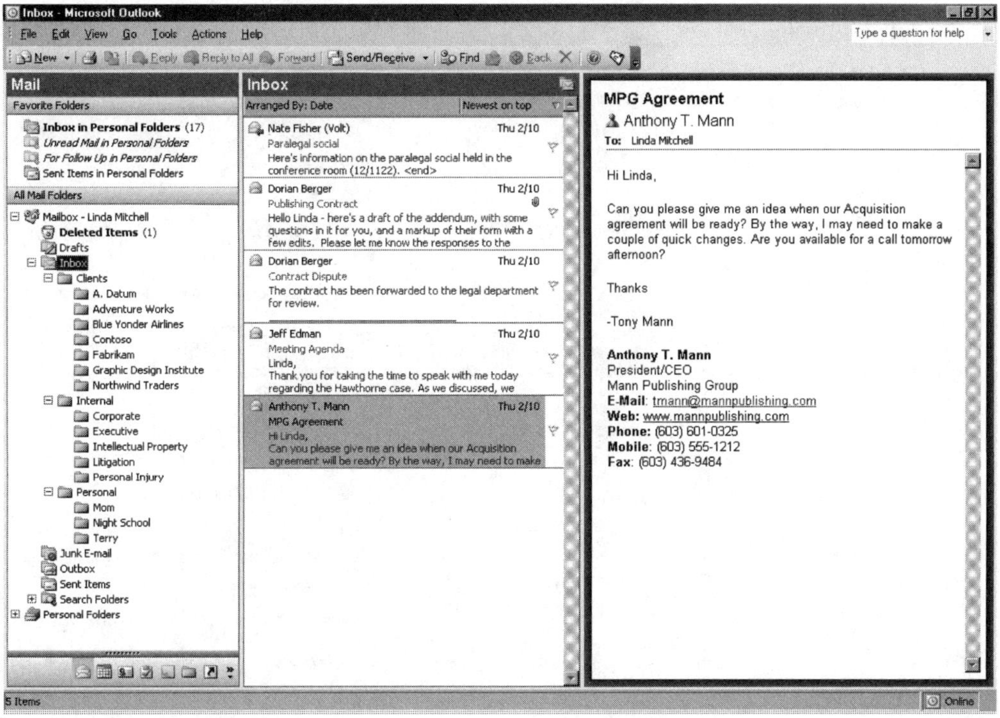

Figure 8.8: Outlook 2003 Message with Reading Pane.

> **⚠ CAUTION**
>
> **The downside to using the Reading Pane is that after the message is viewed for five seconds, the message will no longer be considered unread. This can lead to a situation where you briefly preview a message, but it is now considered read, so you forget to read it again.**

Now that you understand AutoPreview and the Reading Pane, which are different ways to see your messages, you're ready to dive further into views. Outlook 2003 comes out-of-the-box with the views shown in Table 8.2.

View Type	View Name	Description
Inbox (E-Mail)	Messages	Displays all messages
	Messages with AutoPreview	Displays all messages with the AutoPreview window open
	Last Seven Days	Displays only messages that were received in the last seven days
	Unread Messages in This Folder	Displays only messages that have not been read
	Sent To	Displays all messages with the Reading Pane open, with the To address being the first column of data
	Message Timeline	Displays the messages according to the timeline, chronologically from left to right
Calendar	Day/Week/Month	Displays calendar items in days, weeks, and months
	Day/Week/Month View With AutoPreview	Displays calendar items in days, weeks, and months with AutoPreview
	Active Appointments	Displays a listing of all upcoming (active) appointments
	Events	Displays a listing of all appointments that are flagged as all-day events
	Annual Events	Displays a listing of events that recur every year
	Recurring Appointments	Displays a listing of events that recur upon any interval
	By Category	Displays a listing of all events, grouped by category
Contacts	Address Cards	Displays contacts in a shortened card format
	Detailed Address Cards	Displays contacts in a detailed card format
	Phone List	Displays contacts as a list
	By Category	Displays a listing of contacts, grouped by category
	By Company	Displays a listing of contacts, grouped by company
	By Location	Displays a listing of contacts, grouped by Country and Region
	By Follow-Up Flag	Displays a listing of contacts, grouped by flagged items

Table 8.2: Built-In Views in Outlook 2003.

To select a view, simply click the **View⇨ Arrange By⇨ Current View** menu item. You'll see a listing of the possible views shown in Table 8.2. Click the item that is right for you. For example, you may want to view only unread messages. This way, you'll quickly know which ones need a response. To select this option, make sure you are viewing your **Inbox** and click the **View⇨ Arrange By⇨ Current View⇨ Unread Messages in This Folder** menu item.

Conclusion

Microsoft Outlook 2003 has many features for centralizing and managing how you communicate with people. In this chapter, you learned the differences between Outlook and Outlook Express. The features of Outlook include sending and receiving e-mail, managing contacts, and scheduling appointments. You can even create tasks and notes. Each of these activities is managed in a separate program within Outlook 2003. In this chapter, you learned the basics of each of these five programs, what they do, and how they work. You also learned how views work in the Outlook 2003 Mail program. You even discovered how to access your e-mail, appointments, and contacts by using OWA and a Web browser. Make sure to read the referenced chapters to learn more about using certain features of Outlook 2003.

Did you know?

You can create rules that are applied to messages as they are received. A rule is helpful in limiting SPAM because you can have it look for certain words in the subject or the body of the email and immediately delete the message if it contains those words.

Part II

My Tasks

Chapter 9

Conducting Research Safely on the Web

Chapter At A Glance

WHY YOU SHOULD READ THIS CHAPTER:

Like most professions, as a Paralegal you do lots of research. Because security is at the forefront of everyone's mind these days, you need to know what to look for as you conduct your research on the Web. This chapter shows you what to look for when you are conducting research, but explains it in a non-technical way. You'll learn about the many issues relating to visiting Web sites to conduct research, including cookies and security.

PRODUCT OUTLINED IN THIS CHAPTER:

- Microsoft Internet Explorer 6

You have no doubt been to lots of Web sites. In fact, one cannot live without the Web these days. We do absolutely everything on the Web, including banking, surfing, scheduling travel, and of course, research. As a Paralegal, you normally do research all the time using a Web browser, such as Microsoft Internet Explorer, but do you really understand all those confusing technology issues surrounding surfing the Web? This chapter dispels the myths about the Internet not being secure and tells you all about those confusing browser issues, such as cookies, zones, and temporary files.

To Update or Not To Update?

Microsoft continually provides enhancements and security updates to all of its products, including Internet Explorer. There is a misconception that Microsoft products are not secure and that they are full of "holes." In fact the issue is that the more you lock down software to avoid any sort of attack from a hacker, it becomes significantly harder to use from the user's point of view. Therefore, as threats are discovered, Microsoft makes fixes, upgrades, and service packs available to its products but constantly balances ease of use with the vulnerabilities that it discovers from hackers. You or your IT department must make sure that all service packs are applied to maintain the highest level of security on your computer.

Before continuing, make sure you are using the latest version of Internet Explorer. At the time of this writing, the latest version of Internet Explorer is 6.0.2, with Service Pack 2 applied. A service pack is an update to a Microsoft software program that contains fixes and enhancements without needing to upgrade or pay for another version of the software. To see what version you are using, follow these simple steps:

1. Open Internet Explorer by clicking the **Start⇨ Programs⇨ Internet Explorer** menu item.

2. Click the **Help⇨ About** menu item.

3. View the screen that shows the version information, as shown in Figure 9.1.

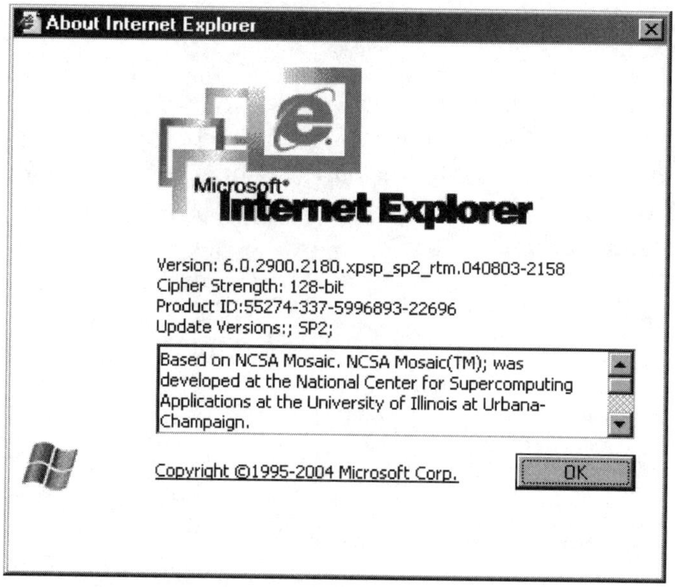

Figure 9.1: About Internet Explorer Window.

There are three things you should take notice of in Figure 9.1:

- **Version** — This version should be at least 6.0.2.
- **Cipher Strength** — This is the level of encryption that the browser can support. If you are going to be sending any confidential information over the Internet, you must ensure the cipher strength is 128-bit. If it is less than this value, it will be possible for a hacker to crack the encryption code and view confidential information.
- **Update Versions** — This version should be at least SP (Service Pack) 2 to ensure the right balance between security and functionality.

4. Click the **OK** button to close the window.

5. If your browser needs updating, click the **Start⇨ Windows Update** menu item to go to the Microsoft Windows Update Web site, where you can download the latest version.

Security Diligence

Ever since 9/11, government officials have been telling us that security is everyone's responsibility. While surfing the Net is less severe than an abandoned bag in the middle of an airport terminal, we must take Internet security seriously. It is the responsibility of a Web site owner (such as `www.LexisNexis.com`) to allow a browser to surf the Web using encryption to protect sensitive information. Sensitive information includes:

- User Names
- Passwords
- Addresses
- Phone Numbers
- Credit Card Numbers

It is your responsibility to make sure that your browser is up-to-date. See the prior section, "To Update or Not To Update." It is also your responsibility to ensure that a Web site uses encryption when you are entering or viewing sensitive information.

There are two simple checks to see if a site uses encryption. The first is to look for a "lock" icon at the bottom of the screen. The second is in the Web address itself. If it begins with **https://** (note the "s") , then the site is secure. Both of these are shown in Figure 9.2.

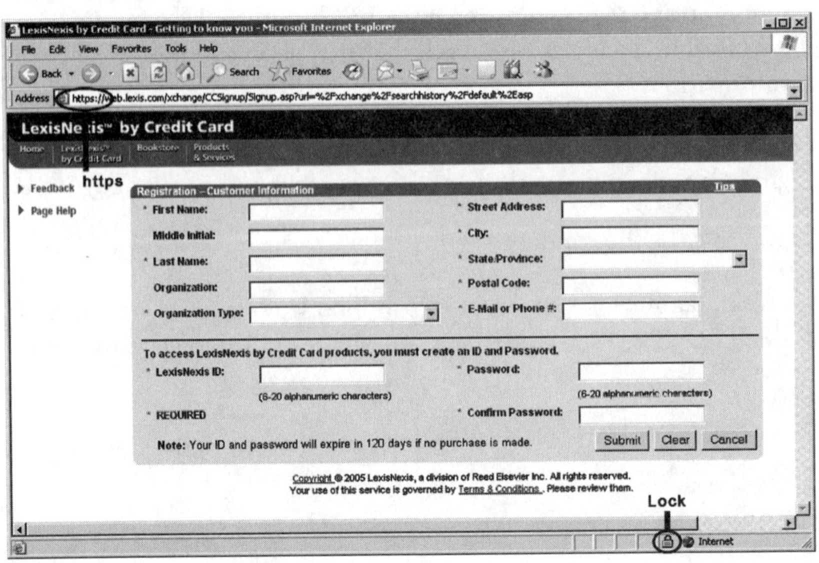

Figure 9.2: Web Page Showing Encryption.

If you ever go to a Web site and enter personal information without the site being secure, you should call the company that runs the Web site immediately. Do not click a **Submit**, **Save**, or **OK** button or else sensitive information will be transmitted without being encrypted.

A Zone is Not Just a Diet

Before you dive into understanding the factors involved in using Internet Explorer to access different Web sites, you need to understand the concept of a zone. A *zone* is a logical region or grouping of Web sites, based on where they are physically located and how well you trust the source. These default zones are available in Internet Explorer 6.0.2:

- **Local Intranet** — Web sites located on your local network. These sites do not have to communicate over the Internet to be accessed.
- **Trusted Sites** — Contains a list of Web sites that you trust not to harm your computer, such as `www.lexisnexis.com`.
- **Restricted Sites** — Contains a list of Web sites that are known or suspected to be harmful to your computer.
- **Internet** — All other sites that don't fall under the other three categories.

For each zone, you can indicate how Internet Explorer should behave when it accesses a Web site within each of these zones. These settings are covered throughout the rest of this chapter.

Cookies Are Not On the Zone Diet!

Cookies sound like something that belongs in your kitchen, not on your computer. However, *cookies* are small files that are stored on your computer that contain information needed on certain Web sites. Much like what you see on the supermarket shelves, some cookies are great, and some are really bad! A cookie can be used to store user ID, password, preferences, personalization, or any other information that you need for frequently visited sites to enhance your experience. For example, suppose you visit a Web site that allows you to select your language of choice. So you don't have to choose the language preference every time you enter the site, chances are software developers wrote a program to allow the language preference to be saved, or stored on your computer. The preference is saved on your computer as a file, or cookie.

OK, so cookies sound like a good thing, right? Well, they can be, but they can also cause problems. Since the writing of cookies on your computer is determined by a computer programmer, you can visit a Web site that puts a malicious cookie on your hard drive. A malicious cookie can contain virtually any information that you don't want it to, such as your name, credit card information, address, or more. Cookies make it possible for unwanted information to be stored and accessed over and over when you visit a Web site.

Protecting Yourself from Cookies

How do you protect yourself? Internet Explorer allows you to indicate whether to accept cookies from Web sites in each zone. By default, cookies are allowed for all zones except the **Restricted Sites** zone. However, if you want to limit cookies for a particular zone, here's how you do it:

1. Open Internet Explorer.

2. Click the **Tools⇨ Internet Options** menu item.

3. Click the **Privacy** tab. Doing so shows you the screen displayed in Figure 9.3.

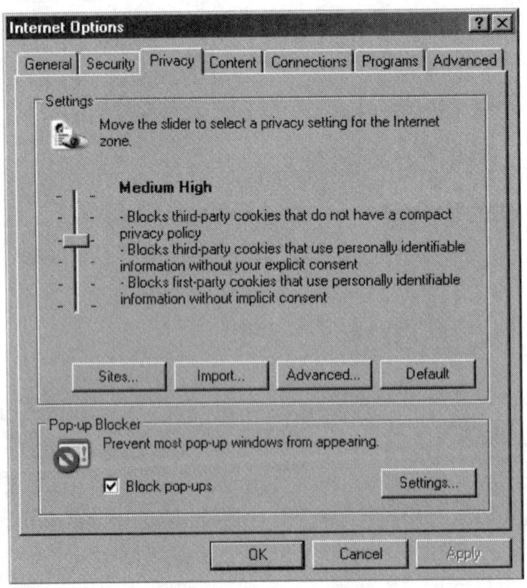

Figure 9.3: Internet Explorer Privacy Options.

4. Move the slider up or down to adjust the settings. Moving the slider up incrementally increases the security of the Internet so that cookies are not accepted. Moving the slider down incrementally decreases the security so that cookies are accepted. For your site, check with your IT department if you are not sure which settings are appropriate to use.

5. Click the **Sites** button to explicitly set a cookie policy for an individual Web site. Clicking this button brings up the screen shown in Figure 9.4.

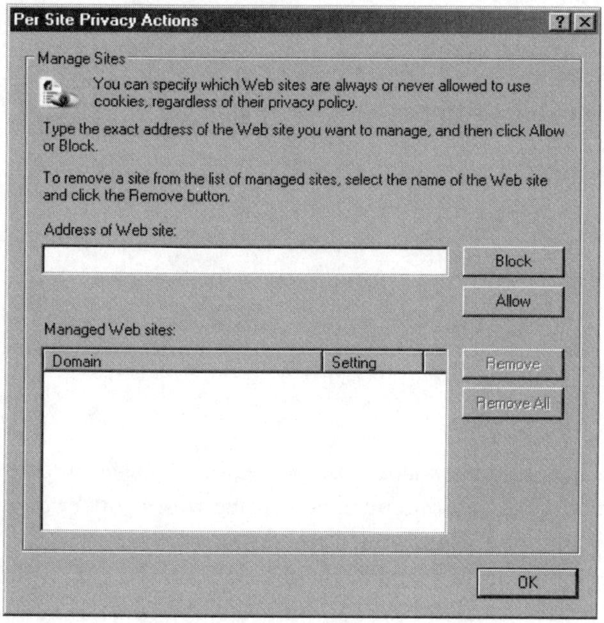

Figure 9.4: Specifying Individual Web Site Settings.

6. Enter the desired Web site address in the **Address of Web site** text box.

7. Click the **Block** button to block all cookies for the entered site, or the **Allow** button to allow all cookies for the entered site.

8. Continue entering settings for each Web site you wish to enter.

9. Click the **OK** button to return to the **Internet Options** screen.

10. Click the **OK** button to close the **Internet Options** screen.

Deleting Cookies

If you are concerned about having cookies on your computer that contain personal information, you can actually delete them. This will only be a factor if you didn't set your cookie policy according to the procedure outlined in the section, "Protecting Yourself from Cookies" earlier in this chapter. If at any point you allowed cookies for untrusted sites, you might have personal information stored on your computer that you didn't intend. Therefore, you should delete your cookies.

To delete cookies, simply follow this procedure:

1. Open Internet Explorer.
2. Click the **Tools⇨ Internet Options** menu item.
3. Ensure the **General** tab is selected, which it will be by default.
4. Click the **Delete Cookies** button. You will be prompted for confirmation before continuing.
5. Click the **OK** button to close the **Internet Options** screen.

Spying on You

Spyware is a term used to describe files that are maliciously placed on your computer to track which Web sites you visit. Spyware on your computer can even force your browser to go to sites that you don't want it to. For example, you point your browser to `www.lexisnexis.com` and instead your browser goes to a search engine Web site or maybe even an adult Web site. This is a very good clue that you have spyware installed on your computer. Spyware is automatically installed by some unscrupulous Web sites. There is nothing good about it. There is no reason for it to be on your computer, except for malicious reasons. Therefore, you must remove it immediately.

To remove spyware, you use a program similar to anti-virus software. This anti-spyware program searches your computer for files that are known to track the actions that you take on your computer. As new spyware tactics are found, updates are made available for free. This is exactly the way anti-virus updates work as well. If you are not familiar with which anti-spyware program to use, check with your IT department. There are a few very good anti-spyware programs, such as Ad-Aware at `www.ad-aware.com`.

Conclusion

When you conduct research on the Web, it is important that you make sure all security updates are installed, so that your personal and client-related information is protected. It is also important that you make sure the "lock" icon is displayed at the bottom of the browser to guarantee that your information is being encrypted as it goes across the Internet. This chapter outlined the security options and considerations to keep in mind when you perform research on the Net, such as https and cookies.

Chapter 10

Taking Notes

Chapter At A Glance

WHY YOU SHOULD READ THIS CHAPTER:

As a Paralegal, you take lots of notes. Technology allows you to save time by using a note-taking program to store notes in an electronic format. Because clicking a loud keyboard is not always appropriate, you can use the handwriting features of OneNote 2003 on a Tablet PC to take notes silently. This chapter shows you the basics of how to take notes with OneNote 2003.

PRODUCT OUTLINED IN THIS CHAPTER:

- OneNote 2003

PRODUCT FEATURES COVERED IN THIS CHAPTER:

- Typing Notes
- Searching Through Notes
- Flagging Notes
- Inserting Outlook Appointments
- Inserting External Files
- Inserting Audio and Video
- Handwriting Notes
- Converting Handwritten Notes into Text

Taking notes is the lifeblood of the legal industry. Without all those legal pads lying around, nobody would ever get any work done. The reality is that most Paralegals don't know they can use technology, such as Microsoft OneNote 2003, to take notes electronically. This saves a tremendous amount of time and effort from having to transcribe those notes into a Word document.

While Chapter 7 gave you a brief introduction into the features of OneNote 2003, this chapter illustrates the mechanics of taking notes in court and in client meetings, options for your notes (such as inserting other documents, video and audio recordings), and converting handwritten notes into text.

NOTE

One thing you need to know about OneNote 2003 is that there is no Save button or menu. OneNote automatically saves your changes, so you never lose any of your notes. However, unless you know this, you'll be searching for the Save button. Microsoft removed the typical Save button because they wanted OneNote 2003 to act like a paper notepad in the real world, where everything you write down is permanently stored.

Typing Notes

Microsoft OneNote can be installed on a typical PC with a keyboard, which means that you enter your notes with a keyboard. In some respects, this is not unlike what you would do with Microsoft Word. The difference is in the types of information that can be easily embedded into your notes and how those notes are stored. OneNote is built specifically for taking notes and incorporating other resources (such as video and audio clips) into your notes.

Probably one of the biggest challenges you'll face in taking notes is how to categorize them. Do you categorize notes by client, by case number, or by document type? It's likely that you or your firm already has a system for categorizing notes. For additional information on how OneNote documents are stored and your categorization options, see Chapter 7.

If you are using OneNote on a PC with only a keyboard (as opposed to a Tablet PC), you can simply click anywhere in the document screen and start typing. OneNote differs from Word in that you can type anywhere on the screen. With Word, you have to manage formatting of the screen and the margins.

Sending a Search Party for Your Notes

Once you have entered your notes, you'll want to search through them to find exactly what you need. Imagine you have collected notes over the course a week with various witnesses or experts. You might want to quickly search through your notes to find a specific term and determine who said it. To search effectively you need to understand how OneNote 2003 structures its files and folders, which is explained in Chapter 7. Understanding the structure of notes is important because it allows you to search within a specific section of your notes or even all of your notes. Limiting your search is known as a search scope. Here are the search scopes available in OneNote 2003:

- **Current Section** — Searches only the current section (tab).
- **Current Folder** — Searches the current folder, including all sections.
- **Current Folder and its Subfolders** — Searches the current folder, including all sections, subfolders and sections within those subfolders.
- **My Entire Notebook** — Searches all OneNote notes.

To bring up the search options, click the down arrow next to the box labeled **Type text to find**. When you do this, you'll see a list of search scopes. These search scopes, along with the text box, are collectively referred to as *searching options* and are shown in Figure 10.1.

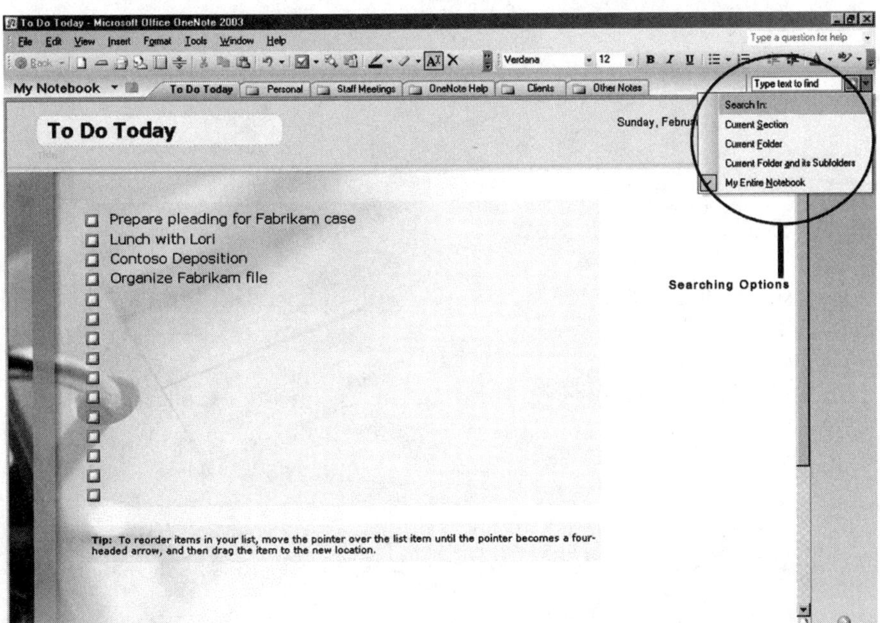

Figure 10.1: OneNote 2003 Searching Options.

To search for an item in your notes, follow these simple steps:

1. Type the desired search phrase into the **Type text to find** box.

2. Click the dropdown arrow and select the desired search scope. For example, if you wanted to search all of your notes, ensure the **My Entire Notebook** option is checked.

3. Click the green "Find" button next to the **Type text to find** box, or press the **Enter** key. You'll see a listing of the items that were found. Simply click on the item in the list provided to immediately jump to the place in your notes where the text was found.

Flagging Notes

Flagging your notes is a way to identify that some action has to be taken on a particular item. *Flagging* is a way to clearly differentiate within a sea of notes that one or more parts of those notes requires some action. For example, you can flag a follow-up for a note taken in a deposition. While OneNote lets you customize the flags used in your notes, these are the ones that come preconfigured:

- To Do
- Important
- Question
- Remember for later
- Definition

To flag a note, simply do this:

1. With the mouse, select all the desired text that you wish to flag. This can be all the text in an area of your notes or a single sentence.

2. Click the desired flag from the **Note Flag** dropdown list on the **Standard** toolbar or click the **Format⇨ Note Flags** menu item and choose from the available flags. The **Standard** toolbar is shown in Chapter 7.

3. Once you choose the desired flag, you'll see an icon that denotes which flag you chose. For example, Figure 10.2 shows an **Important** note flag (which looks like a star) next to an item.

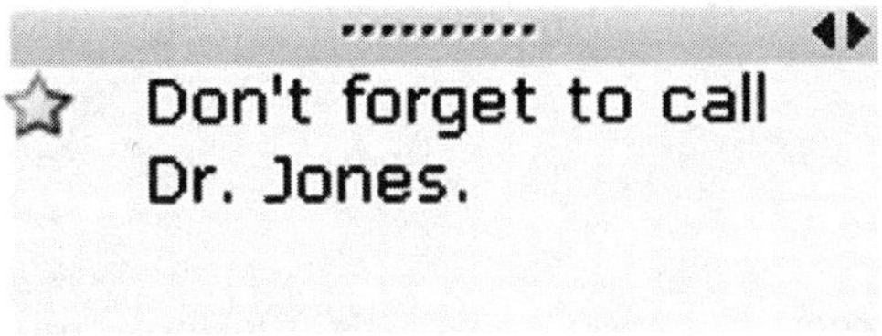

Figure 10.2: Selected Text with Important Note Flag.

That's all there is to using Note Flags.

Inserting Outlook Appointments

To enhance your note-taking capabilities, OneNote lets you insert many types of external data. Because OneNote is part of the Office System, it stands to reason that you would be able to include Outlook appointments in your notes. For example, if you are taking notes for a client called Fabrikam and you know you have a scheduled appointment with an attorney in your firm to go over the case, you might want to insert the appointment into your notes. Figure 10.3 shows what an appointment looks like when it is inserted into your notes.

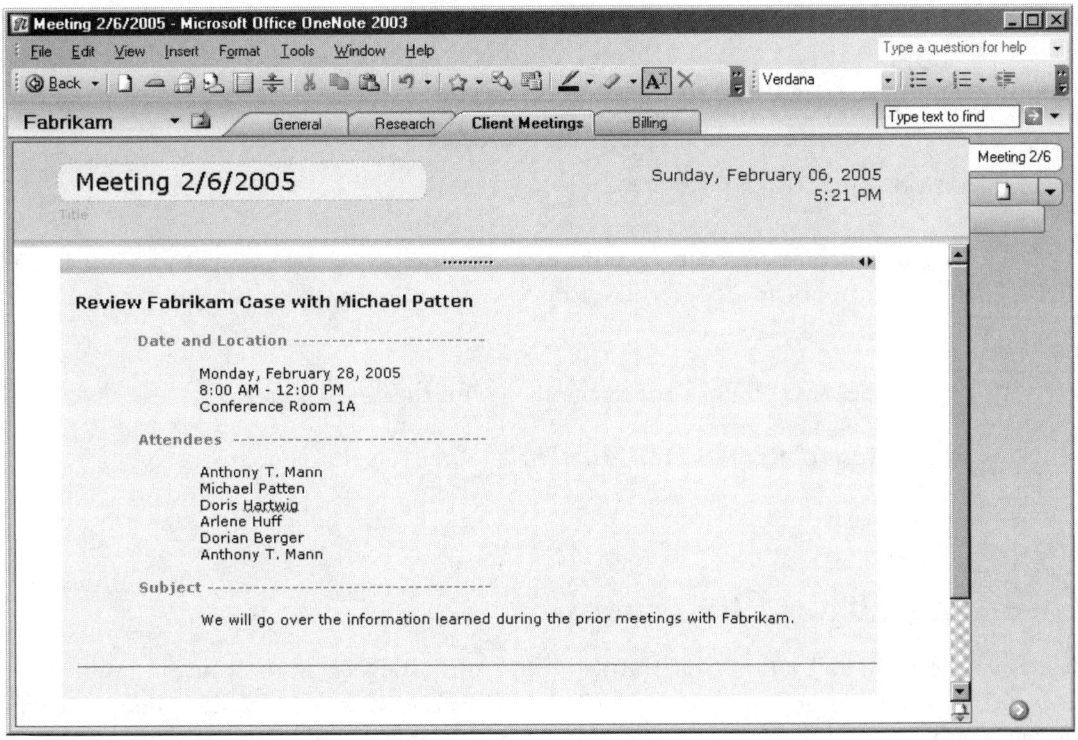

Figure 10.3: Inserting an Outlook Appointment into Your Notes.

To insert an Outlook appointment like the one shown in Figure 10.3, follow these simple steps:

1. Navigate to the desired note.

2. Place the carat in the location where you would like the Outlook appointment inserted.

3. Click the **Insert⇨ Outlook Meeting Details** menu item. You'll see the **Insert Outlook Meeting Details** screen, as shown in Figure 10.4. This screen lets you choose the desired date and view appointments entered into your calendar on that date.

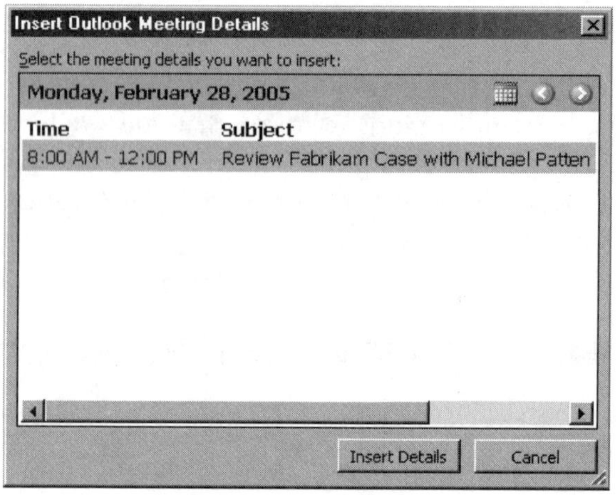

Figure 10.4: Selecting an Outlook Appointment.

4. Navigate to the desired date by clicking either the left or right arrows to advance one date at a time, or click the calendar icon to view a calendar to quickly jump to a specific date.

5. Select the desired appointment that is shown for the selected date.

6. Click the **Insert Details** button. The details of the appointment are inserted into your notes.

Inserting Other Documents

Just as you inserted an Outlook appointment into your OneNote notes, you can insert other documents as well. Again, because OneNote is part of the Microsoft Office System, you can easily insert any common type of document, such as a Word document or Excel spreadsheet.

NOTE

You should know that when you insert a document, OneNote generates a snapshot image of the document. Therefore, you can not make changes to the document image once it is inserted. In addition, if you make changes to the underlying document, they will not be reflected in OneNote. It is a static image.

Suppose you want to insert an Excel spreadsheet containing project billing information into your notes (see Chapter 5 for more information on using this template). Simply click the **Insert⇨ Document as Picture** menu item. You are prompted to select the file to insert. If you insert a spreadsheet, you'll see something similar to what's shown in Figure 10.5.

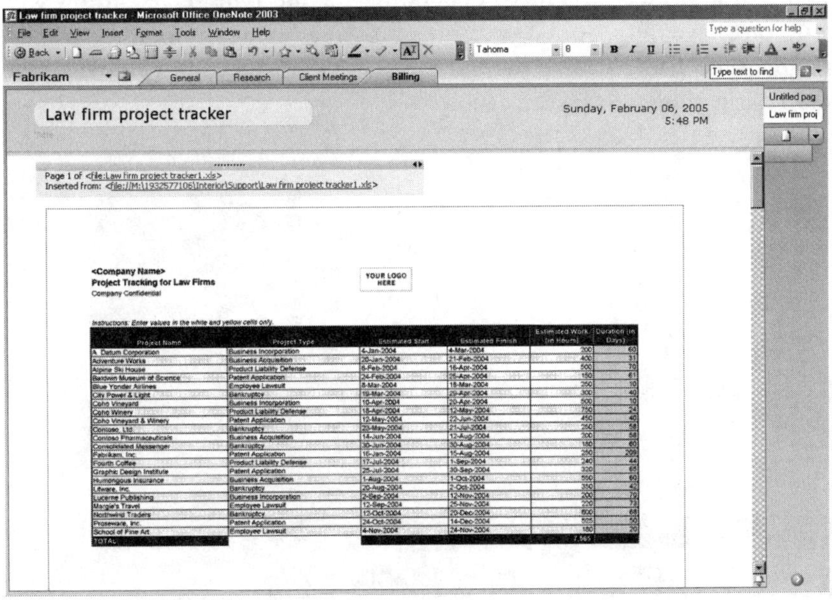

Figure 10.5: OneNote 2003 After Inserting an Excel Spreadsheet.

You can see in Figure 10.5 that even though a picture snapshot of the spreadsheet is inserted, OneNote also inserts links to the original file.

Inserting Audio and Video Recordings

Audio and video recordings can play an important role in legal applications. They can be used to record depositions, interviews, and more. If you use a Tablet PC to run OneNote, you already have a built-in microphone to record audio. If you run OneNote on any other type of computer, such as a desktop workstation or a laptop, you may need to use an external microphone. If you wish to use video recordings, you'll always have to install external video recording equipment. Some Paralegals are using OneNote 2003 to record an audio version of meetings and then take written notes of the meeting as well.

To insert either audio or video recordings into your notes, you only have to follow a few steps, like this:

1. Navigate to the desired note.

2. Place the carat in the location where you would like the audio or video recording inserted.

3. Click the **Tools⇨ Audio and Video Recording** menu item. You can then choose either the **Record Audio Only** or **Record Video**, depending on the type of recording you wish to do. If you don't have the required equipment, such as a microphone or camera, you'll see an error message. Otherwise, a toolbar pops up to enable you to control your recording. This toolbar is shown in Figure 10.6.

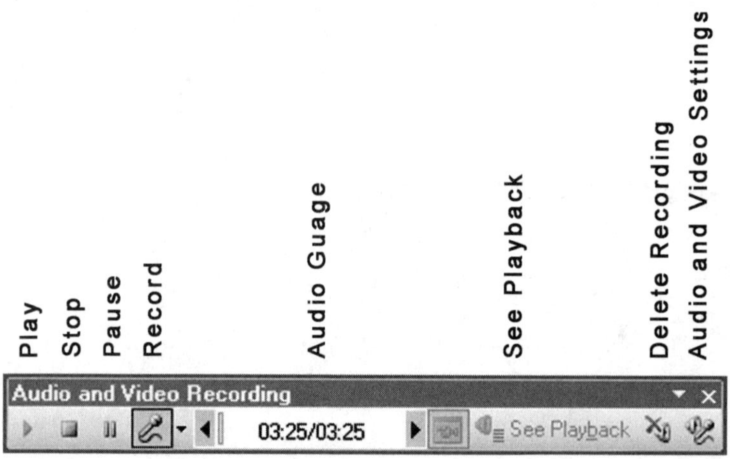

Figure 10.6: Audio and Video Recording Toolbar.

4. Click the **Stop** button when you are finished recording. Your audio recording is inserted into your notes. You'll see a clickable icon to the left of your notes that lets you control the recording, including deleting, appending a new recording, and more.

5. Listen to your recording by clicking the **Play** button on the **Audio and Video Recording** toolbar.

Handwriting Notes

As you learned in Chapter 7, one of the greatest features of OneNote 2003 for Paralegals is the ability handwrite notes onto a computer screen as if you were writing with pen on a pad. You do this with a special stylus and a special type of notebook computer called a Tablet PC. The Tablet PC has a special screen that lets you write on its surface with the stylus. If you are using OneNote 2003, this writing is captured into your notes, so you can take all your notes by writing instead of typing.

The advantage of writing notes directly on the screen is that you don't have to then transpose those notes into an electronic format for storage or collaboration. You'll already have them in an electronic format just by writing on the screen. Another advantage in writing your notes directly on the screen is that you cannot use a noisy keyboard in situations where quietness is essential.

Pulling a New Pen Out of Your Pocket Protector

When you are handwriting your notes onto the screen of a Tablet PC, you have a choice of pen styles and colors. For emphasis, you may use a thicker pen (such as a felt-tip), or a thinner pen for general note-taking. To choose the desired pen type and color, click the dropdown arrow next to the **Pen** button on the **Standard** toolbar. This brings up a pen menu, which looks like the one shown in Figure 10.7.

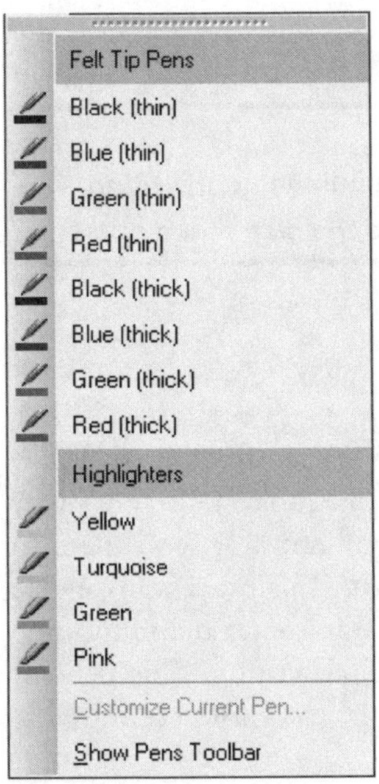

Figure 10.7: The OneNote 2003 Pen Menu.

When you select a given pen, this will be the default pen and color style for anything you subsequently write on the screen (until you choose a new pen). Figure 10.8 shows some of the different pen types.

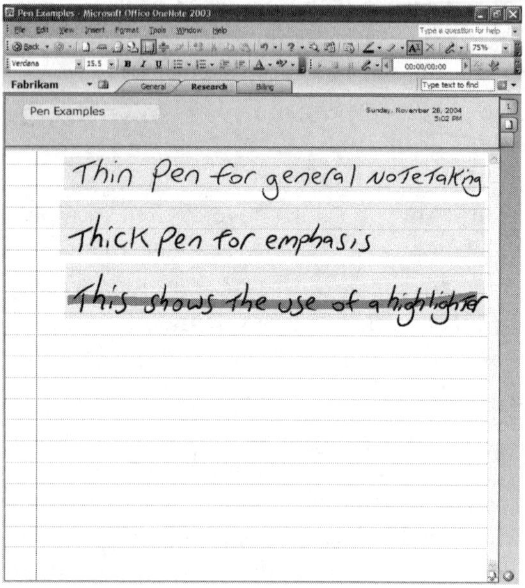

Figure 10.8: Sample Pen Types.

NOTE

Along with a pen selection, you can choose an eraser type to eliminate handwriting on the screen. The Eraser button on the Standard toolbar controls the size of the eraser.

I Can't Read Your Writing!

The only disadvantage in using handwritten notes in OneNote 2003 is that if you have sloppy handwriting on a legal pad, you'll still have sloppy handwriting on the Tablet PC. That's why the authors of this book use a keyboard. If you want to archive your notes or send them to someone else, you may want to convert your handwriting to text first. This process involves a very sophisticated means of reading the curves and spaces in your handwritten text and running an algorithm to do a best guess as to which letters make up your handwriting. This is not a perfect process, so try to be patient. The clearer your handwriting is, the more accurate the process.

> **NOTE**
>
> **Perhaps it should be under the category of "believe it or not," but you can actually search your handwritten notes without converting them to text first. Searching is covered earlier in this chapter.**

To convert your handwritten notes to text, simply click the **Tools⇨ Convert Handwriting to Text** menu item. The conversion process is usually quick, but its accuracy is dictated by how clear your original handwriting is. It is a good idea to go through the converted document and correct any errors that you find, using the mouse and keyboard. An example of a converted document is shown in Chapter 7.

Conclusion

OneNote 2003 provides exceptional features for Paralegals to take notes. Not only can you type your notes by using a keyboard and mouse, you can also handwrite your notes if you use a Tablet PC. This can save much time over transposing notes on legal pads into an electronic format. This chapter covered the basic use of OneNote 2003, including using the keyboard to type notes, searching through your notes, and flagging notes. It covered how to insert Outlook appointments, external files, and audio and video. This chapter also covered how easy it is to handwrite notes and convert those notes into text.

Did you know?

OneNote 2003 can recognize handwriting that is written in more languages than just English. In fact, OneNote 2003 can recognize English, German, French, Japanese, Chinese (Simplified and Traditional), and Korean writing.

Chapter 11

Tracking Document Changes

Chapter At A Glance

WHY YOU SHOULD READ THIS CHAPTER:

As time is always critical, you need to be as efficient as possible. One way to achieve efficiency is to collaborate with multiple people on your legal documents. One way that Microsoft Word enables collaboration on documents is to provide a feature for tracking changes that each user makes to a document. This chapter covers how to track changes in your documents and cautions you about some legal issues surrounding the use of this feature.

PRODUCT OUTLINED IN THIS CHAPTER:

- Microsoft Word 2003

PRODUCT FEATURE COVERED IN THIS CHAPTER:

- Track Changes

To understand the concept of tracking changes, imagine this scenario…

You draft a legal pleading for an attorney named John, who works in your law firm. You need input from John and another attorney, Meredith, on the same document before it can be released to the court. As a Paralegal, it is your responsibility to collate all changes from John and Meredith into one complete document. As the central contact for all changes in a document, you will have to decide which of John's changes and which of Meredith's changes will be incorporated into the final document. To do this, you will have the option of choosing to accept or reject changes made by the attorneys. Microsoft Word will automatically track the changes made by each attorney as the document is accessed by each user. The same scenario can be applied to any other form of document, such as wills, agreements, briefs, leases, memos, and more.

Once you turn on the **Track Changes** feature, you'll notice any change that is made will contain a visual indicator on the screen. This visual indicator is known as a *markup*, because it resembles how you would mark, or correct, text on a piece of paper. For example, if there was a part of a legal pleading as a physical document that was incorrect, an attorney would likely cross out the error and physically write the correction into the document. Microsoft Word allows you to do the exactly the same thing, only electronically. This is known as *tracking changes*.

A Picture is Worth a Thousand Words

Before diving into how the **Track Changes** feature works, let's see what it looks like in action. Figure 11.1 shows a sample legal pleading in Microsoft Word 2003 with changes displayed (marked-up). This document shows three types of changes; inserted text, deleted text, change of format.

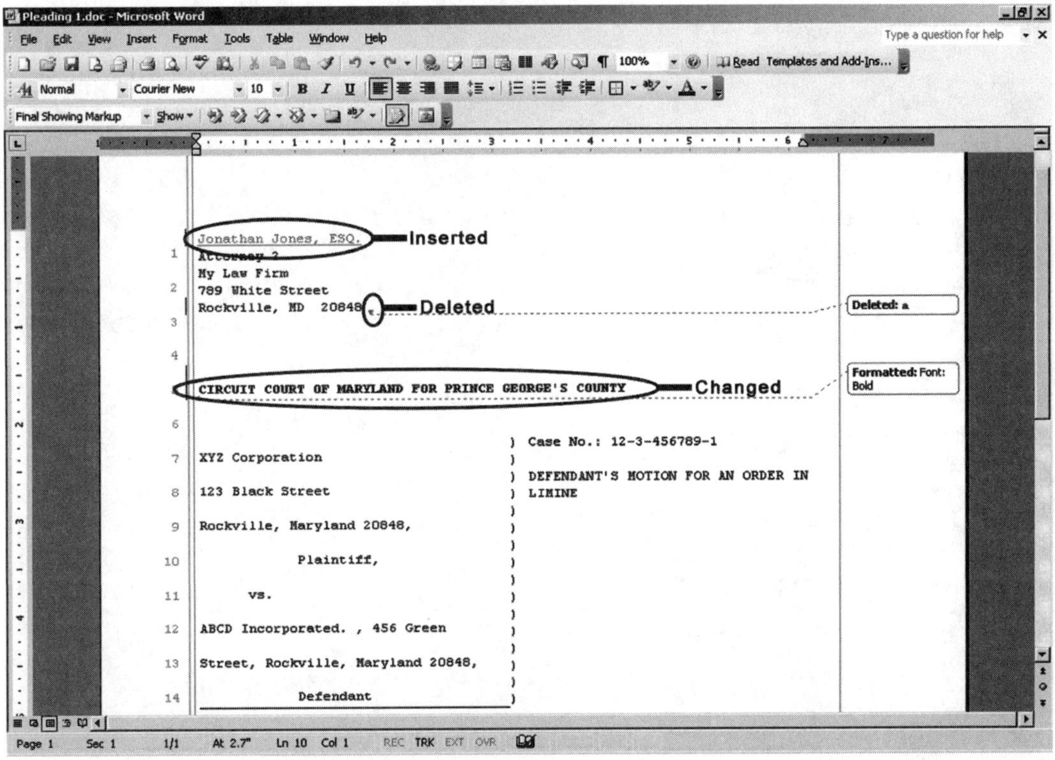

Figure 11.1: Legal Pleading Document Showing Marked-up Changes.

How did those nifty dotted lines and boxes (known as *balloons*) get drawn on the screen? Simple! It happens automatically. As soon as you turn on the **Track Changes** feature in Microsoft Word, each person to make a change to the document will show changes made using the dotted lines and balloons as you see in Figure 11.1.

Where's the "ON" switch?

As you might expect, before you can use the **Track Changes** feature of Word, you must first switch it on. To do so, simply click the **Tools**⇨ **Track Changes** menu item and you're on your way. This menu is shown in Figure 11.2.

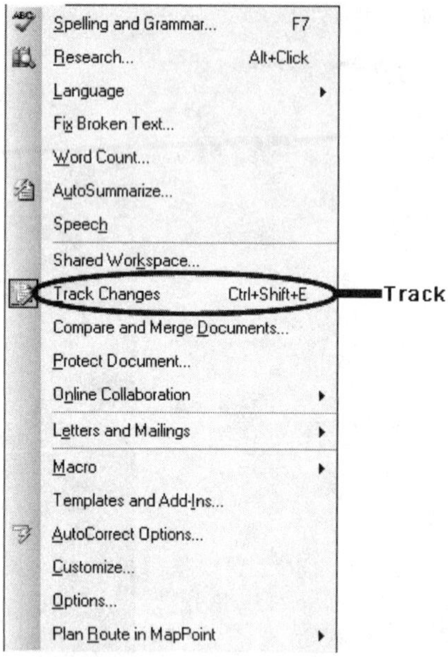

Figure 11.2: Tools Menu Showing Track Changes Selected.

NOTE

It is a very good idea to turn on the Track Changes **feature after you create the initial document, but before you send it around to the attorneys. Attorneys may not know how to use this feature and might forget to turn it on. If that happens and the attorneys work on the document, you will have no way of knowing where the changes are.**

Once the **Track Changes** feature is switched on, by default every change made to a Word document is now reflected for each user by annotating changes in a unique color for each user. Because this book is not printed in color, you cannot see the colors shown in Figure 11.1. Therefore, you should know the first user to make changes to the document will have those changes shown in the color red. Microsoft Word automatically chooses this and subsequent colors for each user that make changes to the document.

Passing the [Tool]Bar

In addition to using menu options with the **Track Changes** feature, Microsoft Word has a special toolbar available to help with managing changes in your documents. This special toolbar is called the **Reviewing** toolbar. It is often easier and quicker to click an icon in a toolbar, rather than navigating a series of menus. This is especially true if any attorney, Paralegal, or Legal Secretary makes many changes to a document. The **Reviewing** toolbar makes managing changes quite easy. Figure 11.3 shows the top of a Word document with a few toolbars enabled, including the **Reviewing** toolbar.

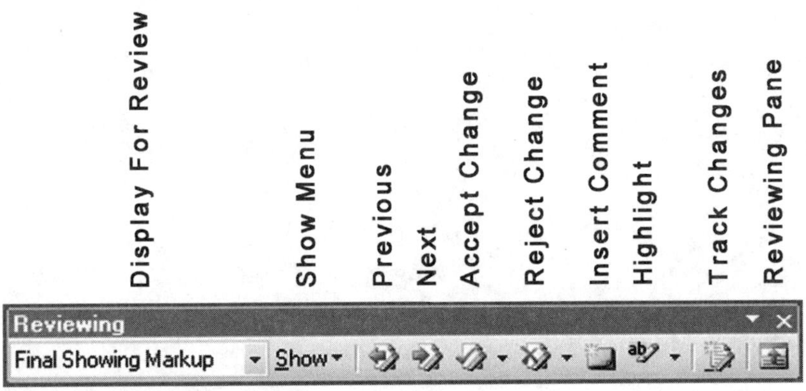

Figure 11.3: Document Showing Reviewing Toolbar.

To show the **Reviewing** toolbar, simply click the **View⇨ Toolbars⇨ Reviewing** menu item. Doing so will show the menu displayed in Figure 11.3. If you wish to move the toolbar, you can drag and drop the menu to another location. The usage of the toolbar items is discussed throughout this chapter.

Being Sneaky with Changes

Suppose you want to track changes in a document, but you don't want it to be obvious. In other words, suppose you need to know which attorney made each change and what each attorney changed, but you don't want to clutter the screen with all the dotted lines and balloons? That too is simple.

If you don't want anyone to see all the marked-up changes, you can simply hide them on the screen, but Word is still on the ball tracking those changes, but just hiding them from view. To hide changes being made, simply click the **View** menu. Doing so brings up the menu shown in Figure 11.4.

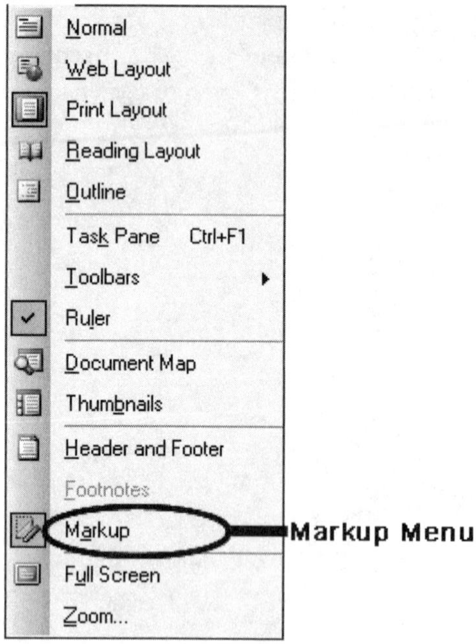

Figure 11.4: View Menu Showing Markup Selected.

By default, the **Markup** menu item is selected (with a box around it). This means that all changes, or *markups*, will be shown on the screen. To hide these changes, simply click the **Markup** menu item and it will toggle to the unselected state (without a box around it). When unselected, no changes will be shown on the screen, even though Word is at your service, tracking changes in the background.

Alternatively, you can select **Final** from the **Display for Review** dropdown menu item in the **Reviewing** toolbar. This too performs the same function as hiding the marked-up text from the users, while continuing to provide the valuable **Track Changes** service.

⚠ CAUTION

When you make changes to a document while using the Track Changes feature, metadata is stored in the document. This metadata should be cleaned and removed from the document before you send the document outside your firm. See Chapter 3 for a discussion of metadata and its removal.

Changes, Changes, Everywhere

Once you construct the initial document, turn on the **Track Changes** feature, send the document around to all attorneys, and receive it back, you will likely see a bunch of changes in the document. So, what in the world do you do with this potentially messy-looking document? It's easier than you think. You have these options:

- **Accept** — Uses the changed text at the current cursor location that was made by another user and incorporates it into the main document.
- **Reject** — Discards the changed text at the current cursor location that was made by another user and reverts back to the original text in the document.
- **Accept All** — Accepts *all* changes in the document at one time. This option is useful when you know for sure that an attorney made all the correct changes. It can save much time over accepting changes one-by-one.
- **Reject All** — Rejects *all* changes in the document simultaneously. It is likely that you will not use this option. The reason it is an unlikely option is that if you didn't trust a user to make changes, you would likely not have sent the document to the user at all.

These options and their usage are discussed in the next two sections.

⚠ CAUTION

Even if you accept changes in a document, someone who is technically savvy can look at the prior changes because they are automatically stored as metadata. These changes could possibly be used against you in court if they are discovered. Therefore, it is essential that you clean and remove the metadata from your documents before you send them out of your firm. Metadata and its removal is discussed in Chapter 3.

Sustained!

After you receive a document back from an attorney, it is likely that you want to actually incorporate, or *accept*, the changes that he or she specifies. After all, the attorney generally knows what needs to be in the final document, such as a legal pleading. You have the option of navigating through the text of the document, change by change, and accepting the change, or accepting all changes wholesale.

To accept changes in a document, follow these steps:

1. Locate the changed text. One way to do this is to simply right-click the changed text itself to reveal the popup menu shown in Figure 11.5.

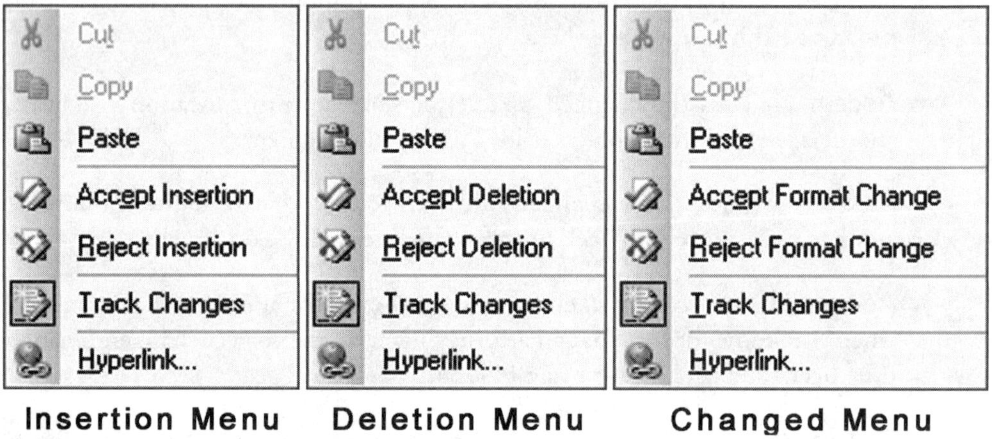

Figure 11.5: Popup Menus That Appear for Inserted, Deleted, or Changed Format Text.

Another way to locate changed text is to click the **Next** button on the **Reviewing** toolbar. See the section, "Passing the [Tool]Bar" earlier in this chapter for information about viewing this toolbar.

2. Accept the change.

If you are using the popup menu, click the **Accept Insertion** menu item for inserted text, **Accept Deletion** menu item for deleted text, or **Accept Format Change** menu item for text that had its format changed. If you are using the **Reviewing** toolbar, click the **Accept Change** button. Either way, the changed text will be incorporated into the document as if it was part of the original document. You'll see all the dotted lines and balloons magically disappear. Alternatively, if you wish to accept all changes, it is much faster to choose the dropdown arrow adjacent to the **Accept Change** menu item, which displays a list of available options, as shown in Figure 11.6.

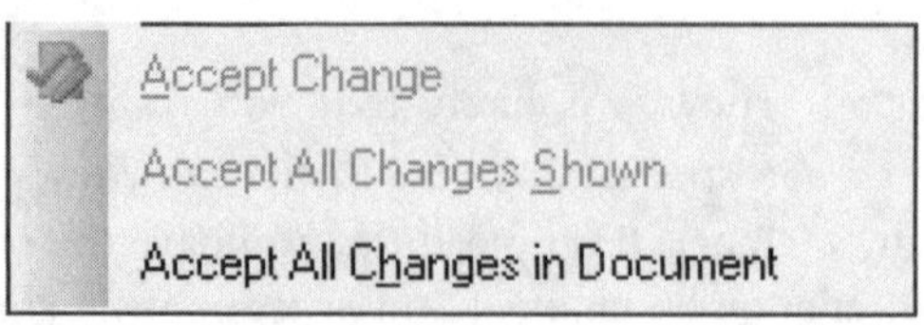

Figure 11.6: Popup Menu Available for Accepting Changes.

Click the **Accept All Changes in Document** menu item to accept each and every change in the document, from all users. If John and Meredith both made changes to the document, all of their changes will be incorporated into the final document using this option. If you wish to accept changes from only Meredith, but not John, you will have to accept changes one-by-one instead.

Objection!

What if you don't want to accept changes, or object to them as it were? What if your attorney or someone else sends you back a document with changes that are wrong or inappropriate? In this case, you'll have to reject the changes. Rejecting an item in a document is just as easy as accepting it, only you click the **Reject Insertion** menu item for inserted text, **Reject Deletion** menu item for deleted text, or **Reject Format Change** menu item for text that had its format changed. If you are using the **Reviewing** toolbar, click the **Reject Change** button. Either way, the changed text will be rejected and the text will revert to its original form. You'll see all the dotted lines and balloons disappear after the change is rejected.

Reviewing is NOT a Pane

Depending on the depth of the changes made to a document, you might not have enough room in the balloon to display all the changes. For example, look at Figure 11.7. It shows a legal pleading where a bunch of text was deleted in the document (as witnessed by the balloon on the bottom-right part of the figure).

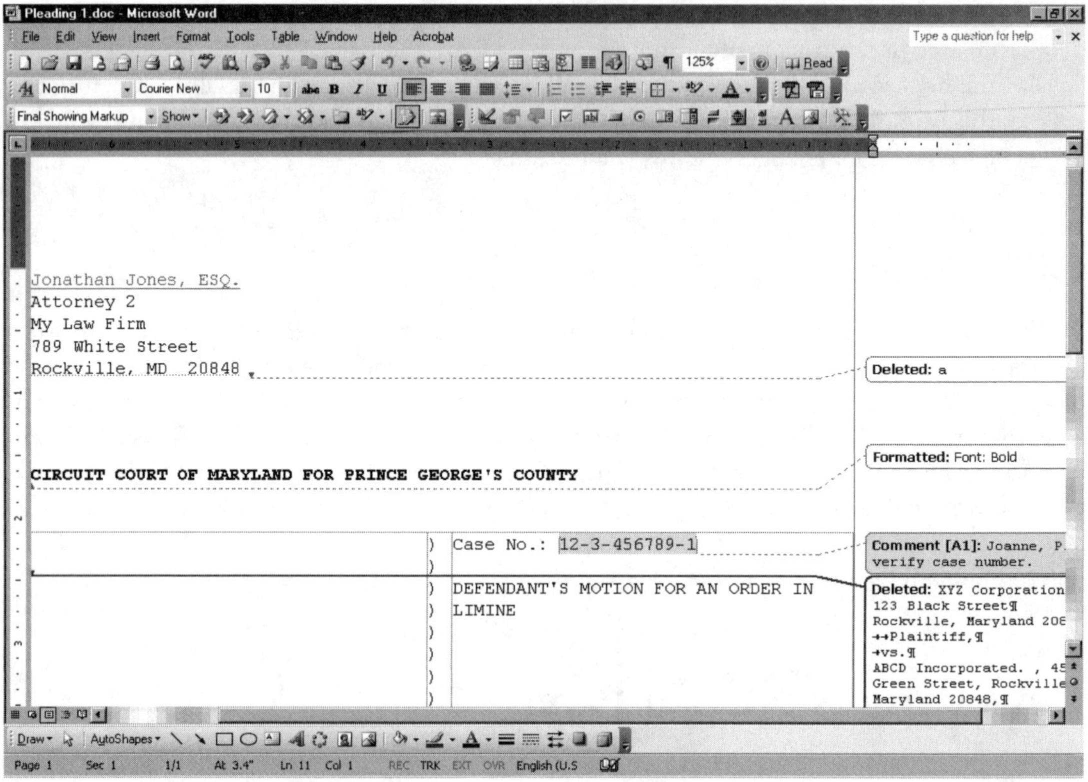

Figure 11.7: Overcrowded Deleted Balloon.

You can clearly see that so much text was deleted that the balloon can't adequately show all the deleted text. Therefore, you can display all the text much easier in a special window called the **Reviewing Pane**, which is shown in Figure 11.8.

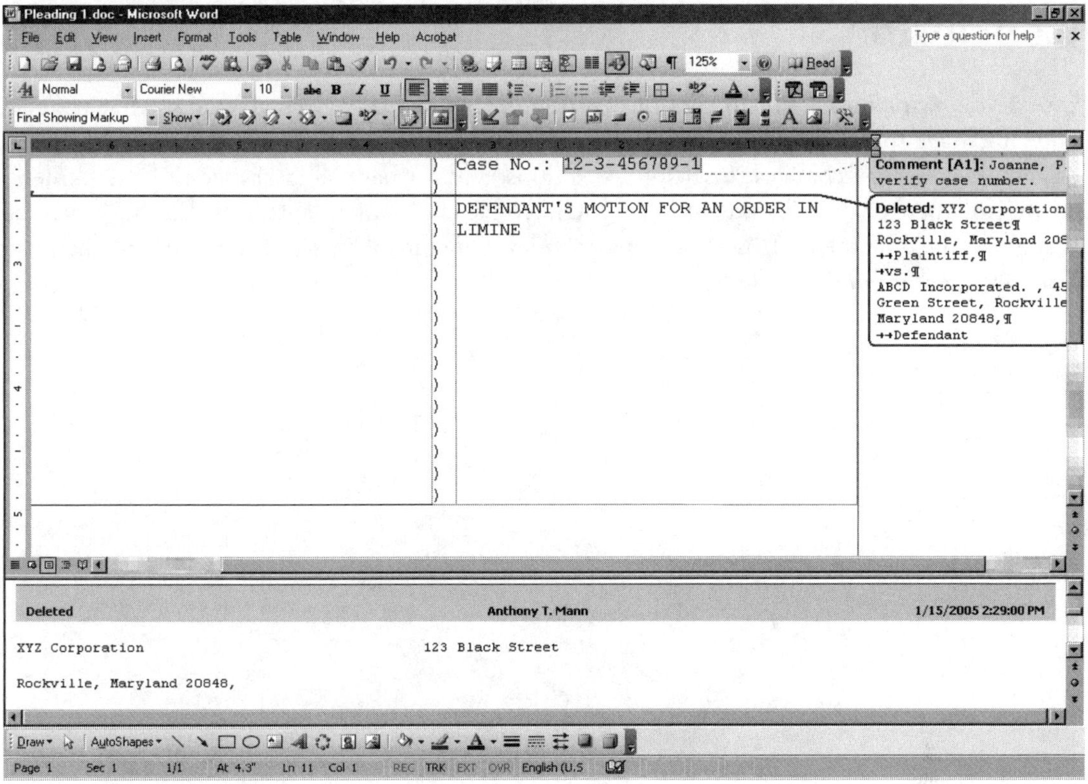

Figure 11.8: Reviewing Pane.

Notice in Figure 11.8, there is a small window at the bottom of the document. This window is called the **Reviewing Pane** and is context-sensitive. This means that the text in the **Reviewing Pane** will change, depending on the location of the cursor. The deleted text is being displayed in the **Reviewing Pane** because the cursor is inside the deleted balloon in the document.

To bring up the **Reviewing Pane**, simply click the **Reviewing Pane** button on the **Reviewing** toolbar. To turn it off, simply click the same button again. The effect of this button is to toggle the window on and off.

Conclusion

Unless you work on all documents by yourself, you will likely need to know what changes someone made to a document. Using the **Track Changes** feature of Microsoft Word 2003, you can graphically view changes (insertions, deletions, and format changes) made to a document. By viewing these changes to a document, you have the choice of accepting or deleting any or all changes in the document. This gives you a great level of control over your documents when you work on them with other people.

Chapter 12

Blacklining and Merging Documents

Chapter At A Glance

WHY YOU SHOULD READ THIS CHAPTER:

There are times when you have multiple documents that need to be compared and merged. You don't have to visually inspect the documents line-by-line. Instead, you can use Microsoft Word 2003 to electronically compare those documents and report differences to you in the form of blacklined documents. You can even merge changes into new documents. This chapter shows you how use Word 2003 to blackline and merge your documents.

PRODUCT OUTLINED IN THIS CHAPTER:

- Microsoft Word 2003

PRODUCT FEATURES COVERED IN THIS CHAPTER:

- Blacklining Documents
- Merging Documents

In Chapter 11, you learned how to track changes in your documents and how Microsoft Word represents those changes on the screen, using balloons and other markups. Now that you have that concept down, you will invariably need to compare two documents in the course of performing your Paralegal duties.

For example, suppose an attorney gives you two legal pleading documents that have the same title, but you need to understand how they are different to know which one to submit to the court. If you have lots of free time, you could compare both of them, word for word. If time is critical, as it is for most of us, you'll want the computer to do it for you. That's where blacklining comes in. But, what if you need parts of each of the documents? You'll need to merge parts of the document together. You're in luck! This chapter covers both of these topics, so put away your black marker or red pen…Microsoft Word is going to do everything for you.

Blacklining your Documents

Blacklining is the process of identifying differences between two documents by showing a black vertical line displayed in the margin where differences exist. This black vertical line is displayed in the margin for each line of text in a Word document that is different between the two documents that you are comparing. To illustrate the concept of blacklining, consider two separate documents, one called **Original** and one called **New**. The **Original** document is shown in Figure 12.1.

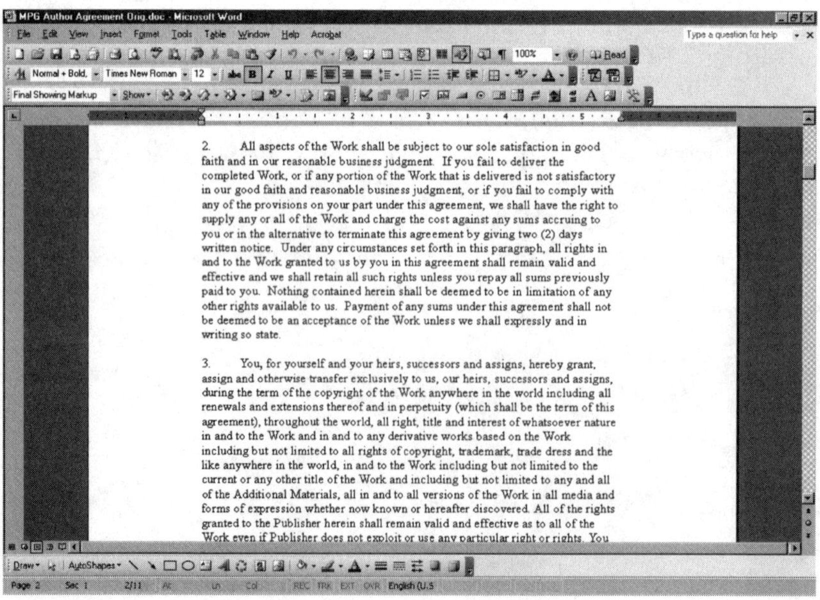

Figure 12.1: Sample Original Document.

The **New** document contains differences from the **Original** document, as shown in Figure 12.2. The changes are circled in Figure 12.2.

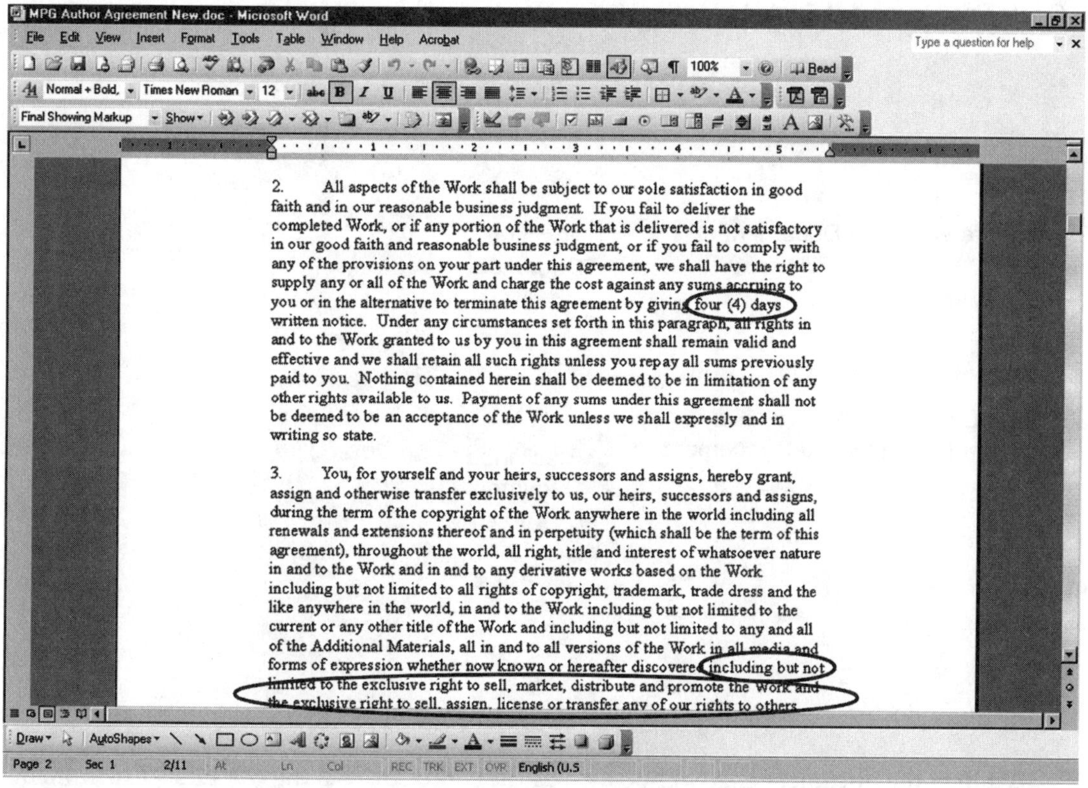

Figure 12.2: Sample New Document.

Before you instruct Word to show you the differences between the two documents, you must understand how you wish to see the changes. In other words, do you want to show the differences between the **New** document and the **Original** document, or vice versa? The way blacklining works in Word is that you first open the **New** document, then compare it with the **Original** document. Word will create a new resulting document that shows the changes between the **Original** and the **New** document. Figure 12.3 illustrates this concept by showing the order that you open documents for comparison in Word.

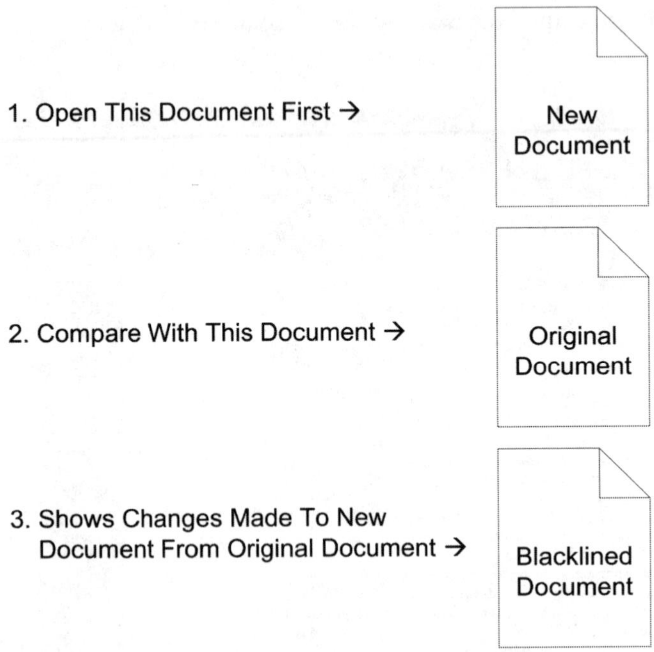

Figure 12.3: Document Comparison Order.

To blackline a document according to Figure 12.3, follow this simple procedure:

1. Open the document that will be used as the source by clicking the **File⇨ Open** menu item and search for the desired document.

2. Click the **Tools⇨ Compare and Merge Documents** menu item. Clicking this menu item brings up the **Compare and Merge Documents** screen, which is shown in Figure 12.4.

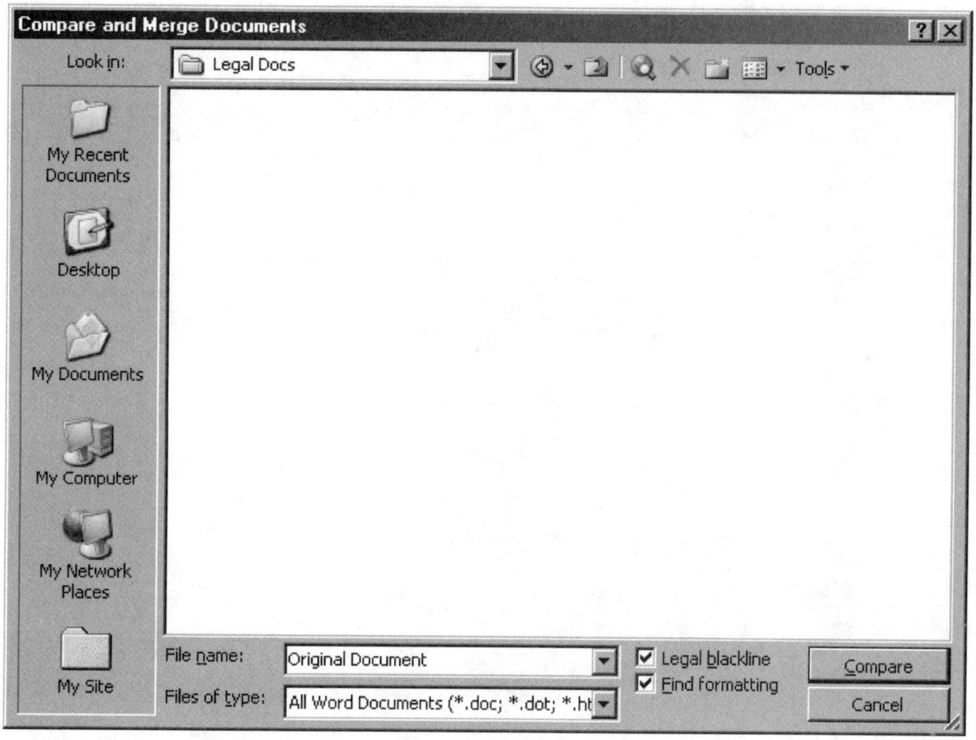

Figure 12.4: Compare and Merge Documents Screen (Showing Compare Button).

3. Ensure the **Legal blackline** option is checked. If the option is NOT checked, the button will display **Merge** instead of **Compare**.

4. Click the **Compare** button. A new document is opened with changes blacklined, as shown in Figure 12.5.

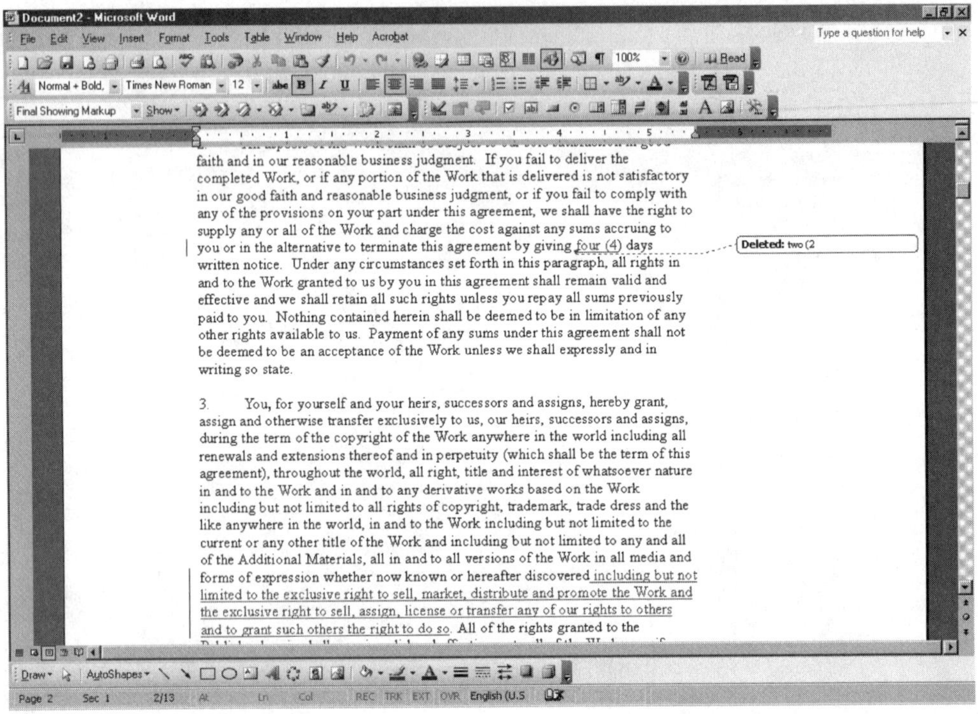

Figure 12.5: Resulting Blacklined Document.

You'll notice in Figure 12.5 that there are two separate areas that are blacklined (as indicated in the left-hand margin). The actual changes are indicated in the document, based on the **Track Changes** options, which are discussed in Chapter 11.

> **NOTE**
>
> **If you reversed the document that is first opened with the one that is compared, the resulting blacklined document would show changes opposite of those shown in Figure 12.5. The first change would be shown as an insert and the second change would be shown as a delete.**

Merging—It's Not Just For Traffic Anymore!

A close cousin to blacklining is merging. Merging your documents simply involves taking two source documents and merging them together into a document. The document can be an existing open document, or a new document. That's it. In the merged document, you'll see all changes that were made between the first and second documents.

Merging can be quite useful in a situation where you download a template from the Microsoft Office Web site and you fill in the areas of the template to make it specific to a client. However, the attorney wants to see what you changed from the original template and you forgot to turn on the **Track Changes** feature (see Chapter 11). You don't have redo anything. You simply merge the changes into a new document, which will highlight the changes. Isn't that simple?

For this example, suppose you have two documents; the original downloaded template named RentalAgreement_Template.doc, and the one you filled-in, named RentalAgreement_Edit.doc. Here's how to merge the two documents:

1. Open the first document that will be used by clicking the **File⇨ Open** menu item and search for the original document (which we called RentalAgreement_Template.doc).

2. Click the **Tools⇨ Compare and Merge Documents** menu item. Clicking this menu item brings up the **Compare and Merge Documents** screen, which is shown in Figure 12.6.

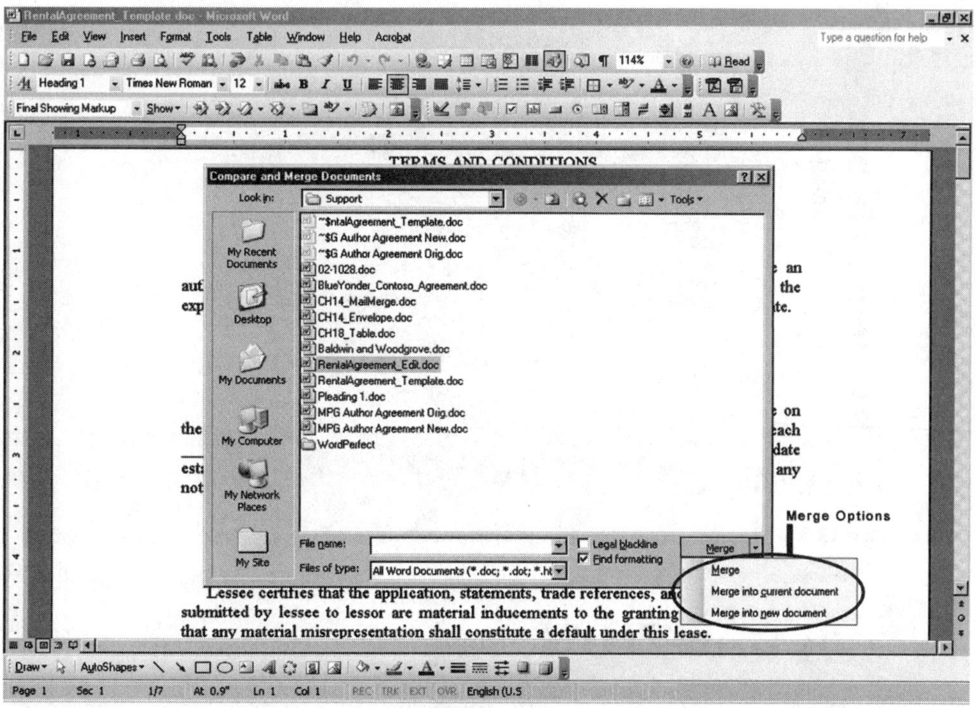

Figure 12.6: Compare and Merge Documents Screen (Showing Merge).

3. Ensure the **Legal blackline** option is *not* checked. If the option *is* checked, the button will display **Compare** instead of **Merge.**

4. Click the dropdown arrow next to the **Merge** button. You'll see a dropdown list of merge options.

5. Click the **Merge into new document** menu item. A new document is opened with the changes shown. To review what the notations on the screen mean for changes in your documents, see Chapter 11. The merged document looks like the one shown in Figure 12.7.

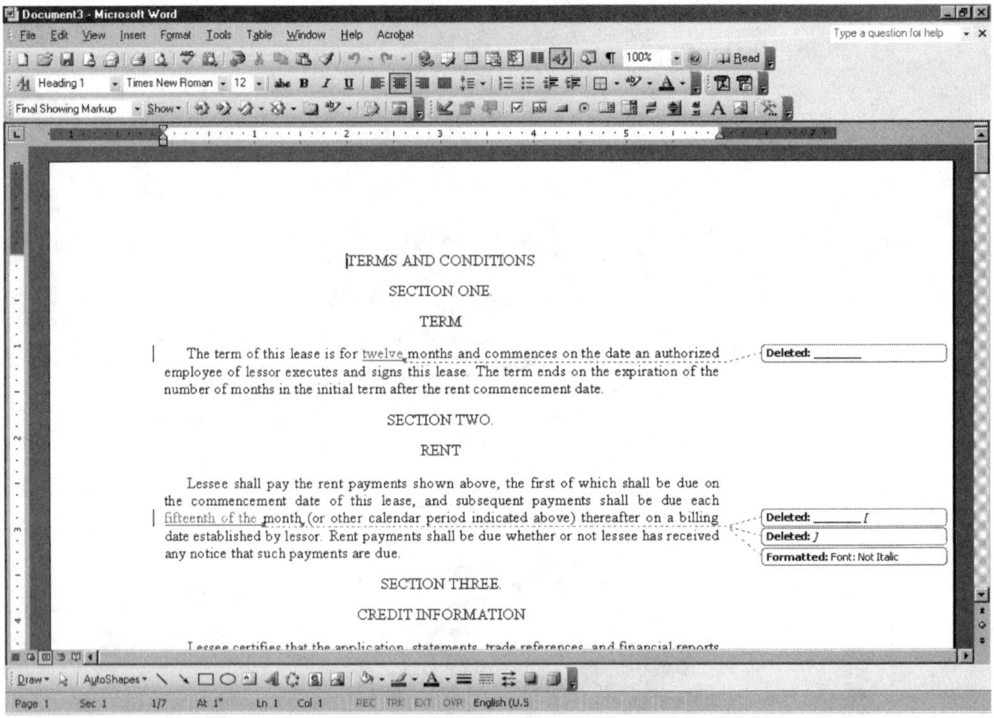

Figure 12.7: New Merged Document Showing Changes.

⚠ CAUTION

When you merge documents, some metadata is stored in the document. This metadata should be cleaned and removed from the document before you send the document outside your firm. Chapter 3 discusses metadata and its removal.

Conclusion

It is inevitable that during the course of performing your Paralegal duties, you will need to compare two Microsoft Word documents. Comparing and outlining changes in a document is referred to as blacklining. Blacklining and its close cousin, merging, are exceptionally easy to do with Word 2003. With a few mouse clicks, documents will be blacklined or merged. This chapter outlined how to perform both of these functions with examples of how each would be used.

Did you know?

When you compare or merge a document that contains tracked changes (see Chapter 11), Word must accept all changes in the document before it can perform the compare or merge.

Chapter 13

Managing Client Contacts

Chapter At A Glance

WHY YOU SHOULD READ THIS CHAPTER:

Managing contacts and client information is one of the most challenging areas that a Paralegal has to deal with. Contact information can be stored in lots of places. In fact, multiple people may have different contact information for the same contact. What information do you trust? This chapter helps you to understand the issues, technologies, and strategies for determining how to deal with contact information.

PRODUCT OUTLINED IN THIS CHAPTER:

- Outlook 2003

PRODUCT FEATURES COVERED IN THIS CHAPTER:

- Outlook 2003 Contact Features

One of the most challenging things you have to do is manage the myriad of contacts that arise in your daily business. For a given client, you might have contact information, other Paralegals might have different contact information, and your attorney might have still separate information—all for the same client! If you don't get this situation under control, your firm might appear to be unprofessional by sending e-mail, snail mail, or overnight documents to the wrong address. Suppose you and an attorney each have a cell phone number for a client, but the client asks you not to ever call on his cell phone. Unless you have a way to update your records and the attorney's records at the same time, there is a chance that the attorney will call the client's cell phone because he doesn't know. There is a better way to manage your contacts! Read on…

Contacts, Contacts, Everywhere!

You know from your daily business that you have contacts absolutely everywhere. Contacts possibly exist simultaneously in these areas:

- Paper address book
- PDA (Personal Digital Assistant)
- Outlook or other e-mail program

What's worse is that your colleagues and attorneys have the same possibilities to store contact information, so the chances of everything being in sync are virtually nil. There is a better way!

Determining a Contact Strategy

To say you must determine a contact strategy probably sounds like a strange concept. The fact remains, if you don't develop a contact strategy, you will continue to have incorrect contacts in multiple locations. In fact, without a contact strategy, when you look up a contact, you won't actually know whether it's correct or not. An attorney might have one address or phone number for a client and you might have another. Which one is correct? Do you even know?

A contact strategy can be quite simple. You need to consider these things:

- Where will the contacts be stored? In other words, will contact information be stored in a single location, such as a common database, or will each person in your firm have contact information for a single contact?

- If contact information is stored individually, who will be the "master" record holder? In the situation where an attorney and you have different information for a single contact, which one will you trust as being accurate?

- What technologies will you use to store your contacts? Table 13.1 illustrates the pros and cons of each possible storage mechanism.

Storage Technology	Pros	Cons
Paper Address Book	Virtually none	Very outdated. Paper address book can be lost and not easily shared with others. It also introduces the possibility of typographical errors when using the contact information.
Excel Spreadsheet	Readily available and can be stored in a common place. Allows users to copy/paste contact information into other programs.	Doesn't continuously communicate with all programs, such as Outlook, although you can import from Excel into Outlook.
Personal Address Book (PAB)	Contacts are stored in a separate physical file, but work seamlessly with Outlook.	Not centrally located, so synchronization of contact information is difficult.
Global Address List (GAL)	Contacts are stored in a central location and are very easy to use and search.	Your IT department needs to install Microsoft Exchange Server as your e-mail server.
Outlook Address Book / Contacts Folder	Contacts are stored in Outlook along with your folders and messages and have replaced Personal Address Books (PABs) in Outlook 2003. However, if you already have a PAB from a prior version, Outlook 2003 can still use it.	Not centrally located, so synchronization of contact information is done manually.
Centralized Contact Manager	Contacts are centrally stored so there is one master record for each contact. Whether your contact manager application integrates easily with Microsoft Office applications depends on which contact manager you're using. They don't all offer the same level of integration.	Can be expensive to purchase. Some contact management programs require licenses for each individual user that accesses the data.

Table 13.1: Contact Management Storage Technology Pros and Cons.

Your contact strategy should, at a minimum, dictate who will update contact information. If your firm uses legal secretaries, perhaps this job is best left to that person. On the other hand, it might be your responsibility to update contact information. If your firm has defined such responsibility, then when new contact information comes into the firm, it is forwarded to this person to update contact information appropriately.

Microsoft Contact Programs

Microsoft has a few different programs that can be used for maintaining contacts. Therefore, it can be confusing to determine which program to use. In many law firms, your choice of program will be based on the decisions that the IT department makes. Your choices are shown in Table 13.2.

Microsoft Program	Description
Outlook Express 6	Free e-mail program that provides basic e-mail functionality, such as sending and receiving e-mail messages, storing contacts, and creating distribution lists. Note: Despite the word "Outlook," Outlook Express is not considered to be part of the Microsoft Office System. Therefore, it is not covered in this book.
Outlook 2003	Contains all features of Outlook Express, but also includes support for using Microsoft Exchange Server as an e-mail server, multiple address books, reminders, and more. Outlook 2003 is not free, but is included in the Microsoft Office system.
Microsoft CRM	Microsoft produces a Customer Relationship Management (CRM) software package, called Microsoft CRM, that can be used to create a holistic view of a customer or client. However, it is not part of the Office System and therefore is not covered in this book.
Business Contact Manager	Perhaps not adequately named, Business Contact Manager (BCM) is a lightweight CRM program that turns Outlook 2003 into an account and business tracking tool. BCM leverages the contact functionality of Outlook 2003, and adds CRM-related features. BCM is included in Office Small Business Edition 2003 and Office Professional Edition 2003.

Table 13.2: Microsoft Contact Management Programs.

NOTE

A more comprehensive list of features and comparisons between Outlook and Outlook Express is shown in Chapter 8.

The technology you are using in your firm usually depends on IT budget and IT staff. Larger firms will likely be running Microsoft Exchange Server as an e-mail server. Therefore, you would use Outlook, which can connect to Microsoft Exchange Server e-mail boxes, whereas Outlook Express cannot. On the other hand, if your firm does not use Microsoft Exchange Server, then you have the choice of using Outlook or Outlook Express. The rest of this chapter assumes you are using Outlook, as Outlook Express is not part of the Microsoft Office System.

Having a Positive Outlook

As Outlook 2003 is the latest incarnation of Microsoft's e-mail program that is part of the Microsoft Office System, the rest of this chapter focuses on using that product (as opposed to Outlook Express). Outlook can do it all, including:

- Sending and receiving e-mail from virtually any e-mail server that is popular today
- Scheduling appointments and meetings
- Use contacts from Exchange Server's Global Address List

- Managing contacts in one or more address books

Making Contact

The first thing you need to manage contacts is a contact manager program, such as Outlook or Outlook Express. Creating Outlook contacts couldn't be easier. You simply click a few menus. If you are used to Outlook Express, creating contacts is done the same way, but the screen will look different. In fact, you can store a lot more information in Outlook than you can in Outlook Express. Here's how you create new contacts:

1. Click the **File⇨ New⇨ Contact** menu item. This brings up a new blank contact screen with the **General** tab shown (see Figure 13.1).

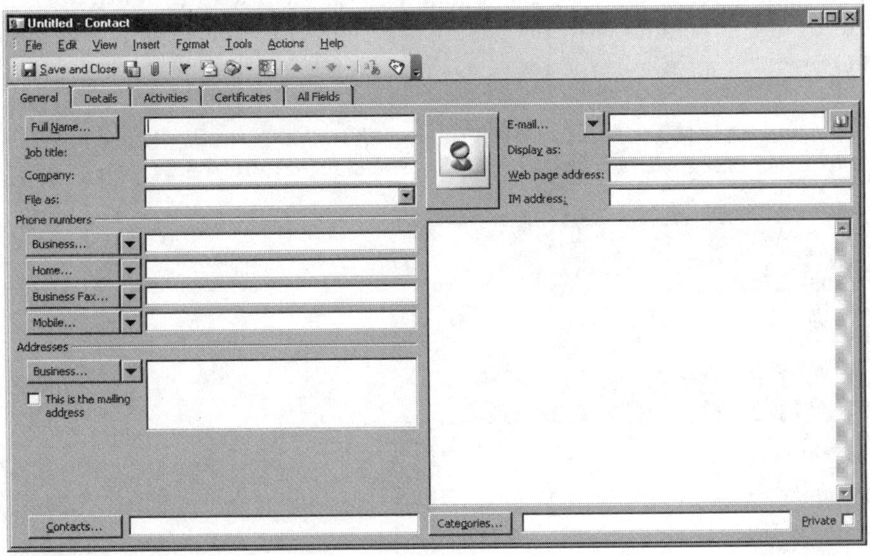

Figure 13.1: Creating a New Contact.

2. Fill in the desired fields for the contact. Notice in Figure 13.1 that you have the basic fields you would expect for a contact, such as name, e-mail, phone numbers, and addresses. Without going through each field, you simply navigate from field to field and fill in the pertinent information about a contact. However, there are a couple of things you should know. Notice the dropdown arrow next to the **Business**, **Home**, **Business Fax**, **Mobile**, and **E-mail** fields. These arrows are used to select a different field to be displayed in that location on the screen if you don't want to use the fields presented. For example, if you don't store home phone numbers for clients, but instead you wish to store pager numbers, you can simply change the **Home** field to a **Pager** field by clicking the dropdown arrow next to the **Home** field and change it. Every field on the screen is optional, except for the full name.

3. Select a picture (optional). If you would like to show the contact's picture in the record, simply click the button icon in the center of the screen and you will be prompted to locate the image file. All popular picture formats are supported. Large pictures will be scaled to the appropriate size for the contact record.

4. Enter comments/notes (optional). In the large box on the bottom right-hand part of the screen, you can enter any kind of notes about the contact that you wish. These notes can be about telephone conversations or any other kind of comment that you want to make and store along with the contact information. This is a great way for Paralegals to note, for example, that a client normally gets in late in the morning and stays at work until 8pm.

5. Select additional contacts (optional). The **Contacts** button at the bottom of the screen can be used to select contacts that should be associated with the current contact. This association can be alternate contacts in case the main contact is on vacation, or any other usage for associating contacts.

6. Select categories (optional). Clicking the **Categories** button brings up a screen to allow you to select categories for this contact, as shown in Figure 13.2.

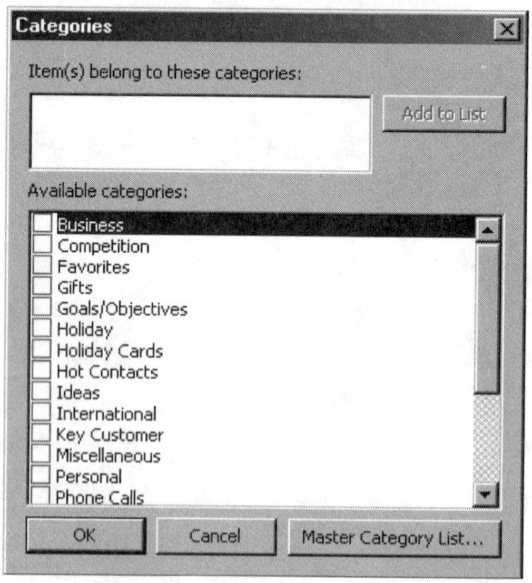

Figure 13.2: Selecting Categories.

The categories shown in Figure 13.2 are just a listing of defaults that are installed as part of Outlook. If you wish to add more categories that are germane to the legal industry, such as **Clients**, **Attorneys**, and **Witnesses**, you can add those by clicking the **Master Category List** button and adding them. Categories are useful for searching contacts that meet certain criteria, so it's a good idea to come up with a strategy for categorizing contacts and be consistent with it.

7. Mark the contact as private (optional). If you click the **Private** check box, the contact cannot be shared. Only you can view this contact.

8. If you plan to view the contact's calendar schedule that will enable you to schedule appointments, click the **Details** tab and enter the contact's **Internet Free-Busy Address** field. More information about how this works can be found in Chapter 15.

9. Click the **Save and Close** button to save your changes and close the screen.

> **NOTE**
>
> **If Outlook was configured to access Exchange Server, your contacts will be stored on the server. Otherwise, your contacts will be stored in the personal folders that were created when Outlook was configured.**

Importing

If you are new to using Outlook 2003, you might have contact information stored in another program. You don't have to retype everything. You can simply import from another program. In fact, you can import from these programs:

- ACT!
- Lotus Organizer
- Microsoft Access
- Microsoft Excel
- Personal Address Book
- Personal Folder File
- Schedule+
- Tab Separated Values
- Comma Separated Values

Importing can be scary if you've never done it before. There can be the sense of "Am I overwriting or deleting something that I don't want to?" Well, fear not! If you work slowly and think about what you are doing, you will be fine.

To import contact information from another program, follow these steps:

1. Click the **File⇨ Import and Export** menu item.
2. From the list provided, select **Import from another program or file.**
3. Click the **Next** button.
4. From the list provided, select the type of program that you are importing from. This corresponds to the list above.
5. Depending on the type of program you choose, you'll be given additional options, such as where to locate the file for importing. Continue with the prompts, based on your selection.
6. Select the option from the following:
    - **Replace duplicates with items imported** — Imported items take precedence, so multiple imports will not create additional records.
    - **Allow duplicates to be created** — Imported items will be duplicated if the same contact already exists in Outlook contacts. This can create lots of duplicate records if you import multiple times.
    - **Do not import duplicates** — Imported items that don't exist will be created, while existing items will be ignored.

Creating Distribution Lists

Distribution lists can be a great time-saver. A *distribution list* is simply a group of contacts. Suppose you have 100 clients and wanted to send a holiday e-mail greeting to all of them. You have the choice of adding all 100 e-mail addresses to the **To** line of your e-mail, or you can create a distribution list to manage all of them.

A distribution list is given a name, such as **All Clients**. Then, you add one or more contacts to the distribution list. From that point forward, all you do is send an e-mail to **All Clients** instead of the individual names.

Here's how you create a distribution list:

1. Select the **File⇨ New⇨ Distribution List** menu item. This brings up the blank screen shown in Figure 13.3.

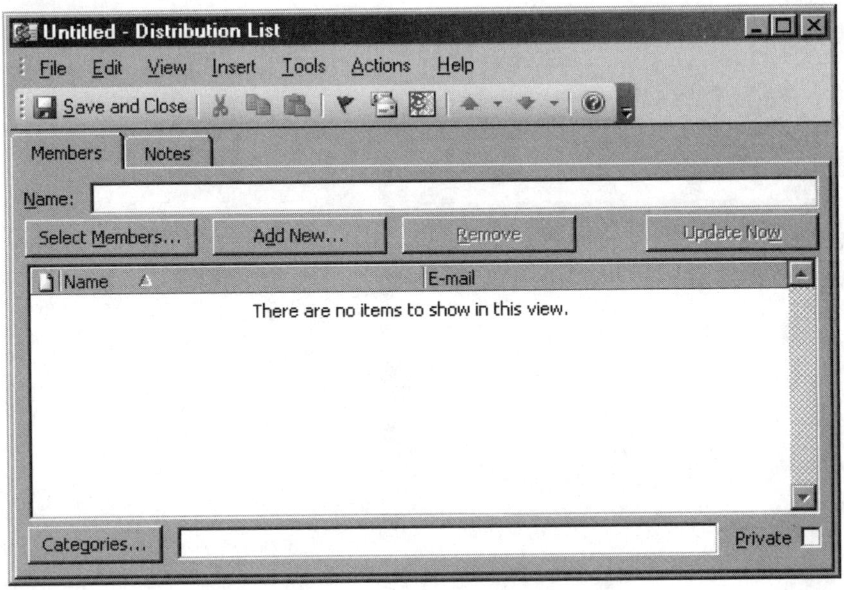

Figure 13.3: Creating a Distribution List.

2. In the **Name** field, give the distribution list a name, such as **#All Clients.**

> **TIP**
>
> **Because distribution list names are sorted alphabetically along with contact names, it is a good idea to precede distribution names with a character that will be sorted at the top of the list. The pound sign (#) is such a character. It has no effect on the performance of your system. It is only for sorting purposes.**

3. Select contact members to add to the distribution list by clicking the **Select Members** button. Clicking this button brings up the screen shown in Figure 13.4.

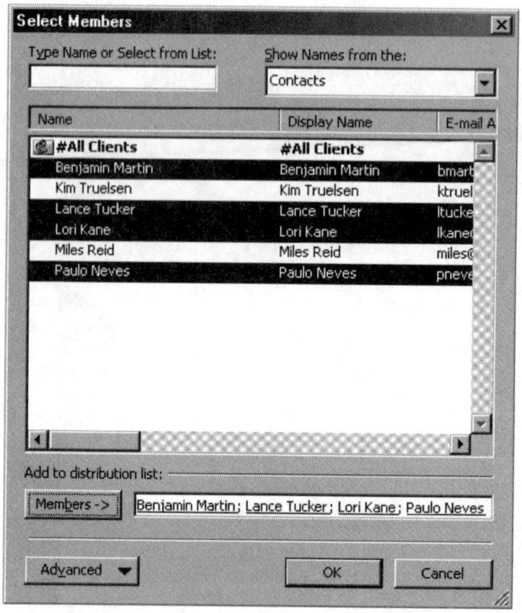

Figure 13.4: Selecting Members for a Distribution List.

4. Click the desired members for the distribution list. To select multiple items, click either the **Shift** or **Ctrl** keys while you click the mouse.

5. Click the **Members** button to select the chosen members.

6. Click the **OK** button to save your choices and close the **Select Members** screen (Figure 13.4) and return to the **Distribution List** screen (Figure 13.3).

I'll Show You Mine if You Show Me Yours

In the long term, you'll spend a lot of time building your contact lists. You enter personal contacts, internal contacts, clients, vendors, partners, and more. Did you realize that you can actually share your contacts? The only caveat to sharing is that your firm must be using Microsoft Exchange Server as your e-mail server. If not, you cannot share your contacts. If Microsoft Exchange Server is being used, you can share your contacts only with someone who has an account within the server. You cannot share contacts outside your firm.

Sharing Your Contacts

If your firm is using Microsoft Exchange Server, here's how you share your contacts with someone else:

1. Right-click the **Contacts** folder in Outlook.
2. Click the **Sharing** menu item. This brings up the screen shown in Figure 13.5.

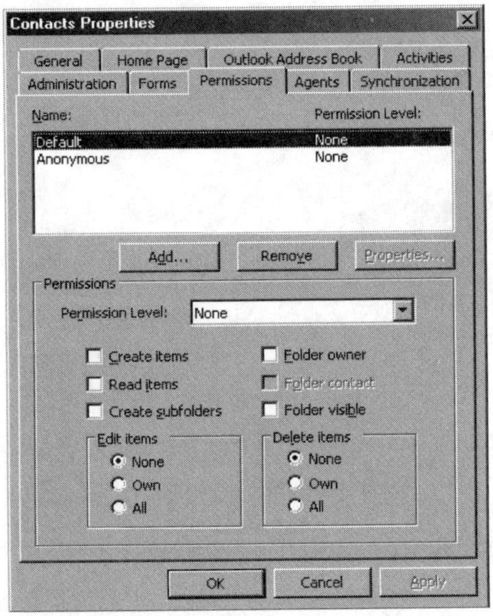

Figure 13.5: Permissions Properties for Contacts in Outlook 2003.

3. Click the **Add** button. You'll see a list of all users that have an Exchange Server account.
4. Select the desired users.
5. Click the **Read** items check box. This allows the selected users to read your contacts.
6. Click the **OK** button to save your changes and close the screen.

After you share your contacts, another user can read them by following the procedure in the next section.

Reading Someone's Shared Contacts

Once someone in your firm has shared their contacts and given you permission to read them, you can configure Outlook to read those contacts. To read someone else's shared contacts, follow this simple procedure:

1. Right-click the **File⇨ Open⇨ Other User's Folder** menu item. This brings up the screen shown in Figure 13.6.

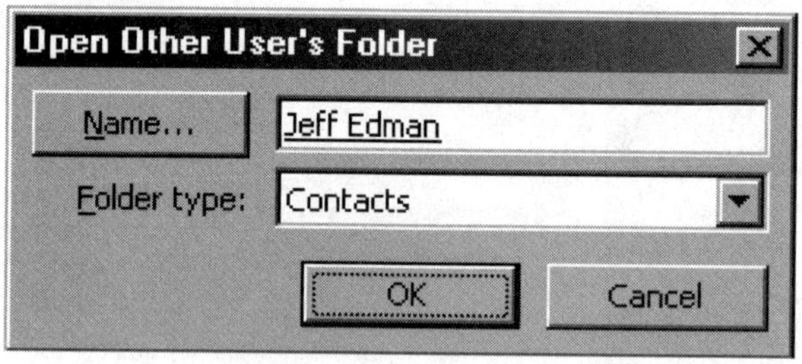

Figure 13.6: Opening Another User's Contacts.

2. Select the desired user's folder to open by clicking the **Name** button and selecting the user who has an account on your Microsoft Exchange Server.

3. Ensure the **Folder type** selected is **Contacts.**

4. Click the OK button. You will now see the other user's contacts.

vCards

A *vCard* is known as a virtual business card. They are generated from an Outlook contact. A vCard is a great way to share contact information for a specific contact. Suppose your firm does business with a certain publishing company and you wish to share that contact information with another Paralegal in a different firm. You cannot share the contact with the other firm, as they wouldn't be using your firm's Exchange Server. Therefore, you can share a vCard. Each contact is represented as a separate vCard.

A vCard is simply a file for a single contact stored in a format that Outlook understands. The format is a .vcf file. Here's how you generate a vCard:

1. Open the contact in Outlook.

2. Click the **File⇨ Export to vCard File** menu item to generate a file that you can e-mail to someone at your leisure.

3. Click the **Actions⇨ Forward as vCard** menu item to immediately forward the open contact to someone.

4. Close the contact.

Signature Templates

While not directly related to contacts, signatures do contain contact information. A signature template contains any of *your* contact information that you want recipients to see when you send them an e-mail. Signature templates typically contain this information:

- Your name
- Position/title
- Phone number
- Web address
- E-mail address

Figure 13.7 shows an example of a signature template.

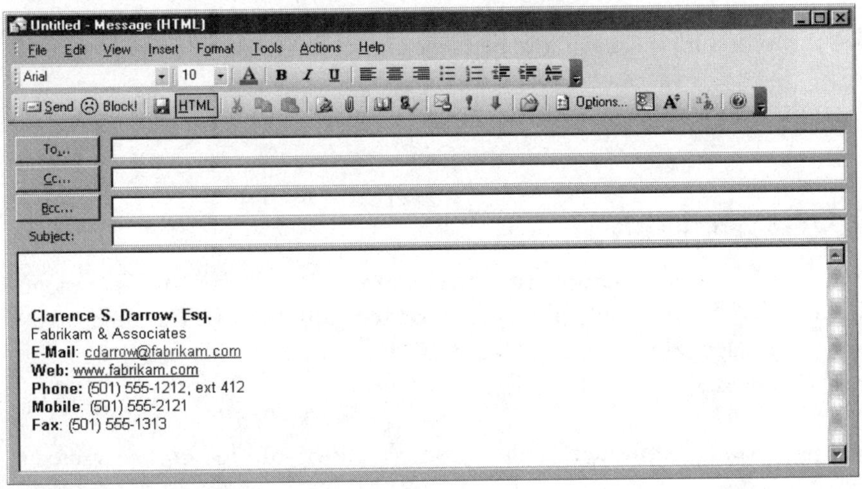

Figure 13.7: Sample Signature Template.

The reason for allowing more than one template could be because you may have different roles or titles within your organization. For example, if sometimes you use the title of **Paralegal** and sometimes **Research Analyst**, you don't want to type this in every time. It is easier to create two signature templates, each with the required information. Then, you simply select the desired signature template when you create a message.

Creating Your Templates

The first step is to create a signature template. To create a signature template, follow this simple procedure:

1. Click the **Tools⇨ Options** menu item. This brings up the **Options** screen.
2. Click the **Mail Format** tab.
3. Click the **Signatures** button. This brings up the **Create Signature** screen.
4. Click the **New** button.
5. Give your new signature a name, which can be your firm name or your job function.
6. Click the **Next** button.
7. Enter your signature information, such as what's presented in Figure 13.7.
8. Click the **OK** button. Your signature is now created, but not selected.
9. Repeat Steps 4 through 8 for each signature that you wish to create.
10. Click the **OK** button to save your changes.

Automatically Using a Template

Once you have created one or more signature templates, you can have your e-mail messages automatically use one, or you can manually choose any of the templates you created at the time of creating an e-mail message. Here's how you have Outlook automatically use a signature template in your e-mail messages:

1. Click the **Tools⇨ Options** menu item. Once again, this brings up the **Options** screen.
2. Click the **Mail Format** tab.

3. If you want new e-mail messages to automatically have a signature, select your new signature in the **Signature for new messages** dropdown list. If the dropdown displays **<None>**, then your new e-mail messages will be created without a signature template, but you will be able to manually apply one after you create your e-mail message.

4. If you want a signature for any message that you forward or reply to, you can select one as you did for new messages, but it is not a standard practice to include a signature when forwarding or replying to messages.

Manually Using a Template

If you are not sure that you want to use a specific signature template all the time, then you can manually choose one at the time you create an e-mail message. To do so, here's how:

1. Create your e-mail message.

2. Place the carat at the location in your e-mail message where you want the signature created.

3. Click the **Insert⇨ Signature** menu item.

3. Select the desired signature from the list provided. The signature will be inserted from the templates you already created. If you make a mistake and you inserted the wrong signature, simply delete the signature text and insert a different signature.

Conclusion

There are lots of ways to manage contacts, but if you use Outlook 2003, your choices become easier, clearer, and simpler. Outlook 2003 has the ability to connect to virtually any e-mail server, such as Microsoft Exchange Server. While you are probably not setting up Outlook on your computer, you should know whether your firm uses Microsoft Exchange Server. There are some additional features available to you if your firm is using Microsoft Exchange Server, such as the sharing of contacts. This chapter outlined the concepts and technologies involved in managing contacts, along with detailed procedures for managing those contacts.

Did you know?

Microsoft makes an add-on product to Outlook 2003 called the Business Contact Manager, or BCM. BCM is used to manage more about your contacts than just their basic contact information. BCM lets you also manage things like call logs and other simple Customer Relationship Management (CRM) needs.

Chapter 14

Sending Bulk Letters

Chapter At A Glance

WHY YOU SHOULD READ THIS CHAPTER

While you may not do it every day, Legal Secretaries and Paralegals are often responsible for sending out bulk letters to clients and vendors. This chapter shows you step-by-step procedures for sending bulk letters in the form of printed letters and e-mail.

PRODUCT OUTLINED IN THIS CHAPTER:

- Microsoft Word 2003
- Microsoft Outlook 2003

PRODUCT FEATURES COVERED IN THIS CHAPTER:

- Mail Merge

If you were to manually address a form letter to each of your clients, it could take so much time that you'd never get your job done. The key to sending out bulk letters using Microsoft Office is to understand the concepts and procedures involved in automating the entire process. Not only can you use Microsoft Word 2003 to create bulk letters and envelopes, but also Outlook 2003 to send bulk e-mails. This chapter is broken into two sections — one for each type of mail merge.

Creating Printed Letters and Envelopes

To create printed letters and envelopes, you would use Microsoft Word 2003. The process is not difficult, but you must understand how to do it, as there are many steps. Word is useful for creating form letters. Then you can use its mail merge feature to merge the form letter with contacts stored in Outlook. As an example, you can use the contacts stored in Outlook for each of your clients to send out holiday letters or news about your firm, such as when you hire a new associate or partner. The process for creating envelopes is similar to that of letters, but each is discussed separately. You can also use mail merge to merge data into your legal documents, such as bulk non-disclosure agreements.

Mail Merging Letters

To help you understand how to create documents for mail merging, let's take a very simple example of creating a holiday letter that you will send out to your clients. The first step is to create the letter that includes placeholder fields. A placeholder field will be used to format the document as if it was a letter, but whose value will be substituted automatically when you run the mail merge process.

To create the letter, you write a Word document as if it was any other document, including formatting, fonts, justification, layout, etc. Figure 14.1 shows a simple document that will be printed on company letterhead, so it appears to be very plain.

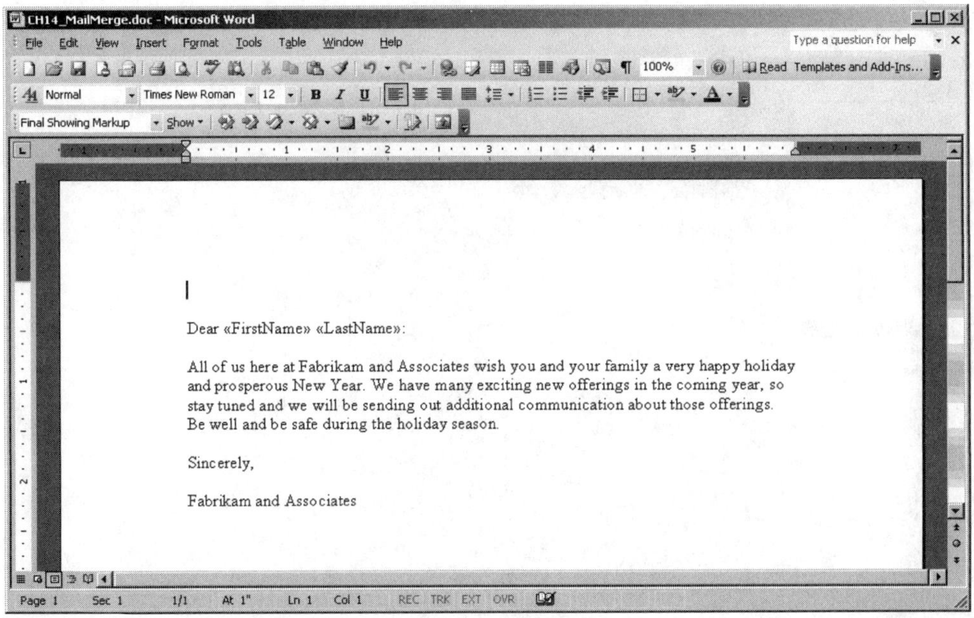

Figure 14.1: Simple Document for Mail Merging.

Notice in Figure 14.1 at the top of the document that there are two placeholder fields called **<<FirstName>>** and **<<LastName>>**. These are special fields that will be substituted when you run the mail merge process. The reason for these placeholder fields is to determine the layout and placement of the fields that will be substituted during the mail merge process.

To enter the placeholder fields, construct your letter as you would any other document and do the following:

1. Place the carat in the location where the placeholder field should be.

2. Click the **Insert⇨ Field** menu item. This brings up the screen shown in Figure 14.2.

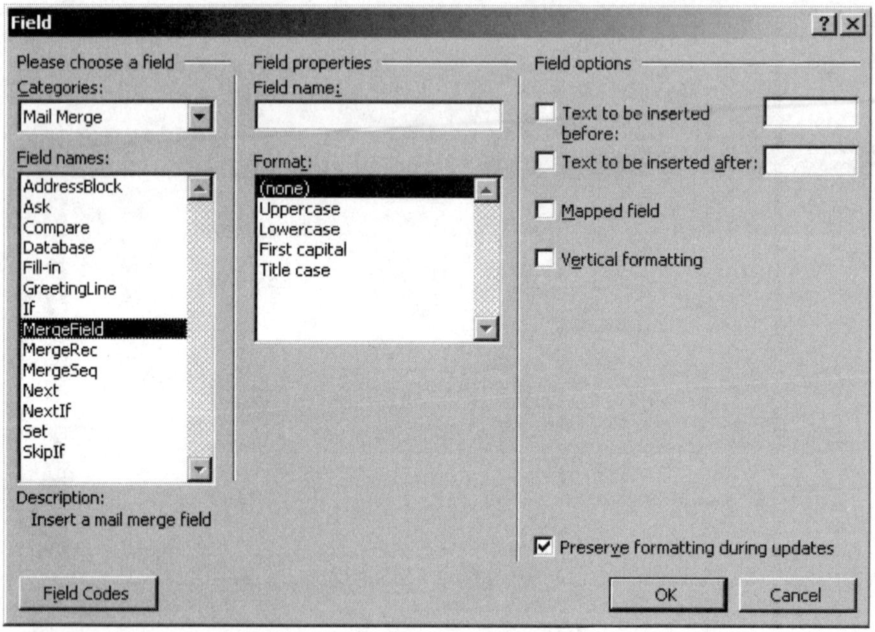

Figure 14.2: Inserting a New Mail Merge Field.

3. In the **Categories** dropdown list, select the **Mail Merge** option.

4. In the **Field names** list, click the **MergeField** item.

5. In the **Field name** box, enter the name of the field as you would like to see it in your document. As an example, the field names for the placeholders in Figure 14.1 are **FirstName** and **LastName**. Do not enter the << or >> characters, as these will be entered automatically by Microsoft Word.

6. Click the **OK** button to insert your field into the document.

7. Repeat Steps 1–6 until you have added each desired placeholder field to your document.

8. Save your document that includes the new placeholder fields.

Merging the Letter

Once you have created your document or letter that contains placeholder fields, you are ready to being the mail merge process. In a series of six steps, Microsoft Word will guide you through the process of selecting the address book from which you will select your recipients for the letter and also assign the fields in the address book to the placeholder fields that you just created. Here's how you do it:

1. Open the document that you created that you wish to mail merge.

2. Open the **Mail Merge** task pane by clicking the **Tools⇨ Letters and Mailings⇨ Mail Merge** menu item. This brings up the task pane shown in Figure 14.3.

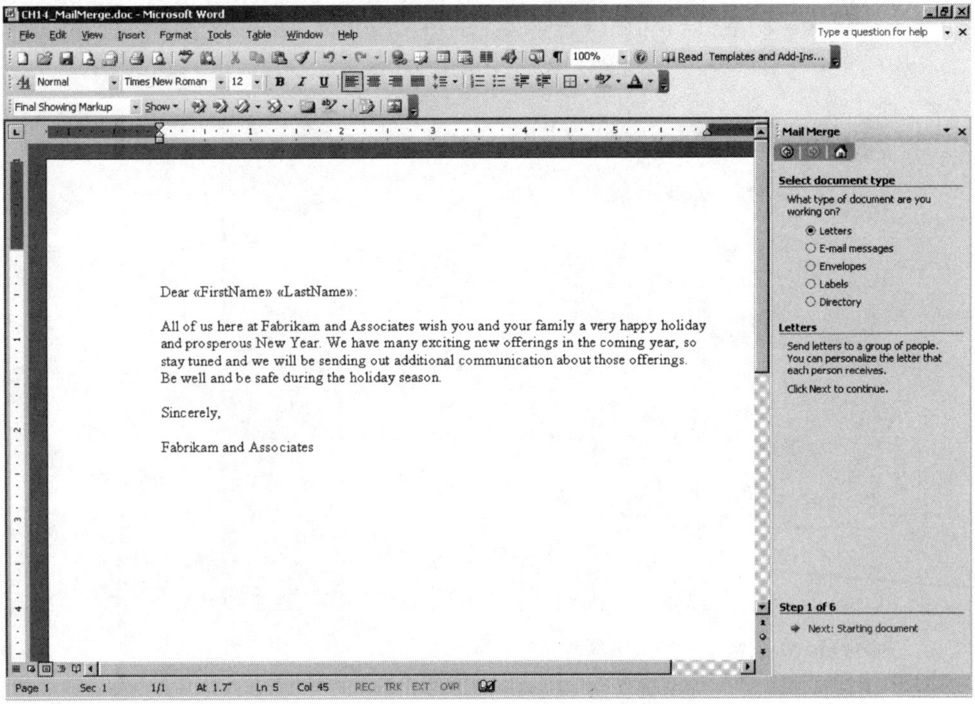

Figure 14.3: Selecting the Document Type (Step 1 of 6).

3. Ensure the **Letters** option is selected and click the **Next** link at the bottom of the screen.

4. In the **Select starting document** step (Step 2 of 6), ensure the **Use the current document** option is selected and click the **Next** link.

5. In the **Select recipients** step (Step 3 of 6), ensure the **Select from Outlook contacts** option is selected and click the **Next** link.

6. Click the **Choose Contacts Folder** option. This will prompt you to select the desired contacts folder on which you will base your mail merge.

7. Click the **Next** link.

8. In the **Write your letter** step (Step 4 of 6), there's nothing to do, as you already wrote your letter if you have followed the steps outlined in this chapter.

9. In the **Preview your letters** step (Step 5 of 6), you will be prompted first to select the contacts that will receive your letters. In the list of addresses shown, simply check the contacts who will be recipients.

10. You are also prompted to map the recently created placeholder field with the appropriate field in the contacts folder. For example, the Word field called **FirstName** needs to map to the Outlook contact **First** field. This mapping is shown in Figure 14.4.

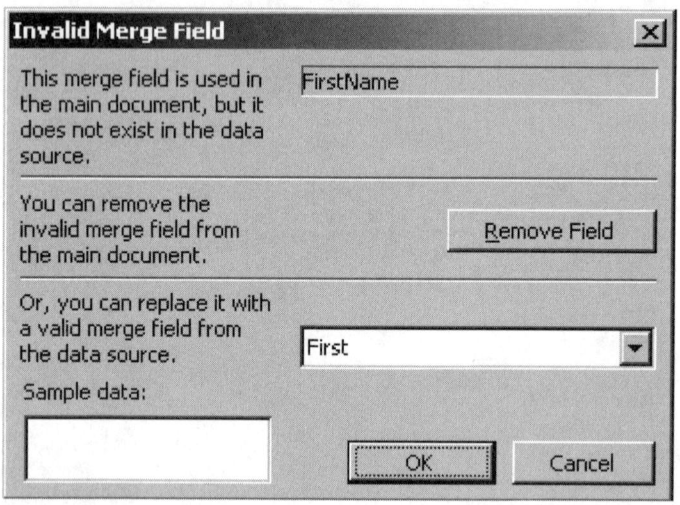

Figure 14.4: Mapping Placeholder Fields to Outlook Fields.

Simply select the desired Outlook field in the dropdown list (called the data source) that will map to the displayed placeholder field. Each unmapped field will be presented automatically.

11. You can scroll through recipients by clicking the << or >> arrows and preview your document, as shown in Figure 14.5.

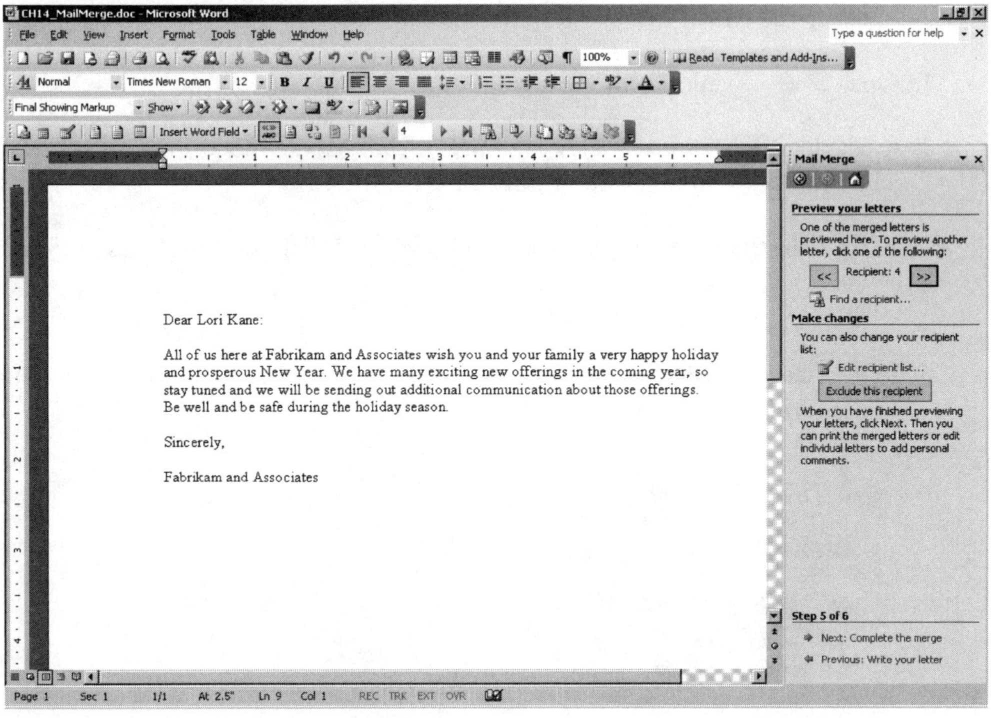

Figure 14.5: Previewing Mail Merged Document (Step 5 of 6).

12. Click the **Next** link.

13. In the **Complete the merge** step (Step 6 of 6), print your letters by clicking the **Print** link.

That's all there is to it. It's a lot of steps, but conceptually very easy. There are other mail merge options that you can choose from, but are not covered in this chapter. If you need more advanced mail merge functionality, check the online help for Microsoft Office, but the steps presented here should help you with most of your needs to mail merge your legal documents, envelopes, and labels.

Printing Envelopes

It is very useful to print envelopes that contain client contact information without having to manually address each of them to individual clients. Alternatively, if you have packages that you are sending to all of your clients, you can have Microsoft Word print the merged client contact information onto labels instead of envelopes. Then you simply peel and apply the labels to your packages. The process for printing labels is virtually the same as it is for envelopes.

To print envelopes for your letters, follow this procedure:

1. Open a new, blank Word document.
2. Click the **Tools⇨ Letters and Mailings⇨ Mail Merge** menu item. This brings up the pane shown on the right-hand side of Figure 14.3.
3. In the **Select document type** screen (Step 1 of 6), click the **Envelopes** option.
4. Click the **Next** link at the bottom of the screen.
5. In the **Select starting document** screen (Step 2 of 6), click the **Change document layout** option, which is shown in Figure 14.6.

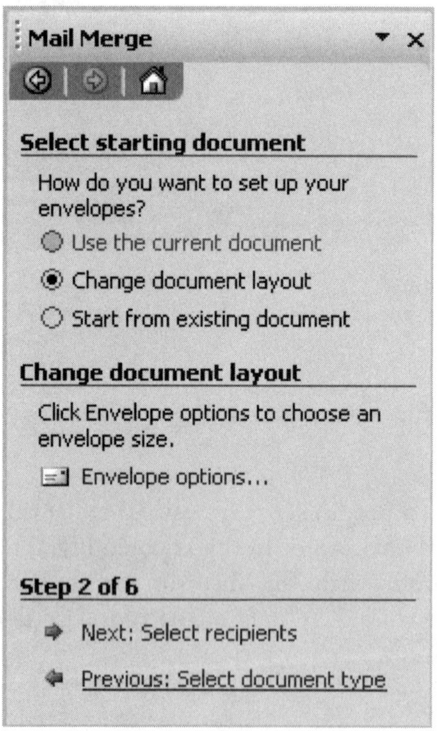

Figure 14.6: Selecting the Starting Document (Step 2 of 6).

6. Click the **Next** link at the bottom of the screen. You'll be prompted for envelope options, as shown in Figure 14.7.

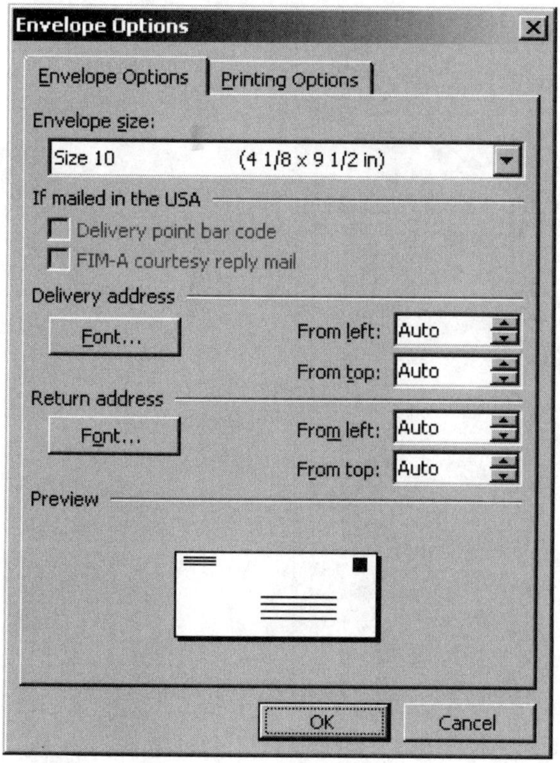

Figure 14.7: Selecting Envelope Options.

7. In the **Envelope Options** screen, you choose the envelope size, adjust the appearance of the delivery and return addresses, and see a thumbnail preview of the envelope. By default, size 10 envelopes are selected, as these are the most common business envelopes.

8. Click the **Printing Options** tab to adjust settings for how you will feed the physical envelopes into your printer, as shown in Figure 14.8.

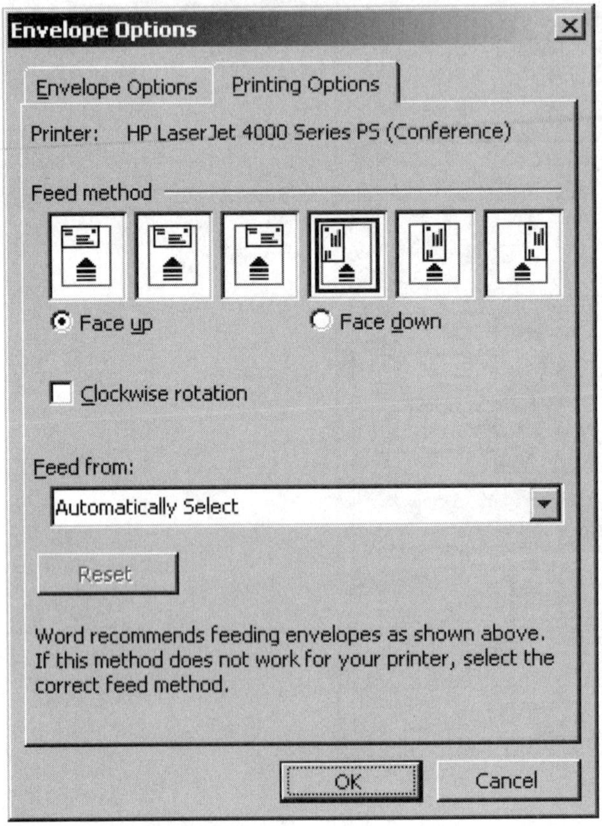

Figure 14.8: Selecting Envelope Printing Options.

By default, envelopes are fed face up and printed as if the text was on the left-hand part of a page. However, depending on your printer and how the envelope feeder attached to your printer operates, you may have to click another feed method.

9. Click the **OK** button to save your changes and continue.

10. In the **Select recipients** screen (Step 3 of 6), click the **Select from Outlook contacts** option, which is shown in Figure 14.9.

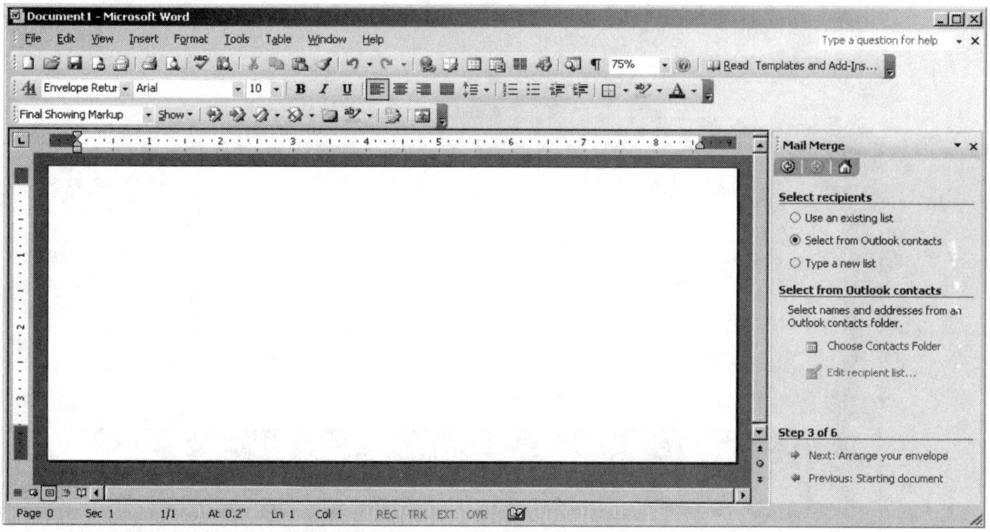

Figure 14.9: Selecting Recipients (Step 3 of 6).

Notice in Figure 14.9, that the document is already formatted as an envelope.

11. Click the **Choose Contacts Folder** option. You will choose the Outlook contacts folder and the specific contacts that will be the recipient of the envelopes. This procedure is performed exactly the same way you did it in the "Merging the Letter" section earlier in this chapter.

12. Click the **Next** link.

13. In the **Arrange your envelope** screen (Step 4 of 6), you will do just that...arrange fields on the screen. If you are using preprinted envelopes, you simply add the recipient's address to the envelope. If you are using plain envelopes and wish to have a return address on the envelope, you can place it there in this step, which is shown in Figure 14.10.

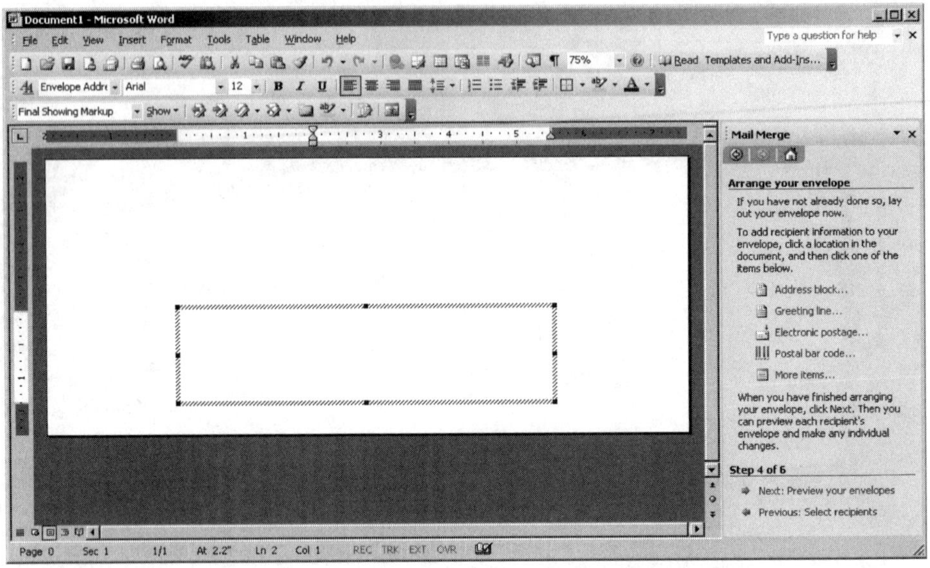

Figure 14.10: Arranging the Envelope (Step 4 of 6).

Notice the rectangular box in Figure 14.10. This box is a frame that Word has automatically placed on the envelope in the area where an address typically appears. Because this frame has no visible borders, to view this box you have to click in the area where the box is located on the screen.

14. Click inside the frame so that you see the carat.

15. In the **Mail Merge** pane, click the **Address block** link. You'll see a special field called **<<AddressBlock>>**. This is a placeholder field for the address fields in your Outlook contacts. If you want to type your firm's return address, simply click outside the frame and the carat should be in the top left-hand corner. You can type your firm's name and address. Because what you type would not be a placeholder field, the text will appear on every envelope exactly as you type it.

16. Click the **Next** link.

17. In the **Preview your envelopes** screen (Step 5 of 6), you can scroll through all of the recipients that were selected from your Outlook address book by clicking the << or >> buttons. If you are not satisfied with the format of the envelope, you can click the **Previous** link and correct the format, font, and other layout issues.

18. Click the **Next** link.

19. In the **Complete the merge** step (Step 6 of 6), print your envelopes by clicking the **Print** link.

NOTE

If you want to create a single envelope, it is not necessary to go through the mail merge process. You can simply click the Tools⇨Letters and Mailings⇨Envelopes and Labels menu item. This shows a single screen where you can select one address from your Outlook address book and print an envelope or label.

Sending Bulk E-mails with Microsoft Outlook 2003

If you have followed the similarities between creating mail merge letters and mail merge envelopes, then it stands to reason that merging Word documents with e-mail recipients should also be a snap. Actually, the process for sending out an e-mail is exactly the same as it is for mail merging a letter, except that instead of sending a document to a printer, you send it to a list of e-mail addresses. These e-mail addresses come from your Outlook contact folder.

To send e-mails based on merging a Word document, follow the same procedure for creating mail merge documents as outlined in "Mail Merging Letters" earlier in this chapter, except:

1. In Step 1 of 6, under **Select Document Type**, select the **E-mail messages** option.
2. In Step 6 of 6, instead of presenting you a **Print** link, you are presented with an **Electronic Mail** link. When you click this link, the screen shown in Figure 14.11 pops up.

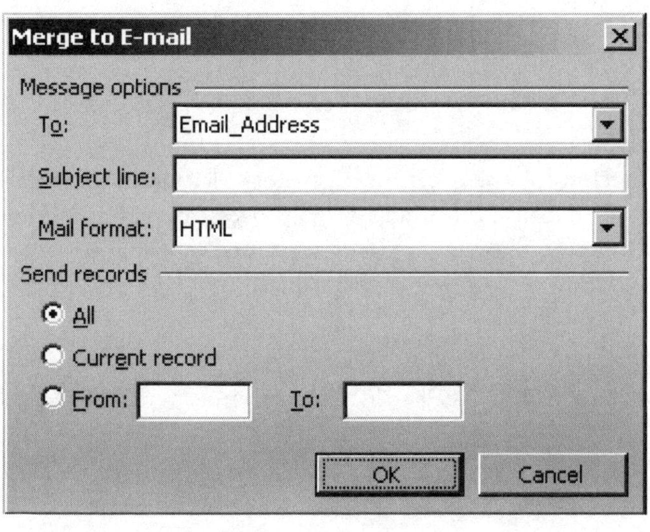

Figure 14.11: Selecting E-mail Options.

3. Ensure the **To** dropdown list reads **Email_Address**. Other options in the dropdown list include fields that you see in the Outlook contacts folder.

4. Enter a value in the **Subject line** field. This value will actually appear as the subject line of the e-mail received by the recipient. Because many SPAM filters look for words that are commonly used in advertising, such as "Special," "Offer," and others, you should avoid a subject line that sounds like SPAM.

5. Choose a value for the **Mail format** field. You can choose from these options:

    - **HTML** — The body of the e-mail is formatted as HTML, which allows very rich formatting. However, some e-mail servers will not process HTML as it may present a security risk. This is the default value.

    - **Plain Text** — The body of the e-mail is formatted as plain text, which does not allow different fonts, bold attributes, lines, or pictures. It is just raw text.

    - **Attachment** — Your e-mail message will be sent with your Word document as an attachment instead of the body of the e-mail.

6. Ensure the **All** option is selected under **Send records**. Since you already chose which records from your contacts folder will be merged, you want to send all of them. In the off-chance that you selected too many records for e-mail recipients, you can limit them further by selecting the **Current record** option, or select a range of specific record numbers in the **From** and **To** fields.

7. Click the **OK** button and your e-mails will be sent. You can see which e-mails were sent by viewing the **Sent Items** folder in Outlook.

Conclusion

Mail Merge is a very powerful technology that can save you lots of time by automating your form letters, envelopes, and more. Because the Mail Merge process merges a document with contact fields, the resulting document will be tailored—and printed or e-mailed—to a specific group of recipients. This chapter showed you how to print mail merge letters, envelopes, and e-mails.

Chapter 15

Scheduling Appointments and Meetings

Chapter At A Glance

WHY YOU SHOULD READ THIS CHAPTER:

As a Paralegal, you will sometimes need to schedule appointments for attorneys or schedule meetings with multiple people, such as clients or others in your firm. While a Legal Secretary may normally perform these functions, there will undoubtedly be many occasions where a Paralegal will need to do this as well. This chapter outlines how easy it is to perform these functions and use the Outlook calendar.

PRODUCT OUTLINED IN THIS CHAPTER:

- Microsoft Outlook 2003

PRODUCT FEATURES COVERED IN THIS CHAPTER:

- Appointments
- Meeting Requests
- Scheduling Appointments for someone else

Using a paper appointment book is not a very efficient way to schedule appointments. Not only could you potentially lose the appointment book, but scheduling appointments requires lots of time on the phone to coordinate everyone's schedule. You can have more time to perform your other Paralegal duties by using technology to schedule your appointments and meetings. Most people use Outlook for email, but it can also handle your appointments and meetings.

Microsoft Outlook has lots of features that enable you to handle your appointments. Not only can you schedule an appointment for yourself, such as court dates, client meetings, and personal appointments, but you can schedule appointments for others. For example, you can schedule appointments for attorneys that you work for. You can also request meetings between multiple parties and check their schedules to see when they are available. This chapter shows you how to manage appointments and meeting requests in Outlook 2003. Figure 15.1 shows Outlook 2003 with a single week's appointments selected.

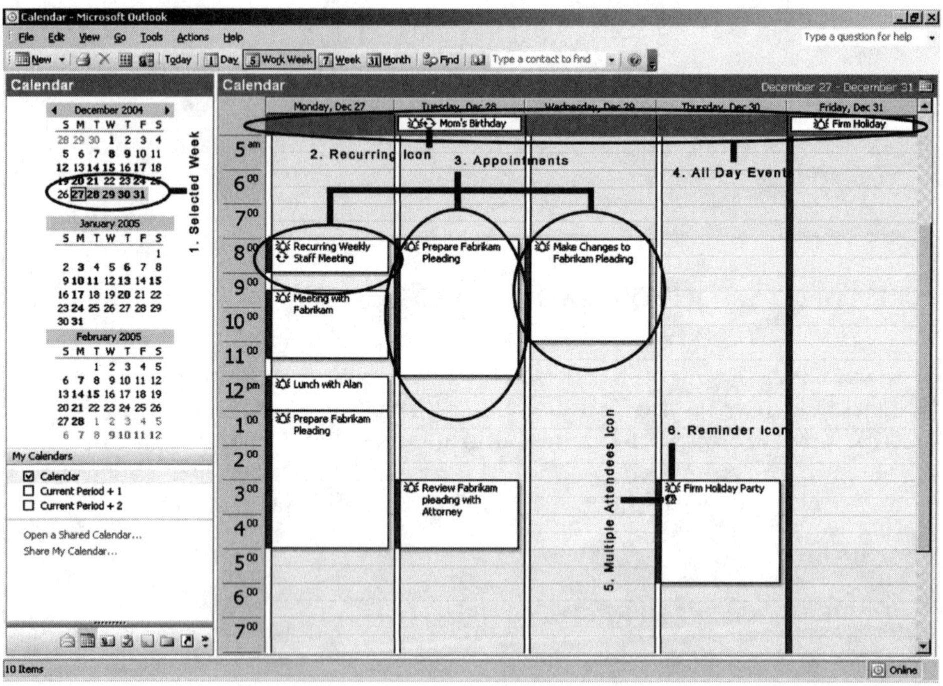

Figure 15.1: Outlook 2003 Appointments.

Figure 15.1 shows the following areas of the screen, which are specifically called out as follows:

- **Selected Week** — The current week represented on the right-hand part of the screen.
- **Recurring Icon** — Indicates the appointment is recurring at some interval. It can occur annually (such as in the case of a birthday) weekly, daily, or at some other interval.

- **Appointments** — Shows each item on the screen as a separate appointment. Even though each item is not circled on the screen, each white area shows a separate appointment.
- **All Day Events** — Items in this area indicate there is no specific start and stop time, but do occur on a specific date.
- **Multiple Attendees Icon** — Indicates the appointment has multiple people attending, or a meeting request.
- **Reminder Icon** — Indicates this appointment will remind you at some predetermined amount of time before the appointment is to occur.

Managing Appointments

The calendar in Outlook 2003 lets you manage your appointments and can optionally remind you when appointments are to occur. This lets you not forget business appointments like court dates and client meetings, or even personal items, such as birthdays and anniversaries.

Suppose you wish to block out four hours of time in your calendar so that you can begin to prepare a legal pleading, draft a will, or some other appointment. Even if you don't need to meet with anyone, it is a good idea to block out the time on your own calendar so that someone else doesn't schedule a meeting with you. When you block out your time, you flag that period of time as being busy.

Creating the Appointment

Here's how you create an appointment in Outlook 2003:

1. Open Outlook 2003.
2. Open the calendar by clicking the **Go⇨ Calendar** menu item.
3. Scroll to the desired month for which you will create the appointment. By default, the current month will already be selected.
4. In the **Calendar** pane on the left-hand side of the screen, click the desired date for which you will create the appointment. The current date is already selected by default. Notice in Figure 15.1 that there is a small square around the **December 27, 2004** date in the left-hand portion of the screen. This indicates the current date.
5. In the right-hand portion of the screen, right-click to reveal a popup menu.

6. Select the **New Appointment** menu item, which brings up the screen shown in Figure 15.2.

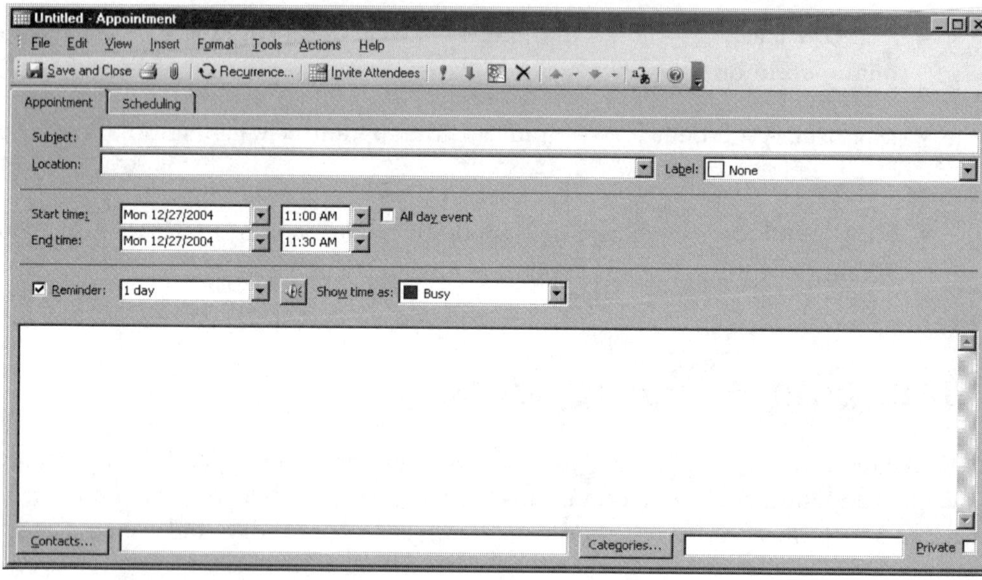

Figure 15.2: Creating a New Appointment.

7. Ensure the **Appointment** tab is selected.

8. Enter data into these fields to create your appointment:

   - **SUBJECT** — This is the value that you see in all of the appointment boxes shown in Figure 15.1. For example, a valid subject might be **Prepare Fabrikam Pleading**. While this field is not required, you really should enter it or you won't be able to read your appointment in the calendar without viewing the detail.

   - **LOCATION** — This field helps you to identify where the appointment will take place. For example, you can enter **My Office, Conference Room 1A, Client Office**, or any other location to help you identify the appointment. This field is not needed in all cases, but if you think it will help to further classify the appointment, you should enter it. You can click the down arrow in this box to select previously entered locations.

   - **LABEL** — By selecting a label from the dropdown list, your appointment will be colored according the selected label. This helps you to make appointments stand out amongst the numerous appointments in your calendar, or to categorize appointments according to color. This is not a required field.

- **Start time** — Select the date and time of the beginning of the appointment.
- **End time** — Select the date and time of the ending of the appointment.
- **All day event** — This box indicates the appointment should not take place at a specific start and end time, but instead take place all day. Clicking this box removes the start and end time from the screen, as it becomes irrelevant. It also blocks the time as **Free** instead of **Busy**.
- **Reminder** — Check box that indicates that you wish to be reminded in advance of the appointment coming due. If you check this box, you can choose the amount of time before the appointment occurs that you wish to be reminded. You can choose from **0 minutes** (at the actual time of the appointment) to **2 weeks** prior to the appointment to be reminded.
- **Show time as** — Dropdown list of how the time for the appointment will be used. This helps others who might want to schedule time with you to understand how your time is blocked. You can choose from:
    - **Free** — You have blocked out a period of time, but you are not busy. This is typical of a recurring appointment that you wish to be reminded of, such as someone's birthday. This is the default value used when you choose the **All day event** check box.
    - **Tentative** — Time has not been confirmed. This is typically used when someone has invited you to attend a meeting, but you have not yet accepted. Therefore, the time is blocked out, but not confirmed.
    - **Busy** — You are busy for the period of time specified. This is the default value for most appointments.
    - **Out of Office** — You have blocked out some time, but will not be in the office.
- **Blank box** — This field lets you enter any type of information that you need for the appointment. For example, if the appointment is to have a conference call with a client, you might want to have the conference call phone number in this box. This is completely optional.
- **Contacts** — Enables you to associate other people in your **Contacts** folder with this appointment. It doesn't invite these contacts to participate in the appointment; it is just for associating a contact with the appointment. For example, you can enter attorney names as a list of contacts for an appointment to draft a pleading. This is an optional field.

- **Categories** — Enables you to categorize the appointment if you wish. For example, you can categorize the appointment according to standard categories, such as **Personal** or **Business**, or even create your own categories, such as **Litigation**, **Real Estate**, etc.
- **Private** — Check box that marks the appointment in such a way that it will not be shared. Nobody will be able to read this appointment. Therefore, if you have a personal medical appointment, you can check this box to ensure that your time is allocated, but nobody else can see the details of the appointment.

9. Click the **Save and Close** button to save your data, close the screen, and enter your values into the calendar.

To Recur or Not To Recur

Many of your appointments might be recurring at some interval. If this is the case, you don't have to enter separate appointments for each and every date. Examples of recurring appointments are:

- Weekly staff meetings
- Weekly client meetings
- Firm holidays
- Your employment anniversary
- Employee and personal birthdays

When you create an appointment (see Figure 15.2), you select recurring properties by clicking the **Recurrence** button. This brings up the screen shown in Figure 15.3.

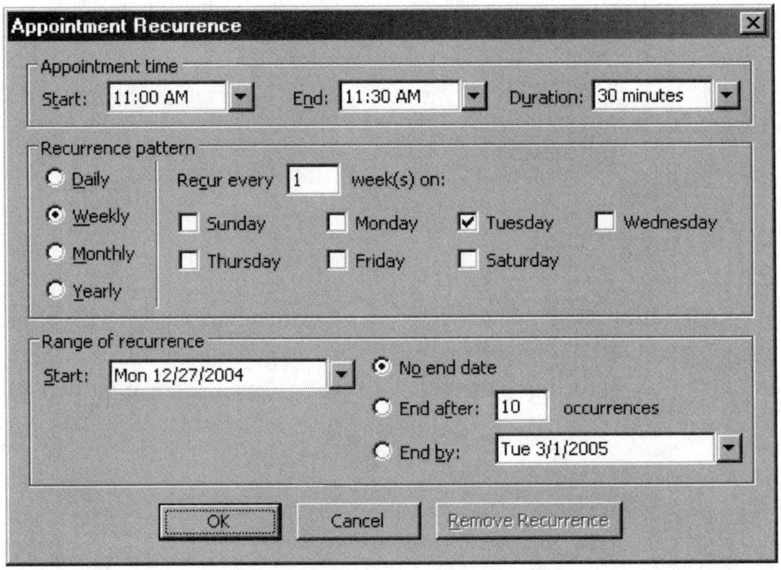

Figure 15.3: Setting Appointment Recurrence.

In Figure 15.3, the **Appointment time** fields are based on the start and end time in the appointment. You can change those times here if you wish, but you can also change them on the screen in Figure 15.2. The main things you need to change on this screen are in the **Recurrence pattern** and **Range of recurrence** sections. The **Recurrence pattern** section contains these options:

- **DAILY** — Lets you select how many days the recurrence should be. By default, the recurrence pattern will be every day. An example of a daily recurrence would be blocking out time for lunch or exercising. You can also select only weekdays under this option.

- **WEEKLY** — Lets you select the how many weeks the recurrence should be. It also lets you select the days within those weeks for the recurrence. By default, the recurrence will be every week on the day that is currently selected when you brought the screen up (see Figure 15.3). An example of a weekly occurrence would be weekly staff meetings or reminders to bill time for legal services.

- **MONTHLY** — Lets you schedule your appointments to occur on a specific day of each month or a specific number of weekdays in the month, such as the fourth Tuesday of each month. Examples of monthly occurrences would be to remind you to send a status report to your supervisor at the beginning of each month, or to back up your e-mail at the end of each month.

- **YEARLY** — Lets you schedule the appointment to occur on a specific day of a specific month each year. An example of a yearly recurrence is someone's birthday.

In the **Range of recurrence** section of the screen, you specify the start and end date of the recurrence. By default, the recurrence will start with the currently selected date and never end. However, you can change the start date and the end date. The end date can be after a certain number of occurrences or a specific date.

Requesting Meetings

Requesting a meeting is not much different from creating an appointment, except that you will ask others to join your meeting. When you create your appointment, you can invite others to attend the meeting by clicking the **Scheduling** tab. This will bring up the screen shown in Figure 15.4.

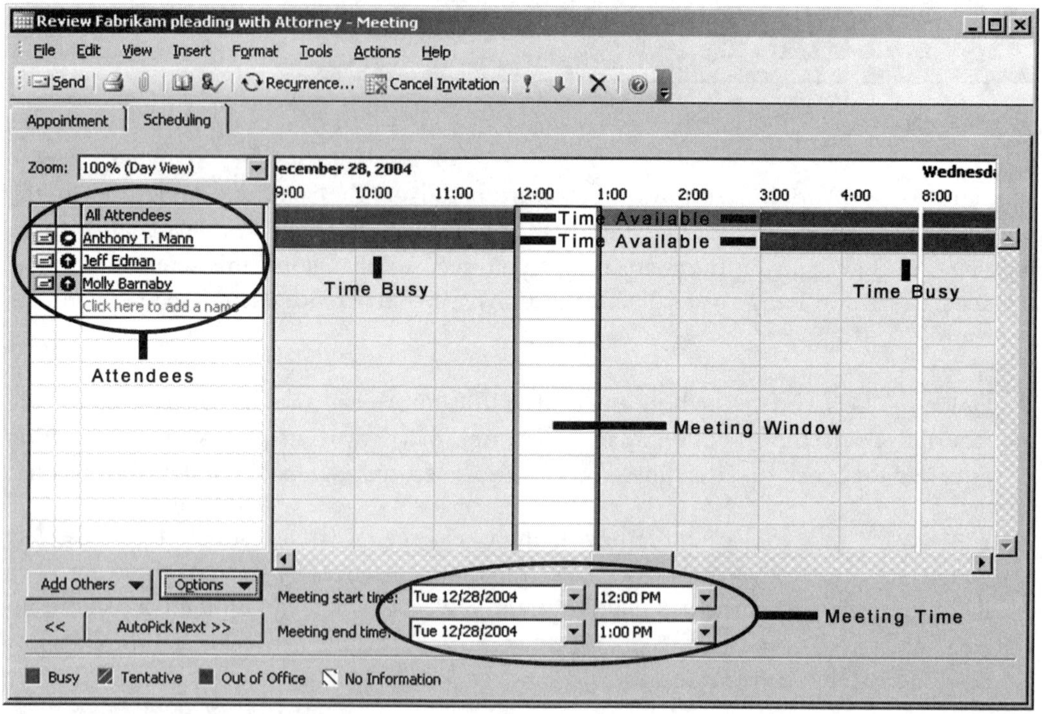

Figure 15.4: Scheduling Meetings with Multiple People.

Figure 15.4 is quite a crowded screen, but when you break it down, it's not so scary. On the left is a vertical listing of all attendees that you wish to invite to the meeting. Any time blocked out with a blue horizontal line is time that has been marked as busy, so you cannot schedule a meeting for anyone for whom the requested time is already blocked out. Any free space in the window means that that time slot is not blocked out by an attendee, so it is available to schedule.

Scheduling the Meeting

The meeting window shown in Figure 15.4 is a vertical view of a time slot for all attendees to see if they are available. Therefore, to schedule a meeting request with multiple people, follow these steps:

1. On the left-hand part of the screen, click the area that reads **Click here to add a name.** Type the name of the person that you wish to attend your meeting. Optionally, you can click the **Add Others** button, then click **Add from Address Book** from the popup menu. This will allow you to choose contacts from your address book.

2. The small icon to the left of the attendee's name is used to indicate whether the attendee is required or is optional for the meeting request. By default the attendee is required, but you can change it by clicking on the icon itself and choosing the desired option from the dropdown list.

3. Continue to add the attendees to your meeting. As you add new attendees, you will see their time schedule on the right-hand part of the screen. If your firm uses Microsoft Exchange Server 2003 to manage e-mail, all attendees that have an account on that e-mail server — such as all firm employees — will immediately have their schedule shown, unless an item is marked **Private.** Private appointments are discussed in "Managing Appointments" earlier in this chapter.

   If your attendees are outside the firm and use another e-mail server, the only way that you will view their schedule is if those attendees use a centralized Free/Busy service. See "Using Free/Busy" later in this chapter.

> **NOTE**
>
> **When you use a Free/Busy service, other people cannot see the details of any of your appointments; they can only see whether you are free or busy. If you are free, someone can schedule your time. If you are busy, they cannot. It's as simple as that.**

4. To see the next available time slot for all attendees, click the **AutoPick Next** button. The meeting window will automatically jump to the next available slot for every single attendee listed. You can also change the time of the appointment manually by adjusting the **Meeting start time** and **Meeting end time** fields.

5. Click the **Send** button to request each individual to attend the meeting. They will receive an e-mail with your request. Additionally, if the attendees use Microsoft Exchange Server as their e-mail server, the requested time will automatically be allocated and scheduled in their Outlook calendar and marked **Tentative**. If they accept the appointment, it will be changed to **Busy**. If they reject the appointment, it will be freed from their schedule.

What Do Attendees See?

When you request that a person attend a meeting, they are sent an e-mail that looks like the one shown in Figure 15.5.

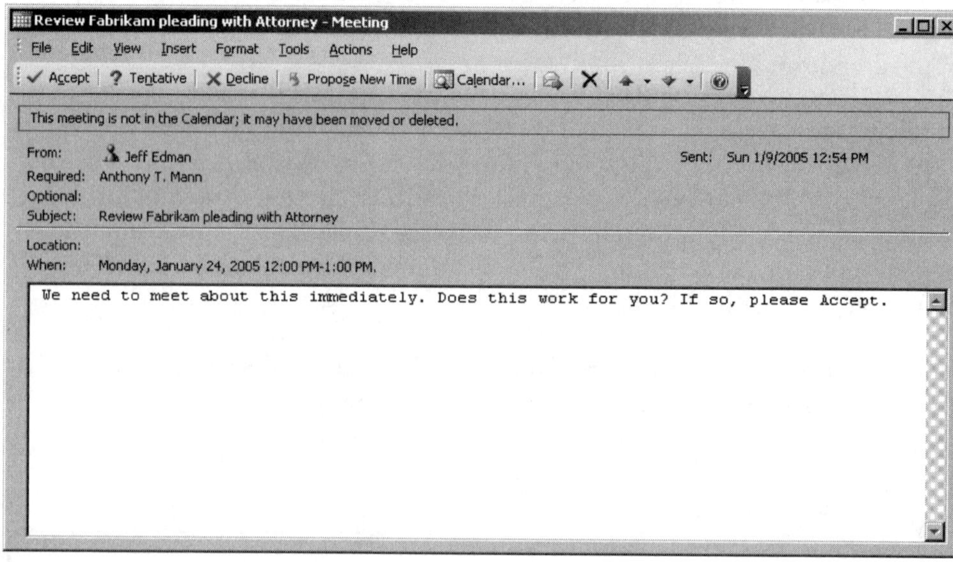

Figure 15.5: Meeting Request E-mail.

Attendees receive e-mails that contain the particulars about the meeting, as you entered them. However, there are a few things in the e-mail that you are probably not familiar with if you've never scheduled a meeting request with Outlook. There are five buttons at the top of the screen that allow the recipient to manage the requested meeting:

- **Accept** — Accepts the requested meeting and places it as a busy appointment if the user's e-mail server is Exchange Server.
- **Tentative** — Conditionally accepts the meeting.
- **Decline** — Declines the meeting outright. It does not suggest a new time. This is a perfectly acceptable response if the attendee is not required.

- **Propose New Time** — Allows the attendee to propose a new time for the meeting, as he or she may have a commitment that is not on the calendar.
- **Calendar** — Opens the calendar to help manage appointments and meeting requests.

When any of these buttons is clicked, you are prompted to send the response to the meeting coordinator.

Reminders

When you create your appointments, either as a single appointment, recurring appointment, or meeting request, one option is to remind you before the appointment comes due. See "Managing Appointments" earlier in this chapter for more information about setting reminders. Periodically, Outlook will pop up a window that contains a list of scheduled appointments that are coming due. Figure 15.6 shows what this reminder screen looks like.

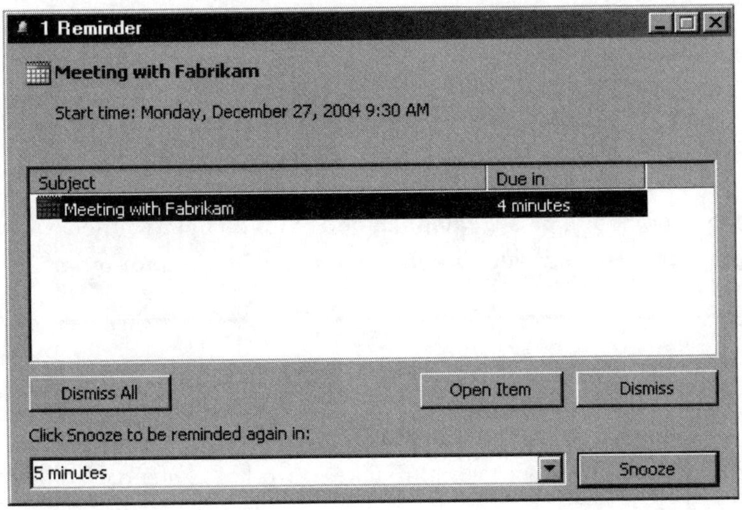

Figure 15.6: Appointment Reminder Screen.

Figure 15.6 shows a single appointment, **Meeting with Fabrikam**, coming due in four minutes. If you don't take action on this item, Outlook will continue to remind you. Therefore, you can click one of these buttons:

- **Dismiss** — Acknowledges the selected item and ensures that Outlook will not remind you about this item again. If it is a recurring item, you will be reminded upon the next occurrence, but not the current occurrence.

- **Open Item** — Opens the item in Outlook and presents a screen that looks the same as the one you used to create the appointment in the first place.
- **Snooze** — Acknowledges the selected item, but Outlook will remind you again in the period of time specified in the **Click Snooze to be reminded again in** dropdown list. You can choose from intervals between **5 minutes** and **2 weeks.**
- **Dismiss All** — Acts the same as the **Dismiss** button, but the action is performed on all items in the reminder screen. Use this option with caution, as you will not be reminded again about any appointment in the list.

Scheduling an Attorney's Time

While this is may be a Legal Secretary's function, sometimes a Paralegal will need to schedule a meeting on behalf of an attorney. The difference between a meeting request and scheduling someone else's time is simply that you won't be involved in the meeting. For example, if you schedule a meeting request with an attorney, the attorney will know to attend, but you will be in the meeting also. What if the attorney asks you to schedule a meeting on his or her behalf with a client? You need to gain access to his or her calendar to do so.

NOTE

Before you can schedule time in someone else's calendar, you must be using either Exchange Server or third-party software that allows scheduling of calendars for other users.

Giving Permission

Before you can access an attorney's calendar, or any one else's, they need to give you permission to do so. For someone to give you permission (or vice versa) to take control of a calendar, follow these simple steps:

1. The person who wishes to share must open Outlook.
2. Select the Calendar folder by clicking the **Go⇨ Calendar** menu item.
3. Select the **File⇨ Folder⇨ Sharing** menu item. This brings up the screen shown in Figure 15.7.

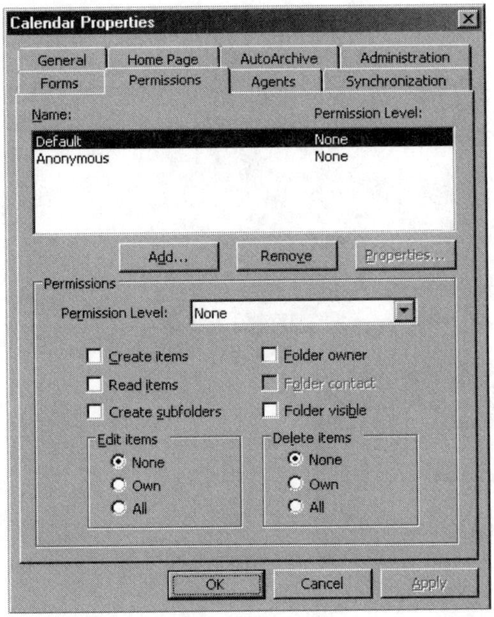

Figure 15.7: Calendar Properties for Sharing.

4. Click the **Add** button and select the users that should have access to the calendar.

5. Click the user in the list of users provided.

6. Select the appropriate permission level for the user from the **Permission Level** dropdown. You'll note that as you click a permission level, individual permissions are checked in the lower portion of the screen. Ensure that the selected user can only do the minimum required for the Calendar folder. For example, if the user does not need to have the ability to delete items from the calendar, ensure **None** is selected under **Delete items**. It is likely that you will select **Author** from the **Permission Level** dropdown, which gives permission to create and read contacts.

7. Click the **OK** button to save your changes and close the screen.

NOTE

You may have to close Outlook and reopen for permission changes to take effect.

Opening a Calendar

Once a user, such as an attorney, has shared his or her calendar with you, you can open the calendar and start scheduling appointments. Assuming you have permission to do so, here's how you open another user's calendar folder:

1. Open Outlook.
2. Click the **File⇨Open⇨Open Other User's Folder** menu item. This brings up the screen shown in Figure 15.8, which enables you to select the folder to open.

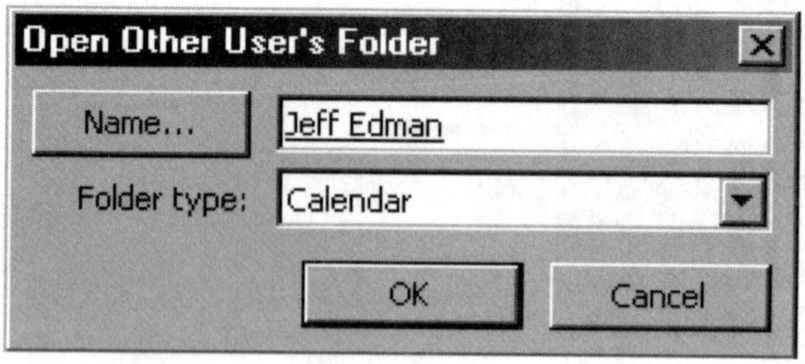

Figure 15.8: Opening Another User's Folder.

3. Click the **Name** button and select the Attorney's name from the list.
4. Select **Calendar** from the **Folder type** dropdown list.
5. Click the **OK** button. This opens the user's calendar. You can then create appointments or meeting requests, as you learned earlier in this chapter.

NOTE

If you were just given permission to access the attorney's Calendar folder, you may have to close Outlook and reopen for permission changes to take effect.

Using Free/Busy

If your firm uses Microsoft Exchange Server as an e-mail server, when you schedule a meeting request, you can automatically find out whether an attendee's time is free or busy in his or her calendar. However, if one or more attendees is not in your organization, an account does not exist for that attendee on your e-mail server. Therefore, you cannot readily find out whether they are available for your meeting without using an external service. This service is called *Free/Busy*.

It simply allows a Calendar folder within Outlook to share with others your time slots that are busy and free for scheduling. Microsoft used to offer this service, but no longer does. However, your firm can provide this service for your clients or you can search for a third-party service on your favorite search engine.

Once you know which Free/Busy service you and your external party will use to publish your free and busy calendar information, you configure it in Outlook like this:

1. Open Outlook.
2. Click the **Tools⇨ Options** menu item.
3. Ensure the **Preferences** tab is selected, which it is by default.
4. Click the **Calendar Options** button. This brings up the **Calendar Options** screen which has a **Free/Busy Options** button on it.
5. Click the **Free/Busy Options** button. This brings up the screen shown in Figure 15.9.

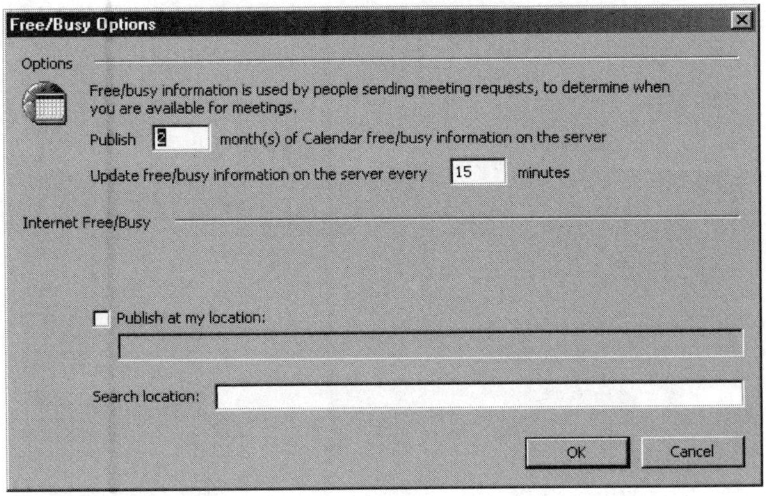

Figure 15.9: Free/Busy Options.

6. Click the **Publish at my location** check box and enter the Web address of the location that will act as the central Free/Busy service.
7. Click the **OK** button to save your choices and close the screen.

Conclusion

One of the greatest features of Outlook is to schedule appointments into your calendar. You can even extend that functionality by creating meeting requests with multiple users. Meeting requests will automatically enter the requested block of time into each person's calendar, so automation really helps make everyone productive. You can even take Outlook calendars one step further and schedule appointments on someone else's behalf. This lets you or a Legal Secretary schedule appointments for attorneys and those appointments will appear in the attorney's calendar. This chapter showed you all about creating appointments and meeting requests, and scheduling appointments on behalf of someone else.

Chapter 16

Securing Documents and Files

Chapter At A Glance

WHY YOU SHOULD READ THIS CHAPTER:

Security of your documents is one of the most important things that you have to think about. You must protect the integrity of information and the identity and private information of clients and attorneys. You don't want to learn that you or your firm is responsible for leaking private information or that someone changed your documents without your knowledge. This chapter explores security-related issues for your Microsoft Office files.

PRODUCTS OUTLINED IN THIS CHAPTER:

- Microsoft Word 2003
- Microsoft Excel 2003
- Microsoft PowerPoint 2003

PRODUCT FEATURE COVERED IN THIS CHAPTER:

- Protection/Security

You already know that security of legal files is of prime importance. Many law firms say they are concerned about security of files, so they instruct their IT (Information Technology) departments, if they have one, to lock down security of servers, disk drives, and folders so that only people in the firm who need access can read and save files. For example, suppose you have a client, ABC Industries, for which you are preparing some legal documents. You want to store the document files on a server called **ClientFiles** on the **M:** drive, in a folder called **Clients\ABCIndustries\Briefs.**

Your IT department ensured that all people in your firm have access to the **ClientFiles** server and the **M:** drive. They also made sure that everyone has access to the **Clients** folder, but only attorneys and Paralegals who work with the **ABCIndustries** client have access to that folder and all folders below (including the **Briefs** folder).

Is this all your firm has to do to make your documents and files secure? It's a great first step, but as a paralegal, you also have a responsibility for the security of files. This chapter is designed to show you how to protect your Microsoft Office files, including Word, Excel, and PowerPoint.

Self-Storage of Your Files

As you know, files are stored in a folder on a disk drive in a server or computer. Each of these things has its own name and security settings, which can be quite confusing as you think about which computer (or server), drive, folder, and file you saved. Figure 16.1 shows how confusing this can be.

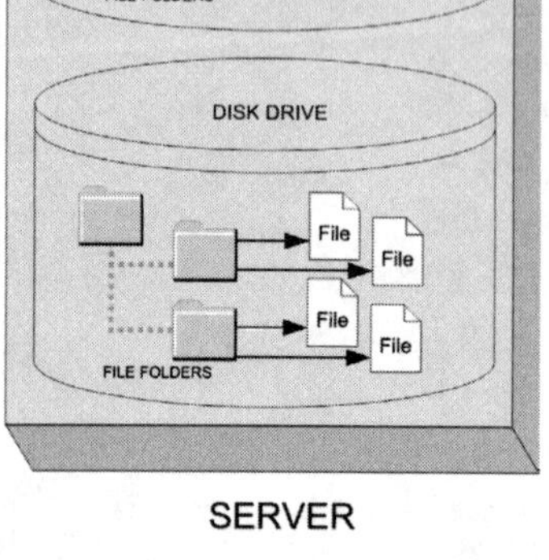

Figure 16.1: Server Containing Drives, Folders, and Files.

Notice in Figure 16.1, there is a single disk drive on a server, which contains folders and files within those folders. Your IT department is responsible for ensuring that only the appropriate users have access to a server, drive, and folder.

Consider the scenario where you have taken the precaution of securing a client's legal document by ensuring that only the required people in your firm have the appropriate permission to access the folder storing the document. However, at the client's request, you email the document to a third party. Since it no longer resides on your firm's server, that same document is now no longer secure and you or your firm could be to blame. Yikes!

To correct this situation, you must secure the document, spreadsheet, or presentation files themselves. Securing a file involves setting some properties that are stored within the file itself, so the security settings stay with the document, regardless of where it resides or who you send it to. Want to see how it's done? Read on...

To Protect and Serve

Protecting your Microsoft Office documents is very easy to do, but depending on which Office program (Word, Excel, or PowerPoint) you are trying to protect, there are different procedures involved. This is mostly because the amount of protection available is dictated by the very nature of the file itself. For example, there are more protection options available to Excel 2003 files than Word 2003 files.

Protecting Word 2003 Documents

Protecting Word 2003 documents from unauthorized changes is very simple. To protect a document, follow these steps:

1. Click the **Tools⇨ Protect Document** menu item. This brings up the **Protect Document** screen, as shown in Figure 16.2.

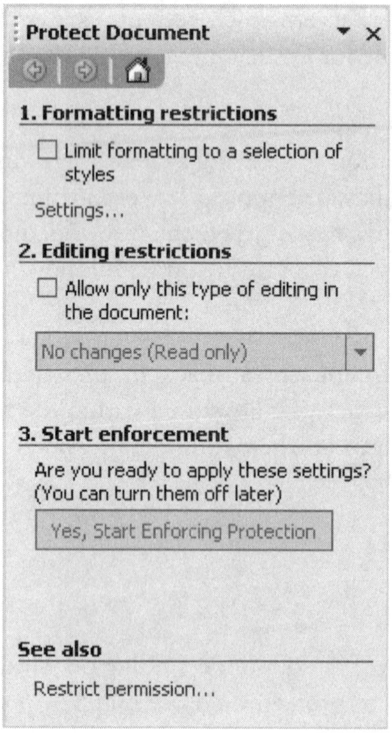

Figure 16.2: Protect Document Screen.

The screen is divided into three sections:

- **FORMATTING RESTRICTIONS** — Limits users to formatting with a selection of Word styles. You will likely not need to change the settings in this section, as it doesn't prevent someone from being able to edit the document — it only prevents them from formatting a style.
- **EDITING RESTRICTIONS** — Limits users' ability to edit the document.
- **START ENFORCEMENT** — Begins protection of the document based on formatting and editing restrictions chosen.

2. Choose the editing restrictions by clicking the **Allow only this type of editing in the document** option. Once you do this, you'll see a dropdown of editing choices, as follows:

   - **TRACKED CHANGES** — Allows anyone to make changes to the document, but changes will be tracked. For more information about tracked changes, see Chapter 11.

- **Comments** — Allows users to only make comments in the document, but not edit it.
- **Filling in forms** — Allows users to only enter values into form fields.
- **No changes** — Does not allow anyone to make changes to the document unless they know the password to unprotect it. This is the default option.

3. Specify optional exceptions to the option chosen in Step #2. You can specify exceptions, allowing specific people—and nobody else—to make changes to the document. A really cool feature of Word 2003 is that these optional users can be allowed to edit only parts of a document. To do this, simply highlight a part of the document and click the group or users that should have the ability to edit the selected part of the document. If you don't see a user (individual) that you would like to assign, simply click the **More users** link and enter the user's login ID or email address.

4. Click the **Yes, Start Enforcing Protection** button. You are prompted to supply a password, as shown in Figure 16.3.

Figure 16.3: Start Enforcing Protection.

5. You can opt to enter a known password, which must be entered by a user before protection can be removed, or you can opt to allow authenticated users to remove document protection.

> **NOTE**
>
> **An authenticated user is one who has successfully logged into their computer or the network attached to their computer.**

6. Click the **OK** button after you choose the desired method and your document will be protected.

7. To unprotect the document, click the **Tools⇨ Unprotect Document** menu item. You'll be prompted for the password before you can unprotect the document.

Protecting Excel 2003 Spreadsheets

Microsoft Excel 2003 has lots of protection options. We won't go through them all, since as a Paralegal you probably spend most of your time in Microsoft Word 2003. However, you should know about them, so here we go…

With Excel 2003, you have the choice of protecting these things:

- Entire worksheet
- Ranges of cells
- Workbook and all of its worksheets

Suppose you have an Excel spreadsheet that you downloaded from the Microsoft Office Web site to track your law firm's projects (using the Law Firm Project Tracking Template), as shown in Figure 16.4.

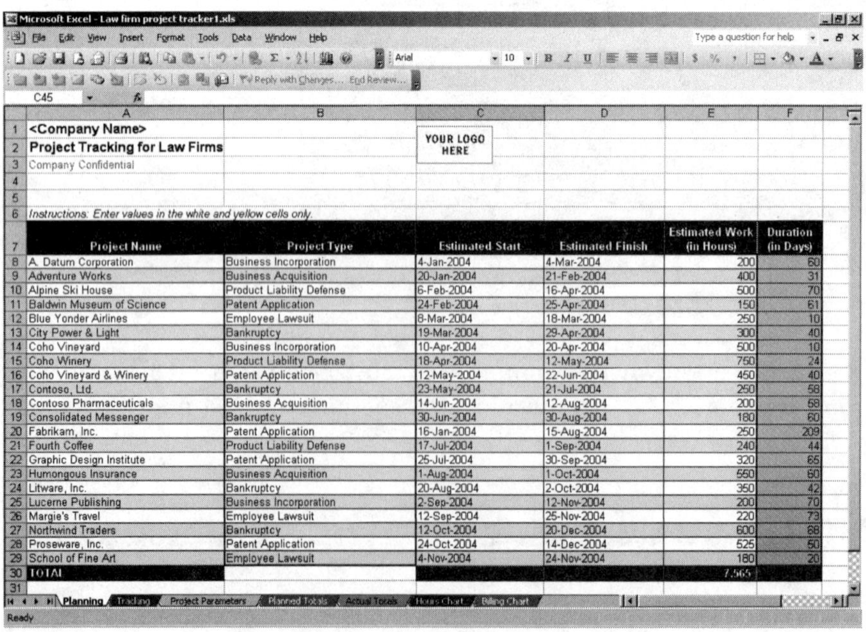

	A	B	C	D	E	F
1	<Company Name>		YOUR LOGO HERE			
2	Project Tracking for Law Firms					
3	Company Confidential					
4						
5						
6	*Instructions: Enter values in the white and yellow cells only.*					
7	Project Name	Project Type	Estimated Start	Estimated Finish	Estimated Work (in Hours)	Duration (in Days)
8	A. Datum Corporation	Business Incorporation	4-Jan-2004	4-Mar-2004	200	60
9	Adventure Works	Business Acquisition	20-Jan-2004	21-Feb-2004	400	31
10	Alpine Ski House	Product Liability Defense	6-Feb-2004	16-Apr-2004	500	70
11	Baldwin Museum of Science	Patent Application	24-Feb-2004	25-Apr-2004	150	61
12	Blue Yonder Airlines	Employee Lawsuit	8-Mar-2004	18-Mar-2004	250	10
13	City Power & Light	Bankruptcy	19-Mar-2004	29-Apr-2004	300	40
14	Coho Vineyard	Business Incorporation	10-Apr-2004	20-Apr-2004	500	10
15	Coho Winery	Product Liability Defense	18-Apr-2004	12-May-2004	750	24
16	Coho Vineyard & Winery	Patent Application	12-May-2004	22-Jun-2004	450	40
17	Contoso, Ltd.	Bankruptcy	23-May-2004	21-Jul-2004	250	58
18	Contoso Pharmaceuticals	Business Acquisition	14-Jun-2004	12-Aug-2004	200	58
19	Consolidated Messenger	Bankruptcy	30-Jun-2004	30-Aug-2004	180	60
20	Fabrikam, Inc.	Patent Application	16-Jan-2004	15-Aug-2004	250	209
21	Fourth Coffee	Product Liability Defense	17-Jul-2004	1-Sep-2004	240	44
22	Graphic Design Institute	Patent Application	25-Jul-2004	30-Sep-2004	320	65
23	Humongous Insurance	Business Acquisition	1-Aug-2004	1-Oct-2004	550	60
24	Litware, Inc.	Bankruptcy	20-Aug-2004	2-Oct-2004	350	42
25	Lucerne Publishing	Business Incorporation	2-Sep-2004	12-Nov-2004	200	70
26	Margie's Travel	Employee Lawsuit	12-Sep-2004	25-Nov-2004	220	73
27	Northwind Traders	Bankruptcy	12-Oct-2004	20-Dec-2004	600	68
28	Proseware, Inc.	Patent Application	24-Oct-2004	14-Dec-2004	525	50
29	School of Fine Art	Employee Lawsuit	4-Nov-2004	24-Nov-2004	180	20
30	TOTAL				7,565	
31						

Figure 16.4: Law Firm Project Tracking Template for Excel.

Depending on the roles within your organization, you may determine that you must protect one of the worksheets (Planning, Tracking, Project Parameters, etc.) from being edited. To protect a worksheet, simply do this:

1. Select the worksheet so that it is active.

2. Click the **Tools⇨ Protection⇨ Protect Sheet** menu item. This brings up the screen shown in Figure 16.5.

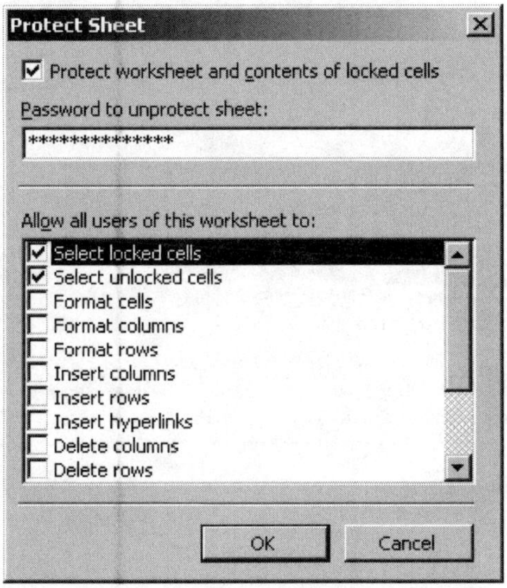

Figure 16.5: Protecting an Excel [Work]Sheet.

3. Enter a password that will be needed to unprotect the sheet into the **Password to unprotect sheet** field. There is no minimum number of characters required to protect a worksheet.

4. Optionally select the actions that users can perform while the sheet is locked. You can choose from the options shown in Table 16.1:

User Actions	Description
Select locked cells	Allows a user to select a cell that is locked. A locked cell prevents unauthorized users from changing the value or formatting of a cell when it is protected. This option is checked by default. See note below.
Select unlocked cells	Allows a user to select a cell that is not locked. This option is checked by default. See note below.
Format cells	Allows the formatting (font, color, alignment, etc.) of a cell.
Format columns	Allows the formatting of a column of cells
Format rows	Allows the formatting of a row of cells.
Insert columns	Allows a user to insert a column into a worksheet
Insert rows	Allows a user to insert a row into a worksheet.
Insert hyperlinks	Allows a user to insert a hyperlink (Web address) into a cell.
Delete columns	Allows the deletion of a column from a worksheet.
Delete rows	Allows the deletion of a row from a worksheet.
Sort	Allows sorting of data in a worksheet using the DataSort menu item.
Use AutoFilter	Allows the use of the AutoFilter command, which automatically allows a user to limit the data displayed by populating a list of distinct values of data in a range.
Use PivotTable reports	Allows a user to run reports, based on Excel's Pivot Table feature.
Edit objects	Allows a user to edit objects, such as images.
Edit scenarios	Allows a user to edit "what-if" scenarios, whose functionality is built into Excel 2003.

Table 16.1: Actions Available to a User When an Excel Sheet is Protected.

NOTE

Because (by default) you can select locked and unlocked cells, the default behavior is to allow any cell to be selected. Remember, if the spreadsheet is unlocked with a password, then a user can perform any action. Therefore, the actions that you select here will apply to a sheet that is still under protection.

5. Click the **OK** button to protect your sheet.

6. To unprotect the sheet, click the **Tools⇨ Protection⇨ Unprotect Sheet** menu item. You'll be prompted for the password before you can unprotect the sheet.

Protecting PowerPoint 2003 Presentations

Microsoft PowerPoint is a great program for showing presentations to clients, within your own firm, and sometimes in court. Just as with Excel and Word documents, you may have the need to protect your PowerPoint presentations from unauthorized usage. Doing so is easy, but protection is set differently than it is from within Word 2003 or Excel 2003.

In PowerPoint 2003, you only have the option to specify a password to open the presentation and/or a password to modify the presentation. From within PowerPoint 2003, here's how you protect a presentation from unauthorized usage:

1. Click the **Tools⇨ Options** menu item.
2. Click the **Security** tab. You'll see the screen shown in Figure 16.6.

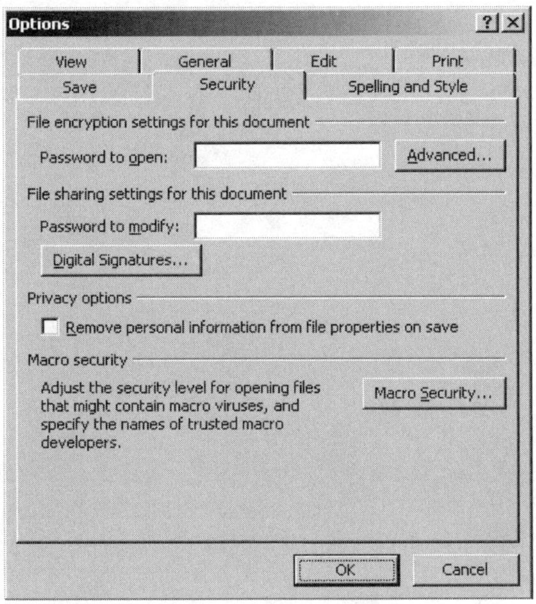

Figure 16.6: Security Options for PowerPoint 2003.

3. To require a password for a user to open the PowerPoint presentation, enter a password in the **Password to open** field.
4. To require a password for a user to modify the PowerPoint presentation, enter a password in the **Password to modify** field.
5. Click the **OK** button to save your changes. You'll be prompted to reenter any changed passwords. Once you do, your PowerPoint presentation will be protected.

6. To remove password protection, simply open the **Options** screen again and clear the password fields.

Conclusion

This chapter outlined how to secure your Word 2003, Excel 2003, and PowerPoint 2003 files. Even though your IT department is responsible for controlling the security of server, files, and folders, security of individual files is your responsibility. If you consider the security of your Microsoft Office files and not just defer security responsibility to your IT department, you can always be assured that a file will still be secure, even if it is sent outside your firm. If you are using prior versions of Microsoft Office, there is similar protection built-in, but you have fewer security options available. Please keep the security of your files always in the forefront of your mind.

Chapter 17

Structuring Documents

Chapter At A Glance

WHY YOU SHOULD READ THIS CHAPTER:

The format of your legal documents is critical. If your documents are not formatted correctly, they might even be rejected by a court. There are layout issues that you must consider to make your document look right. However, before you can dive into the layout and formatting of your content, you must understand how to structure your overall document, regardless of actual content. This chapter shows you how to structure your documents in preparation for formatting the content inside the documents.

PRODUCT OUTLINED IN THIS CHAPTER:

- Microsoft Word 2003

PRODUCT FEATURES COVERED IN THIS CHAPTER:

- Miscellaneous formatting features

At the summit of all legal formatting techniques is page formatting. Page formatting affects the overall size and orientation of your document or sections within a document. While you can format a page at any time, it helps to format a page in the beginning because it will affect the layout of everything else on the page. In this chapter, you'll first see how to format your documents and then you'll learn how to apply what you learned to some specific formatting examples.

Formatting your page is done on the **Page Setup** screen, which is made up of three tabs. Bring up this screen by clicking the **File⇨ Page Setup** menu item. Before we dive into the nitty-gritty of setting up your documents, look at Figure 17.1. Portions of the image are intentionally blurred to clearly show the significant areas of the figure. It maps the terminology used in setting up your pages with the area of a document that represents the term.

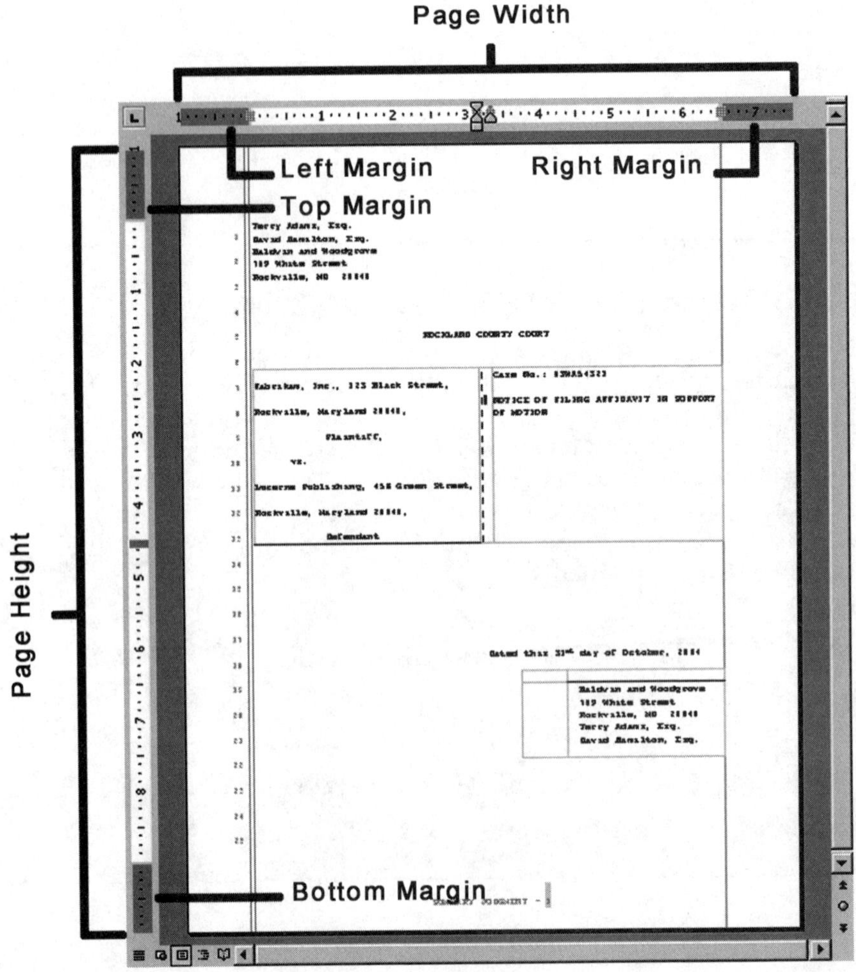

Figure 17.1: Page Setup Locations and Terminology.

Margins Tab

The **Margins** tab is the first tab on the **Page Setup** screen. This tab contains fields that control the margins and orientation of the document. Figure 17.2 shows the **Margins** tab.

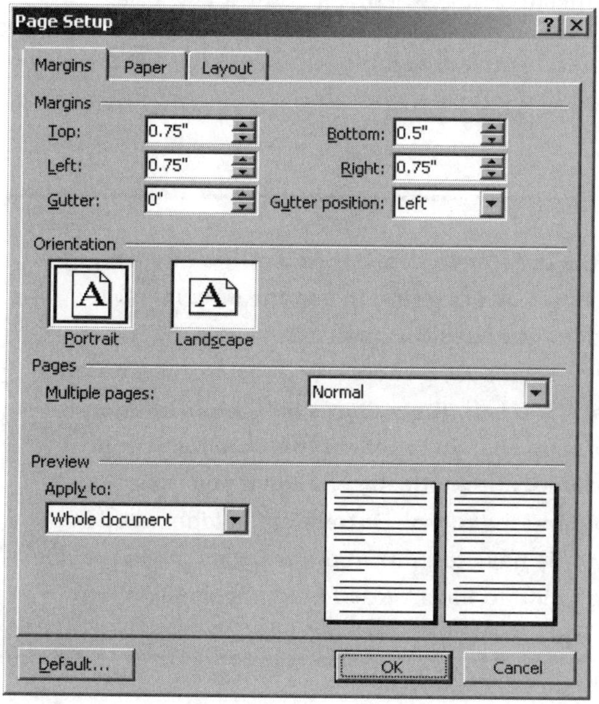

Figure 17.2: The Margins Tab on the Page Setup Screen.

The fields on the **Margins** tab are:

Margins

- **Top** — Amount of space in the top margin. 1" is the default value when you create a new page.
- **Bottom** — Amount of space in the bottom margin. 1" is the default value when you create a new page.
- **Left** — Amount of space in the left margin. 1.25" is the default value when you create a new page.

- **RIGHT** — Amount of space in the right margin. 1.25" is the default value when you create a new page.
- **GUTTER** — Amount of additional space in either the left or right margin, depending on the gutter position. Much like the gutter in a bowling lane, this area is not considered part of the active text area. 0" is the default value when you create a new page.
- **GUTTER POSITION** — The position of the gutter as specified in the **Gutter** field. Position can either be **Left** or **Right**, with **Left** being the default value.

> **NOTE**
>
> **You might be wondering what the difference is between a gutter and a margin. The answer to this depends on how you are going to use the document. A gutter set at .5" in the left position may have the same effect as a .5" left margin. However, there is one important difference. If you resize margins with the mouse by dragging the rulers, the Left, Right, Top, and Bottom margins on the Margins tab will automatically change to reflect this manual action. On the other hand, the gutter will not automatically change if you resize the margins with the mouse by dragging the rulers. Gutters are seldom used in legal documents. You normally only have to think about margins in your legal documents. However, if you are going to have a document physically bound, gutters may come into play as well.**

Orientation

- **PORTRAIT** — Pages are taller than they are wide. This is the default orientation.
- **LANDSCAPE** — Pages are wider than they are tall.

Pages

- **MULTIPLE PAGES** — Controls how the document will be formatted with multiple pages. Here are your choices:
    - **NORMAL** — Each page uses the same margin settings. This is the default value.

- **Mirror margins** — Left and right pages will have opposite (or mirrored) margins. For example, if you specify a left margin of 1.25" and you are currently looking at a left-hand (even) page number, the right margin will automatically be 1.25" as well so that they are mirrored. However, mirror margins are almost never used in legal documents.
- **2 pages per sheet** — Every sheet of paper will be divided in half to produce two separate pages. This is helpful in situations where, for example, you have two labels on a sheet of paper. This option is seldom, but sometimes, used in legal documents.
- **Booklet** — Sheets will be bound and folded as a booklet. If you choose this option, you'll have an additional choice of how many pages make up the booklet. Booklet is almost never used in legal documents.

Preview

- **Apply to** — Dictates how the changes made on the **Margins** tab will affect your document. You can choose from these options:
  - **Whole document** — Resets the settings for the entire document, including all pages.
  - **This point forward** — Resets the settings not for the entire document, but only on the current page and all pages after the current page. This can be a useful setting if you plan to have multiple size pages or different orientations in the same document. It can lead to very undesirable results if you use this option without understanding its implications.

Paper Tab

The **Paper** tab is the second tab on the **Page Setup** screen. This tab contains fields that control the paper size that you wish to use in the document. It also controls where the paper is loaded into the printer. Many printers have multiple paper trays, so you can specify which tray the paper is loaded into. Figure 17.3 shows the **Paper** tab.

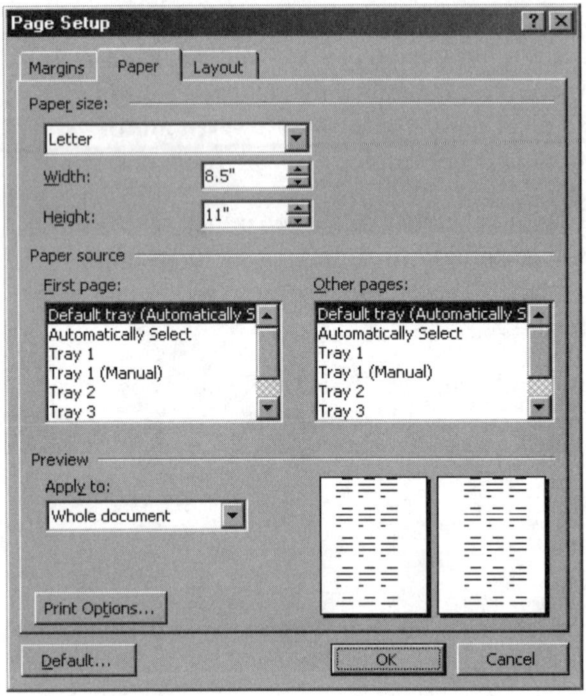

Figure 17.3: The Paper Tab on the Page Setup Screen.

The fields on the **Paper** tab are:

Paper size

- In the dropdown list provided, select the size of paper that you will use. This affects how the entire document will be laid out. Letter is the default value, but you can also choose from many popular sizes, including **Legal**, **A4**, **A5**, and **Custom size.**

- **Width and Height** — Specifies the width and height of the paper. You only need to alter these values if you choose **Custom size** as the paper size. Otherwise, Word knows the size of the paper, based on the size chosen in the dropdown list. For example, a letter-sized document is always 8.5" X 11". The only thing that can change for a letter-sized document is the orientation that you select on the **Margins** tab. If you choose a **Landscape** orientation, the **Width** and **Height** will be reversed.

Paper source

- **First page** — Specifies the tray in the printer that contains the paper for the first page of the document only. You may wish to print the first page on a special stock of paper or letterhead, which could be loaded into a different tray in the printer. If this is not the case, ensure that the value selected in the **First page** field is the same as the value selected in the **Other pages** field.

Preview

This area shows a basic picture preview of how the options you chose on the **Paper** tab affect the document. See "Preview" under "Margins Tab" earlier in this chapter for more information.

Layout Tab

The **Layout** tab is the third and final tab on the **Page Setup** screen. This tab contains fields that control the layout of your document. It controls sections, headers, footers, and vertical alignment on a page. Figure 17.4 shows the **Layout** tab.

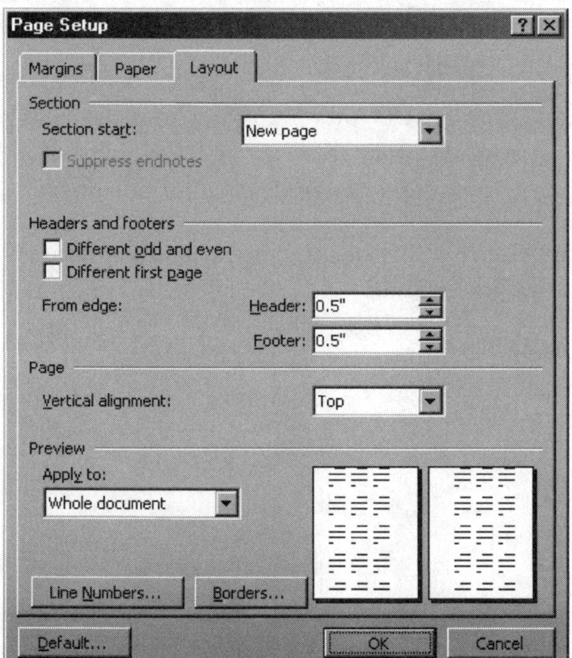

Figure 17.4: The Layout Tab on the Page Setup Screen.

The fields on the **Layout** tab are:

Section

A *section* is a region that logically divides a page or a document. One section can contain formatting that is different from another section. Sections do not affect things like fonts, but they do affect anything that is related to layout, such as columns.

- **Section start** — Specifies when new sections will automatically be created. You can choose from these options:
    - **Continuous** — No new pages will be created.
    - **New column** — Starts a new section when a new column is created on a page.
    - **New page** — Starts a new section when a new page is created (either even or odd). This is the default option.
    - **Even page** — Starts a new section when a new even page is created. The **Even page** option is rarely used in legal documents.
    - **Odd page** — Starts a new section when a new odd page is created. The **Odd page** option is rarely used in legal documents.
- **Suppress endnotes** — If checked, this option will prevent Word from displaying endnotes in the current section, but will instead display them in the following section. This option is not enabled unless you have footnotes or endnotes in your document.

A section is typically used in a situation where the formatting of a document needs to change. Conditions which will cause you to start a new section include:

- Page numbering format change (such as roman numerals to arabic numbers)
- Header or footer changes
- Orientation changes
- Page size changes

As an example, suppose you are preparing an agreement, which includes a cover page, a Table of Contents, body, and exhibits. The cover page, Table of Contents, and body may use one page numbering format. However, you have an exhibit, which must use another page numbering format. This one detail will force you to create a new section.

There's really nothing to creating new sections if you format the document to use a **New page** for the **Section start** field. If you do this, each page will be in its own section. Therefore, to change the orientation of the new section, simply place the cursor on the desired page and click the **File⇨ Page Setup** menu item and change the orientation.

Headers and footers

- **Different odd and even** — If checked, your document will contain a different header for an odd page than it does for an even page. This is useful in situations where you are producing a book or booklet, where the title of the document is on the left-hand (even) page and the chapter title is on the right-hand (odd) page. This type of header and footer is almost never used in legal documents.

- **Different first page** —If checked, your document will have a different header on the first page of the document than it does on every other page. This is useful in situations such as letters where your firm information is printed only on the first page, but not subsequent pages. This is also useful when you don't want the page number to appear on the first page of your legal documents.

- **Header (From edge)** — Specifies the distance from the top of the page to the beginning of the header. The default is .5" (one-half inch).

- **Footer (From edge)** — Specifies the distance from the bottom of the page to the end of the footer. The default is .5" (one-half inch).

Page

- **Vertical alignment** — Specifies how the text is aligned vertically between the top and bottom margins. You can choose from **Top**, **Center**, **Justified**, and **Bottom**. The **Justified** setting is only effective if the current page has a full page of text. It is almost never used in legal documents. If the current page is not full, this setting has the same effect as choosing **Top**.

Preview

This area shows a basic picture preview of how the options you chose on the **Layout** tab affect the document. See "Preview" under "Margins Tab" earlier in this chapter for more information. However, there are two additional buttons on the **Layout** tab that aren't on the other tabs. They are **Line Numbers** and **Borders**, both of which are covered in Chapter 18.

Putting it all Together

So far in this chapter, you learned about a lot of options to structure your legal documents, so here you'll see how to put it all together. As an example, suppose you wanted to create an agreement that contains these sections:

- Title Page
- Table of Contents
- Body
- Exhibit A

The rest of this chapter is dedicated to showing you how to create these sections. The procedures do not specify any text that goes into these sections, as that would just cloud the issue of managing document formats at this point. The next four headings show how to create the four sections listed above, but first create a new document by following these steps:

1. Open Microsoft Word.
2. Create a new document by clicking the **File⇨ New** menu item. A new document is created. This will allow you to follow the rest of the steps presented in this chapter.

Creating the Title Page

The title page (Section 1) is used to simply give a title to your document. A title page normally doesn't have a header or footer and the text is centered on the page horizontally and vertically. Since you already opened a new document, the blank page is now the title page. Here's how you configure the title page:

1. Type the title of your document, such as `AGREEMENT TO PURCHASE PROPERTY`.
2. Center your text horizontally by clicking anywhere within the title text and clicking the **Center** icon on the **Formatting** toolbar.
3. Center your text vertically by clicking the **File⇨ Page Setup** menu item.
4. In the **Vertical alignment** dropdown list, choose the **Center** option.
5. Click the **OK** button.

Your title page, configured as Section 1, is now created with its text centered horizontally and vertically.

Creating the Table of Contents Page

The Table of Contents (TOC) itself is generated automatically by Word, according to the heading styles you use in your document. Creating the TOC is shown in Chapter 22. However, to configure the page that will contain the TOC (Section 2), you will likely need a header to display the centered heading **Table of Contents**, along with a footer containing a roman numeral for the centered page number.

Here's how you configure the TOC page:

1. Click the **Insert⇨ Break** menu item and select the **Next page** option to create a new section break (Section 2).
2. Click the **File⇨ Page Setup** menu item.
3. Change the **Vertical alignment** dropdown list to use the **Top** option.
4. Open the header by clicking the **View⇨ Header and Footer** menu item.
5. Type the text of your header, such as `Table of Contents`.
6. Center your header by clicking the **Center** icon on the **Formatting** toolbar.
7. Disconnect the header for the Table of Contents section (Section 2) by ensuring the **Link to Previous** button on the **Header and Footer** toolbar is not clicked. (This button is outlined in Chapter 19). Therefore, changes in section 1 will not affect Section 2.
8. Click the **Switch Between Header and Footer** button on the **Header and Footer** toolbar. You'll now be looking at the footer of Section 2.
9. Click the **Insert Page Number** button on the **Header and Footer** toolbar.
10. Click the **Format Page Number** button on the **Header and Footer** toolbar.
11. Change the **Number format** dropdown list to be a lowercase roman numeral (**i, ii, iii,** ...).
12. In the **Start at** field, select the number with which to begin the numbering. You will likely need to ensure the number is **1**.

13. Center your page number by clicking the **Center** icon on the **Formatting** toolbar.

14. Click the **Close** button on the **Header and Footer** toolbar.

You have now configured Section 2, which is the Table of Contents page that contains a centered text header and a centered roman numeral footer.

Creating the Body

The body is the largest section in your document, but for purposes of example, it will be a single page. The body in this example (Section 3) uses the same centered header on every page in the section. The centered footer contains the page number of the section, but is omitted on the first page of the section. This is a likely scenario when you create your own legal documents, and the recommended technique is to use a different header and footer on the first page. There are lots of steps involved in configuring the body, so you might want to grab a cup of coffee. Then, create the body like this:

1. Click the **Insert⇨ Break** menu item and select the **Next page** option to create a new section break (Section 3).

2. Type any desired text in the body of the document, but for the purposes of example, this text is not relevant, so it is skipped.

3. Create a new page within the current section by clicking the **Insert⇨ Break** menu item and selecting the **Page break** option. This new page will be used to have a different header and footer within the same section.

4. Move the cursor back to the first page of Section 3.

5. Click the **File⇨ Page Setup** menu item.

6. Click the **Layout** tab.

7. Select the **Different first page** option.

8. Open the header by clicking the **View⇨ Header and Footer** menu item.

9. Disconnect the header for the body section (Section 3) by ensuring the **Link to Previous** button on the **Header and Footer** toolbar is not clicked.

10. Type the text of your header, such as `Property Purchase Agreement`.

11. Center your header by clicking the **Center** icon on the **Formatting** toolbar.

12. Click the **Switch Between Header and Footer** button on the **Header and Footer** toolbar. You'll now be looking at the footer of the first page of Section 3.

13. Ensure there is no text in the footer for the first page in this section.

14. Click the **Switch Between Header and Footer** button on the **Header and Footer** toolbar. You'll now be looking back at the header of the first page of Section 3.

15. Click the **Show Next** button on the **Header and Footer** toolbar.

16. Type the same header as you did in Step 10. From this point forward, every subsequent new page in the body will use this header text and formatting.

17. Click the **Switch Between Header and Footer** button on the **Header and Footer** toolbar. You'll now be looking at the footer of the second page of Section 3.

18. Click the **Insert Page Number** button on the **Header and Footer** toolbar.

19. Click the **Format Page Number** button on the **Header and Footer** toolbar.

20. Change the **Number format** dropdown list to be arabic numerals (**1, 2, 3, …**).

21. In the **Start at** field, select the number with which to begin the numbering. You will likely need to ensure the number is **2** because you skipped the page number on the first page in the section.

22. Center your page number by clicking the **Center** icon on the **Formatting** toolbar.

23. Click the **Close** button on the **Header and Footer** toolbar.

Creating Exhibit A

Not all legal documents have exhibits, but if you need one, it is likely to have different formatting requirements for the footer page numbers. The following example scenario for Exhibit A continues the header from the previous section, but uses different footers.

Here's how you configure the Exhibit:

1. Click the **Insert⇨ Break** menu item and select the **Next page** option to create a new section break (Section 4).

2. Open the header by clicking the **View⇨ Header and Footer** menu item.

3. Because you want to use the header from the previous section, ensure the **Link to Previous** button on the **Header and Footer** toolbar is clicked.

4. Click the **Switch Between Header and Footer** button on the **Header and Footer** toolbar. You'll now be looking at the footer of the first page of Section 4.

5. Click the **Insert Page Number** button on the **Header and Footer** toolbar.

6. Click the **Format Page Number** button on the **Header and Footer** toolbar.

7. Change the **Number format** dropdown list to be arabic numerals (**1, 2, 3, ...**)

8. In the **Start at** field, select the number with which to begin the numbering. Because this is an Exhibit (or Appendix), you will likely need to restart the page numbering, so enter a value of **1**.

9. Center your page number by clicking the **Center** icon on the **Formatting** toolbar.

10. Instead of displaying the page number by itself, you may desire to preface your footer page numbering with the letter "A-" such as **A-1**, **A-2**, etc. If you do, you can simply type the preface in the footer before the page number field.

11. Click the **Close** button on the **Header and Footer** toolbar.

Your document is now formatted according to complex section breaks that you are likely to encounter in many legal documents.

Conclusion

Before you embark on the challenging task of formatting the content of your documents, you must understand how to format the document itself. This includes things like page size, orientation, and other configuration information. This chapter showed you how to configure your documents in preparation for formatting the content, which is shown in Chapter 18.

Chapter 18

Formatting Content

Chapter At A Glance

WHY YOU SHOULD READ THIS CHAPTER:

As you may know, it can be very challenging to format the content inside your documents, especially legal pleadings. Legal pleadings require line numbers, borders, specially formatted text, and more. While the Legal Pleading Wizard shown in Chapter 23 can create much of this for you, it can be extremely beneficial for you to understand how to create these documents manually. This will heighten your awareness as to how Microsoft Word formats documents and will lead to higher productivity in the long run. This chapter shows you how to format complex documents using tables, line numbers, borders, and more. Even though a litigation practice area may benefit most from the example pleading shown in this chapter, other practice areas (such as Corporate, Trusts and Estates, and Real Estate) can apply some of the principles outlined as well.

PRODUCT OUTLINED IN THIS CHAPTER:

- Microsoft Word 2003

PRODUCT FEATURES COVERED IN THIS CHAPTER:

- Miscellaneous formatting features

One of the biggest challenges that you face as a Paralegal is formatting your documents. This is especially true if you are not very familiar with Microsoft Word, or if you are more familiar with the ins and outs of WordPerfect. After reading this chapter, you'll know the majority of what's important in formatting your documents. While you can get much of this information by reading online help or a large 800-page book, we have carefully distilled the content to only the information that you are likely to need as a Paralegal.

Once you have specified all the formatting options for your document, such as page size, orientation, and margins (see Chapter 17), you are ready to begin constructing your document. This short chapter does not outline each and every possible way to format your content, but does focus on the issues and formatting challenges that a Paralegal faces. In this chapter, you'll learn how to format your legal documents by using Word tables, line numbering, page borders, double spacing, and columns.

Word Tables

Word Tables (sometimes just known as tables) are probably the most useful and effective layout tool that you will need to use as a Paralegal. Tables allow you to easily line up your text so that it displays nicely on your page. To illustrate the point, take a look at Figure 18.1, which is a sample pleading.

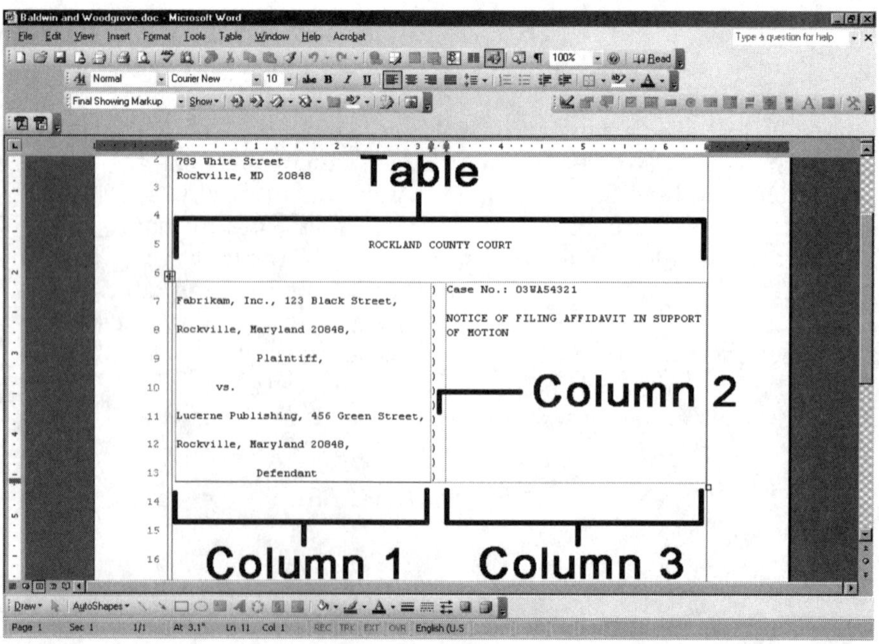

Figure 18.1: Word Table Inside a Document.

Notice that there is one table on the page, which consists of three columns. The first column contains a caption box for the pleading. The second column is a narrow column that contains the delimiters on the right of the caption box. These can be solid lines, left parenthesis, equal sign, or something else required by the court. The third column contains the case number and title. If it was not for the table displayed on the page, it would be difficult or impossible to line up the text in this fashion.

Crafting Tables is not Just for Carpenters

If you want to create a table, you need no special woodworking abilities. You simply need to click a few mouse buttons. You can create a table before or after you place text into the document. However, it's a little easier if you create the table first. To create a new table, follow these steps:

1. Place the cursor where you would like the table to be created.

2. Click the **Table⇨ Insert⇨ Table** menu item. You'll see the screen shown in Figure 18.2.

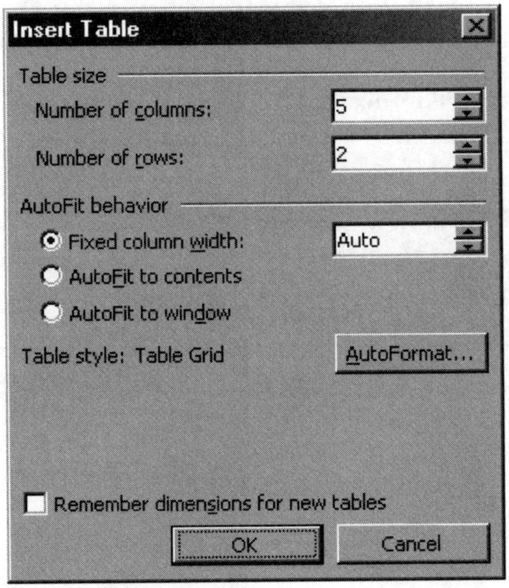

Figure 18.2: Insert Table Screen.

3. Enter the number of columns and rows you would like your table to have. While you can adjust the number of columns and rows later, it is best if you decide on a number now. It very easy to add new rows later, but a little trickier to add new columns. Therefore, at least try to know the number of columns needed. Remember that in Figure 18.5 there are two columns. Therefore, you would enter the number **3** in the **Number of columns** field. Make a best guess for the number of rows in the **Number of rows** field.

4. Specify how you would like the columns to be formatted with these options:

   - **FIXED COLUMN WIDTH** — Every column will use the same column width and is calculated based on the amount usable of space between the margins, divided by the number of columns that you specify in the **Number of columns** field. This is the default option.

   - **AUTOFIT TO CONTENTS** — Each column is sized to the longest content that is contained within any row inside the column. If there are not enough contents to fit the entire width of the page, the table will not be expanded to fit the width of the page.

   - **AUTOFIT TO WINDOW** — Each column is sized to the longest content that is contained within any row inside the column, but will also be expanded to fit the width of the page (or window).

For your legal documents, it is likely that you will format your tables by simply using the **Fixed column width** option with **Auto.** This also allows you to resize columns after the text is placed in the table.

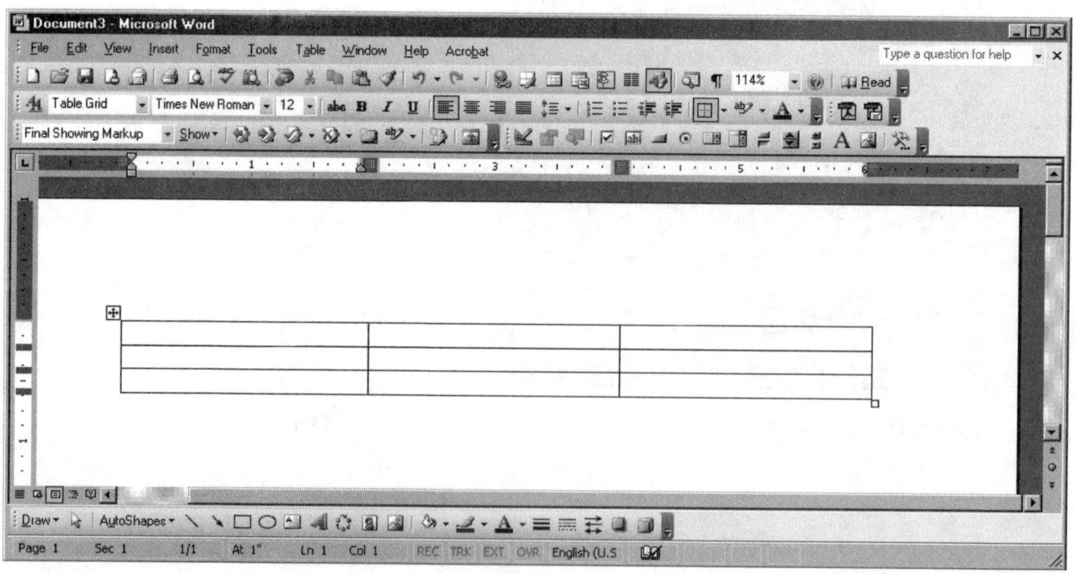

Figure 18.3: Document After Inserting a New Table with Three Columns and Three Rows.

Sending Your Table to the Tailor

Once your table is created, you can size it according to your specifications. This can be a difficult thing to do and there are many different ways to do it. Therefore, it is important for you to understand the concepts. If you place the carat inside a table cell (by clicking in any cell), you'll see the rulers for both the rows and columns in the table appear in the margins. See Figure 18.4 for a detailed look at the location of these rulers.

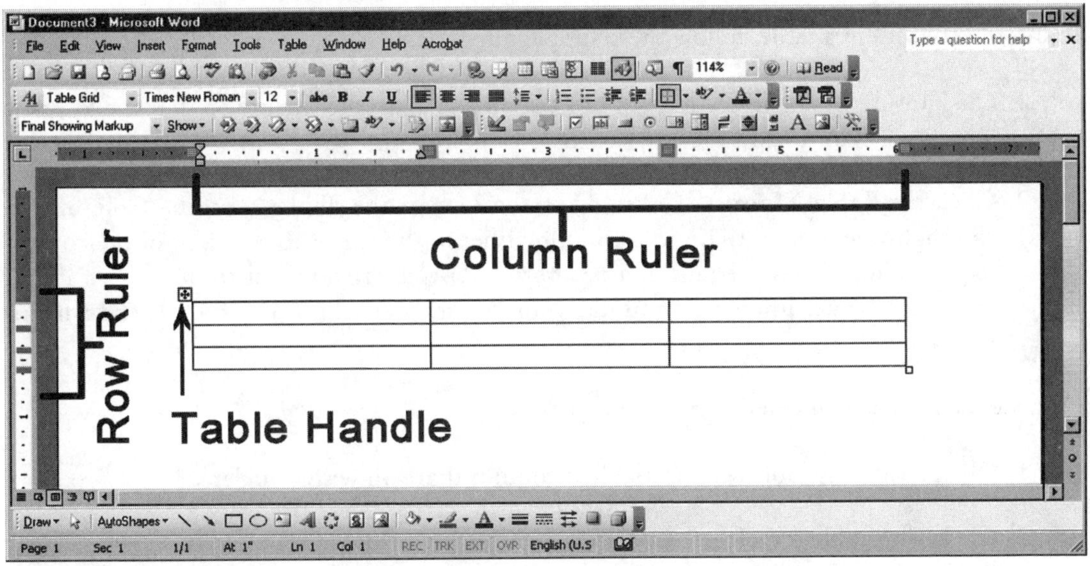

Figure 18.4: Rulers and Table Handle After Clicking Inside Table.

You'll also notice in Figure 18.4 that there is a small box called a table handle. If you click this box, it's just like selecting the entire table. If you right-click this box, you'll be presented with options for the table. This is covered further in the section, "Changing Properties," later in this chapter.

The rulers presented in Figure 18.4 might be confusing at first, but it actually makes a lot of sense. Any gray area on the ruler represents the location of the line that separates a column or a row. The white areas between these gray areas represent the size of the column or row. Therefore, if you want to make the size of a column larger, in the column ruler, place your mouse over the gray area in the ruler that represents the line between columns in your table and drag the column to the desired width. You'll see the column resize. This works just as well for a row using the row ruler. Another way for you to resize is to manually indicate what the size of a column should be. This is covered in the section, "Changing Properties," later in this chapter.

Inserting and Deleting Columns

If you didn't know how many columns your table should have when you created it, or you wish to change the number of columns, you certainly can do that, but it might throw off the size of the table itself. Imagine a scenario where you have five columns in a table and you remove two of them. The remaining three columns will be larger, as the size of the overall table will not change.

To insert a column in a table, follow these simple directions:

1. Click inside any table cell located in a column that is either before or after the location where you want to add the new column.

2. Click the **Table⇨ Insert⇨ Columns to the Left** or the **Table⇨ Insert⇨ Columns to the Right** menu item to insert a column either to the left or to the right of the current location. You will not be given a prompt to verify that you want to do this, so if you make a mistake, immediately undo your action by clicking the **Edit⇨ Undo** menu item.

Likewise, here's how you delete a column in a table:

1. Click inside any table cell located in a column that you wish to delete.

2. Click the **Table⇨ Delete⇨ Columns** menu item and the column becomes history. Again, if you inadvertently deleted a column, simply click the **Edit⇨ Undo** menu item.

Inserting and Deleting Rows

Inserting or deleting rows is very similar to inserting or deleting columns. However, there are different considerations to keep in mind concerning the size of the tables. If you insert a row in a table, the size of the table will grow vertically, which can affect the layout of your document. Likewise, if you delete a row, the size of the table will shrink accordingly.

To insert a row in a table, follow these simple directions:

1. Click inside any table cell located in a row that is either above or below the location where you want to add the new row.

2. Click the **Table⇨ Insert⇨ Rows Above** or the **Table⇨ Insert⇨ Rows Below** menu item to insert a row either above or below the current location.

Likewise, here's how you delete a row in a table:

1. Click inside any table cell located in a row that you wish to delete.

2. Click the **Table⇨ Delete⇨ Rows** menu item to delete the current row.

Changing Properties

Once you know where the table handle is located (see Figure 18.4), you can do some very interesting things. By right-clicking this table handle and selecting the **Table Properties** menu item, you can change any of the following properties of the table very easily:

- **TABLE** — Properties of the table itself, such as borders and shading.

- **ROW** — Properties of one or more rows in the table.

- **COLUMN** — Properties of one or more columns in the table.

- **CELL** — Properties of the currently selected cell.

Each of the above properties is displayed on one of four tabs. All four tabs are shown in Figure 18.5.

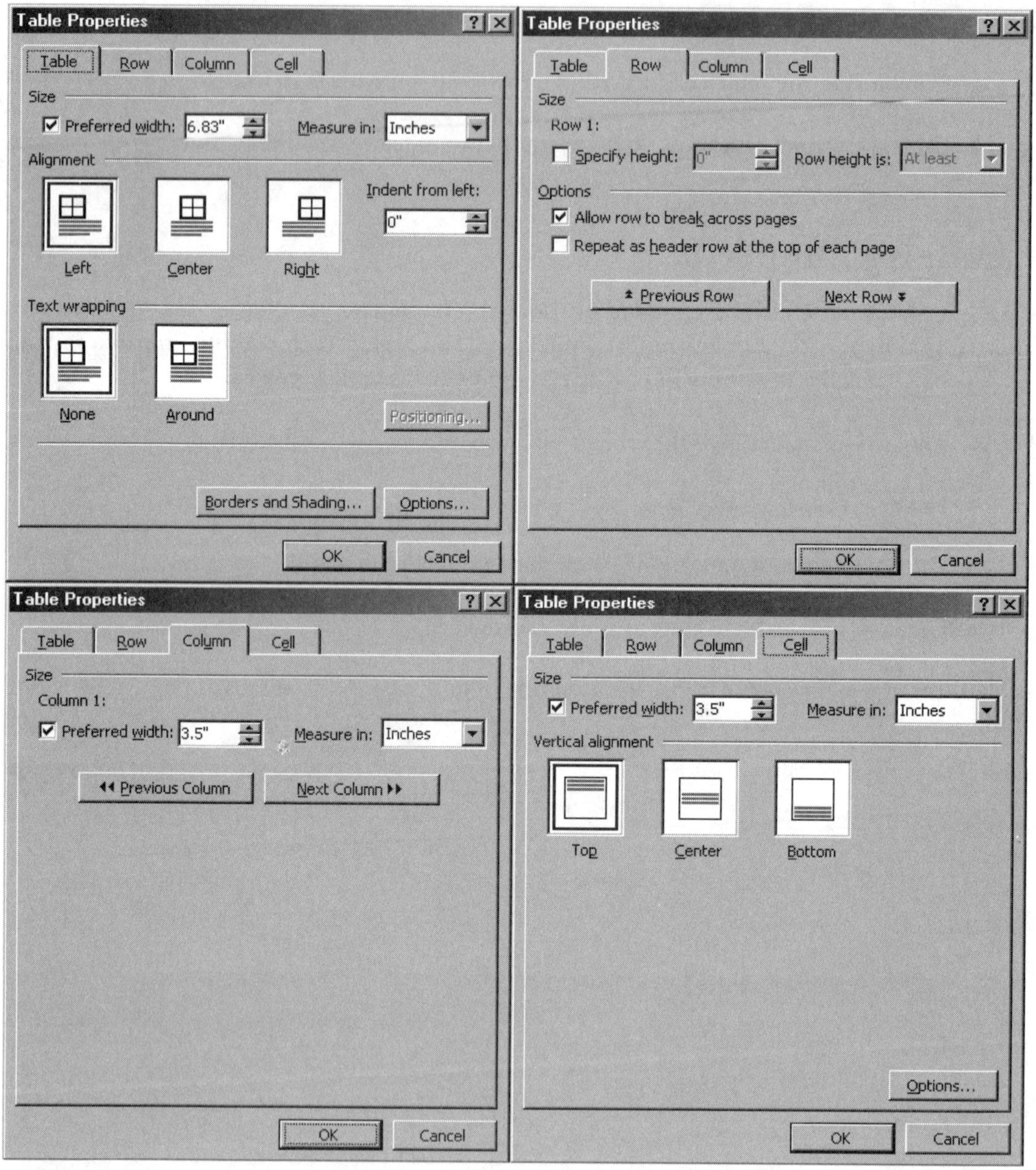

Figure 18.5: Four Tabs of the Table Properties Screen.

In each of the four tabs, there are many similarities. Basically, all four tabs control the alignment and position of the table. The **Table** tab allows you to specify the overall size of the table. To specify the size, click the **Preferred width** check box and enter the desired width. The **Table** tab also allows you to specify **Left**, **Center**, or **Right** alignment for the horizontal alignment of each cell in the table, with **Left** being the default value. The **Table** tab has an additional option that specifies how text will wrap around pictures. By default, text will display on the next line after a picture, but you can have it wrap around the text as well.

The **Row** tab allows you to specify properties of every row in the table. You navigate from one row to another by clicking the **Previous Row** and **Next Row** buttons. As you navigate each row, the screen indicates the current row. In Figure 18.5, the current row is displayed as **Row 1**, so any settings that you change affect only the first row. To change the height of the current row, click the **Specify height** check box and enter the desired height in the adjacent boxes.

The **Column** tab allows you to specify the properties of every column in the table. You navigate from one column to another by clicking the **Previous Column** and **Next Column** buttons. As you navigate each column, the screen indicates the current column. In Figure 18.5, the current column is displayed as **Column 1**, so any settings that you change affect only the first column. To change the width of the current column, click the **Preferred width** check box and enter the desired width values in the adjacent boxes.

The **Cell** tab allows you to enter a preferred width, just as the **Table** and **Column** tabs do. It also lets you specify alignment, but unlike the **Table** tab, the alignment specified here is the vertical alignment of the contents of a cell. This will include graphics and text. You can choose from **Top**, **Center**, and **Bottom**, with **Top** being the default value.

Table Borders

By default, every cell in a table has a border. In other words, there is a thin black line in the left, top, right, and bottom part of each cell. If you are using a table simply to format text, it is very likely that you want no borders at all. This way, the final document will not even show a table at all when it is printed. To remove table borders, follow this procedure:

1. Right-click the table handle.
2. Choose the **Borders and Shading** menu item.
3. Ensure the **Borders** tab is clicked. This brings up the screen shown in Figure 18.6.

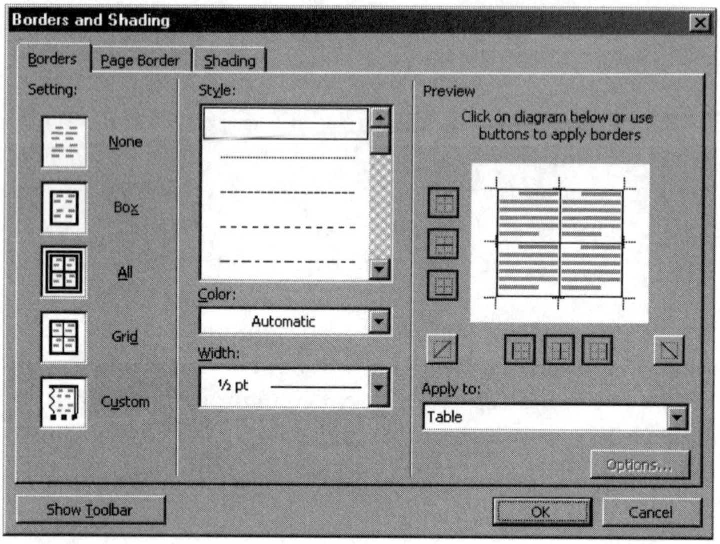

Figure 18.6: Configuring Table Borders.

4. Click the **None** box under the **Setting** label.

5. Click the **OK** button.

NOTE

While not covered in this chapter due to complexity and space constraints, you can select any border size, color, and position for any cell column, row, or table. You can even mix-and-match borders. For example, you can have a thick blue line on the right border of cells in one column, but a thin black line on the left border of cells in the same column.

TIP

With borders removed, you may think that you should not see any lines at all in your tables. What you do see is lines shown in light gray instead of black. You should know that after you remove borders the lines shown are for your reference only. They will not show on a printed page. If you want to test it, you can go to the File⇨ Print Preview menu item, which will show exactly the way the document is to be printed. You'll notice there are no lines in the printed table.

Entering Text into a Table

Once your table is created and formatted, you can simply enter text the way you need it to appear. If you are trying to create a caption box similar to the one shown in Figure 18.1, you enter the text on three separate rows. Figure 18.7 shows a manually configured Word table with three rows.

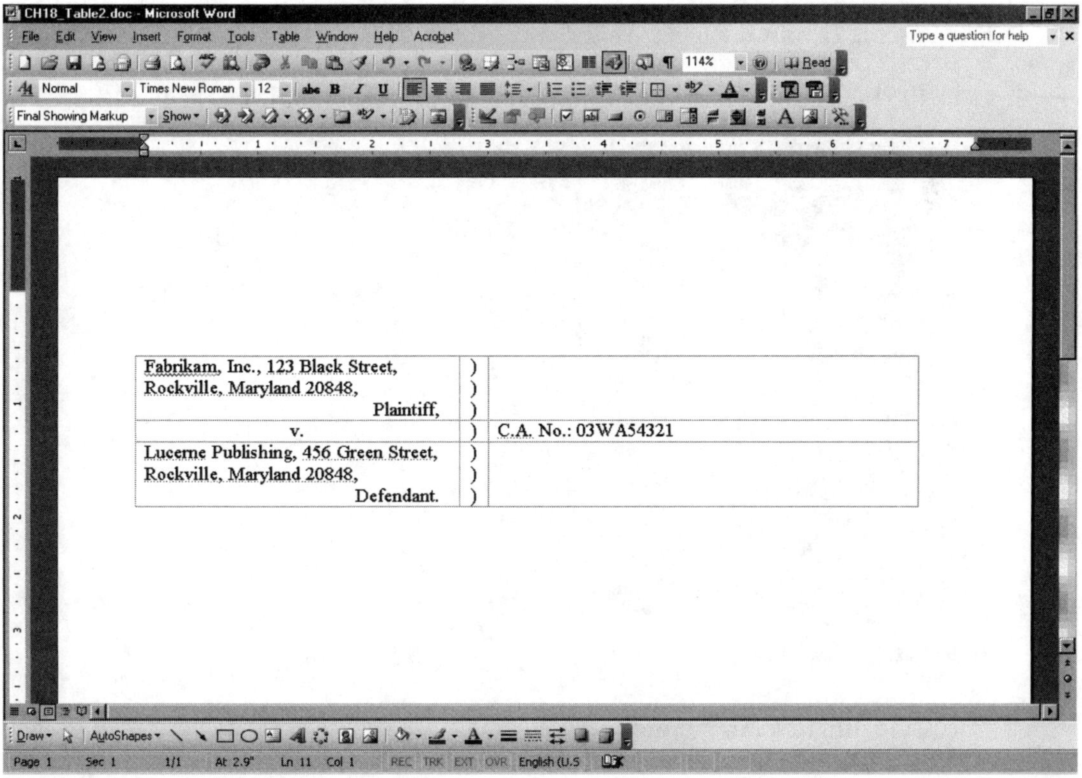

Figure 18.7: Manually Configured Legal Pleading Table.

OK, so the table shown in Figure 18.7 doesn't look pretty. In fact, you may be thinking, "This looks nothing like a legal pleading!" In fact, it is the beginning. While you can use the Legal Pleading Wizard (see Chapter 23) to do this entire configuration for you, it is a good idea to understand how it is done so that you can tweak your own documents and lessen your frustration with formatting tables.

Take a Number, Please!

Some legal documents, such as those used in litigation, need to have line numbers in the left-hand margin. Some Paralegals actually type the line numbers by hand. On a 50-page document, this can be exceedingly tedious and can introduce error. Have the computer do it for you. It's only a couple of mouse clicks to get it done, so you should know how…like this:

1. Bring up the **Layout** tab of the **Page Setup** screen. This was shown in Figure 18.4.
2. Click the **Line Numbers** button. This brings up the screen shown in Figure 18.8.

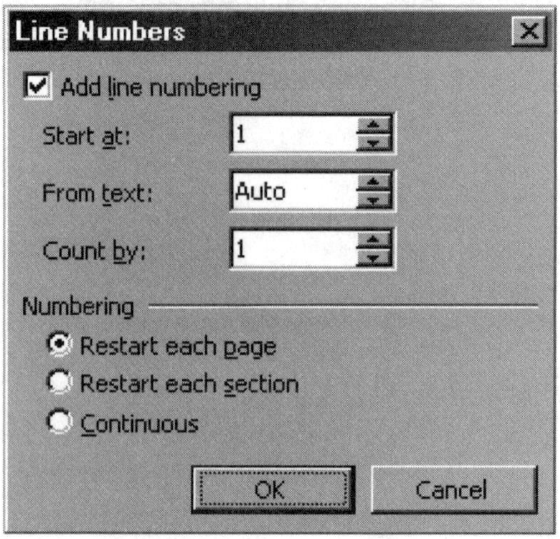

Figure 18.8: Page Layout Line Numbering Options.

3. Check the **Add line numbering** check box.
4. Accept all the default options by clicking the **OK** button. Doing so will start all line numbers at the number 1 and increment each by 1. Upon each new page, the line numbers are reset. This is generally the behavior you need in your legal documents. If you are creating a document that needs to have line numbering at another increment, such as every five lines, you would simply change the **Count by** field to a value of 5.

Going South of the Border

Figure 18.1 shows a legal pleading that contains a left-hand, double-line border. While this pleading was created using the Legal Pleading Wizard (See Chapter 23), you can certainly format your documents manually to contain borders that you are likely to see in legal pleadings.

Typically, you need to configure a double vertical line border in the left-hand margin and a single vertical line border in the right-hand margin. Since this is a non-standard border configuration, you'll need to set a few special options. To configure the left and right borders, follow this procedure:

1. Click the **Format⇨ Borders and Shading** menu item.
2. Click the **Page Border** tab. This brings up the screen shown in Figure 18.9.

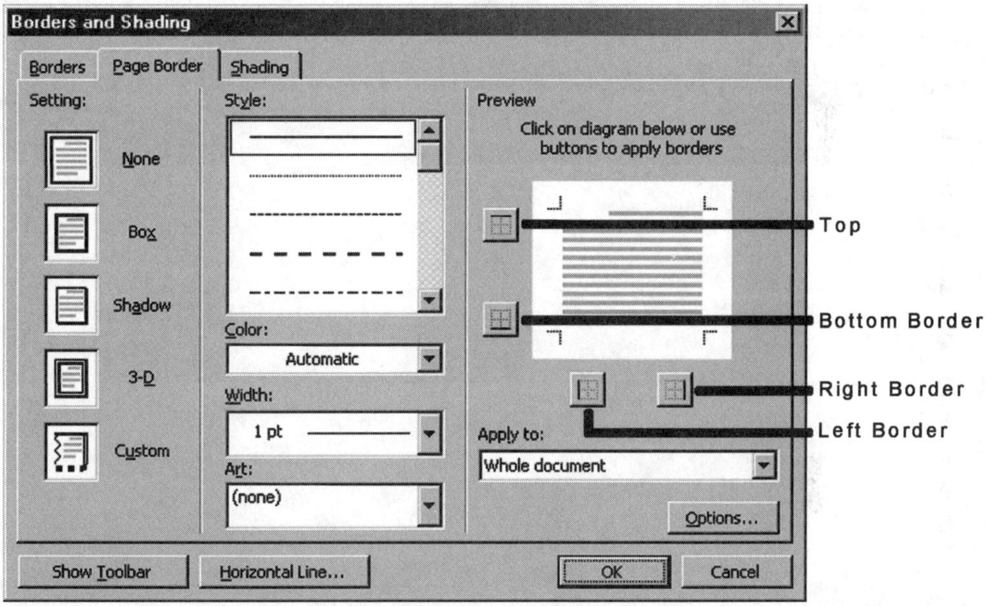

Figure 18.9: Page Borders and Shading Options.

While this screen looks very complicated, just follow the rest of the steps to create the aforementioned borders.

3. To begin the process of selecting the left-hand border, in the **Style** list, scroll down to the double line.
4. Select the desired line width in the **Width** dropdown list. For example, a **1 1/2 pt** width may be acceptable for the left-hand border of your pleading.
5. Click the left border button. This will assign the selected style to the left border.
6. To begin the process of selecting the right-hand border, in the **Style** list, scroll down to the single line.
7. Select the desired line width in the **Width** dropdown list. For example, a **1 pt** width may be acceptable for the right-hand border of your pleading.

8. Click the right border button. This will assign the selected style to the right border.

9. Click the **OK** button to assign the borders.

The above configured borders can be seen in Figure 18.10, along with automatic line numbering.

Figure 18.10: Resulting Page after Configuring Borders.

Notice in Figure 18.10 that there is a double line in the left border and a single line in the right border. This is the result of following the preceding procedure.

NOTE

If the left-hand double line border appears to run through the automatic line numbers, you can adjust the spacing of where the borders are drawn. To do so, click the Options **button shown in Figure 18.9 and change the** Measure from **dropdown list to a value of** Text **and increase the** Left margin**.**

Are You Seeing Double?

Many legal documents need to have text double-spaced. Configuring double-spacing is very simple to do. Here's how:

1. Select the text that needs to be double-spaced.
2. Click the **Format⇨ Paragraph** menu item.
3. Ensure the **Indents and Spacing** tab is selected.
4. Under the **Spacing** section, select **Double** in the **Line spacing** dropdown.
5. Click the **OK** button.

Your selected paragraphs will now be double-spaced, taking into account the font and font size that is used. For example, double-spacing on a 20 point font is not the same as double-spacing on a 10 point font. However, it happens automatically when you select the **Double** option.

Writing a Legal Column

Another popular formatting technique in law firms is to use columns of text, just the same way a newspaper or magazine does. Typically, columns are used in corporate documents, leases, and more.

To format your document to use columns, follow this procedure.

1. Place the cursor in the area of a page where you would like to configure columns.
2. Click the **Format⇨ Columns** menu item. This brings up the screen shown in Figure 18.11.

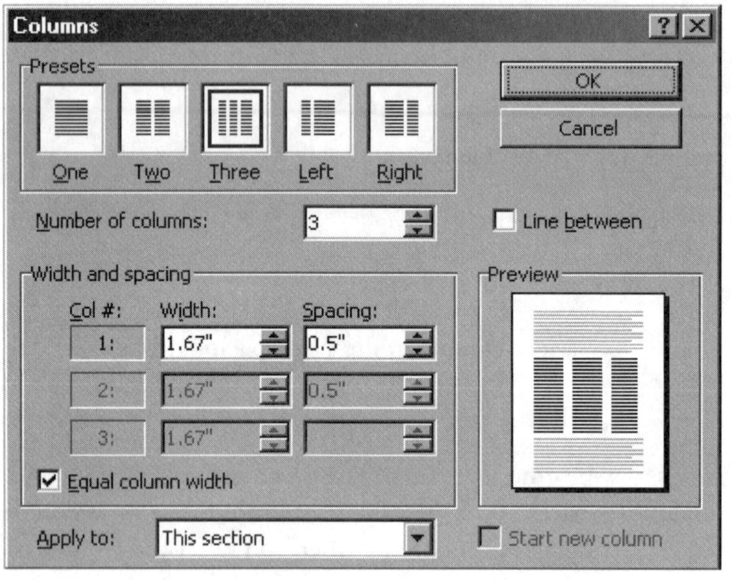

Figure 18.11: Configuring Columns.

3. In the **Number of columns** field, enter the number of columns you wish to configure. You can configure up to twelve columns. However, it is most common to configure one, two, or three, so you can click the corresponding **Preset** picture if desired.

4. If you would like a thin vertical line to appear between columns, check the **Line between** check box.

5. For each column, you can enter the desired width (in inches), or accept just the default value, as you can change it later. The default value is dependent on your page margins.

6. If every column should have the same width, check the **Equal column width** check box. If this box is checked, only Column 1 width and spacing is enabled because all other column values become irrelevant. On the other hand, if you uncheck the **Equal column width** check box, all column width and spacing boxes become enabled and you can change the values if desired.

7. Probably most important is the **Apply to** dropdown list. If you choose **This section**, the column will be created only in the current section. This is likely the option that you want because you probably don't want columns to be created in the entire document.

8. Click the **OK** button to save your changes, close the screen, and configure the section with columns.

To remove your column configuration, simply place the mouse cursor in the area that contains the column-formatted text and bring up the same configuration screen. This time, select the preset labeled **One**, or enter the number **1** into the **Number of columns** field and click the **OK** button. Your text will be formatted as a single column, which is how your default documents are formatted when they are created.

Conclusion

Formatting your documents to conform to strict legal standards can be quite challenging. This is especially true if you come from a WordPerfect environment and don't have much experience using Microsoft Word. Because formatting can easily be a book in its own right, this chapter focused only on the major formatting tasks that you will need to know as a Paralegal who needs to create litigation and other documents. Because tables are one of the most common ways to format text in a Word document, this chapter focused mostly on creating and formatting tables. It also showed you how to configure the document pages themselves, as well as automatic line numbering and double-spacing.

Did you know?

You can format your entire document by using themes. A theme is a collection of settings, such as backgrounds and styles. Themes may not be appropriate for your law office, but you can use them for personal documents. Themes can be seen by clicking the **Format⇨Theme** menu item in Microsoft Word 2003.

Chapter 19

Configuring Headers and Footers

Chapter At A Glance

WHY YOU SHOULD READ THIS CHAPTER:

Headers and footers are a very important (and often misunderstood) feature of Microsoft Office. They are a very powerful way for you to automatically have text placed at the top or bottom of the screen without interfering with the body text. There are some challenges with headers and footers if you are using multiple sections in your documents. This chapter shows you how to manage headers and footers.

PRODUCT OUTLINED IN THIS CHAPTER:

- Microsoft Word 2003
- Microsoft Excel 2003
- Microsoft PowerPoint 2003

PRODUCT FEATURES COVERED IN THIS CHAPTER:

- Headers and Footers

Suppose you are preparing a set of documents for an attorney to take to court. You accidentally bump the table and a several sheets fall to the floor. Which set of documents do they belong to? Without headers and footers, you may not know. Headers and footers provide vital information about a document, such as date, time, file name, file location, case number, and more. Headers and footers are needed in virtually every kind of document. A *header* is a reserved area of the top of a document that contains text that is automatically placed in the reserved area. Likewise, a *footer* is a reserved area at the bottom of the page. Headers often contain things such as document names, section names, and firm names. Footers usually contain document names, document numbers, page numbers, and dates. Too often, people who are not familiar with how headers and footers work will manually type header and footer information into each page of a document. This becomes very unmanageable, especially in large documents. Therefore, after reading this chapter, you'll be able to properly use headers and footers.

Word 2003

As a Paralegal, you are certain to write documents using Word 2003. Often, these documents are complex, and are made up of multiple sections. Each of the sections might have different header and footer requirements. After reading this chapter, you'll be able to configure headers and footers, even in complex documents. To start with, Figure 19.1 shows two sections in a legal document with different headers and footers. Then you'll see how to create them easily. Portions of the image are intentionally blurred to clearly show the significant areas of the figure.

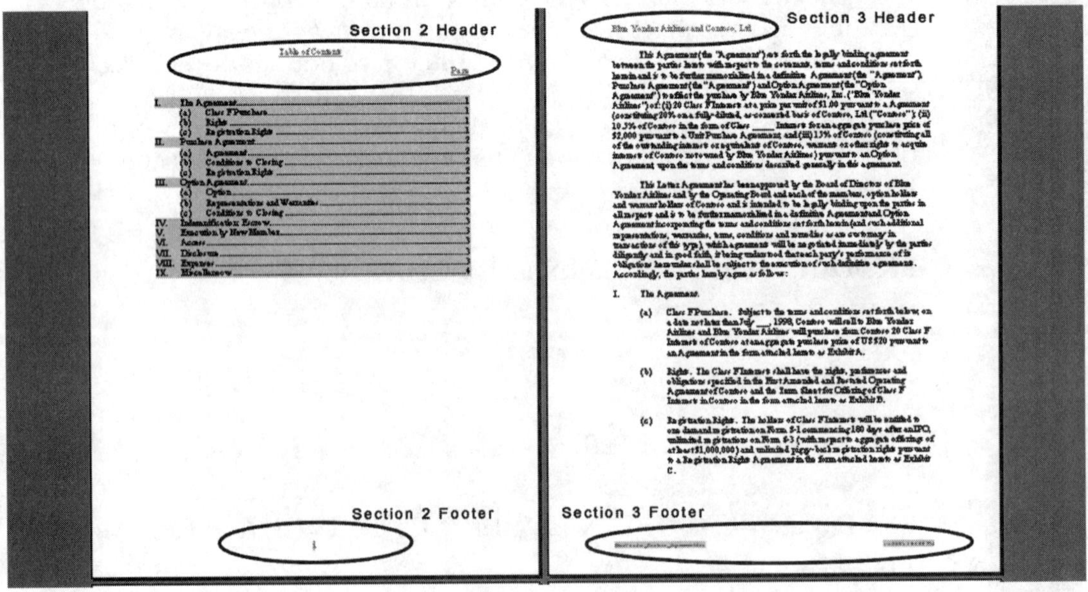

Figure 19.1: Headers and Footers in Two Sections of a Document.

The left-hand page in Figure 19.1 shows the Table of Contents for the document. The header contains the words "Table of Contents," but also contains a label for the column of page numbers, simply called "Page." The footer contains a page number in roman numeral format.

NOTE

The reason you would want to have the heading called "Page" in the document header is because if the Table of Contents spans multiple pages, the header information will automatically span pages also.

The right-hand page is the beginning of the long agreement part of the document. It has a header that is different from the Table of Contents. It contains the names of the parties in the agreement. The footer is not a roman numeral, but instead the file name of the document on the left and the current date/time on the right.

While your legal documents will surely have different requirements for headers and footers, the example shown in the agreement in Figure 19.1 is a good representation of the types of issues you'll face in your complex documents. Before you read the rest of this chapter, it is assumed that each of the different parts of your document that contain different footers are already constructed as different sections of the document. Sections are very easy to create and are discussed in Chapter 17. In fact, sections can be created automatically when you create new pages.

When you manage headers and footers, you use the **Header and Footer** toolbar, which you open by clicking the **View⇨ Header and Footer** menu item. This opens the header within the current section and also brings up the **Header and Footer** toolbar, which is shown in Figure 19.2.

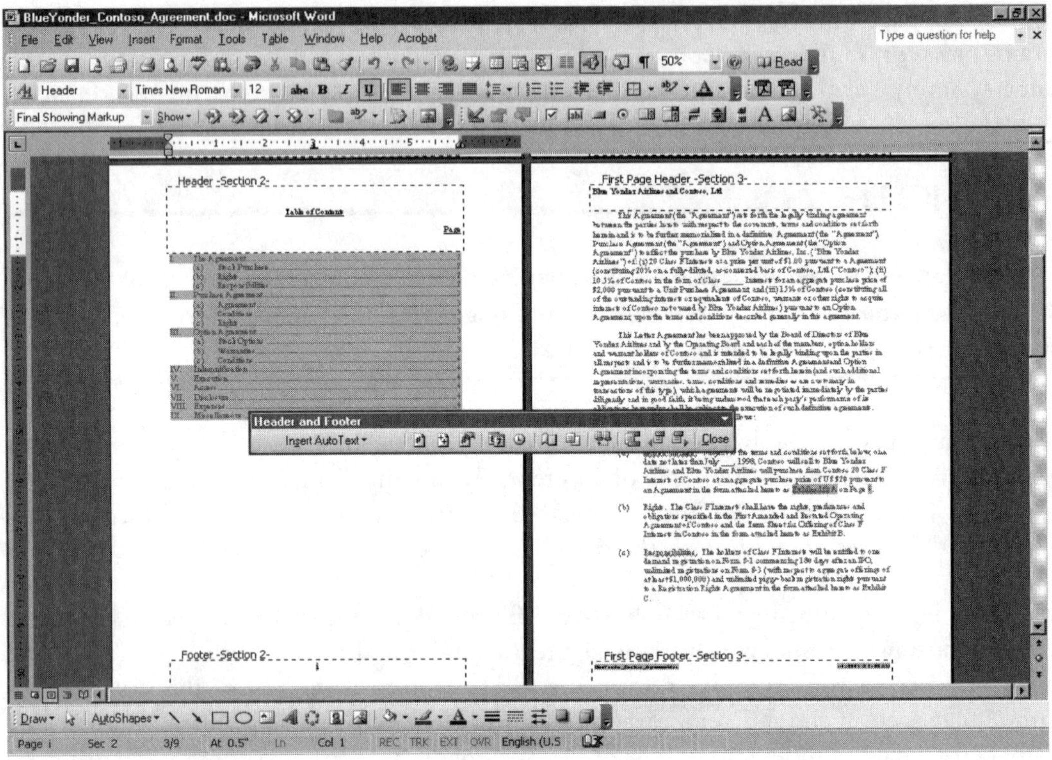

Figure 19.2: Editing Headers and Footers.

There's a lot going on in Figure 19.2, but it's very understandable. Two adjacent pages are shown, each in its own section. You can see this where the headers and footers are automatically labeled **Section 2** and **Section 3**. (This automatically happened when you created a new section in the document.) The dotted outlined boxes that appear at the top and bottom of each page are used to show the header and footer areas when you clicked the **View⇨ Headers and Footers** menu item. Finally, a toolbar magically appeared to help you navigate and format the headers and footers in your document. Figure 19.3 shows a closer look at the **Header and Footer** toolbar.

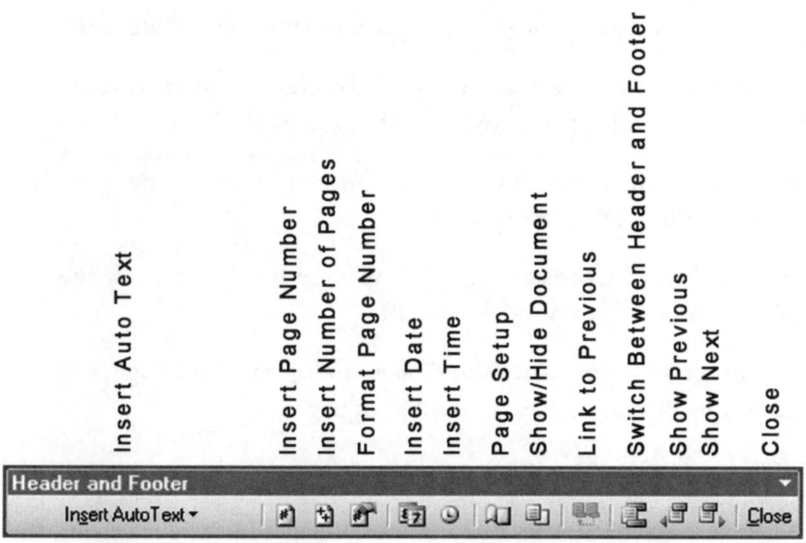

Figure 19.3: Header and Footer Toolbar.

Because headers and footers are so important to your legal documents, here is a detailed listing of each of the tools in the **Header and Footer** toolbar:

- **INSERT AUTO TEXT** — Inserts special text that is stored along with the document. Special text can be a combination of actual text and variables. A variable is substituted with constant values by Word 2003. For example, if you want a page to read "Page 1 of 5" then the "1" and the "5" are variables, as these values must be free to change as your document grows or shrinks. On the other hand, "Page" and "of" are constant values. You can choose from these Auto Text options:

    - **PAGE** — This is the same as clicking the **Insert Page Number** button.

    - **AUTHOR, PAGE #, DATE** — Inserts not only the author of the document, but also the page number and the date of the last save. This is a very convenient feature whereby the author is left-aligned, the page number is centered, and the date is right-aligned.

    - **CONFIDENTIAL, PAGE #, DATE** — Inserts the constant value "Confidential," the page number, and date of the last document save. Again, the first value is left-aligned, the second is centered, and the third is right-aligned.

    - **CREATED BY** — Inserts the constant value "Created by," followed by the name of the person who initially created the document.

    - **CREATED ON** — Inserts the constant value "Created on," followed by the date the document was initially created.

- **Filename** — Inserts the actual name of the file as it exists on your hard disk.
- **Filename and path** — Inserts the actual name of the file as it exists on your hard disk plus the file location, also known as the *path*.
- **Last printed** — Inserts the constant value "Last printed," followed by the date and time the document was last printed.
- **Last saved by** — Inserts the constant value "Last saved by," followed by the name of the person who last saved the document.
- **Page X of Y** — Inserts the constant value "Page," followed by the page number, the constant "of," and the total number of pages.

- **Insert Page Number** — Inserts the current page number within the document.
- **Insert Number of Pages** — Inserts the total number of pages in the document. This number is automatically updated when you add or remove pages in the document.
- **Format Page Number** — Allows you to indicate how you want the page numbers formatted. You can choose from roman numerals, letters, or numbers. You can even indicate whether you want the numbering to restart or continue from the previous section. This option gives you tremendous flexibility in presenting your documents because the sections can follow a completely different format from each other, but also be numbered as if they are part of a complete document that you present to the court or a client.
- **Insert Date** — Inserts the current date.
- **Insert Time** — Inserts the current time.
- **Page Setup** — Opens the **Page Setup** screen. This screen is shown in Chapter 17.
- **Show/Hide Document Text** — Temporarily toggles between showing body text on the screen (the area outside the headers and footers) and hiding that text. Hiding the text may make it easier for you to concentrate on formatting your headers and footers without becoming distracted.
- **Link to Previous** — Enables you to use the header or footer from the previous section. This button is only enabled if your document contains more than one section. Remember, one of the biggest reasons to create multiple sections in a document is to use different headers and footers. However, if you don't want to configure a separate footer for a section, but you want to use the previous one instead, this is the way to

do it. Clicking the **Link to Previous** button will automatically use the header or footer (depending on the current active area) from the previous section without needing to do anything else. With most legal documents, you will likely not use this option.

- **SWITCH BETWEEN HEADER AND FOOTER** — Alternates the active area between header and footer (and vice versa) on the same page.
- **SHOW PREVIOUS** — Moves to the previous header or footer, depending on the current carat location. If the header is active, the **Show Previous** button will move to the header on the previous page and make it active. Likewise, if the footer is active, the **Show Previous** button will move to the footer on the previous page and make it active.
- **SHOW NEXT** — Acts exactly as the **Show Previous** button, but moves to the next page instead of the previous page.
- **CLOSE** — Closes all headers and footers and also the toolbar. Any changes that you made in those headers and footers will be displayed in the document, but they won't be saved until the document itself is saved.

It is important to realize that any of the fields in the previous list can appear in a header or footer. It's up to you as the document creator to determine what is required in the headers and footers of your documents.

Heading Word Off at the Pass

Knowing how the **Header and Footer** toolbar works, you can create the header shown in Figure 19.1 by following these directions:

1. Position the carat anywhere on the page that contains the section for which you will create or modify the header. You may need to insert a new section break by clicking the **Insert⇨ Break** menu item and choosing from the desired section break types. Section breaks are covered in Chapter 17.
2. Open the **Header and Footer** toolbar. This opens a blank area for the header.
3. To create a header that reads "Table of Contents," simply type `Table of Contents` in the header.
4. Format this line by centering it. You can do this by simply clicking the **Center** button in the **Formatting** toolbar (not on the **Header and Footer** toolbar). If you don't see this button, refer to Chapter 4.

5. To create a line that reads "Page," press the **Enter** key twice and type `Page`, but don't press the **Enter** key again. Note that if you press the **Enter** key again, a new line is created in the header and it may appear taller than you expect.

6. Format this line by right-aligning it. You can do this by simply clicking the **Right Align** button in the **Formatting** toolbar.

7. Ensure the **Link to Previous** button on the **Header and Footer** toolbar is not selected. Unselecting this option ensures that the current section does not use the header or footer values from the previous section. This is a very important concept to grasp, as using it incorrectly can cause many headaches for your header and footer formatting.

8. Click the **Show Next** button on the **Header and Footer** toolbar to jump to the header in the next section. This section, according to Figure 19.1, simply shows a brief title for the document.

9. Enter your brief title, such as `Blue Yonder Airlines and Contoso, Ltd.`

10. If you have additional headers to enter, continue to click the **Show Next** button and enter those headers the same way.

That's it for the header. You're now ready to move on to the footer, which is discussed next.

Ensuring Your Footers Don't Stink

Effective footers are just as important as effective headers. You need to know what is required by the court or your client, but probably more important is that you actually use the footers (and headers) to communicate effectively and not just fill space on the page.

Footers are entered just like headers are. To continue with the example shown in Figure 19.1, here's how you enter the footers:

1. Position the carat anywhere on the page that contains the section for which you will create or modify the footer.

2. Open the **Header and Footer** toolbar if it is not already open.

3. Ensure the **Link to Previous** button is not selected.

4. Click the **Switch Between Header and Footer** button.

5. In Figure 19.1, the footer in Section 2 is the page number shown in roman numerals. Click the **Insert Page Number** button.

6. If the page number isn't shown in roman numerals, click the **Format Page Number** button and select the roman numeral option in the **Number format** dropdown list.
7. Format this line by centering it. You can do this by simply clicking the **Center** button in the **Formatting** toolbar (not on the **Header and Footer** toolbar). If you don't see this button, refer to Chapter 4.
8. Click the **Show Next** button on the **Header and Footer** toolbar to jump to the footer in the next section. This section, according to Figure 19.1, shows the document file name on the left and the current date and time on the right.
9. Click the **Insert Auto Text** button.
10. Click the **Filename** option. You'll see the file name appear in the footer. Click the **Left Align** button on the **Formatting** toolbar.
11. Press the **Tab** key to move the carat to the center position in the footer.
12. Press the **Tab** key one more time to move the carat to the right position in the footer.
13. Click the **Insert Date** button.
14. Press the space bar. If you do not do this, the time will appear immediately after the date, with no spaces.
15. Click the **Insert Time** button.
16. Click the **Close** button.
17. If you have additional footers to enter, continue to click the **Show Next** button and enter those footers the same way.

Your footer will now be formatted according to the one shown in Figure 19.1.

Excel 2003

Excel 2003 headers and footers are similar, but not as robust. Excel 2003 headers and footers are not divided into sections. In fact, headers and footers are displayed on every page, but the same concept applies to Excel 2003 as it does to Word 2003. Here's how you configure headers and footers in Excel 2003:

1. Open Excel 2003.

2. Click the **View⇨ Header and Footer** menu item. This brings up the screen shown in Figure 19.4.

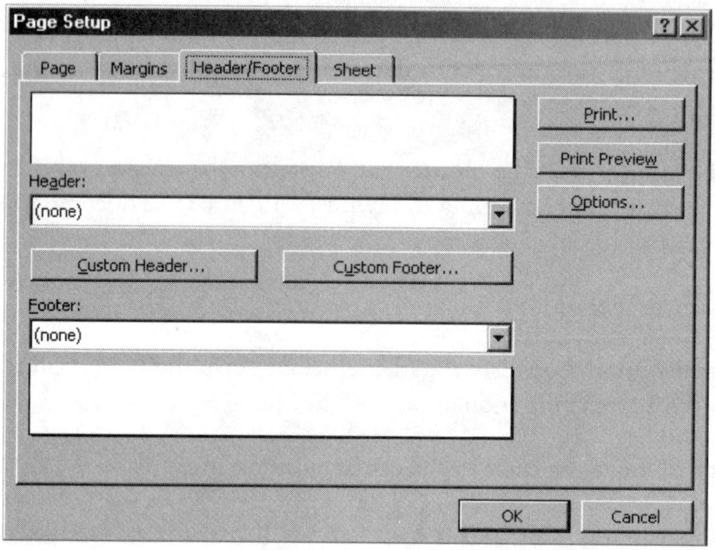

Figure 19.4: Excel 2003 Headers and Footers.

3. Select the desired header from the **Header** dropdown list.

4. If you don't see the header that you would like to use, click the **Custom Header** button and enter your header information, which brings up the screen shown in Figure 19.5. Note that every time you create a custom header, the custom information is stored in the **Header** dropdown list for easy selection next time.

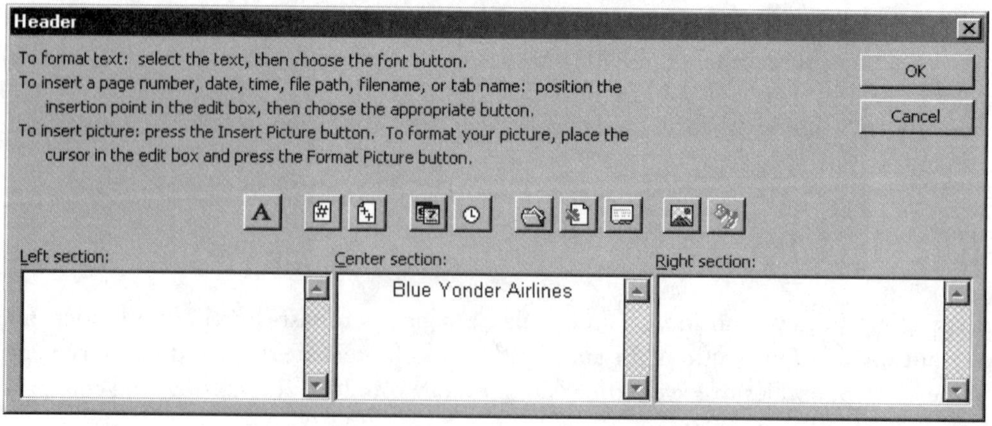

Figure 19.5: Customizing an Excel 2003 Header.

5. The screen is divided into three sections: left, center, and right. Choose from the desired buttons to select special fields as you did in the Word 2003 **Header and Footer** toolbar. You can also enter constant text, such as that shown in Figure 19.5.

6. Click the **OK** button to close the **Header** screen and save your changes.

7. Repeat the same procedure for the footer.

PowerPoint 2003

Like Excel 2003, the support for headers and footers in PowerPoint 2003 is not as robust as it is in Word 2003. However, unlike Excel 2003, where headers and footers are exactly the same on every page, PowerPoint 2003 allows you to create separate headers and footers for each slide. You can also create separate headers and footers for notes and handouts.

⚠ CAUTION

Surprisingly enough, the term "header" doesn't mean the same thing in PowerPoint 2003 as it does in Word 2003 or Excel 2003. In PowerPoint 2003, information that you may wish to place in a header, such as the date, must be placed at the bottom of the page instead. To get around this limitation, some people use backgrounds that contain the desired information already in the image.

To create headers and footers in PowerPoint 2003, follow these steps:

1. Open PowerPoint 2003.

2. Click the **View⇨ Header and Footer** menu item. This brings up the screen shown in Figure 19.6.

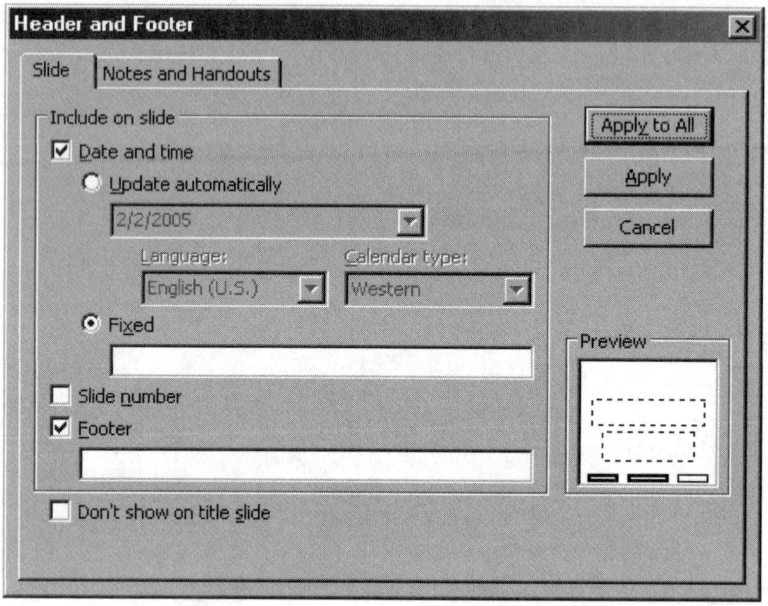

Figure 19.6: Customizing PowerPoint 2003 Slide Header and Footer.

3. Select the items to display at the bottom of your PowerPoint slides. You can choose from:

   - **Date and time** —Inserts the date and time in the bottom-left part of the slide, based on the option you choose. You can click the **Update automatically** option to have the date and time always reflect the current date and time, or select the **Fixed** option and enter the date and time to display.

   - **Slide number** — Inserts the slide number in the bottom-right part of the slide.

   - **Footer** — Inserts custom text that you type in the text box provided. This text will appear in the center on the bottom of the slide.

4. Click the **Apply to All** button to apply your changes to every slide in the PowerPoint slide deck.

5. Click the **Apply** button to apply changes only to the current slide.

Conclusion

Headers and footers can be extremely powerful ways to format your documents according to court specifications or for clients. Headers and footers enable you to save a tremendous amount of time by automatically placing information in a reserved area at the top or bottom of your Word 2003 documents. Configuring your Word documents to use headers and footers means that you typically have multiple sections in complex documents. Multiple sections allow you to format headers and footers differently in the same document for ultimate flexibility. There is less robust support for headers and footers in Excel 2003 and PowerPoint 2003, but it is supported. This chapter showed the detailed steps to follow for configuring headers and footers in the Microsoft Office 2003 products.

Did you know?

You can use almost all formatting features of Word 2003 inside your header and footer. This includes font names, sizes, colors, justification, and more.

Chapter 20

Managing Styles

Chapter At A Glance

WHY YOU SHOULD READ THIS CHAPTER:

If you find yourself creating the same types of documents all the time, you'll probably love to learn that there is a way to apply consistent formatting to your documents. This is accomplished in Word 2003 by defining and applying Word Styles. This chapter shows you how to create and manage your styles.

PRODUCT OUTLINED IN THIS CHAPTER:

- Microsoft Word 2003

PRODUCT FEATURES COVERED IN THIS CHAPTER:

- Word 2003 Styles

As a Paralegal, you probably find yourself creating the same types of documents over and over again. Such documents include agreements, pleadings, wills, and more. To ensure consistent formatting, you should consider using Word 2003 Styles. *Styles* are a way for you to manage a collection of settings that you apply to a given use of the text in a document. This collection of settings includes font names, font sizes, spacing, indentation, and more. You give each collection of settings a name, which will be referred to simply as style. For example, you might have defined **Heading 1**, **Heading 2**, **Heading 3**, and **Body** styles. Assigning a style to your document text applies all the formatting and settings that make up the style. Styles can be configured to affect entire paragraphs, specific characters, tables, and listings. When the style is created, you specify what type of style you are creating. In this chapter, you'll learn how to create and apply styles to your legal documents.

NOTE

Prior to Word 2002, directly formatting your text within your paragraphs could cause many problems, such as footnotes becoming fractured. Using styles prevented this problem. However, it is still a very good practice to use styles to format your legal documents.

The settings that you can set for a style are stored in these basic categories:

- **FONT** — Font name, size, color, character spacing, and text effect options
- **PARAGRAPH** — Alignment, indentation, and paragraph spacing options
- **TABS** — Tab stop positions
- **BORDER** — Border and shading options
- **LANGUAGE** — Selects the language for the style
- **FRAME** — Text frame and wrapping options
- **NUMBERING** — Bullets and numbering options
- **SHORTCUT KEY** — Selects a shortcut key for the style to be applied

When you create a style, you specify any or all of the options in the above categories. The main advantage in using a style is that you apply it to text or a paragraph and you can get it to look a certain way with just one mouse click. This can help you to format your legal documents according to any standard, such as your firm's, that of a court, a client, and more.

It's difficult to say how many styles you need for your legal documents and what you should name your styles. The answer to this question certainly depends on the types of documents you draft, such as pleadings, wills, and real estate agreements. For a pleading, you may need to have styles that specify formatting for:

- Attorney name
- Firm name
- Double-spacing the body of the document
- Signature block
- Footer
- Caption box

On the other hand, for a rental agreement, you may need to have styles that specify formatting for:

- Document title
- Attorney name
- Firm name
- Section name
- Section number
- Body text
- Signature block
- Numbered list
- Page number

The bottom line is that you need to determine which styles make sense for the types of documents that you are creating. Also, if the documents are created for litigation, you probably need to create your styles to make sure they conform to courtroom document specifications.

You've Got Style

You can apply a style to text in one of two ways — from the **Style** dropdown list in the **Formatting** toolbar or from the **Styles and Formatting** task pane. What's the difference you may ask? Both let you select an existing style, but only the **Styles and Formatting** task pane lets you create a new style. There is one other difference. The **Style** dropdown list from the **Formatting** toolbar shows a listing of all styles, but the **Styles and Formatting** task pane shows each style in the correct font with a preview of formatting options, such as boxes, underlines, bold, and more. Take a look at Figure 20.1. It shows how to apply a style from both the **Style** dropdown list in the **Formatting** toolbar and the **Styles and Formatting** task pane.

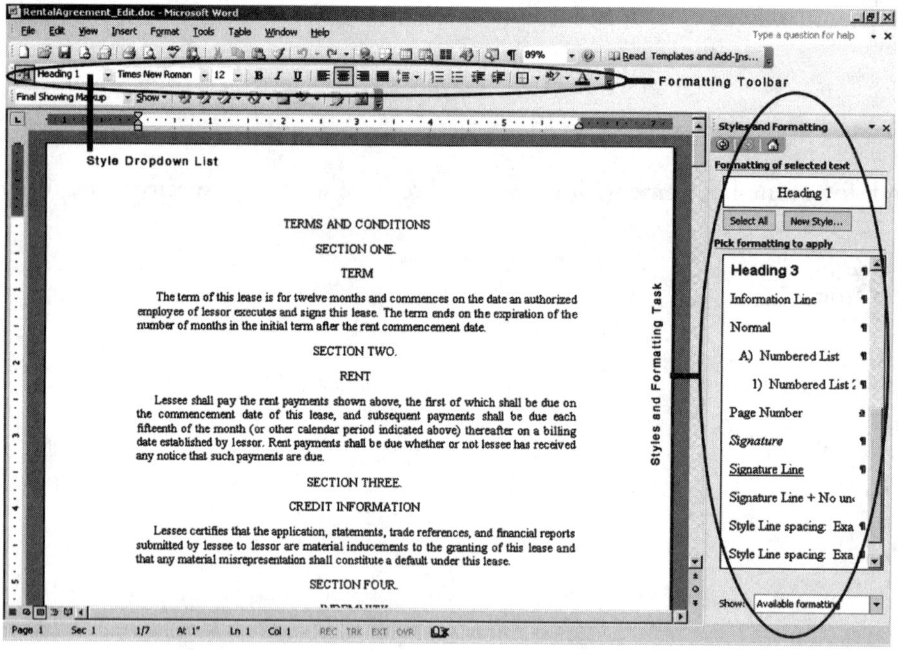

Figure 20.1: Applying a Style.

Because the **Styles and Formatting** task pane has everything you need to select and create styles, the rest of this chapter assumes that you are using this means of managing styles in your documents.

To apply a style to your text, follow these simple steps:

1. Open the desired document in Microsoft Word.

2. Select the desired text that will have the style applied. Alternatively, you can place the carat anywhere in a paragraph (without selecting any text) and the style will be applied to the entire paragraph.

3. Open the **Styles and Formatting** task pane (if it is not already open) by clicking the **Styles⇨ Styles and Formatting** menu item.

4. Find the style name that you wish to apply by scrolling within the **Styles and Formatting** task pane.

5. Click the desired style name. Depending on the type of style, you'll see your paragraph, selected characters, table, or list change to reflect the characteristics of the style.

Everybody Can Be More Stylish

You can easily create your own styles for use in your legal documents. However, before you do, you first have to know how to configure your text manually, because after all, a style is simply a collection of formatting options. If you don't know how to alter the formatting settings within Word to make the text appear the way you want, you won't be able to configure your style correctly, so make sure you know what to do to make your text appear correctly.

To create a style, follow this procedure:

1. Open the **Styles and Formatting** task pane.

2. Click the **New Style** button, which brings up the **New Style** screen. The way the screen looks depends completely on the options chosen on the screen. Each is shown later in the next step.

3. Fill in or select data for these fields:

   - **NAME** — Enter the name of your style. This is the name that you will see in all lists that present styles.

   - **STYLE TYPE** — Select the way the style will be used. You can choose from **Paragraph**, **Character**, **Table**, or **List**. The default type for your styles is **Paragraph**, as this is the most common type to create in your legal documents. However, a **List** style type runs a close second. A **Paragraph** style type is just like it sounds; it is applied to an entire paragraph, while a **List** style type applies to numbered lists. As your legal documents are likely to have many numbered lists, such as paragraph numbers, you will be using this type of style.

   - **STYLE BASED ON** — Select an existing style that will be used as a starting point for the new style. This will prevent you from having to create the style from scratch. The **Style based on** field is not available for a **List** style type.

- **STYLE FOR FOLLOWING PARAGRAPH** — Select an existing style that will be automatically applied to the paragraph immediately following the one on which you apply a style. The **Style for following paragraph** field is available only for the **Paragraph** style type.

- **FORMATTING** — Enables you to configure basic style options, but depends on the type style you selected in the **Style type** field.

  For paragraph styles, you can specify formatting that affects a paragraph as a whole. You can specify things like font name, font size, font color, bolding, italicizing, and underlining. You can also specify the alignment of the paragraph, such as left-aligned, center-aligned, right-aligned, and justified (left-aligned and right-aligned). Furthermore, you can indicate line spacing options for your paragraphs including single-spacing, double-spacing, and triple spacing. Paragraph spacing options are also included to allow more or less spacing between the paragraph for which you defining a style and the following paragraph. To learn where each of these options is located on the screen, simply hold the mouse over the buttons and you'll see a tool tip balloon that tells you what the button does. Paragraph styles are defined for things like document titles, body text, or even to setup a pleading caption box. Paragraph styles are the most common type of style that you will use in your legal documents. Figure 20.2 shows the options available for a paragraph style.

NOTE

In each of the screens shown in Figures 20.2 through 20.5, the top circles point out the Style type **field and the bottom circles indicate the formatting options available for each** Style type.

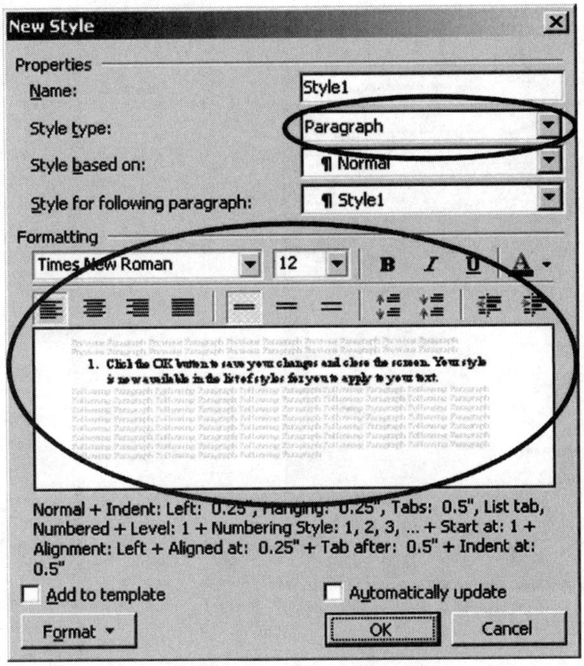

Figure 20.2: Formatting Options for Paragraph Styles.

Similar to the way paragraph styles change the characteristics of an entire paragraph, a character style applies only to selected characters in your document. There are fewer options available to a character style because one or more selected characters are not affected by spacing or alignment. However, you can specify the font name, font size, bolding, italicizing, underlining, and font color for the character style. A character style is sometimes used in legal documents for citations. Figure 20.3 shows the options available for character styles.

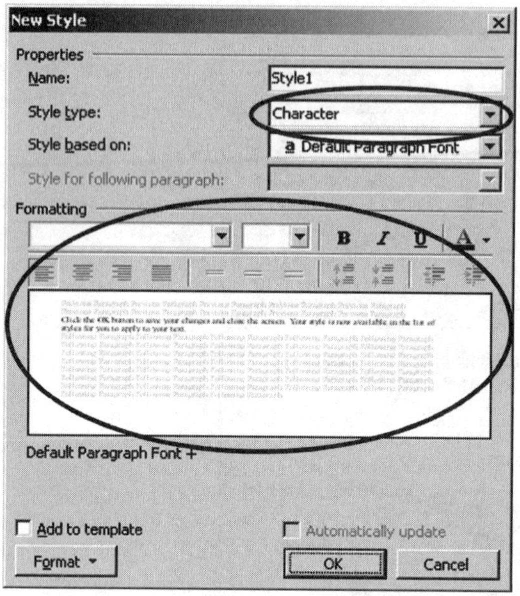

Figure 20.3: Formatting Options for Character Styles.

Table styles affect how a Word table behaves. Not only can you specify the things that paragraph styles allow, but you also configure a style to include line widths, line colors, justification of the cell contents, and more. Tables can be useful to help you configure caption boxes that are used in pleadings. Tables are discussed further in Chapter 18, but the options for a table style are shown in Figure 20.4.

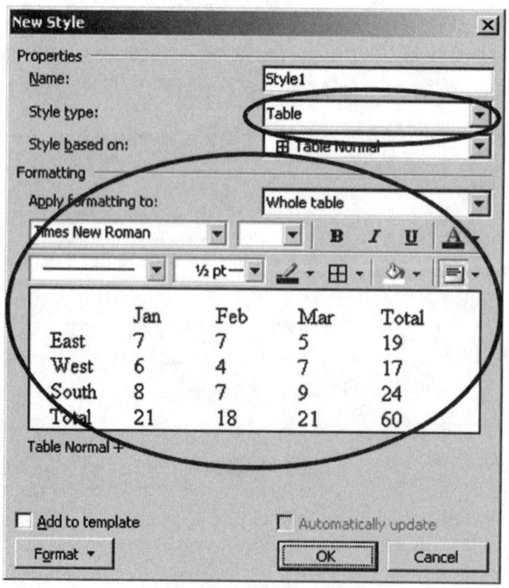

Figure 20.4: Formatting Options for Table Styles.

A list style affects the formatting of a numbered or bulleted list. As all types of legal documents contain numbered and bulleted lists, it can be helpful to define styles that automatically format these items. You can specify the number or bulleting style, the font name, font size, font color, indenting options, and more. Figure 20.5 shows the list style options available in Word 2003.

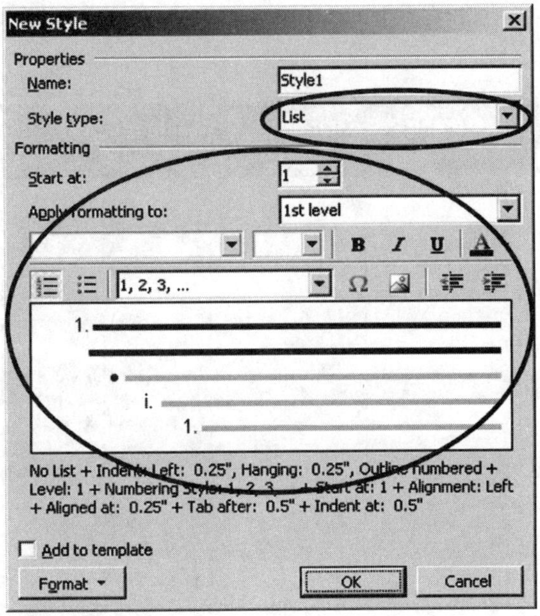

Figure 20.5: Formatting Options for List Styles.

- **ADD TO TEMPLATE** — Check this box if the currently selected template is to contain your new style. Unless you attach a new template, the new style will be saved to the **Normal** template.

⚠ CAUTION

Updating the Normal template will affect the styles available when you create a new document. This may be a desired effect for your firm, but chances are you don't want to select this option.

- **AUTOMATICALLY UPDATE** — Check this box if you want any manual formatting changes to selected text to automatically update the style applied to that text.

⚠ CAUTION

Using this option might cause your style to be updated when you didn't intend for it to be.

- **FORMAT** — This button presents more advanced formatting options. Table 20.1 shows which advanced formatting option categories are available for each **Style type**.

Advanced Formatting Options	Paragraph	Character	Table	List
Font	X	X	X	X
Paragraph	X		X	
Tabs	X		X	
Border	X	X		
Language	X	X		
Frame	X			
Numbering	X			X
Shortcut Key	X	X		X
Table Properties			X	
Borders and Shading			X	
Stripes			X	

Table 20.1: Advanced Formatting Option Categories for Each Style Type.

Because they are the most common formatting types that you will likely encounter, more details about **Paragraph** and **List** formatting types are described later in this chapter.

4. Click the **OK** button to save your changes and close the screen. Your style is now available in the list of styles for you to apply to your text.

Specifying Paragraph Formatting Options

It is likely that you'll need to create a style for preparing your documents to go to court. For example, you may need to create a style called **LegalBody**, which simply formats a paragraph to use the Courier New font with a size of 12 points. To do so, follow this procedure:

1. Create a new style and name it **LegalBody**. The creation of new styles is covered in the section "Everybody Can Be More Stylish."

2. Specify **Paragraph** in the **Style type** dropdown list.

3. In the **Formatting** section of the screen, select **Courier New** in the dropdown list of fonts.

4. Select **12** in the dropdown list of font sizes.

5. You can also specify any additional formatting features that you wish your style to have, such as centered justification, double-spacing, and more.

6. Click the **OK** button to create your style. It is now available to select for use with a paragraph.

NOTE

It is impossible to cover each and every formatting option in a single chapter, so it's best that you understand the concepts and the mechanics of how to build your styles.

Specifying List Formatting Options

In addition to specifying paragraph formatting options, as a Paralegal you probably need to specify styles and options that apply to lists. Many paragraphs in legal documents are numbered, as in the case of a contract. You may wish to create a style called **LegalBodyNum**, which uses a Times New Roman font with a size of 12 points and uses arabic numerals (1, 2, 3, etc.), starting at the number 1. Here's how you create the style:

1. Create a new style and name it **LegalBodyNum**.

2. Specify **List** in the **Style type** dropdown list.

3. Select **1** in the **Start at** field.

4. In the **Formatting** section of the screen, select **Times New Roman** in the dropdown list of fonts.

5. Select **12** in the dropdown list of font sizes.

6. Select **1, 2, 3...** in the dropdown list of numbering options.

7. You can also specify any additional formatting features that you wish your style to have, such as centered justification, double-spacing, and more.

8. Click the **OK** button to create your style. It is now available to select for use with a paragraph. Every time you apply your style to a subsequent paragraph, it will receive a successive number.

Bulleting and numbering is covered further in Chapter 21.

NOTE

There are other non-Microsoft tools available for formatting your numbered lists, such as the NumberingSuite from SoftWise. For more information, visit their Web site at `www.SoftWise.net`.

Modifying and Deleting Styles

To modify or delete a style, do the following:

1. Move the mouse over the desired style in the **Styles and Formatting** task pane. You'll see a dropdown arrow on the right-hand side of the name of the style.
2. Click the dropdown list arrow.
3. Click the **Modify Style** or **Delete** menu item. If you modify a style, you specify properties exactly the same way you did when you created the style. If you delete a style, you are prompted to confirm the deletion first.

Conclusion

Word 2003 Styles offer a great way to configure your formatting options into a convenient package. One you configure a style, you can apply it to any text in your documents and the text will automatically adopt all characteristics, formatting, and options that are defined in the style. While Word 2003 comes with some styles already built into the **Normal** template, you can easily create your own — provided that you know how you want your paragraphs and text formatted. The bottom line is…if you don't know how to manually format your documents, you won't be able to create a style to do it for you. Therefore, it is very important to know how to format your documents manually. Chapters 18, 19, and 21 can help you understand formatting your documents. This chapter showed you how to create, modify, and delete Word 2003 Styles for use in your legal documents.

Chapter 21

Bulleting and Numbering

Chapter At A Glance

WHY YOU SHOULD READ THIS CHAPTER

Bulleting and Numbering is a very important mechanism in formatting your legal documents. Almost all legal documents have paragraphs that are numbered and contain bulleted lists of items. This chapter shows you how to use Microsoft Word 2003 to format the numbers and bullets in your legal documents.

PRODUCT OUTLINED IN THIS CHAPTER:

- Microsoft Word 2003

PRODUCT FEATURES COVERED IN THIS CHAPTER:

- Bullets and Numbering

At first glance, numbering seems to be different from bulleting. In fact, they are quite similar. Numbering refers to a numbered list and bulleting refers to a bulleted list. You see, both numbering and bulleting are just lists of items. When you construct your legal documents, it is very easy to switch between numbers and bullets (and vice versa).

Bullets and numbering have traditionally been a problem for many Paralegals. Microsoft Word alone can handle bullets and numbering, but sometimes gets quite complex for legal documents. There are some third-party numbering software packages that automate legal document numbering, such as Innova from SoftWise (`www.SoftWise.net`).

To illustrate using Microsoft Word's numbering features, Listing 21.1 shows a simple numbered list (appearing in roman numerals) which you might see in a purchase agreement:

```
I.          The Agreement
II.         Purchase Agreement
III.        Option Agreement
IV.         Indemnification
V.          Execution
VI.         Access
VII.        Disclosure
VIII.       Expenses
IX.         Miscellaneous
```

Listing 21.1: Sample Numbered List in Roman Numeral Format.

Alternatively, Listing 21.2 shows the exact same numbered list with the numerals appearing in arabic format:

```
1.    The Agreement
2.    Purchase Agreement
3.    Option Agreement
4.    Indemnification
5.    Execution
6.    Access
7.    Disclosure
8.    Expenses
9.    Miscellaneous
```

Listing 21.2: Sample Numbered List in Arabic Format.

Notice the difference in horizontal spacing between the numbering in Listing 21.1 and 21.2. There is less space between the number in Listing 21.2 than there is in Listing 21.1. This is because the roman numerals take more space than the arabic numerals and so the text is pushed to the next tab location. These are the types of things you need to keep in mind as you consider how to use numbering and bulleting in your documents.

Being Gun-shy About Bulleting

Bullets are used to list items where the numeric sequence of those items is not significant. Most legal documents use numbering because specific paragraphs can then be referenced by number. When a paragraph or item is bulleted, you cannot specifically locate that item, as all bullets look the same.

Bullets are sometimes used in simple documents, such as memos, letters, and brochures. They are not typically used in other types of legal documents that require complex numbering.

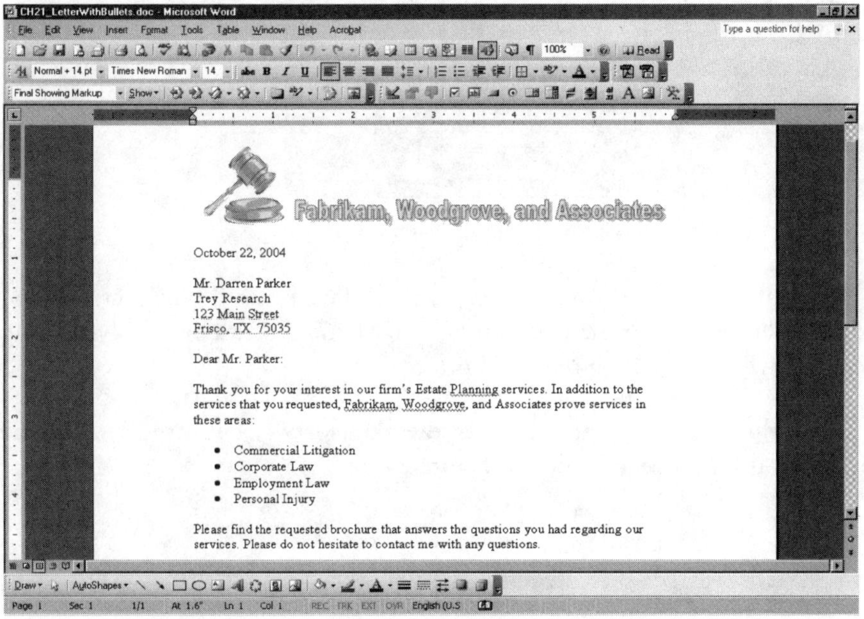

Figure 21.1: Example of Bullets in a Document.

To create a bulleted list, follow these steps:

1. Type your text with one item on each line.
2. With the mouse or keyboard, select the lines of text that you want to bullet.

3. Click the **Bullets** button on the **Formatting** toolbar. For more information about where this button is located, see Chapter 4. The selected lines of text are now presented as bullets.

4. To change the format of the bullets, click the **Format⇨ Bullets and Numbering** menu item. This brings up the screen shown in Figure 21.2.

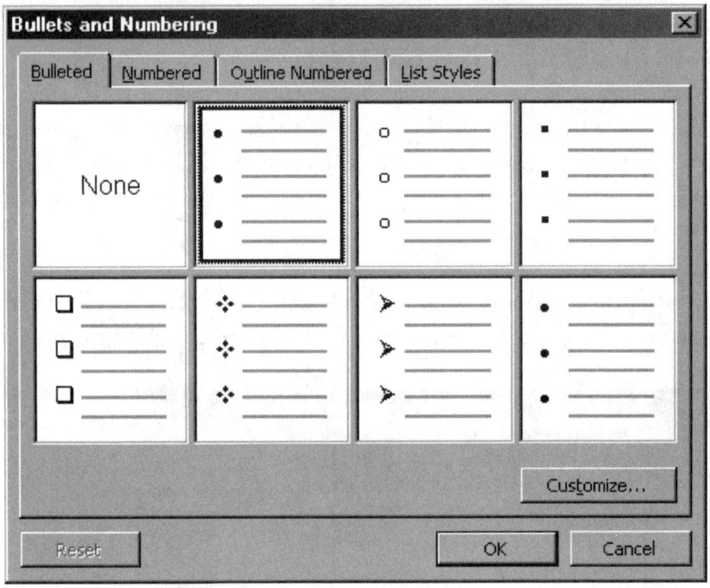

Figure 21.2: Configuring Bulleted Items in the Bullets and Numbering Screen.

5. By default, round bullets are used when you click the **Bullets** button. However, you can select any of the bullet formats presented in the seven pictured boxes by simply clicking the desired bullet style and clicking the **OK** button.

6. To specify any additional parameters besides the bullet style, click the **Customize** button. This brings up the screen shown in Figure 21.3.

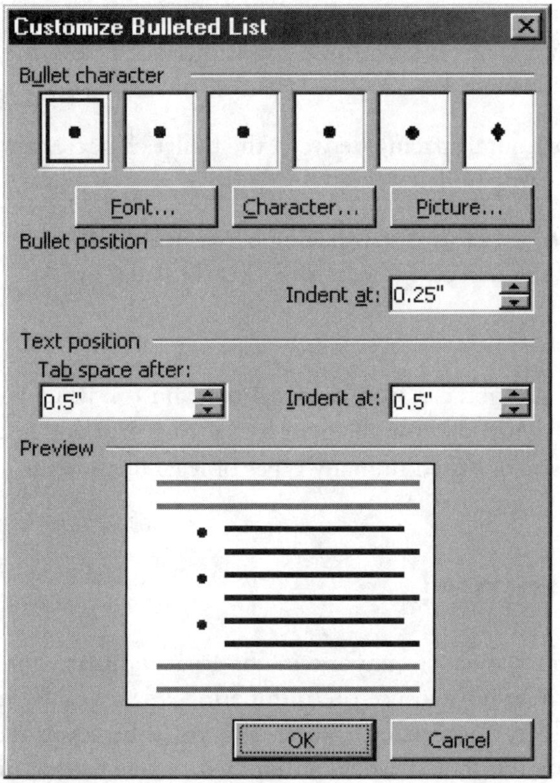

Figure 21.3: Customizing Bulleted Lists.

When you customize your bulleted lists, you can choose from these options:

- **Bullet Character** — Series of six picture boxes that are used to select the bullet character to be displayed.
- **Font** — Font used for the bullet character. By default, the Symbol font is used, but you may have a bullet character that resides in a different font.
- **Character** — Further options for the bullet character if the six picture boxes aren't sufficient.
- **Picture** — Allows you to select an image to be used as a bullet character. This is probably not applicable to legal applications.

- **INDENT AT (BULLET POSITION)** — Horizontal spacing before the bullet character starts. The default is one quarter inch and is measured from the start position of the previous line.
- **TAB SPACE AFTER** — Horizontal spacing between the bullet character and the start of the text on the first bulleted line.
- **INDENT AT (TEXT POSITION)** — Horizontal spacing between the bullet character and the start of the text on lines after the first bulleted line.

Bulleted lists are really that easy. Typically, you can just use the **Bullets** button when you need a bulleted list in a legal document. Now that you know all about formatting your documents with bullets, let's move on to numbering, which is used in many types of legal documents.

Word's Got Your Number!

Automatic numbering should be a great friend to anyone in the legal industry, but it is not without its challenges. You have to know how to use the numbering feature of Word or you may become frustrated at times. Well, fear not! After reading this, you'll be comfortable with formatting your Word documents using numbered lists. If you only have one level of numbered items, such as the one shown in Listing 21.1, numbering is quite simple. It starts to get more complex when you have multiple levels of numbering.

One Level

If you know that you are going to have only one level of numbering in your document, such as a simple letter or memo, you can read this section. However, if there is any possibility that you will use the document with more than one level, it is a good idea to follow the procedure listed under "Multiple Levels" later in this chapter. If your Word document has a single level of numbering, as does the example shown in Listing 21.1, you can easily format the text using Word's numbering features, like this:

1. Type your text with one numbered item on each line.
2. With the mouse or keyboard, select the lines of text that you will want to be numbered.

3. Click the **Numbering** button on the **Formatting** toolbar. For more information about where this button is located, see Chapter 4. The selected lines of text are now presented as sequential numbers.

4. To change the format of the numbers, click the **Format⇨ Bullets and Numbering** menu item. This brings up the screen shown in Figure 21.4.

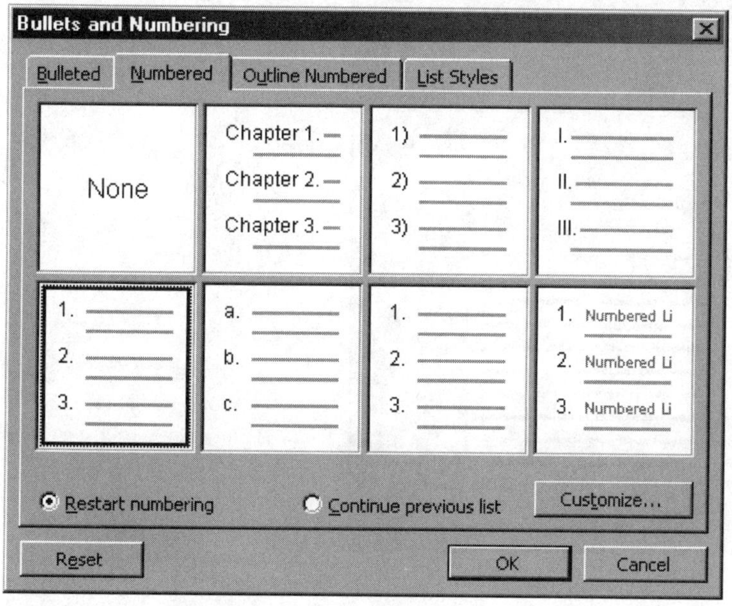

Figure 21.4: Configuring Numbered Items in the Bullets and Numbering Screen.

5. By default, numbered items use a numeral format, followed by a period when you click the **Numbering** button. However, you can select any of the numbering formats presented in the seven pictured boxes by simply clicking the desired style and clicking the **OK** button.

6. If there is a previous numbered list in your document, the **Restart numbering** and **Continue previous list** options become enabled. Select the **Restart numbering** option if you want the current list to begin at number **1**. Otherwise, if you want the list to continue with the next number from the previous list, click the **Continue previous list** option.

7. To specify any additional parameters besides the number style, click the **Customize** button. This brings up the screen shown in Figure 21.5.

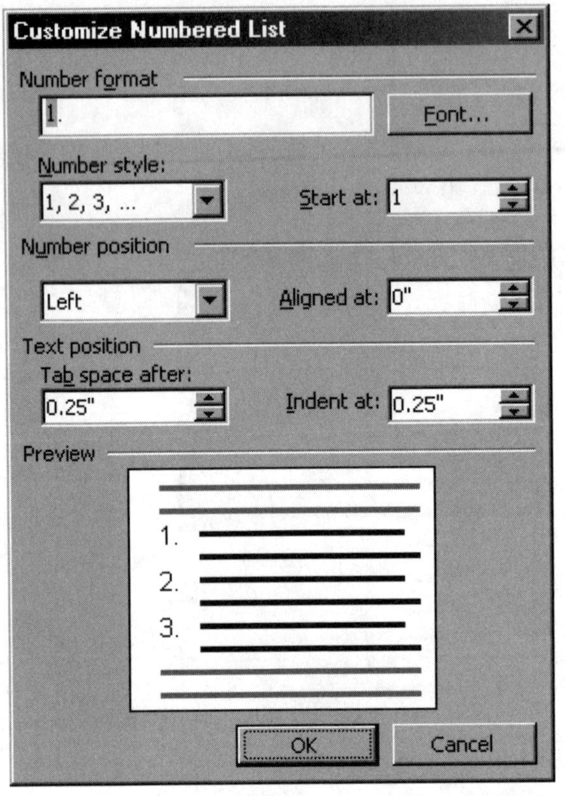

Figure 21.5: Customizing Numbered Lists.

When you customize your numbered lists, you can choose from these options:

- **NUMBER FORMAT** — How the number will be formatted. By default, the number is formatted with a period after it, but you can format it in any way that is required in your documents. Examples include right parenthesis, dashes, spaces, tabs, arrows, and more. You can also choose the font of the number by clicking the **Font** button.

- **NUMBER STYLE** — Format of the numbers in the numbered list. By default, arabic numerals are selected, by you can also choose from roman numerals, letters, and more from the dropdown list.

- **START AT** — Number with which the list should start. By default, this is the numeral **1**.

- **NUMBER POSITION** — Position of the number in the numbered list, either **Left**, **Center**, or **Right**, with **Left** being the default value.

- **ALIGNED AT** — Horizontal spacing before the number starts. The default is one quarter inch and is measured from the start position of the previous line.
- **TAB SPACE AFTER** — Horizontal spacing between the number in the numbered list and the start of the text on the first numbered line.
- **INDENT AT** — Horizontal spacing between the number and the start of the text on lines after the first numbered line.

Numbered lists are easy if you are not going to have complex documents with multiple levels of numbered lists. If you are, that's when the confusion can start. The next section shows you how to manage multiple levels.

Multiple Levels

Since most legal documents contain multiple levels of numbering, the documents start to become more difficult and complex as you increase the number of levels of numbering. While it may be unlikely in legal documents, multiple levels of numbering may intersperse bulleted lists as well. An example of a legal agreement with multiple levels of numbering is shown in Figure 21.6.

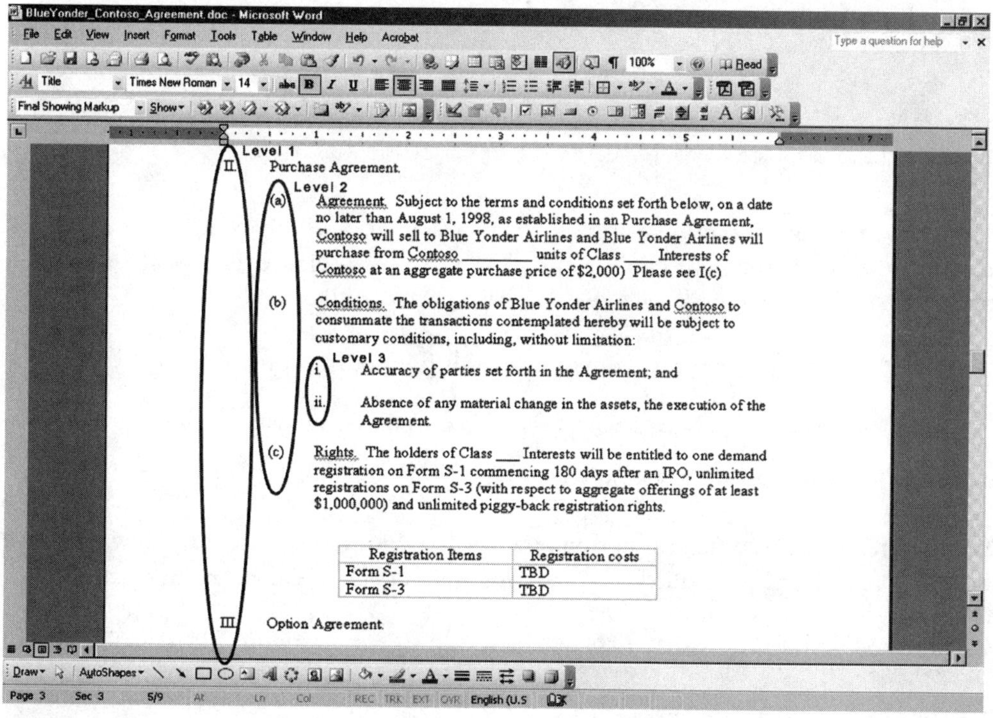

Figure 21.6: Agreement with Multiple Numbering Levels.

Using multiple levels of numbering is known as an *outline numbering*. This is because when you structure a document in the way shown in Figure 21.6, it forms an outline. To configure your document to use the outline format in Figure 21.6, follow these steps:

1. Click the **Format⇨ Bullets and Numbering** menu item. This brings up the screen shown in Figure 21.7.

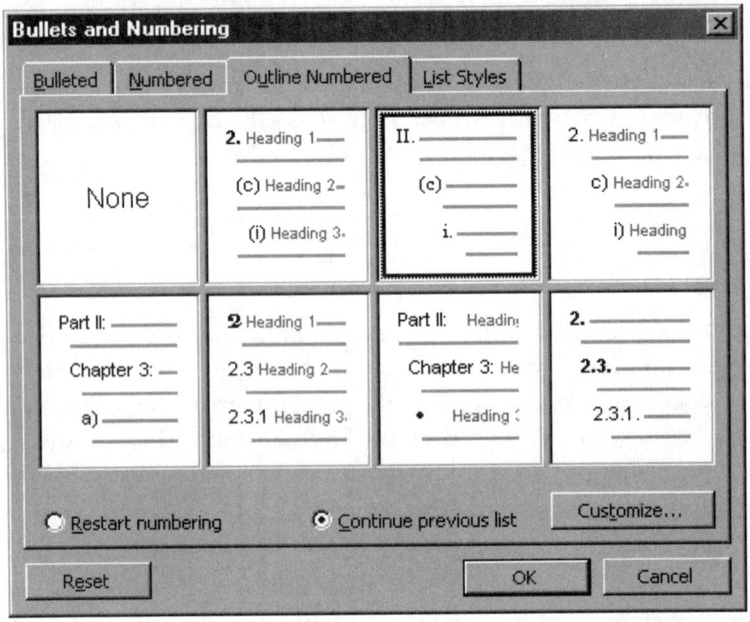

Figure 21.7: Configuring Outline Numbered Items in the Bullets and Numbering Screen.

2. From the seven outline numbering schemes presented, you can choose one and click the **OK** button to save your choices and close the screen. Figure 21.7 shows a selected numbering scheme that will have the first level presented like this:

   - **FIRST LEVEL** — Uppercase roman numerals followed by a period
   - **SECOND LEVEL** — Lowercase letters encased in parentheses
   - **THIRD LEVEL** — Lowercase roman numerals followed by a period

3. If you don't see an outline numbering scheme that you want to use, or you want to see how levels lower than the third level are configured, click the **Customize** button.

4. Click the **More** button, which displays the screen shown in Figure 21.8.

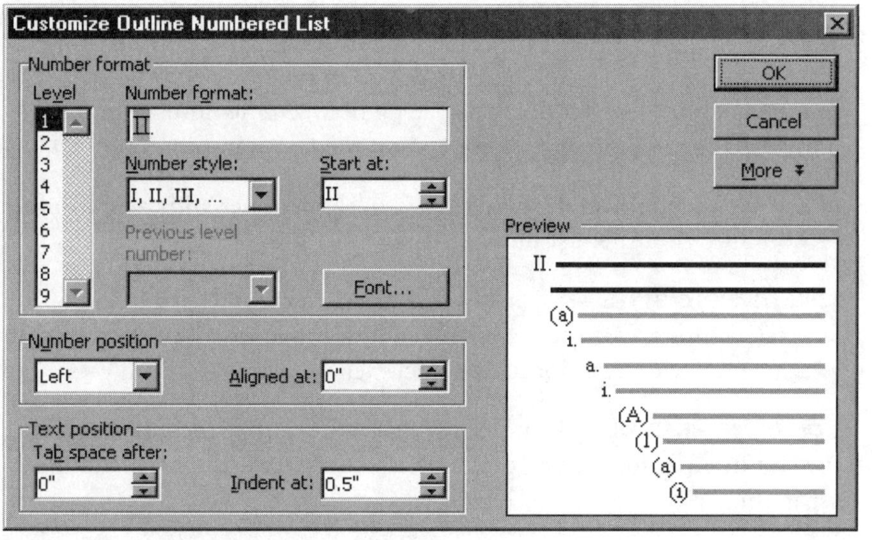

Figure 21.8: Customizing Outline Numbered Lists.

Figure 21.8 is quite busy, but it's important that you understand how this screen works.

- **LEVEL** — Numbered outline level that is used to configure the screen. As you select a different level, all values in the screen will change to reflect the configured values at that level. For example, if you click **1**, the **Number format** and **Number style** displayed will be that for level 1. If you click **2**, the same fields will reflect the values for level 2, etc.

- **NUMBER FORMAT** — How the number will be formatted. Examples include a period, right parenthesis, dashes, spaces, tabs, arrows, and more. You can also choose the font of the number by clicking the **Font** button.

- **NUMBER STYLE** —Format of the numbers in the numbered list. Choices include arabic numerals, roman numerals, letters, and more from the dropdown list.

- **START AT** — Number with which the list should start. By default, you'll see the number of the item that was selected when the screen was brought up.

- **PREVIOUS LEVEL NUMBER** — Used to display the number of the previous level selected in this dropdown list. Most legal outlines do not specify a value for this field.

- **NUMBER POSITION** — Position of the number in the numbered list, either **Left**, **Center**, or **Right**, with **Left** being the default value.

- **ALIGNED AT** — Horizontal spacing before the number starts. The default is zero inches and is measured from the start position of the previous line.
- **TAB SPACE AFTER** — Horizontal spacing between the number in the numbered list and the start of the text on the first numbered line.
- **INDENT AT** — Horizontal spacing between the number and the start of the text on lines after the first numbered line.
- **LINK LEVEL TO STYLE** — Specifies that the currently selected level is associated with a Word style. It is a good idea to always have each level linked to a style to have a well-formatted document.
- **FOLLOW NUMBER WITH** — Indicates what will separate the number with the text heading for the paragraph. A tab character is the most common separator.
- **LISTNUM FIELD LIST NAME** — Used for complex programming and should normally not be used.
- **LEGAL STYLE NUMBERING** — Forces numbering to use an arabic style, such as **1.1**, **2.3.1**, etc.
- **RESTART NUMBERING AFTER** — Dropdown list of levels after which numbering for the currently selected level will restart. This can be very useful in creating Interrogatories.
- **APPLY CHANGES TO** — Enables you to specify how to apply changes made to the numbering scheme. Normally, changes are applied to the whole list.

5. To continue configuring the outline list shown in Figure 21.6, click **1** under the **Level** field.
6. Ensure the **Number style** field reads **I, II, III,** ….
7. Ensure the **Number format** field has a period after the uppercase roman numeral. If not, simply type the period into the field.
8. Click **2** under the **Level** field.
9. Ensure the **Number style** field reads **a, b, c,** ….
10. Ensure the **Number format** field has the letter surrounded by parentheses. If not, type parentheses around the letter.
11. Click **3** under the **Level** field.

12. Ensure the **Number style** field reads **i, ii, iii, ...**.

13. Ensure the **Number format** field has a period after the lowercase roman numeral. If not, simply type the period into the field.

14. After you configure your numbered outline options, click the **OK** button to save your changes and close the screen.

15. Type one paragraph of text.

16. If your paragraph needs to be indented, click the **Increase Indent** button on the **Formatting** toolbar. For more information about where this button is located, see Chapter 4. Alternatively, you could press the **Home** key followed by the **Tab** key. You'll notice that the indented text starts to formulate the numbered list according to the format you already specified.

17. If your paragraph needs to be outdented, click the **Decrease Indent** button on the **Formatting** toolbar. Alternatively, you can press the **Home** key, followed by the **Shift + Tab** keys. You'll notice the text move to the left and become part of the numbering in the previous level.

18. Continue entering your text and indenting or outdenting it as appropriate for your document. When you are finished entering your text, your numbered list will now look like it does in Figure 21.6.

Everyone Wants to Feel Special

There are a couple of special options and procedures available to your numbered and bulleted lists that you should know about to avoid any possible frustration. Here are the special options available to you:

- **Changing from Numbers to Bullets** — To change from numbers to bullets, click anywhere in a numbered item and click the **Bullets** button on the **Formatting** toolbar. You should use this option with caution, as it may adversely affect your outline numbering scheme.

- **Changing from Bullets to Numbers** — To change from bullets to numbers, click anywhere in a bulleted item and click the **Numbering** button on the **Formatting** toolbar. You should use this option with caution, as it may adversely affect your outline numbering scheme.

- **RESET NUMBERING** — If your numbering at a level continues from the previous list and you want it to start at the number **1**, right-click the number itself (not the text adjacent to the number) and click the **Restart Numbering** menu item from the popup menu.

- **CONTINUE NUMBERING** — If your numbering at a level starts at the number **1** and you want it to continue from the previous list, right-click the number itself (not the text adjacent to the number) and click the **Continue Numbering** menu item from the popup menu.

Conclusion

Almost all legal documents — such as agreements, pleadings, and wills — contain numbered lists and perhaps bulleted lists. Bulleting and Numbering can be easy in a simple document, but can be complex if you have multiple levels of bullets and numbered lists. This chapter showed you how to easily format your documents to use bullets and numbered lists. It also showed you how to format your complex legal documents by formatting your numbered lists to have multiple levels, which is known as an outline numbered list. This is how your numbered lists start to become complex. However, after reading this chapter, you know all about how to format complex numbered lists in your legal documents.

Chapter 22

Cross-Referencing

Chapter At A Glance

WHY YOU SHOULD READ THIS CHAPTER:

Cross-references can be very important in your legal documents. Cross-references call out another location in the document, but are maintained by Word 2003. After reading this chapter, you'll understand how to create cross-references to locations in a document, Table of Contents, and also to create footnotes and endnotes.

PRODUCT OUTLINED IN THIS CHAPTER:

- Microsoft Word 2003

PRODUCT FEATURES COVERED IN THIS CHAPTER:

- Cross-references
- Footnotes and Endnotes
- Table of Contents

Cross-references provide a useful way to reference another part of any legal document. For example, in an agreement, you may have a cross-reference to Exhibit A at the end of the same document. The advantage of using a cross-reference is that Microsoft Word 2003 maintains a link to the reference in case the page number or title of the reference changes. Cross-references can even be created as a hyperlink, so you can simply press the **CTRL** key and click on the link to jump to a specific place in the document. Footnotes and endnotes are close cousins to the cross-reference. These are very useful in legal documents to give proper credit to resources. The best way to understand cross-references, footnotes and endnotes, and Table of Contents is to see them in action, so read on...

Cross-References

Cross-references are a very effective way to manage internal references to parts of your legal documents. Before you use cross-references, you have to make sure your headings are set up correctly.

Heading in the Right Direction

In Chapter 20, you learned all about Word styles. The reason you need to first understand about Word styles is that any text configured as a heading style (Heading 1, Heading 2, etc.) can easily be cross-referenced throughout the rest of your document.

The rest of this chapter uses the example of a legal acquisition agreement with a specific document outline, formatted with roman numerals using the **Heading 1** style, while the level below that ((a), (b), (c), etc.) uses the **Heading 2** style. The legal acquisition agreement outline looks like this:

```
I.      The Agreement
        (a)     Stock Purchase
        (b)     Rights
        (c)     Responsibilities
II.     Purchase Agreement
        (a)     Agreement
        (b)     Conditions
        (c)     Rights
III.    Option Agreement
        (a)     Stock Options
        (b)     Warranties
        (c)     Conditions
IV.     Indemnification
V.      Execution
```

```
VI.     Access
VII.    Disclosure
VIII.   Expenses
IX.     Miscellaneous
X.      Exhibit A
```

Using Cross-References

As long as your overall document is structured correctly using Word heading styles, creating a cross-reference is simple. Before showing you how to create the cross-reference, consider this paragraph in the agreement:

> Stock Purchase. Subject to the terms and conditions set forth below, on a date not later than July ___, 1998, Contoso will sell to Blue Yonder Airlines and Blue Yonder Airlines will purchase from Contoso 20 Class F Interests of Contoso at an aggregate purchase price of US $20 pursuant to an Agreement in the form attached hereto as Exhibit A on page 6.

Notice at the end of the paragraph is a reference to Exhibit A and the page number that it is on. Exhibit A is at the end of the same document, so you might think it's acceptable to just type Exhibit A and its page number at the end of the paragraph. That's certainly fine if you are absolutely 100% positively sure that this exhibit will never change its title and location. Well, as we all know, anything that can change…will!

What if a new exhibit is placed before Exhibit A and the current Exhibit A moves to Exhibit B? Now, your title and page numbers are both wrong. You'll have to manually go through your document and update all the cross-references. Therefore, it is not a good practice to manually type cross-references. It is a good practice to get used to how cross-references work and always use them.

Once you create a cross-reference in Microsoft Word 2003, the document semi-automatically updates any title and page number, so you don't have to worry about your document being incorrect (which could make you or your firm appear unprofessional). It is updated semi-automatically because although Word 2003 keeps track of all the references, they are not automatically updated. You have to "tell" Word to update the reference.

Creating Cross-References

Since you now understand why manually entering cross-references is a bad thing, it's time to learn how to do it right. Here's how you create a cross-reference in Microsoft Word 2003:

1. Open the desired document, such as the aforementioned legal acquisition agreement.

2. Position the carat in the paragraph where you would like to make a cross-reference to another part of the document. Using the prior example, you would place the carat right after this part of the paragraph:

```
...attached hereto as
```

3. Click the **Insert⇨ Reference⇨ Cross-reference** menu item. This brings up the screen shown in Figure 22.1.

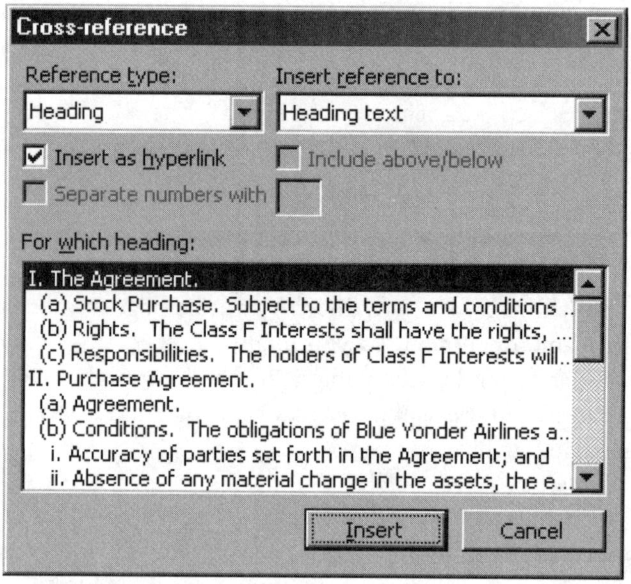

Figure 22.1: Inserting a Cross-Reference.

4. In the **Reference type** dropdown list, ensure that **Heading** is selected. This will ensure that all headings already configured in the current document will be listed in the **For which heading** list.

5. Ensure that **Heading** text is selected in the **Insert reference to** dropdown list. This will insert the heading part of the reference (rather than the numeric reference — such as 1.1, IV, etc. — or the page number reference).

6. In the **For which heading** list, click the desired reference. Using the example as presented earlier, you would scroll down until you see **Exhibit A** and select that item.

7. Ensure the **Insert as hyperlink** check box is checked. This gives the ability to press the **CTRL** key while you click the link, which makes Word automatically jump to the

referenced text. This can be a real time saver in your legal documents so you don't have to go searching for referenced items. You simply click them.

8. Click the **Insert** button. This inserts the reference to the title of the heading.

9. Following the same example, since we want to insert a reference that reads **Exhibit A on Page 6** after the newly created cross-reference to **Exhibit A**, you now must type `on Page`.

10. Bring up the cross-reference screen again by clicking the **Insert⇨ Reference⇨ Cross-reference** menu item.

11. Keep the **Reference type** dropdown list as **Heading**.

12. This time, in the **Insert reference to** dropdown list, select **Page number**.

13. Scroll down to the **Exhibit A** listing in the **For which heading** list again.

14. Ensure the **Insert as hyperlink** check box is checked.

15. Click the **Insert** button. This inserts the page number reference.

After you add the two cross-references, the paragraph looks like it does in Figure 22.2.

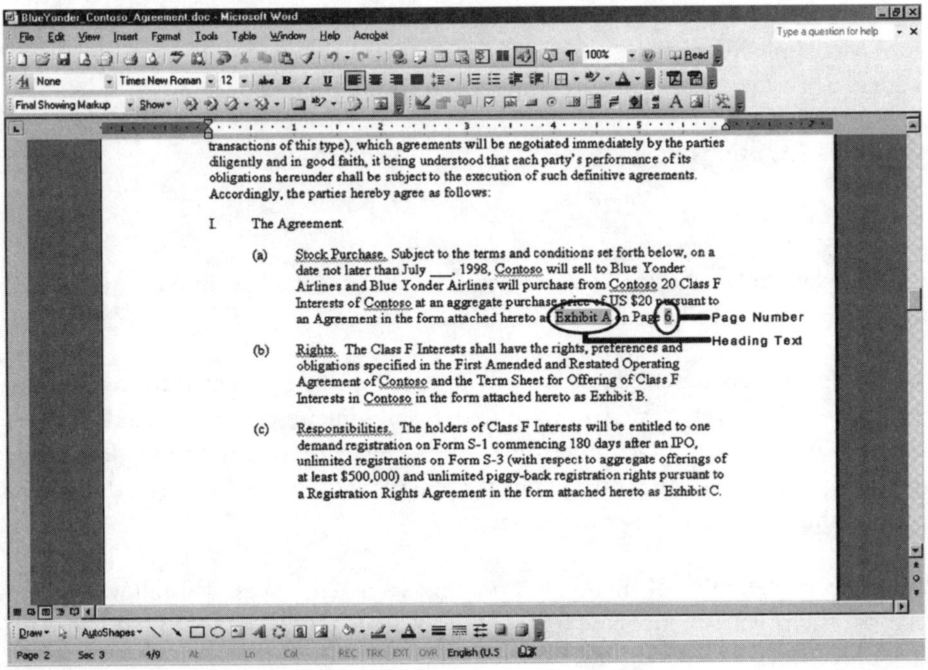

Figure 22.2: Paragraph After Adding Two Cross-References.

Pulling the Trigger on Semi-Automatic References

Word 2003 keeps track of all cross-references so that any changes can be updated in your document. However, these updates don't take place automatically as you would expect; they are only semi-automatic. To update your references, you can update a single reference or all references in the document. You only need to update your references when something changes. For example, if you change the title **Exhibit A** to **Attachment A**, the cross-reference will need to be updated.

Single References

To update a single cross-reference, simply right-click the cross-reference and select the **Update Field** menu item from the popup menu. You'll see the text in the paragraph change to reflect the new changes.

All References

Before you proof or send out any document, it is a good idea to update all references in the document. This ensures that everything in the document is up-to-date. This applies not only to cross-references, but also to Table of Contents.

You can configure Microsoft Word to automatically update all references when you print the document or request a print preview of the document. To configure this option:

1. Click the **Tools⇨ Options** menu item.
2. Click the **Print** tab.
3. Ensure the **Update fields** check box is selected. This ensures that a printed or previewed document will automatically update all fields.

The drawback to having your document automatically updated is that it can be time-consuming for large documents to update every time you want to print. If you are working on a document and printing lots of drafts, this can be cumbersome. Additionally, checking the **Update fields** option does not ensure that the document references are updated when you send a document via e-mail. Therefore, this is not a perfect procedure.

It is a good idea to get in the habit of manually updating your references. This allows you to control all aspects of when the references are updated. To update all references in a document, follow this simple procedure:

1. Open the desired document.
2. Click the **Edit⇨ Select All** menu item or press the **CTRL + A** keys to select all text in the document. This includes all fields, such as cross-references and Table of Contents.
3. Press the **F9** key. All references will be updated in the document.
4. Click anywhere in the document or move the carat with the keyboard arrow keys to unselect all text in the document.

Footnotes and Endnotes

A footnote is a reference to text in the document where the source of that text is noted at the bottom of the same page. An endnote is similar to a footnote, except that the reference is not on the same page; it's at the end of the document.

Footnote and endnote references will automatically sequentially number and keep track of the referenced text. This way, if a new footnote or endnote is created, the reference number associated with the reference will be updated immediately—not only in the text of the document, but also in the footnote or endnote itself. An example of a footnote is shown in Figure 22.3.

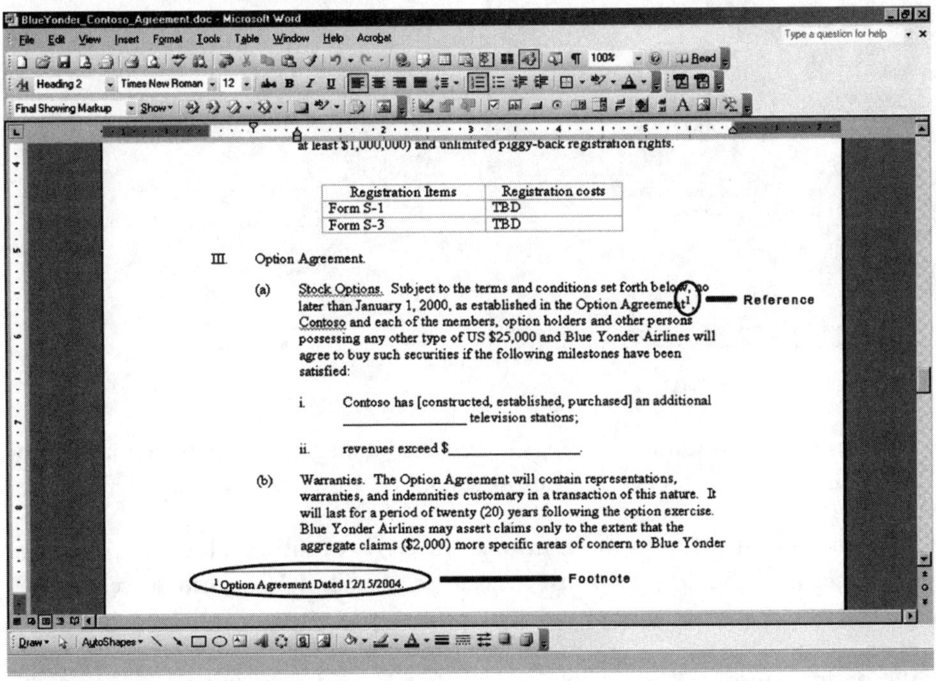

Figure 22.3: Word 2003 Footnotes in Action.

In Figure 22.3, notice the reference with the numeral **1**. This was created automatically, as was the same numeral in the footnote itself (at the bottom of the screen).

Here's how you create footnotes in your own documents:

1. Open the desired Word 2003 document.
2. Select the text in the document for which you will create the footnote reference. In Figure 22.3, the term **Option Agreement** was selected before the footnote was created.
3. Click the **Insert⇨ Reference⇨ Footnote** menu item to open the screen shown in Figure 22.4.

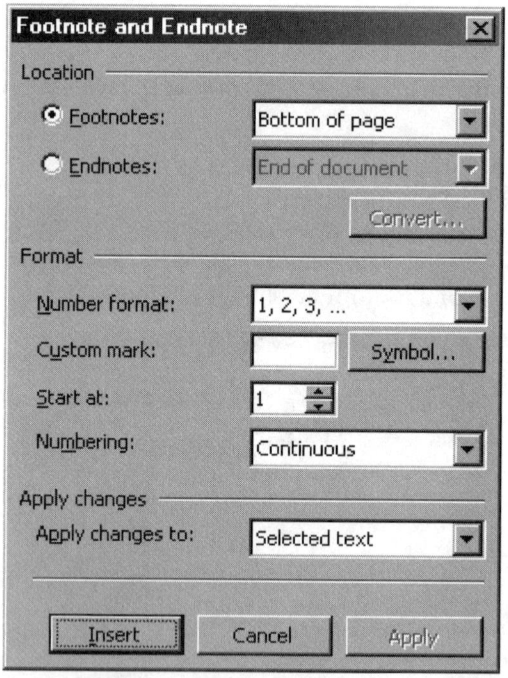

Figure 22.4: Creating Word 2003 Footnotes.

4. Ensure the **Footnotes** option is selected. On the other hand, if you want the note to be at the end of the document, click the **Endnotes** option instead.
5. Select the desired location for the footnote or endnote. By default, for footnotes, **Bottom of page** is selected in the dropdown list. Endnotes have **End of document** selected by default in the dropdown list.
6. Select the desired number format in the **Number format** dropdown list. Normally, footnotes and endnotes use arabic numerals (1, 2, 3, …).

7. Click the **Insert** button. The numeral reference is automatically entered at the end of the selected text. The same numeral is automatically entered at the bottom of the page with the carat blinking.

8. Type the desired footnote. (The footnote in Figure 22.3 reads **Option Agreement Dated 12/15/2004**).

9. Continue with every footnote needed in the document.

Endnotes are created exactly the same way as footnotes, except that you select the **Endnotes** option in Figure 22.4 instead of **Footnotes**.

Creating a Table of Contents

Some legal documents, such as agreements, contain a Table of Contents (TOC) page after the title page. You don't have to manually type all the page number references in the TOC. Microsoft Word can automatically generate a TOC because it is just another kind of cross-reference. It works by referencing the headings that you have already configured throughout your document. The page numbers and headings for the TOC are updated just like any other cross-reference field that is discussed throughout this chapter. Creating a TOC is easy to do in Microsoft Word, as long as you have applied heading styles throughout your document, such as **Heading 1** and **Heading 2** to the headings in your document.

Here's how you create a TOC in Microsoft Word:

1. Position the carat at the location in your document that will receive the TOC.

2. Click the **Insert⇨ Reference⇨ Index and Tables** menu item.

3. Click the **Table of Contents** tab. This brings up the screen shown in Figure 22.5.

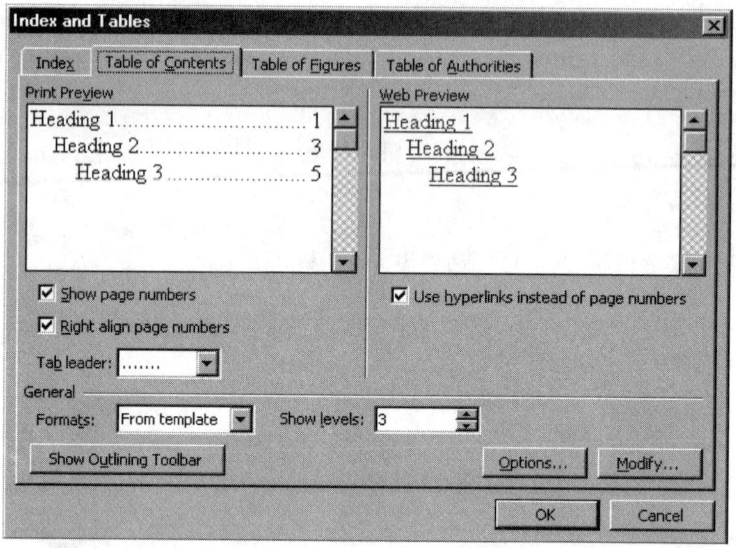

Figure 22.5: Creating Word 2003 Table of Contents.

4. To create a standard TOC, you can accept all of the default options. These options will display three levels of headings, so your document may need to display more or less, depending on the depth your document goes into. If you wish to change the levels displayed within the TOC, change the number of levels in the **Show levels** field.

5. Click the **OK** button to create the TOC.

Your TOC needs to be updated just like any other cross-reference in Microsoft Word. Refer to the section, "Creating Cross-References" to learn how to update your TOC.

Conclusion

This chapter showed you how to create cross-references, footnotes, and endnotes. Cross-references are important features of Microsoft Word 2003. They are used to create references to internal parts of your documents—either by text reference, page number, or heading number. Once references to sections in your internal documents are created, they can easily be updated to account for changes in the document. Footnotes and endnotes are close cousins to cross-references. One part of a document that is flagged as a reference will also create an endnote or a footnote to that reference.

Chapter 23

Drafting Legal Pleadings

Chapter At A Glance

WHY YOU SHOULD READ THIS CHAPTER:

Paralegals play many different roles in law firms, depending on their specific practice area. If you work in Corporate or Estate Planning practice areas, you probably don't deal with pleadings. However, Paralegals that focus on litigation will probably need to draft legal pleadings and briefs. This chapter shows how to draft legal pleadings using Microsoft's Legal Pleading Wizard, which guides you through the steps of creating pleadings.

PRODUCT OUTLINED IN THIS CHAPTER:

- Microsoft Word 2003

PRODUCT FEATURE COVERED IN THIS CHAPTER:

- Legal Pleading Wizard

Chapter 3 showed you how to download and install templates in Microsoft Office and Chapter 4 showed you which templates were available for Microsoft Word. Specifically for pleadings, these templates are available on the Microsoft Office Web site:

- Pleading form with 25 lines
- Pleading form with 26 lines
- Pleading form with 28 lines
- Pleading form with 32 lines
- Legal Pleading Wizard

If you are a Paralegal in a litigation practice area of a law firm, you will likely want to learn about these templates. Even if they don't exactly suit your needs, you can use these templates as a starting point, and then customize the resulting document that is created by using the templates or the wizard. This chapter shows how to draft legal pleadings by using the Legal Pleading Wizard, available as a free download from the Microsoft Office Web site. See Chapter 3 for more information about downloading and installing the templates.

Pleading the Fifth

The easiest way to construct a legal pleading is to use the Legal Pleading Wizard. This is a special program that is available from the Microsoft Office Web site that prompts and guides you through a series of steps and automatically formats pleadings as Microsoft Word templates. After the wizard creates the template, it will launch another wizard to fill in data by creating a document based on that template. If that was too confusing, just think of this as a two-task process, which we'll call A and B. In fact, these two separate tasks are not actually labeled on the screen.

Task A: Creating a Pleading Template

The first of two tasks in creating your legal pleading is to allow the Legal Pleading Wizard to create a pleading template. It will create a template for each court that you will need to create pleadings for.

NOTE

Even though you use the Legal Pleading Wizard to carry out two separate tasks (to create a template and to create a document based on that template), these separate tasks are not displayed on the screen. It will, however, be obvious when you look at the figures shown in this chapter that there are two distinctive screens (tasks), each with its own set of steps.

Here's how you use the Legal Pleading Wizard, which automatically starts Task A:

1. Make sure you download the Legal Pleading Wizard. Refer to Chapters 3 and 4 to see how to do this.

2. In Microsoft Word, click the **File⇨ New** menu item. A blank window is opened with the **New Document** pane being displayed as well, which is shown in Figure 23.1.

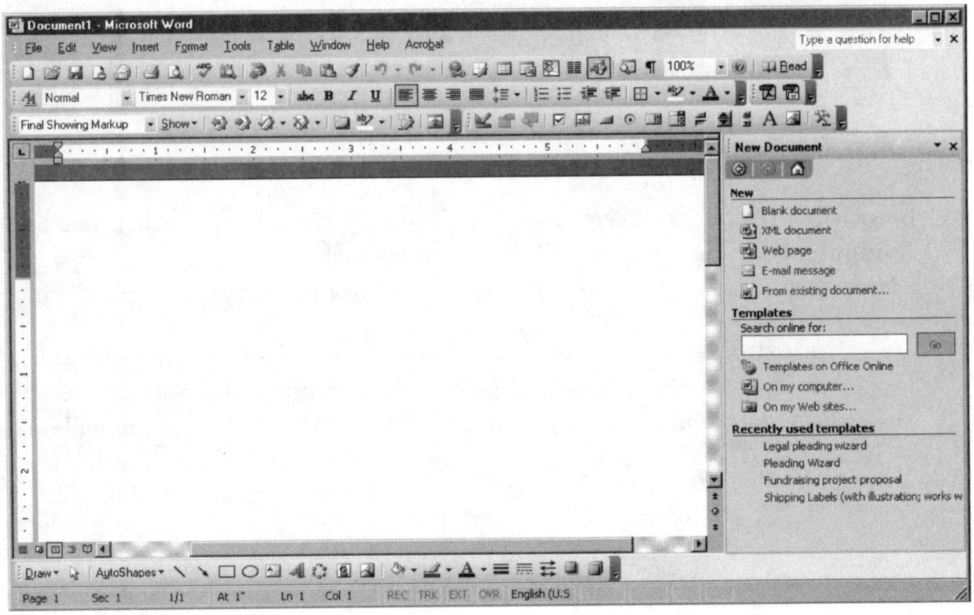

Figure 23.1: Blank Document and New Document Pane.

3. In the **Templates** section of the **New Document** pane, click the **On my computer...** link. This opens the **Templates** window, which categorizes the available templates into groups.

4. Click the **Legal Pleadings** tab. You should see the Pleading Wizard. If you don't see it, you have not correctly downloaded and installed it.

5. Either double-click the **Pleading Wizard** or select it and click the **OK** button. The wizard starts and guides you through a series of steps. The first step of the wizard is shown in Figure 23.2.

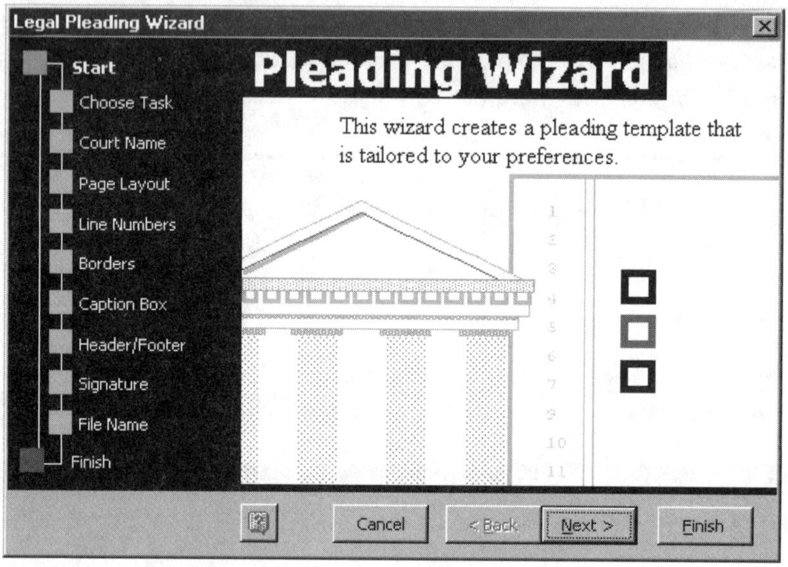

Figure 23.2: Legal Pleading Wizard.

You'll notice that there are nine steps in using the wizard (even though they aren't numbered). In each step, you'll enter data or make choices. After each step, click the **Next** button to save your choices and proceed to the next step.

- **Choose Task** — This step is used to indicate how you would like to use the wizard. As mentioned earlier, you can store multiple court-specific templates that can be reused, so you must specify the type of template you will be using in this step, which is shown in Figure 23.3.

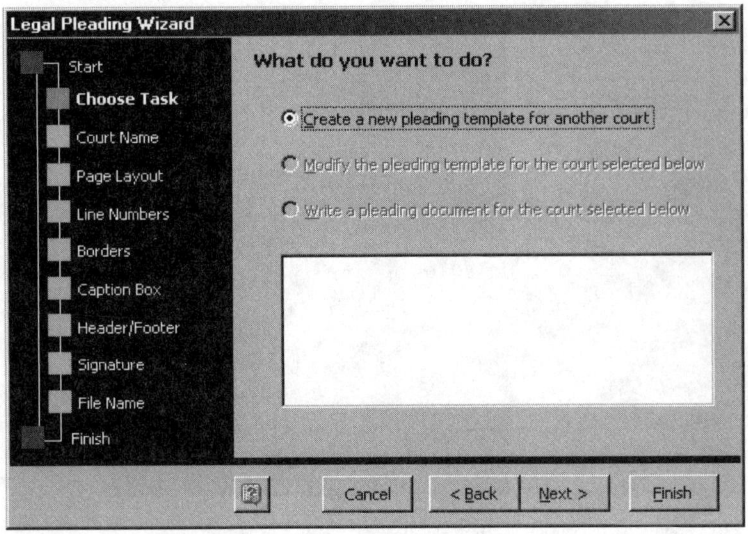

Figure 23.3: Choosing a Task in the Legal Pleading Wizard.

Figure 23.3 shows that you have these three choices:

- **CREATE A NEW PLEADING TEMPLATE FOR ANOTHER COURT** — Indicates that you will be creating a new template and specifying the layout and values for that template. If this is the first time you are running the wizard, this will be the only option available to you.

- **MODIFY THE PLEADING TEMPLATE FOR THE COURT SELECTED BELOW** — If you have run the wizard before, the name of the court for which you created a prior template will appear in this list. If you wish to modify a template, simply click the desired template in the list provided. If you have not run the wizard before, this list will be blank and the option will be disabled.

- **WRITE A PLEADING DOCUMENT FOR THE COURT SELECTED BELOW** — Similar to the Modify option, the name of the court will appear in the list, if you have run the wizard before. This option indicates that you do not wish to modify the template, but simply to use it and create a new document.

• **COURT NAME** — This step is used to specify the name of the court as it should appear on the pleading. It will also appear in the list of available templates the next time you run the wizard. As shown in Figure 23.4, enter the name of the court in the text box provided and choose how it should be aligned, either **Left**, **Center**, or **Right**.

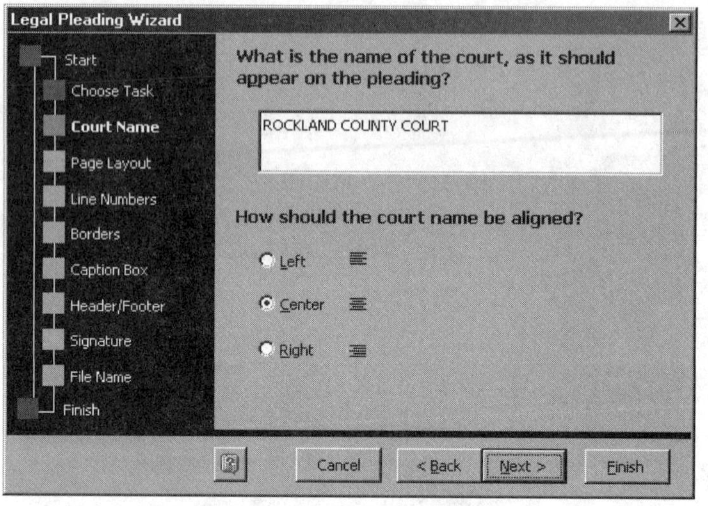

Figure 23.4: Choosing a Court Name in the Legal Pleading Wizard.

- **PAGE LAYOUT** — There are numerous values that you specify in this step, shown in Figure 23.5, which dictates the layout of the pleading. These values are very specific to the way the court expects to see the pleadings.

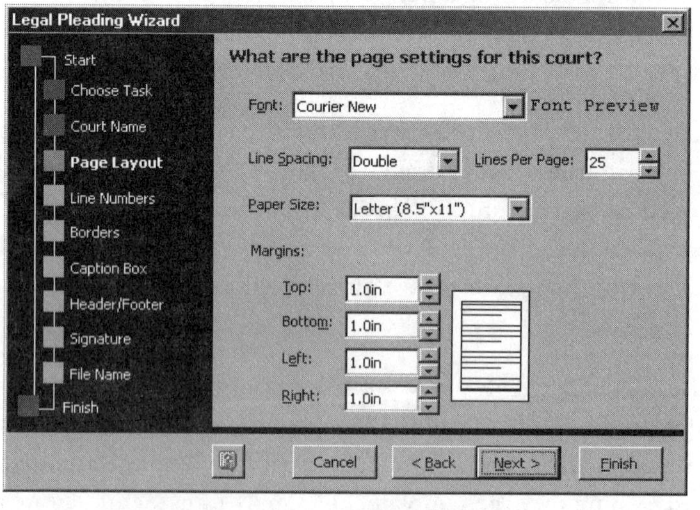

Figure 23.5: Choosing a Page Layout in the Legal Pleading Wizard.

Choose the desired **Font**, **Line Spacing**, and **Lines Per Page** settings that are appropriate for your court. Also select the **Paper Size** and **Margins** that your court requires.

NOTE

The default font is Courier New. The Courier family of fonts is known as a *non-proportional* font. A non-proportional font uses the exact same amount of space for each character. In other words, an "i" takes the same space as a "W". On the other hand, a *proportional* font uses less space for an "i" than it does for a "W". Check with your court to determine which font they require.

- **Line Numbers** — This step, shown in Figure 23.6, is used to indicate how line numbers should appear in your pleading. The number of lines is specified in the **Page Layout** step.

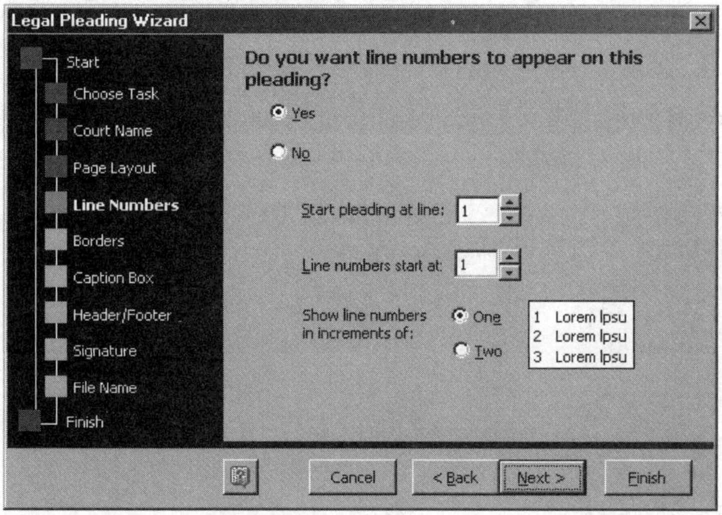

Figure 23.6: Choosing Line Number Settings in the Legal Pleading Wizard.

If your court requires line numbers, under **Do you want line numbers to appear on this pleading?**, click the **Yes** option, otherwise click the **No** option. If you choose the **Yes** option, specify at which line number the pleading and line numbers begin. By default, each is set to a value of **1**.

- **Borders** — This step is used to indicate how the left and right borders should appear. As shown in Figure 23.7, the default values are to have a double vertical line in the left border and a single vertical line in the right border. If you wish to change either of these settings for your court, simply click the desired values (**Double**, **Single**, or **None**).

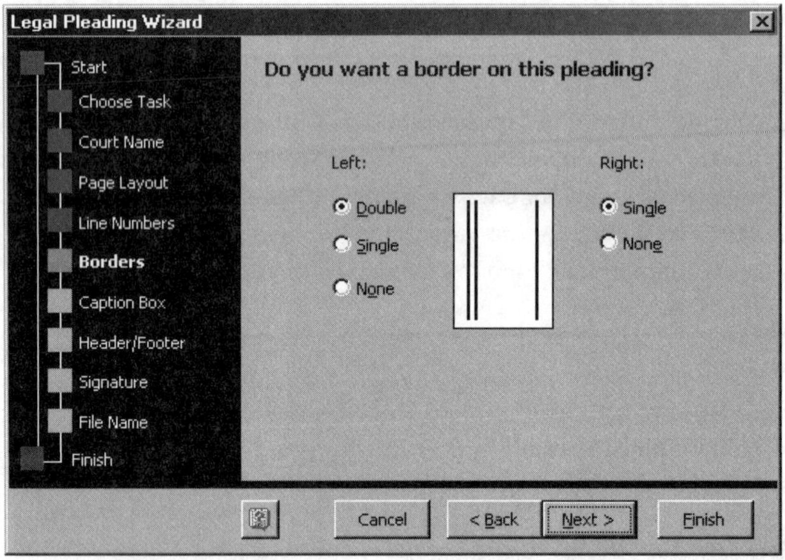

Figure 23.7: Choosing Borders in the Legal Pleading Wizard.

- **Caption Box** — While it may not be immediately apparent, Figure 23.8 shows the styles available for the caption box to be displayed on the pleading.

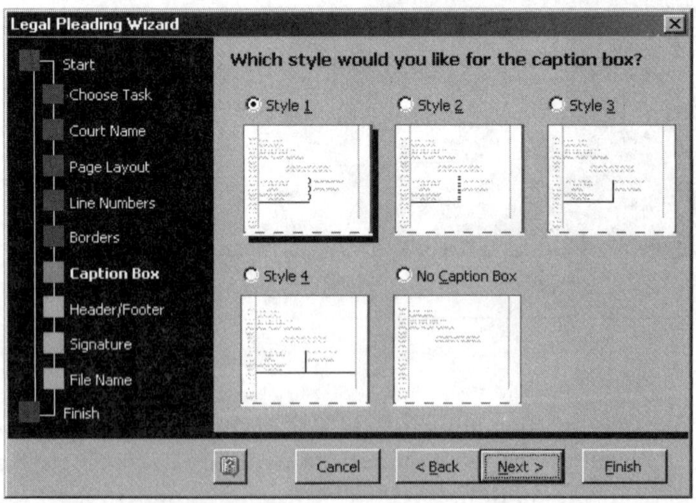

Figure 23.8: Choosing Caption Box Style in the Legal Pleading Wizard.

These styles are available:

- o **Style 1** — This is the default style and shows a left parenthesis ")" on the right of the caption with a solid horizontal line halfway across the page under the caption.

- o **STYLE 2** — Shows a colon ":" on the right of the caption with a solid horizontal line halfway across the page under the caption.
- o **STYLE 3** — Shows a solid vertical line on the right of the caption with a solid horizontal line halfway across the page under the caption.
- o **STYLE 4** — Shows a solid vertical line on the right of the caption with a solid horizontal line the whole way across the page under the caption.
- o **STYLE 5** — Shows no caption box at all.

- **HEADER/FOOTER** — This step is used to specify which fields of information you want to display on the first page of the pleading (the header) and at the bottom of each page of the pleading (the footer), as shown in Figure 23.9.

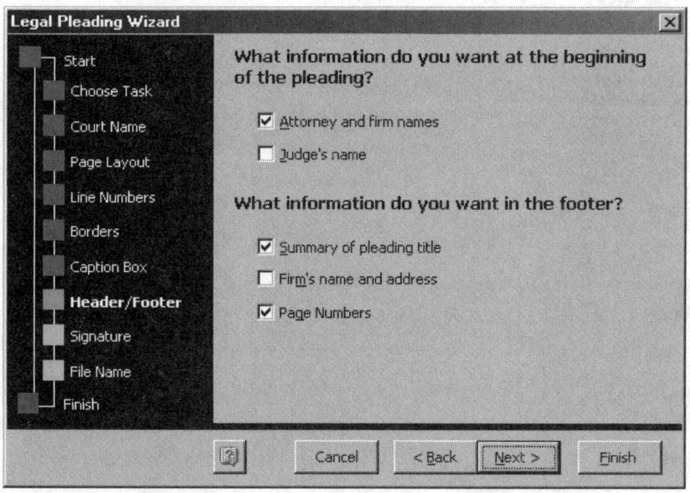

Figure 23.9: Choosing Header and Footer Options in the Legal Pleading Wizard.

On the first page, you have the choice of displaying:

- o **ATTORNEY AND FIRM NAMES** — These names will be specified after you finish all nine steps.
- o **JUDGE'S NAME** — The judge's name will be specified after you finish all nine steps.

In the footer of each page, you can include:

- o **SUMMARY OF PLEADING TITLE** — Displays the pleading, such as **Motion for Hearing**. The actual pleading is specified after you finish all nine steps.

- o **FIRM'S NAME AND ADDRESS** — Displays the firm's name and address on all pages in the footer. This too is specified after you complete the wizard.
- o **PAGE NUMBERS** — Displays automatic page numbers.

- **SIGNATURE** — This step (shown in Figure 23.10) is used to indicate how you will use a signature block on the first page of the pleading. By default, a signature will be used, along with the date.

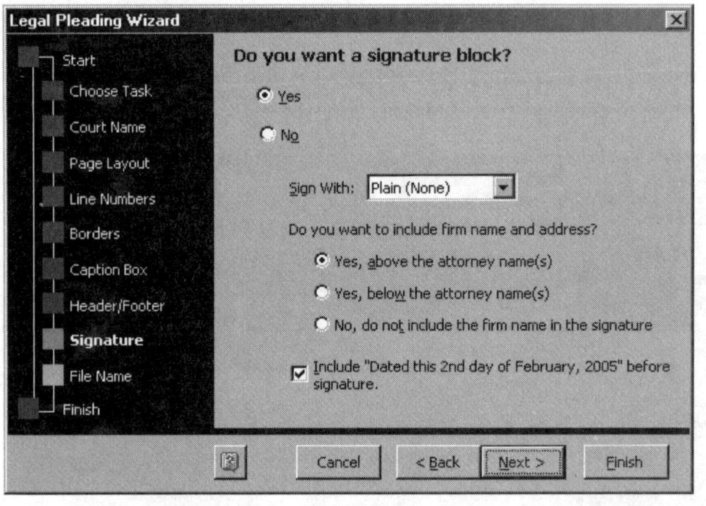

Figure 23.10: Choosing Signature Options in the Legal Pleading Wizard.

If you don't want to include a signature, click the **No** option, which makes all other options on the screen disappear. Otherwise, if you want to include a signature, specify these options:

- o **SIGN WITH** — Signs the pleading by prefacing your name with no prefix, **By**, **By:**, or **X**. The wizard will automatically place a line for your signature just after this prefix. You can also type a special prefix into the field even though it may not be presented in the dropdown list.
- o **YES, ABOVE THE ATTORNEY NAME(S)** — Includes the signature as specified in the **Sign With** option, but includes it above the attorney names.
- o **YES, BELOW THE ATTORNEY NAME(S)** — Includes the signature as specified in the **Sign With** option, but includes it below the attorney names.

- **No, do not include the firm name in the signature** — Omits a signature from the pleading.
- **Include <Current Date> before signature** — Includes the current date on which the pleading is created. This appears one line before the signature line.

- **File Name** —This last step in Task A is to specify the file name used for the template. Remember, Task A (including all nine steps) was to have the wizard simply create a Word 2003 template—not to fill the template with data. Therefore, this template needs a name. Word templates have a .dot file extension, which stands for document template. Because each template is usually created for a specific court, the default file name is the name of the court, as specified in the **Court Name** step, followed by **.dot**. This is shown in Figure 23.11. You can change it if you wish. You do not specify a location on your hard drive, as all templates are stored in a predefined location.

TIP

Templates are stored in this folder location on your computer: `<drive>:\Documents and Settings\<username>\Application Data\Microsoft\Templates\Legal Pleadings.`

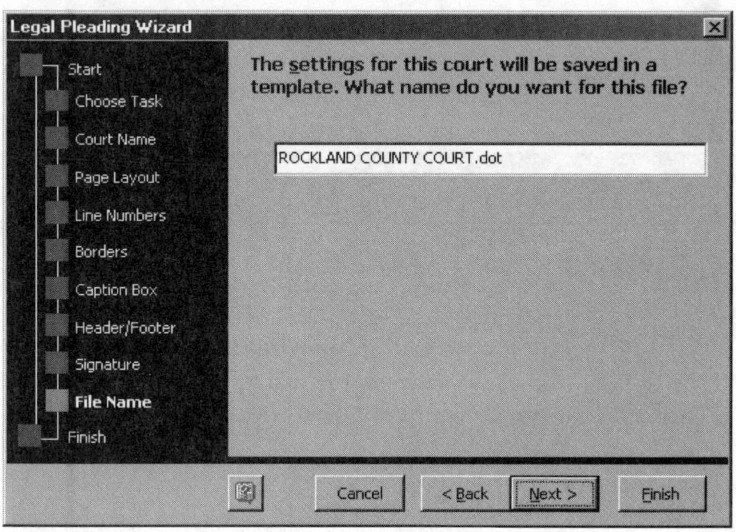

Figure 23.11: Choosing the Template File Name in the Legal Pleading Wizard.

- Click the **Next** or **Finish** buttons to have the wizard begin Task B.

Task B: Creating a Document Based on the Newly Created Template

After you complete Task A, which is to create a legal pleading template using the Legal Pleading Wizard, you create a document based on that template and fill in the pertinent data, such as your firm's name, your name, the title of the pleading, etc. When you click the **Next** or **Finish** buttons using the wizard shown in Task A, a new wizard will be launched to guide you through the process of creating the document based on your new template.

Here's how the second wizard works, which begins Task B, as shown in Figure 23.12.

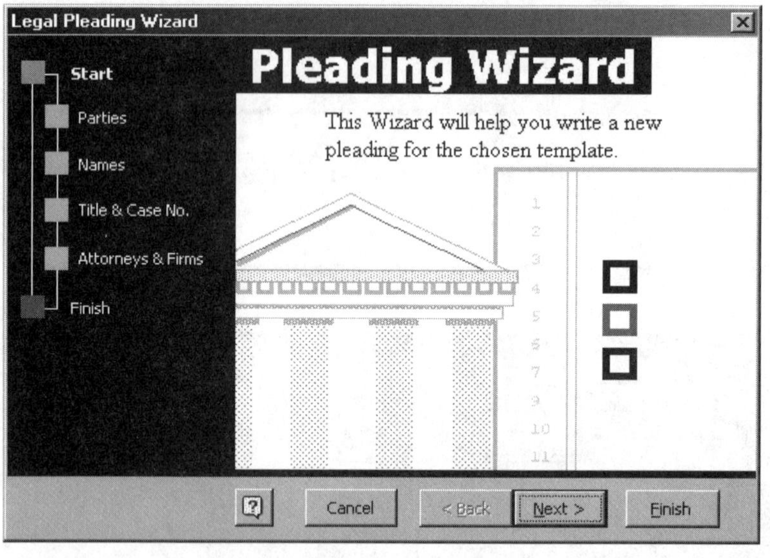

Figure 23.12: Beginning Task B with the Legal Pleading Wizard.

Much like the wizard in Task A has nine steps, Task B's wizard has four steps (even though they aren't numbered on the screen). Again, in each step, you'll enter data or make choices in each step, then click the **Next** button to save your choices and proceed to the next step. These are the four steps:

1. **Parties** — Used to indicate the type of parties that are to be specified on the pleading, as shown in Figure 23.13:

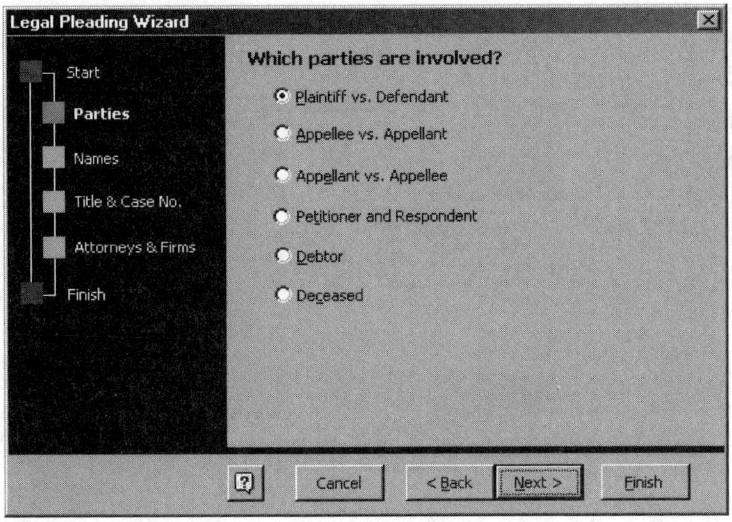

Figure 23.13: Choosing the Parties Involved in the Pleading.

Choose from these possible parties on the pleading:

- Plaintiff vs. Defendant
- Appellee vs. Appellant
- Appellant vs. Appellee
- Petitioner and Respondent
- Debtor
- Deceased

2. **Names** — Enter the plaintiff and defendant names (and sometimes addresses) for the parties chosen in the prior step, as shown in Figure 23.23. You can either type the name (and address, if needed) by hand or select the address from your Outlook or Outlook Express address book. To learn how to manage contacts that you can use here in this wizard, see Chapter 13.

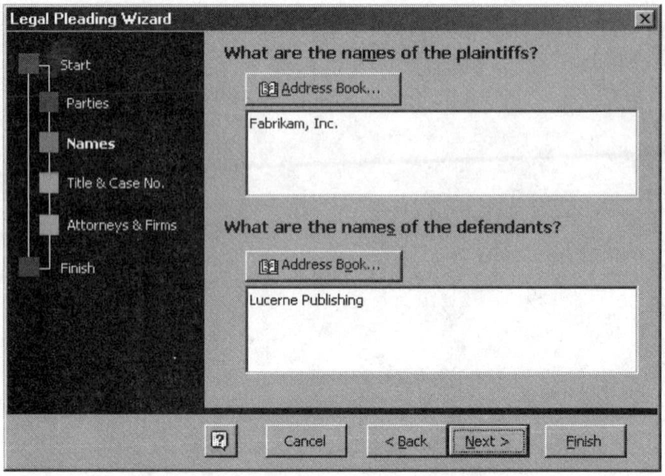

Figure 23.14: Entering the Names of the Parties Involved.

3. **Title & Case No.** — Enter the title and case number, as shown in Figure 23.15.

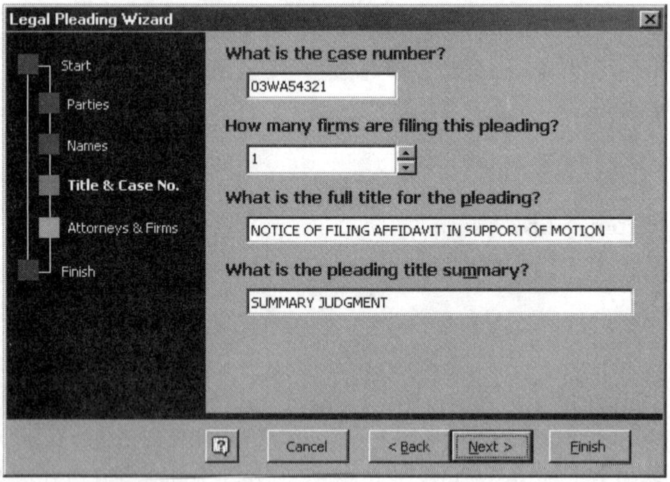

Figure 23.15: Entering Case Number and Title.

In Step 3, fill in the following fields, all of which are used on the final form:

- **What is the case number?** — This is the case number as assigned by the court.
- **How many firms are filing this pleading?** — Enter the number of firms involved in filing the pleading. The default is 1.

- **WHAT IS THE FULL TITLE FOR THE PLEADING?** — This is used on the first page of the pleading.

- **WHAT IS THE PLEADING TITLE SUMMARY?** — This is used in the footer of each page of the pleading. If the court in which this pleading will be filed requires the pleading title in the footer, enter it here.

4. In the last step, you enter the names of the attorneys of record. For each additional firm that you chose in Step 3 (under **How many firms are filing this pleading?**), you see an additional step under which you specify attorney and firm names. Step 4 is shown in Figure 23.16.

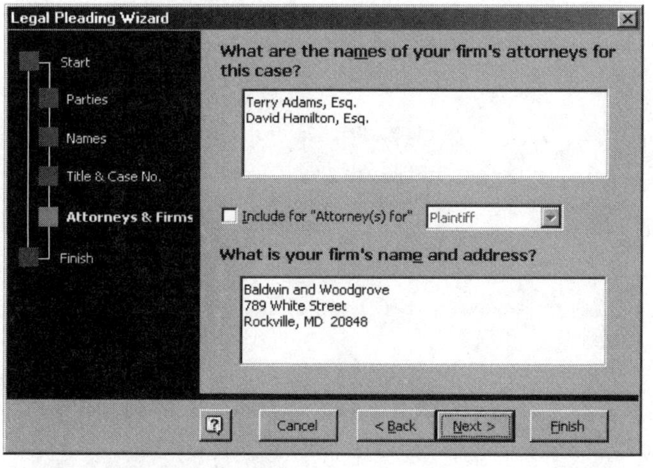

Figure 23.16: Attorney and Firm Names.

These fields are available under Step 4:

- **WHAT ARE THE NAMES OF YOUR FIRM'S ATTORNEYS FOR THIS CASE?** — This field is used to indicate the attorney's names for a single firm. If you specified more than one firm in Step 3, you will be prompted for the additional firm name(s) after you click the **Next** button.

- **INCLUDE FOR "ATTORNEY(S) FOR"** — Check this box if you wish to include attorneys for the Plaintiff, Appellee, Appellant, Petitioner, Debtor, Deceased, Defendant, Respondent.

- **WHAT IS YOUR FIRM'S NAME AND ADDRESS?** — Enter the name and address of your firm. Remember, if you chose more than one firm in Step 3, you will be prompted for those firms after you click the **Next** button.

5. Click the **Finish** button. You'll see all your choices nicely presented in a pleading document, configured with the choices you made using the two wizards. Make sure you save your new document with your desired file name.

Because you must be dying to know how the format looks in the resulting document, here you go. It's shown in Figure 23.17.

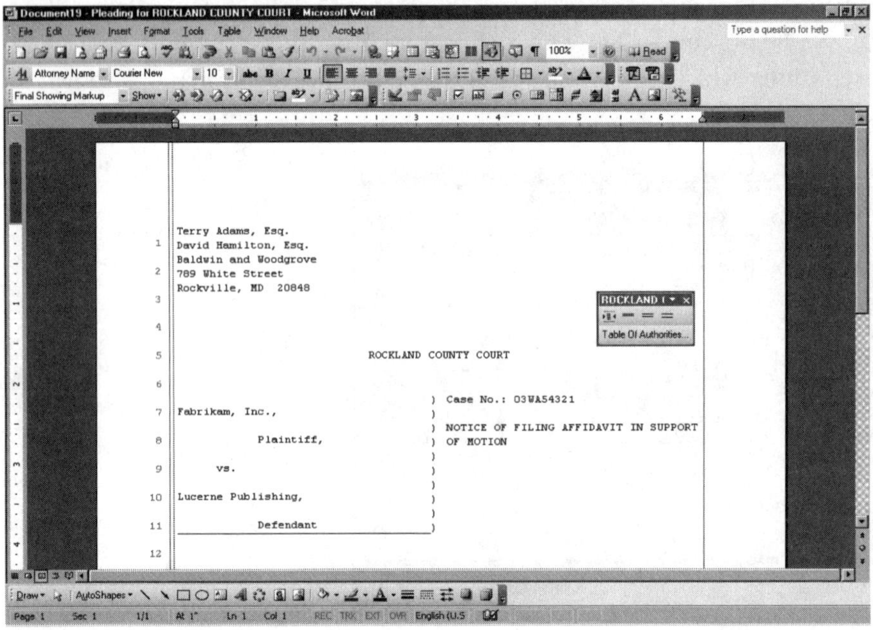

Figure 23.17: Resulting Document After Using the Legal Pleading Wizard.

Reusing Templates

If you recall, when you created a new template using the Legal Pleading Wizard, you were prompted for a file name. Believe it or not, this is for a reason. The reason is that this file name is used as a template to create documents for the same court, with the same format (number of lines, court name, etc.). To reuse a template that you've already created, simply create a new document, based on templates located on your computer (as you did back in Figure 23.1). This time, when you click the **Legal Pleadings** tab, you'll see your new template located in the folder, as shown in Figure 23.18.

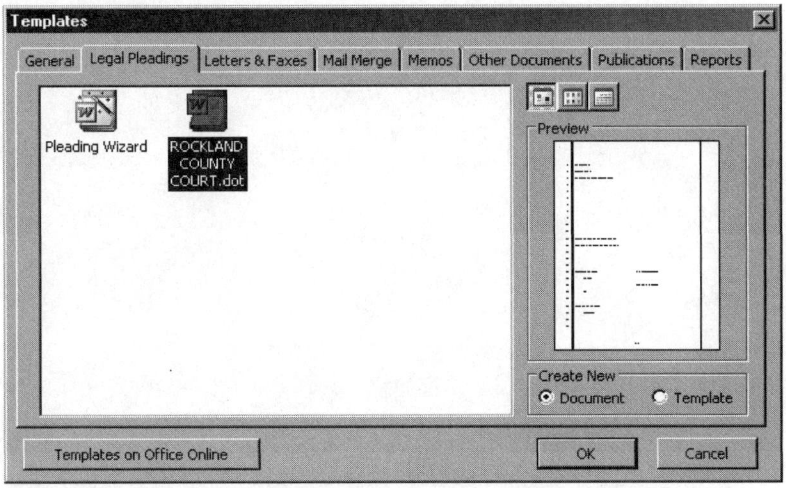

Figure 23.18: Legal Pleadings Templates, Showing Newly Created Template.

This time when you click the **OK** button, the wizard will guide you through only Task B, which is used to indicate specific parties, firms, and titles used for the court. Refer to the earlier section, "Task B: Creating a Document Based on the Newly Created Template."

Conclusion

This chapter walked you through using the Legal Pleading Wizard to automate the process of creating a pleading. As you know, formatting legal documents, such as pleadings, to make them suitable for submission to a court can be quite challenging. Using the Legal Pleading Wizard from Microsoft dramatically simplifies the creation of pleadings. Not only can you choose how many lines should appear in the document, but also the attorneys, firms, parties involved, and more. It even lets you save the settings as a template that you can use later. If you want to know more about how to manually structure and format your documents, see Chapters 17 and 18.

Did you know?

If you didn't want to use the Legal Pleading Wizard to guide you though the process of creating a pleading, you could use one of the free pleading templates available from Microsoft. There are 25, 26, 28, and 32-line pleading templates that will format your documents, but you have to supply the information manually.

Chapter 24

Generating a Table of Authorities

Chapter At A Glance

WHY YOU SHOULD READ THIS CHAPTER:

A Table of Authorities is commonly found in legal briefs and reply briefs. It lists citations found in your document. If you create documents that need a Table of Authorities, this chapter shows you everything you need to know to make it simple.

PRODUCT OUTLINED IN THIS CHAPTER:

- Microsoft Word 2003

PRODUCT FEATURES COVERED IN THIS CHAPTER:

- Table of Authorities

A Table of Authorities (TOA) is a listing at the beginning of a brief or a reply brief that lists all the references used in a document, such as cases, statutes, and other sources. These references appear at the beginning of the document in alphabetical order, not in page number order like a Table of Contents does. You can create TOA in Microsoft Word 2003 fairly easily. Before you dive into creating TOA, take a look at what one looks like, as shown in Figure 24.1.

> **NOTE**
>
> **The examples shown in this chapter were taken largely from the Reply Brief of Petitioner in the case of NORFOLK SOUTHERN RAILWAY COMPANY (Petitioner) v. JAMES N. KIRBY PTY LTD D/B/A/ KIRBY ENGINEERING, MMI GENERAL INSURANCE, LTD. (Respondents), No. 02-1028 from** `FindLaw.com`**. While the information contained herein is public information, full credit is to be given to** `FindLaw.com` **for their easily searchable database.**

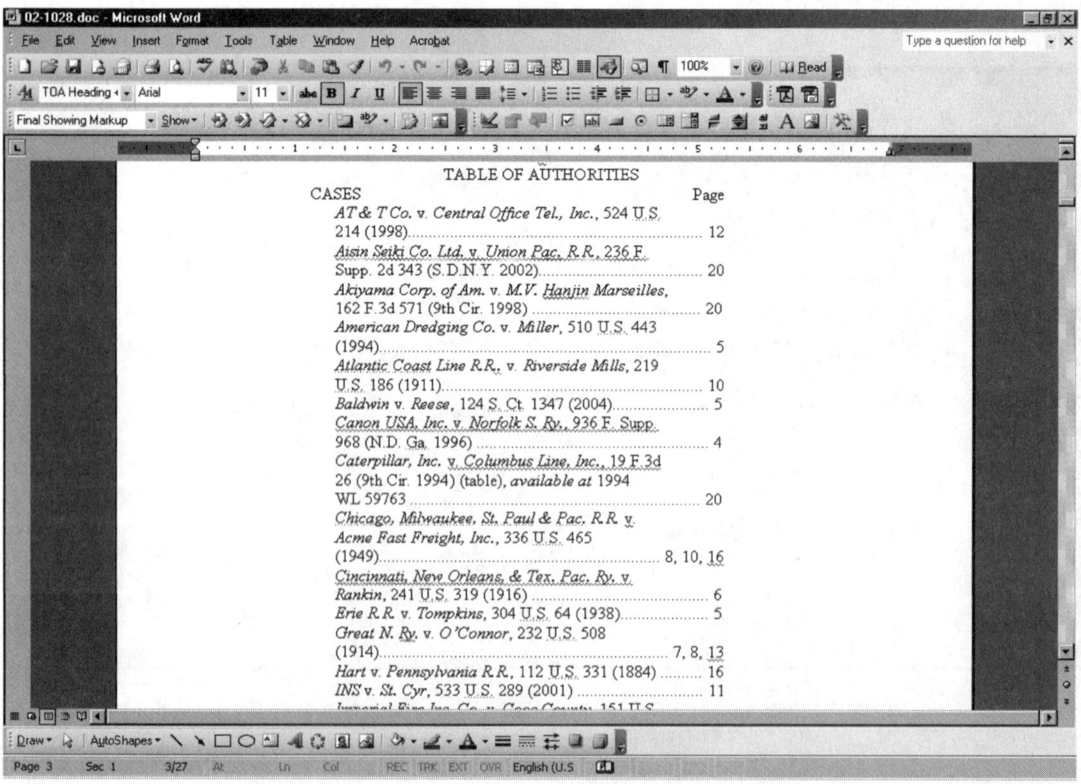

Figure 24.1: Sample Table of Authorities.

The TOA is generated from a list of citations that you indicate from within the document itself. After your brief or reply brief is written, make sure you add footnotes to your document if they are required. Footnotes are covered in Chapter 22. These footnotes will likely be used in marking the citations. It is possible, depending on the type of document you are creating, that you won't have any footnotes in your document. Then, you'll be ready to begin flagging your cases listed in the document and marking them as citations.

Citations are classified into categories. Figure 24.1 shows a category called **CASES** that lists all citations within that category in alphabetical order. Microsoft Word allows up to 16 different categories, with these being default categories:

- Cases
- Statutes
- Other Authorities
- Rules
- Treatises
- Regulations
- Constitutional Provisions

Citations are Not Just for Police

When you flag cases or statutes in your document to include in the TOA, you mark these references as a citation. A citation can have a long or short form. Typically, the first usage of a citation is the long form, but subsequent usages can be the short form. This, of course, depends on what the court expects as a format for your briefs or reply briefs.

Creating and Editing Citations

Creating citations is very easy to do in Microsoft Word 2003. Again, these citations will be used to generate the TOA. To create, or *mark* citations, follow these easy steps:

1. Select the complete text that will be used to mark the long citation. An example is shown in Figure 24.2.

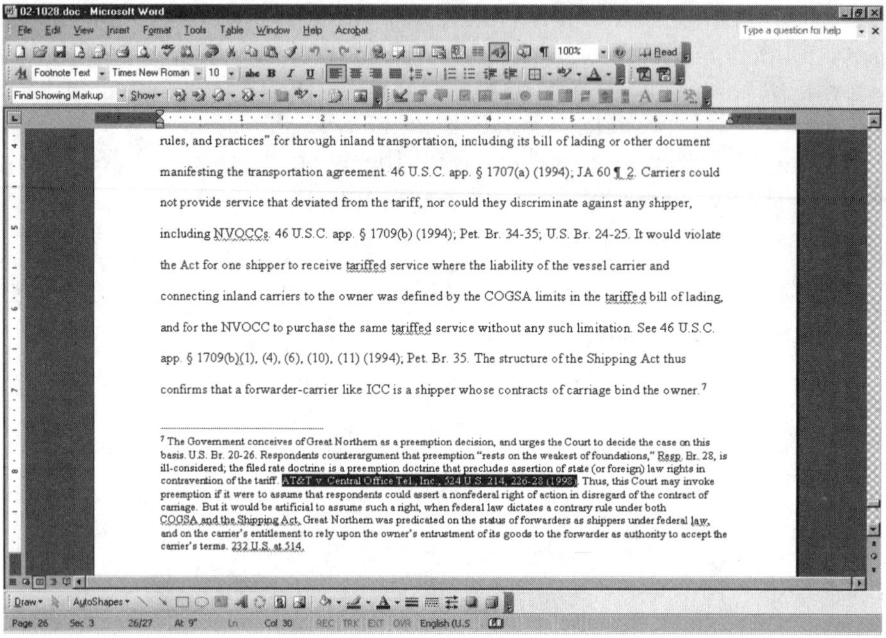

Figure 24.2: Selecting the Long Citation.

2. Press the **ALT** + **Shift** + **I** keys to bring up the **Mark Citation** screen. There is no menu item to bring up this screen, so make sure you press the correct keys. The **Mark Citation** screen is shown in Figure 24.3.

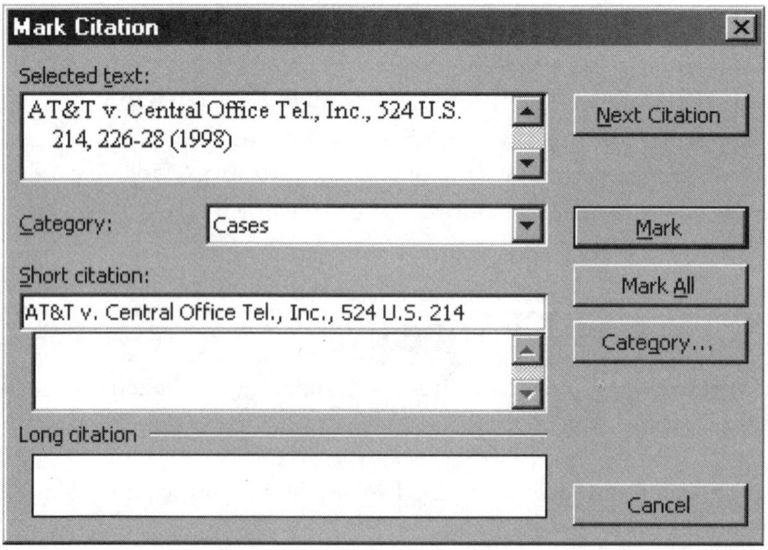

Figure 24.3: Marking Citations.

3. Replace the text in the **Short citation** field with whatever makes sense for the short citation. For example, the short citation might be just **AT&T v. Central Office Tel., Inc., 524 U.S. 214**. The **Long citation** field will automatically be entered when you click the **Mark** button.

4. Select the desired category, or create your own by clicking the **Category** button. Creating your own categories is covered in the section "Managing Categories" later in this chapter.

5. Click the **Mark** button. This will mark your citation, but does not create the TOA. The reason you want to select the desired category before this step is to avoid the last used category being automatically used by default. Therefore, make sure to select your category before clicking the **Mark** button.

6. If you wish to edit a citation, you can click the **Next Citation** button or select the citation from the **Short citation** list. You can edit only the short citation or category for the text.

7. Click the **Close** button. After you mark your citation, the **Cancel** button changes to a **Close** button.

8. Repeat the process for each citation. Most often, after the first long citation is marked, thereafter in the document the citation must be marked and referenced as a short citation instead of a long citation. This is done by selecting the desired short citation from the dropdown list.

9. Create or update your TOA, as shown in "Do You Have Authority?" later in this chapter.

Managing Categories

A citation can be classified as one of sixteen possible categories. When you mark your citation, you choose from one of these categories, or you create your own. To manage your own categories, click the **Category** button on the **Mark Citation** screen (see Figure 24.3). This brings up the screen shown in Figure 24.4.

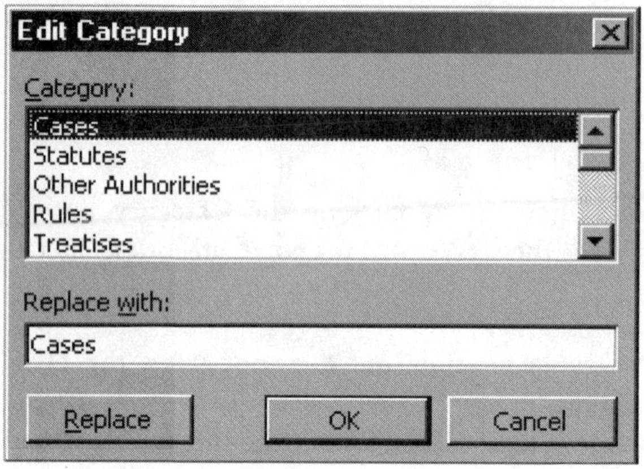

Figure 24.4: Editing Categories.

Because you can use only sixteen possible categories, each is listed in the **Category** list in Figure 24.4. The first seven items are configured when you installed Microsoft Word. If you want to change any of the first seven, or configure the remaining nine categories, follow this simple procedure.

1. Click the desired category in the **Category** list.
2. In the **Replace with** text box, enter the text that should appear as the category.
3. Click the **Replace** button to replace the category.
4. Continue replacing each category as desired.
5. Click the **OK** button when you are finished to save your changes and close the screen. The new categories will become available on the **Mark Citation** screen.

NOTE

If a new category is created after the TOA has been inserted into the document, then citations marked with the new category will not show up in the TOA by simply updating the TOA field. The TOA field would need to be deleted and recreated in order for the new category to show up.

Deleting Citations

Deleting citations is not very straightforward. It would be nice if you could edit a citation by bringing up the **Mark Citation** screen and clicking a **Delete** button, but this is not possible. To delete a citation, you have to show the field codes, select them, and delete them. Here's how you do it:

1. Show field codes by clicking the **Show/Hide** button on the **Standard** toolbar. If you are not sure where this button is located, refer to Chapter 4, as it shows this button. This shows special codes after the text that you marked as a citation. For example, this text is the marked citation shown in Figure 24.3:

   ```
   {TA \l "AT&T v. Central Office Tel., Inc., 524 U.S. 214, 226-28 (1998)" \s
   "AT&T v. Central Office Tel., Inc." \c 1}
   ```

   While you don't need to know everything about the special codes in the marked citation, you do need to know what it looks like because you must select the entire thing to delete the citation.

2. Select the entire field code, beginning with the { character and ending with the } character.

3. Click the **Delete** or **Del** key.

4. Update your TOA, as shown in the following section.

Do You Have Authority?

After you create all citations in your brief or reply brief, you are ready to create the Table of Authorities. This table will read all the special citations that you entered and magically create the TOA. Creating the TOA is quite simple as long as you have your citations correctly marked. To create the TOA, follow this procedure:

1. Place the carat at the location where the TOA should be inserted. This may be a blank page at the beginning of the document.

2. Click the **Insert⇨ Reference⇨ Indexes and Tables** menu item.

3. Click the **Table of Authorities** tab. This brings up the screen shown in Figure 24.5.

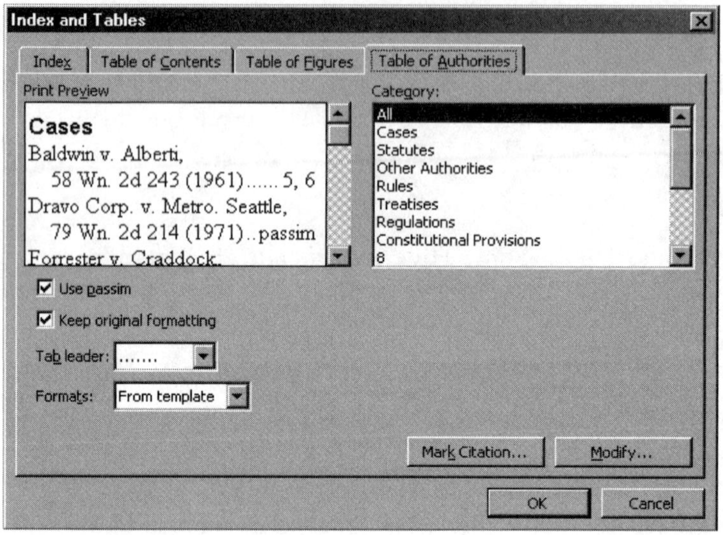

Figure 24.5: Creating a Table of Authorities.

4. Select the desired categories to use in the TOA. By default, all categories are used to generate the TOA, but if you want only one category, click that category in the **Category** list.

5. Choose the desired format in the **Formats** dropdown list. You'll see a preview of each format as you scroll through the choices.

6. Click the **OK** button to create the TOA and close the screen.

NOTE

If you wish to update the TOA, simply right-click anywhere on the TOA and click the Update Field menu item from the popup menu. Alternatively, you can highlight the TOA field and press the F9 key. However, if any formatting changes are made directly to the TOA itself, those changes will be lost each time the TOA is updated. For example, if the attorney prefers that the case names are italicized in the TOA and direct formatting is applied to the text in the TOA, when the field is updated again the direct formatting will be lost.

Conclusion

Table of Authorities (TOA) are commonly found in legal briefs and reply briefs. They are used to cite references to cases, statutes, and other sources in your legal documents. A TOA is created with just a few simple mouse clicks, but it requires that you properly mark each citation in your legal document first. This chapter showed you how to mark your citations and create the TOA.

Did you know?

If additional citations have been marked and you right-click one of the sections in the TOA and choose **Update Field**, only added citations for that section get updated. Any new citations marked for any other section will not get updated. In order to ensure that all TOA sections are updated, you must highlight the entire TOA and press the **F9** key.

Chapter 25

Converting WordPerfect Documents

Chapter At A Glance

WHY YOU SHOULD READ THIS CHAPTER:

In recent years, Microsoft Word has been adopted by the legal industry as the word processing program of choice. Because WordPerfect used to be the leading program, most law firms have legacy WordPerfect documents lying around. To prevent you from having to retype your documents, you can convert from WordPerfect to Word format, but there are things that you need to take into consideration so you don't lose formatting or data. This chapter describes the process of converting WordPerfect documents into Word documents.

PRODUCT OUTLINED IN THIS CHAPTER:

- Microsoft Word 2003

PRODUCT FEATURE COVERED IN THIS CHAPTER:

- Converters and Filters

During the process of interviewing Paralegals for this book, one of the most common requests we found was the need to convert WordPerfect documents to Microsoft Word formatted documents. So, this chapter focuses on this one task. You're not going to believe how easy it is.

How Perfect is WordPerfect?

Even if your firm uses Microsoft Word, you undoubtedly have WordPerfect documents lying around. You receive WordPerfect documents from clients, attorneys, sample templates on the Internet, and many other scenarios. As Microsoft Word has become the word processing program of choice for the legal industry, it wasn't too long ago that this wasn't the case. WordPerfect has a long legacy in the legal industry. Therefore, you should know that if you have any WordPerfect documents in your organization, you can certainly convert them into a Word format. You don't have to retype them from scratch.

The problem in the past has been the inability to convert from a WordPerfect format to a Word formatted document. If you want to leverage the power of Microsoft Office without losing your current documents, fear not! Help is on the way. A law firm cannot simply discard its legacy documents, so this chapter is dedicated to showing how to convert from the WordPerfect format to the Word format.

Do You Have What it Takes?

To convert WordPerfect documents to Word documents, you need a special converter that knows how to read the WordPerfect format. Fortunately, one such converter comes free with the Microsoft Office System. However, this is an optional component that may not have been installed as part of your Microsoft Office System installation. To save on disk space, when you install the Microsoft Office System products, not every program and option is installed to your hard drive. Instead, programs are installed with one of the options shown in Figure 25.1.

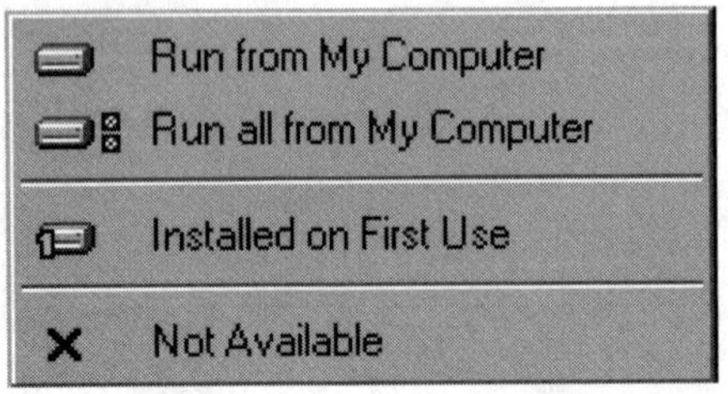

Figure 25.1: Installation Options.

As shown in Figure 25.1, these options are available for each program, converter, and feature of Microsoft Office 2003:

- **Run from My Computer** — Installs the program, feature, option, or converter on your hard drive, which makes it available continuously.
- **Run all from My Computer** — Installs every possible feature of Office 2003. Using this option consumes the most disk space on your computer, but will not slow you down and force you to find the Office 2003 CD.
- **Installed on First Use** — Does not install the option onto your hard drive, but will prompt you for the Office 2003 CD to install the feature when used.
- **Not Available** — Does not make the feature available at any time.

To begin with, see if you have the necessary converter installed. To do this, follow these steps:

1. Open the Windows Control Panel. This is normally done by clicking the **Start⇨ Settings⇨ Control Panel** menu item. However, depending on your configuration and permissions, this menu may not be shown. If not, check the Windows help file to see how to enable this menu.
2. Double-click the **Add or Remove Programs** icon.
3. Scroll down to locate the **Microsoft Office Professional Edition 2003** entry in the list of installed programs.
4. Click the **Change** button. After a few seconds, this brings up the **Maintenance Mode Options** screen, as shown in Figure 25.2.

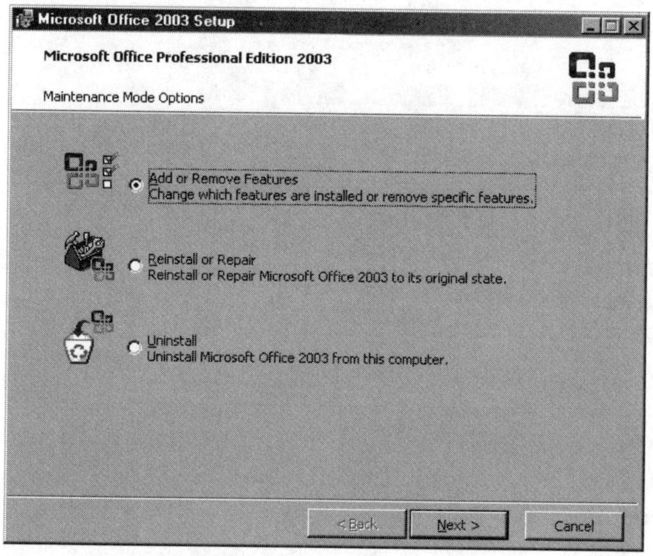

Figure 25.2: Maintenance Mode Options Screen.

5. Ensure that the **Add or Remove Features** option is selected.

6. Click the **Next** button to continue.

7. Click the **Choose advanced customization of applications** option.

8. Click the **Next** button.

9. In the **Advanced Customization** screen, expand the **Microsoft Office** entry by clicking the + icon, if not already done.

10. Expand the **Office Shared Features** entry.

11. Expand the **Converters and Filters** entry.

12. Expand the **Text Converters** entry. Doing so will show the screen depicted in Figure 25.3.

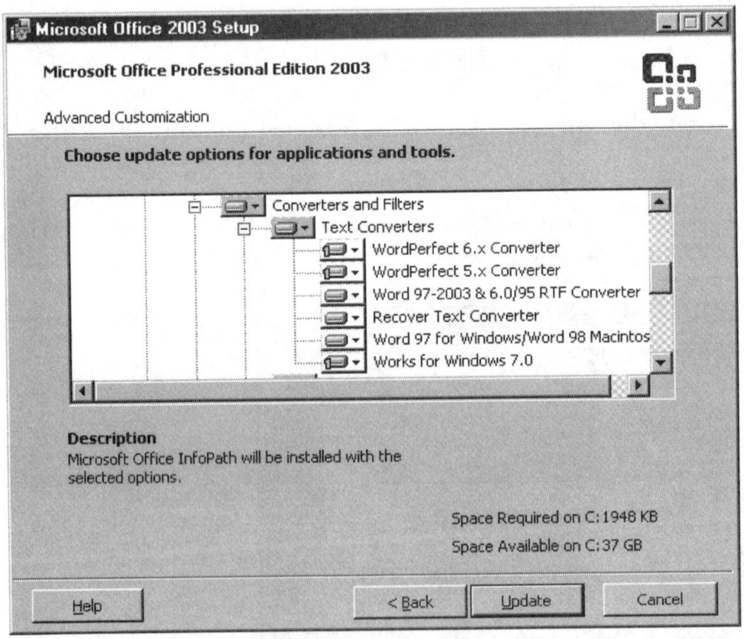

Figure 25.3: Text Converters Available in Office 2003.

13. Ensure that the **WordPerfect 6.x Converter** and the **WordPerfect 5.x Converter** options are set to either **Installed on First Use** (which it should be by default), or **Run from My Computer**. If neither option is selected, choose it now.

14. Click the **Update** button.

NOTE

Because there can be complex formatting features in your WordPerfect documents, sometimes Microsoft Word doesn't do the greatest job of converting all of them. There are other third-party converter products on the market which provide additional capabilities over those provided in the Microsoft Word converter, but they are not free. One such product is DocXchange from Microsystems (`www.microsystems.com`) and another, called CrossWords, from Levit & James (`www.levitjames.com`).

Converting WordPerfect Documents

After you have made sure that the WordPerfect converters are installed or will be installed on first use, you are ready to begin the process of document conversion. It's simpler than you may think. Here's how you convert your WordPerfect documents into Word documents.

1. Open the WordPerfect document from within Microsoft Word by clicking the **File⇨ Open** menu item.

2. In the **Files of type** dropdown list, select the type of file to be either **WordPerfect 5.x (*.doc)** or **WordPerfect 6.x (*.wpd;*.doc)**, as shown in Figure 25.4.

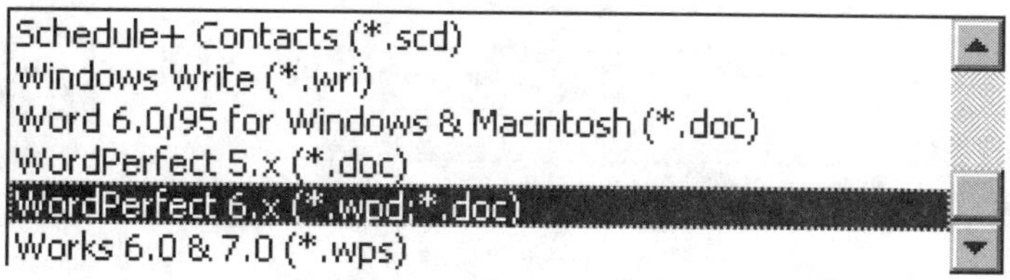

Figure 25.4: Selecting the WordPerfect File Type.

3. Locate, navigate to, and select the desired WordPerfect file to open.

4. Click the **Open** button. If the converter is set to be installed on first use, you will see the message shown in Figure 25.5.

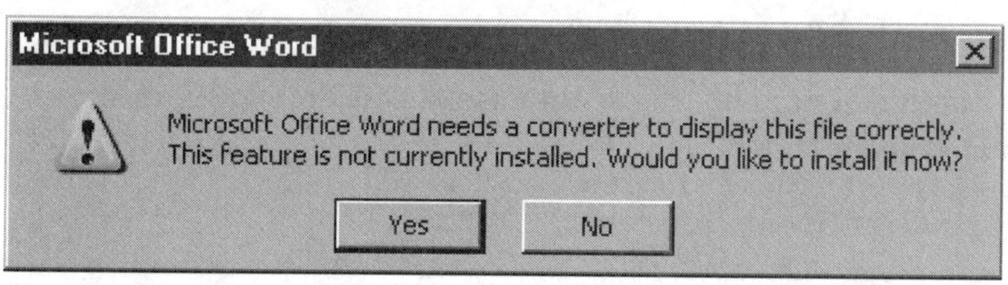

Figure 25.5: Warning Message When Set to Install Converter on First Use.

5. Click the **Yes** button to install the converter. Have your original CD nearby to find the installation files when you are prompted. After the installation program finds the installation files on the CD, all required files will be installed to convert from WordPerfect to Word.

6. Your WordPerfect document will be opened in Microsoft Word. An example WordPerfect document to request the release of medical records is shown as a Word document in Figure 25.6.

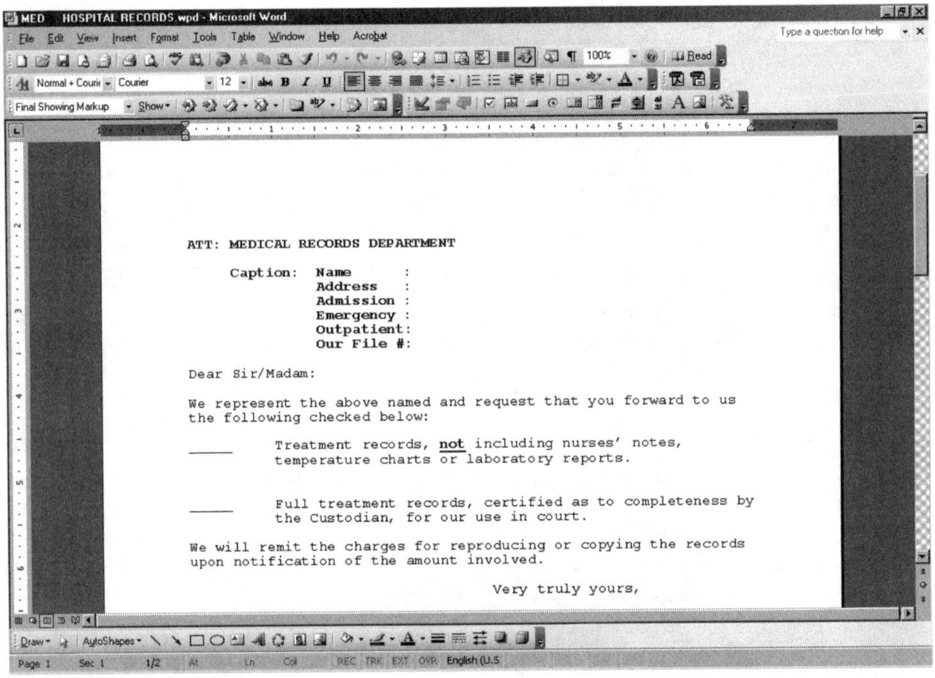

Figure 25.6: WordPerfect Document Displayed in Microsoft Word.

7. Save the file as a Word document. If you don't do this, the document will be stored as a WordPerfect document. You definitely don't want to do that, being that you worked so hard to covert to Word. To save the document in Microsoft Word format, follow these simple steps:

   - Click the **File⇨ Save As** menu item.
   - In the screen that pops up, ensure the **Save as type** dropdown list shows **Word Document (*.doc)**.
   - Give your file an appropriate name.
   - Click the **Save** button.

Reformatting WordPerfect Documents

Now that you have converted a WordPerfect document to a Microsoft Word document, format or reformat the documents in any way you see fit. Depending on the complexity of your WordPerfect documents, you may have lost some of the formatting or special features of the document. However, Microsoft has done its best to ensure that the documents are converted correctly with minimal effort on your part. Some of the possible formatting problems that you'll need to correct include:

- **INVALID SECTION BREAKS** — Breaks for sections and their options might not be converted correctly.
- **AUTOMATIC LINE NUMBERING PROBLEMS** — Automatic line numbering options in WordPerfect might need to be reapplied in Word.
- **INCONSISTENT HEADERS AND FOOTERS** — Placement and formatting of header and footer text and options may be wrong, depending on complexity.
- **INVALID COMPATIBILITY OPTIONS** — Depending on the compatibility options (the **Compatibility** tab under the **Tools⇨ Options** menu), the WordPerfect compatibility options might be set incorrectly, and therefore affect conversion.

If you need to reformat the document in any way, you can do so now. The document is now in Word format and has all the features and functionality of any Word document. For example, you can change margins, backgrounds, fonts, spacing, and any other attributes you need to in order to satisfy your firm's requirements for how your documents should look.

TIP

Although it should be used as a last resort, if you are having major formatting problems in your converted WordPerfect documents, you can opt to keep the text only and manually reformat the entire document. To do this, simply copy all text in the document by following this quick procedure:

1. **Click the** Edit⇨ Select All **menu item to select all text in the document.**
2. **Click the** Edit⇨ Copy **menu item to copy all the selected text.**
3. **Click the** Edit⇨ Paste Special **menu item and choose the** Unformatted Text **option. This will paste the contents of an entire document into a new one, but without formatting. Again, this option should be used as a last resort only.**

Conclusion

The process of converting WordPerfect documents into Word documents is very simple, but it requires a special converter that exists on the original Microsoft Office installation CD. This converter is probably not already installed, so you need to have your CD handy when you try to open a WordPerfect document in Microsoft Word. The rest is simple because it happens automatically. Because it is so simple to convert your documents, you no longer have to avoid using Microsoft Word just because you have a library of old WordPerfect documents.

Part III

Extras

Glossary

All-Day Event	An Outlook calendar entry that does not start or stop at a specific time of day. All-Day Events are normally entered as "free" time, instead of "busy" time.
AutoPreview	Shows the first few lines of data to enable you to partially view Outlook messages and tasks. With AutoPreview turned on, you'll be able to quickly see messages and tasks, but will use approximately three times the space on the screen.
Balloons	Bubble that appears in Word when Track Changes is turned on, showing the comments or changes you made to the document. The balloon refers to a specific area of text in the document.
Blacklining	Process of comparing documents and labeling changed areas of the document with a vertical black line in the margin.
Bullets	Series of related items that are presented sequentially but are not numbered. The icon representing the bullet is typically a small solid circle, but can be any icon.
Carat	Insertion point that represents where text is to be entered from the keyboard. The carat is typically represented on the screen as an "I".
Collaboration	Process of multiple people working together on a document.
Cookie	Small file that stores information from a Web site onto your workstation. Cookies can be malicious by storing personal information, but they can also store user preferences that can make Web site navigation easier and faster.

Cross-reference	One area of a document that references another. Most types of cross-references, such as Table of Contents and Table of Authorities, can be automatically updated.
Cursor	Graphical object on the screen that moves with the mouse. Typically, when you move the cursor and click the left mouse button, it places a carat in the cursor location.
Distribution List	Stores multiple e-mail addresses that will receive a bulk mailing.
Flagging	Specific area of a OneNote 2003 note that is marked with an icon to call special attention.
Footer	Area at the bottom of a page in a Word document, Excel spreadsheet, or PowerPoint presentation that repeats on every page of a document or section. Word also allows you to specify whether the footer is to appear on only odd or even pages.
Free/Busy	Information that another user can see from your Outlook calendar to indicate whether your schedule is free or busy at a specific period of time. Other users cannot see specific data about appointments you have—only whether you are free or busy.
Handouts	Slides that are printed and distributed to others in a meeting. Handouts are in a different format than online PowerPoint slides in that they provide areas for attendees to take notes.
Header	Area at the top of a page in a Word document, Excel spreadsheet, or PowerPoint presentation that repeats on every page of a document or section. Word also allows you to specify whether the header is to appear on only odd or even pages.
Hyperlink	A clickable area of text that immediately jumps to another location or document. Typically, hyperlinks point to web page addresses. Hyperlinks are sometimes known simply as links.
Indent	Process of moving the text of a document inward (to the right) to the next available tab stop or defined location. Indenting is typically done for paragraphs, bullets, and numbering.

Justified	Alignment of text whereby the left margin and the right margin are consistently aligned. Most books, including this one, are justified in this way.
Mail Merge	Process of combining, or merging, a predefined form (such as a letter) with addressee information. The result is a series of form letters, labels, or other document type that goes to multiple recipients.
Mark	Process of flagging a citation for use in a Table of Authorities.
Markup	Term given to text that has been edited by using the track changes feature. If a document contains changes, it is said to be "marked-up."
Metadata	Personal or other information that is stored inside a Word document, Excel spreadsheet, or PowerPoint presentation. This information consists of the original file name, who modified it, company information, and more.
Microsoft Office System	Set of tools and technologies that comprise a complete suite of interoperable programs. There are many programs in the Microsoft Office System, but this book covers only five of them; Word, Excel, PowerPoint, Outlook, and OneNote.
Non-proportional Font	Font whose letters occupy the same amount of space. For example, a "W" occupies the same space as an "i".
Notes	Program in Outlook that lets you create Sticky Notes for use on your computer. Notes also refer to the mechanism by which you write or type into OneNote 2003.
Numbering	Series of related items that are presented sequentially where the order of items is significant and are preceded with a numerical representation.
Outdent	Process of moving the text of a document outward (to the left) to the previous available tab stop or defined location. Outdenting is typically done for paragraphs, bullets, and numbering.

Outline Numbering	Multiple levels of numbering and/or bullets in a Word document. Each level can use a different format. This is the process by which most legal Word documents are formatted.
Parallel Process	Process that occurs in tandem with another so no one process blocks another.
Path	Folder location on your hard drive where files are stored.
Pivot	Process of swapping rows for columns in an Excel Worksheet.
Placeholder Field	Defined field that holds the place of an actual value when mail-merging documents.
Presentation	PowerPoint slides that you show to an audience on the computer monitor.
Proofing tools	Built-in tools to Microsoft Office, such as spell checking and grammar checking.
Proportional Font	Font whose letters do not occupy the same amount of space. For example, a "W" occupies more space than an "i".
Range function	Excel programmatic function that acts on a range of cells.
Reveal Formatting	Special pane in Word that shows the formatting characteristics of the selected text.
Root	Highest possible level in a Path. For example, the root of your C: drive is the highest possible level where you can place files and folders.
Searching Options	Area of OneNote 2003 that lets you perform searching functionality.
Section	An area of a document that is used to define formatting. The formatting of one section of a document can be completely different from another. Sections in Word documents provide the flexibility you need to assemble a complex document within a single file.

Serial Process	Process that occurs sequentially after another. Therefore, if there is a hold-up in one process, it will hold-up the other process.
Service Pack	Installable software that is used to fix bugs, holes, or to add features. Microsoft sometimes releases services packs for its operating systems (Windows 98, Windows XP, etc.) and for its Office products.
Slide Deck	Same as a PowerPoint presentation.
Slides	Same as a PowerPoint presentation.
Spyware	Malicious software that can be downloaded from the Web for the sole purpose of tracking your purchasing habits, Web sites visited, and perhaps to even hijack your personal or financial information. You should run anti-spyware software on your computers.
Styles	Collections of formatting characteristics, such as font names, sizes, justifications, spacing, and more. Highly recommended for your legal documents.
Stylus	Special pointing device that is safe to use on a Tablet PC.
Task Pane	Area of the right-hand part of the screen for many Microsoft Office programs that helps guide you through tasks. The task pane can be shown by pressing the **CTRL + F1** keys.
Templates	Predefined forms that give you a head-start in creating your own documents. Templates are available for all Microsoft Office programs. Many are available specifically for the legal industry for free.
Tracking changes	Process of having Microsoft Word store the revisions that you or someone else makes to a document. Others can view the individual changes to the document and either accept or reject them.
vCard	Virtual Business Card for use in Microsoft Outlook. It is very convenient to send or receive a vCard so that contact information does not have to be retyped.

Viewer	Free, lightweight versions of most Microsoft Office programs that are free. Viewers can be very helpful for your clients that receive Office documents from you for which they don't have the installed program.
View	A predefined way to see data on the screen, such as which columns to display and how to filter the data displayed.
Workbook	Excel container that houses one or more worksheets.
Worksheet	Excel spreadsheet that contains rows and columns. One or more worksheets are contained in a workbook.
Zone	Area of a network that your Web browser accesses. For example, you can access an internal network called an *Intranet* or the public Internet. A zone can even be designated as a trusted or private site.

Legal References

Among the many legal professionals that were interviewed and consulted during the production of this book, the authors wish to extend special recognition to the following individuals and firms (in alphabetical order):

Mark Callahan
Paralegal
Nutter, McClennen & Fish, LLP
World Trade Center West
Boston, MA 02210
(617) 439-2000
www.nutter.com

Jean Champagney
Director of Client Services
SoftWise Corporation
53 Hamilton Avenue
Staten Island, NY 10301
www.SoftWise.net
sales@SoftWise.net

Felicia S. Chappell
Executive Assistant
Siskind Susser, PC
5400 Poplar Avenue, Suite 300
Memphis, TN 38119
901.682.6455
www.visalaw.com

Jennifer Colman
Nutter, McClennen & Fish, LLP
World Trade Center West
Boston, MA 02210
(617) 439-2000
www.nutter.com

Julia C. Forbes
Paralegal and IS Special Projects
Mintz Levin Cohn Ferris Glovsky and Popeo PC
Boston, Washington DC, Reston, New York,
Los Angeles, Stamford and London
www.mintz.com

Jonathan Nelson
Attorney at Law
Law Offices of Jonathan Robert Nelson
20 Exchange Place, 43rd Floor
New York, NY 10005
(212) 593-5775
www.attorneynelson.com

Lori Ann Page
Project Coordinator
SoftWise Corporation
53 Hamilton Avenue
Staten Island, NY 10301
www.SoftWise.net
sales@SoftWise.net

Steven D. Strauss
The Strauss Group
www.MrAllBiz.com
sstrauss@MrAllBiz.com

Suzanne Scanlon
Litigation Technology Specialist
Goodwin Procter LLP
Exchange Place
Boston, MA 02109
Tel: (617) 570-1000
www.goodwinprocter.com

Index

NOTE

Locators followed by a *t* indicate tables.

P

V

W

Z

Notes

Notes

Notes

Notes

Notes

Notes

Need to dazzle 'em with daring document automation?
Observe the stunning symmetry, the perfect arc, the graceful suspension.
While you master the art of juggling, why not add a flawless disappearing act?
OUT-OF-SIGHT®
METADATA MANAGEMENT UTILITY
innova™
DOCUMENT AUTOMATION PLATFORM

IMPORTANT NOTICE
REGISTER YOUR BOOK

Bonus Materials

Your book refers to valuable material that complements your learning experience. In order to download these materials you will need to register your book at `http://www.agilitypress.com`.

This bonus material is available after registration:

- Additional Legal Templates
- Advanced Chapters
- Keyboard Shortcut References

Registering your book

To register your book, follow these 7 easy steps:

1. Point your browser to:
   `http://www.agilitypress.com`.
2. Create an account and login.
3. Click the **My Books** link.
4. Click the **Register New Book** button.
5. Enter the registration number found on the back of the book (see Figure A).
6. Confirm registration and view your new book on the virtual bookshelf.
7. Click the spine of the desired book to view the available downloads and resources for the selected book.

Figure A: Back of your book.